THE PRAGMATICS OF INSIGNIFICANCE
Chekhov,
Zoshchenko,
Gogol

STUDIES OF THE HARRIMAN INSTITUTE
Columbia University

THE PRAGMATICS
OF INSIGNIFICANCE
Chekhov,
Zoshchenko,
Gogol

Cathy Popkin

Stanford University Press
Stanford, California
1993

Stanford University Press
Stanford, California

© 1993 by the Board of Trustees of the
Leland Stanford Junior University

Printed in the United States of America

CIP data appear at the end of the book

To J.D. with gratitude
To R.M. with joy

Acknowledgments

This book was completed with the generous assistance of several institutions. I am especially grateful to the National Endowment for the Humanities, the American Council of Learned Societies, and the Kennan Institute for Advanced Russian Studies for the fellowship support that facilitated the writing of the manuscript. Much of my research was funded by grants from the International Research and Exchanges Board, the Dartmouth College Faculty Research Committee, and the Council for Research in the Humanities at Columbia University. Special thanks are due the Department of Slavic Languages at Columbia for generously defraying the costs of the illustrations.

I appreciate as well the permission I have been granted to reproduce copyrighted material. The *New York Post* has been most kind, and the *Los Angeles Times* Syndicate and the United Press Syndicate have both been extremely forthcoming. I owe particular thanks to Joy Weiner of the *New Yorker* for her invaluable assistance in obtaining the magazine's consent to use its artwork. An earlier version of Chapter 1 was published in Rolf-Dieter Kluge, ed., *Anton P. Čexov: Werk und Wirkung* (Otto Harrassowitz, 1990), and portions of Chapters 4 and 5 appeared in Susanne Fusso and Priscilla Meyer, eds., *Essays on Gogol: Logos and the Russian Word* (Northwestern University Press, 1992). I gratefully acknowledge the publishers' permission to incorporate that material into the present book.

Above all, I want to thank my colleagues and friends whose support has sustained me. I have benefited immeasurably from the suggestions of those who read all or parts of the manuscript at various times. My foremost debt in this regard is to William Mills Todd III, who has also been a source of friendship, encouragement, and wise counsel at every stage. Gary Saul Morson generously provided a meticulous assessment and critique that has improved the book in innumerable ways. Amy Mandelker graciously took time from her many responsibilities to offer both a nuanced reading and much-needed reassurances. Robert Belknap, too, set his own work aside to help improve mine. Barry

Scherr was kind enough to comment on an earlier version of the manuscript. Elizabeth Allen and Irina Reyfman have not only read my work, but have been steadfast friends as well. Richard Gustafson's support has been invaluable. And Robert Maguire has provided the kind of encouragement and understanding that only someone else working on Gogol could give.

I am most grateful to Helen Tartar of Stanford University Press for the confidence she has shown in me and for the editorial wisdom she has shared so generously. I am indebted as well to Kirsten Painter for her peerless indexing, and to Andrew Hicks and Jill Roese for their spirited help with proofreading. Thanks also to Christina Weinberg for expediting my work with her superb research assistance.

This book would never have been completed without the insight and forbearance of several people, and I owe them more than I can say. I thank my parents, Alice and Harold Popkin, for their patience and my sister, Noreen Honeycutt, for her unerring sense of perspective. Bette Weneck has my gratitude for her friendship and for her uncanny ability to understand what made the process of writing difficult. More than anyone else, Jimmy David made that process comprehensible and sustainable; I thank him as well for his formal permission to cope poorly every once in a while. On such occasions, it was Raj Menon who had to cope with me. For this, and for much, much more, I thank him with all my heart.

Contents

Guide to Notation ... xi

Introduction: Triviality and Tellability ... 1

1 Anton Chekhov: Reinventing Events ... 17

2 Mikhail Zoshchenko: Great Strides and Trivial Indiscretions ... 53

3 Zoshchenko and the Politics of Perceptibility ... 93

4 Nikolai Gogol: Distended Discourse and the Pragmatics of Elaboration ... 125

5 Gogol's Coats and Clutter: Content and Its Discontents ... 159

Conclusion: Too Little and Too Much—Story and Discourse and the Pragmatics of Insignificance ... 211

Notes ... 221

Works Cited ... 259

Index ... 277

Guide to Notation

I have followed the modified Library of Congress system of transliteration to render Russian words and names, substituting commonly used anglicized forms where they are more familiar (Dostoevsky, Tolstoy, Gogol, Bely, Gorky). I have retained the transliterated forms in Russian language citations.

In quoted material, spaced ellipsis points (. . .) indicate *my* omissions; closed suspension points (...) belong to the texts themselves.

THE PRAGMATICS OF INSIGNIFICANCE
Chekhov, Zoshchenko, Gogol

INTRODUCTION

Triviality and Tellability

DIARY OF A CAT

TODAY Today I got some food in a bowl. It was great! I slept some, too.

TODAY Played with yarn. Got some food in a bowl. Had a good nap.

TODAY Slept, food, yarn. Fun!

TODAY I played with a shoelace. Ate, slept. A good day.

TODAY Slept. Ate some food. Yum.

TODAY Food in a bowl. Yarn galore. Dozed for quite a while.

TODAY Had a good nap. Then food in a bowl. Then yarn.

R. Chast

© 1987 Roz Chast
originally in The New Yorker Magazine, Inc.
All Rights Reserved.

Everyone tells stories. And from the most accomplished novelist polishing a manuscript for publication to the child reporting on a day at school, nearly everyone develops a sense of what is "worth telling." Very few of us would bother to recount every aspect of our daily routine, like the earnest feline diarist; fewer still would expatiate indefinitely on that "food in a bowl," even if we did see fit to mention it. Normally we single out significant events for narration, and in telling our tales, we tend to limit the potentially infinite spectrum of details to what is essential for an appreciation of those events.

And yet we can name major works of literature that seem to do just the opposite, canonical "greats" devoted to nothing more monumental than a sneeze or a galosh, others that detail for pages on end the contents of countless bowls and plates, glasses and goblets, casseroles and tureens, none of which bears the slightest connection to the matter at hand. What makes any of this even remotely worth telling? Can it be that we demand less from our literary texts than from our casual conversations?

On the contrary, rules Mary Pratt in her pioneering study of literature as a kind of "speech act." The non-participating audience of literary narrative, having voluntarily relinquished its turn-taking privileges, is entitled to expect more of a presentation than the interlocutor who can interrupt at any time.[1] Still, the very presence (and identity) of that potential interrupter in the conversational setting imposes immediate standards for what is "significant" enough to tell and how exhaustive a treatment it warrants. Someone new in town is more likely to appreciate directions to the business district than somebody who has been living there for years. A friend of Maria's is apt to be more interested in her new address than someone who has never met her. And while many of her friends might ask her about the state of her manuscript, her editor may care to hear about her revisions in considerably greater detail. We tend (or at least intend), without giving it too much thought, to contribute information that is not only new but also has some relevance for the listener. H. P. Grice's "Conversational Maxims" provide an explicit and systematic statement of those imperatives to which most speakers adhere unconsciously in the spirit of efficiency and cooperation (with varying degrees of success):

I. *Maxims of Quantity*

  1. "Make your contribution as informative as is required (for the current purposes of the exchange)."

2. "Do not make your contribution more informative than is required."
. . .
II. *Maxims of Quality*
Supermaxim: "Make your contribution one that is true."
Maxims: 1. "Do not say what you believe to be false." 2. "Do not say that for which you lack adequate evidence."
III. *Maxims of Relation*
1. "Be relevant." . . .
IV. *Maxims of Manner*
Supermaxim: "Be perspicuous."
Maxims: 1. "Avoid obscurity of expression." 2. "Avoid ambiguity." 3. "Be brief (avoid unnecessary prolixity)." 4. "Be orderly."[2]

These maxims are compelling as long as we share their underlying assumption, namely that the purpose of a given speech act is "a maximally effective exchange of information."[3] But while this generally holds for what Pratt calls "assertible" utterances—assertions that anticipate or answer questions and thus provide true and nonobvious information presumed to be relevant to the hearer[4]—it is not universally the case, even in the presence of the most exacting interrupters.

Much of what passes for conversation between friends, for instance, provides no new information at all; rather, it reiterates and reconfirms an already articulated—and probably shared—opinion. "He's such a jerk," I rehearse about someone for whom the antipathy is general. "I know," returns my interlocutor, with no apparent disappointment at the old news.

Or to what extent is my principal purpose really "to inform" when I regale my dinner guests with an account of Maria's moving-day misadventures, particularly if these guests are not acquainted with her or her reputation? And why must I be concise, provided my listeners continue to be entertained (i.e., as long as they do not interrupt with William Labov's dreaded "so what?"[5])? Obviously there are other purposes of communication than the efficient exchange of information, and a substantial portion of our verbal performance consists of matter that is not strictly relevant. In fact, there exists an entire category of utterances whose only relevance is what Pratt refers to as their "tellability." "Assertibility" is a function of a statement's capacity to *inform*; "tellability," on the other hand, underwrites the verbal *display* of something felt to be simply "unusual, contrary to expectations, or otherwise problematic." The "tellable" may or may not provide news, but it does inspire imaginative involvement. The index of a statement's tellability is its power to invite contemplation, evaluation, and ultimately an interpretation of the state of affairs it represents.[6]

The fact that Maria has moved, then, is assertible only to those who know her, but it may be tellable to a more general audience if the circumstances surrounding her relocation are in some sense unusual or problematic. Conversely, even for Maria's friends, "Maria has moved" is not assertible if they are already aware of her new residence. And yet this long-established fact could be tellable, even if no new or nonobvious information is exchanged: if the account itself is related in a novel fashion, those eager interlocutors are likely to remain receptive.

Clearly literary narrative, too, aspires more to "tellability" than to "assertibility." A literary text need not be informative in the sense of providing any immediately relevant information. Neither must it be true. And it certainly need not be maximally efficient. As Pratt emphasizes, "Text-internally, the literary speech situation admits of enormous elaboration, accumulation of detail, and even pure repetition. . . . Indeed, one might say that what literary works chiefly do is elaborate on the state of affairs they posit. . . . Finally, literary works can be repeated in their entirety. As with natural narratives, we can choose to hear the good ones again and again."[7]

The essential distinction, in other words, is not between literature and conversation, but rather between verbal performance that *asserts*, and verbal performance that *tells*, whether it does it in writing or out loud. Most narrative—whether natural or literary—operates in the realm of the *tellable*; like dinner-party entertainment, literary narrative strives not principally to inform, but to inspire contemplation and evaluation, if in a less identifiable audience.

Thus relieved of the constraints of assertibility (as neatly articulated by Grice), literary narrative enjoys a certain license in both pertinence of subject matter and economy of delivery. But neither does this mean that "anything goes," any more than it does in the presence of listeners armed with a handy "so what?" By virtue of long-standing tenets of literary theory that hold that a work of serious literature must treat a subject of some "importance," by virtue of well-established generic conventions of epic proportions, tragic downfalls, the "unerhörte Begebenheit," and so forth,[8] and because, quite simply, an author must capture and maintain the interest of the reader, a literary narrative must display something "worth telling" in order to be "worth reading." Readers may be unable to interrupt the speaker if they are bored, but they can always interrupt their reading. What, then, is required to sustain the reader's imaginative involvement? What, finally, makes something tellable?

This book addresses the question of what is worth telling by looking at texts that raise it themselves—works by Chekhov, Zoshchenko, and Gogol that foreground their own choice of material that is not inherently significant or otherwise newsworthy. Although the notion of "inherent" significance is problematic, to say the least, I consider texts that select *flagrantly* small-scale, provocatively trivial material, texts that *force* the issue of significance and tellability. By spinning tales of yarn and sneezes, these works challenge not only our intuitive but also our literary-critical sense of what is worth telling and worth reading.

Some of these texts defy our sense of proportion by presenting a *story* constructed around an ostensibly small and inconsequential event. Others affront convention and intuition at the level of the *discourse* by deploying detail that seems insignificant or extraneous. Because a trivial story presents very different problems from a trivia-laden discourse, these diverse manifestations of "insignificance" will be dealt with separately here. But first, the distinction between the two levels of narrative must be made with precision.

Story and discourse correspond in my usage to the "what" and the "how" of narrative, respectively. "Story" refers to what happens (and to whom it happens, and where, when, and why it happens); "discourse" refers to the arrangement and presentation of that story content in a particular text. "Discourse" can be said to encompass both the *dispositio* and *elocutio* of the narrative events, while "story" is equivalent to the *inventio*. This final Latin term is especially apt because it emphasizes what I will stress below, namely, that far from being some preexistent but amorphous raw material that acquires meaning only through its subsequent discursive treatment, the story is itself a meaningful construct. It is devised to reveal some aspect of the organization of the world.[9] Story models the relationships between the members of that world's population. It forms a map of the fictional world that locates value systems and their adherents. And ultimately, story works by disrupting its own order: the story's events involve a change in the state of affairs established as "normal." Events, by definition, threaten the status quo.

At the level of *story*, we will see, the *event* is the locus of tellability.[10] And the degree of significance of an event is inseparable from the nature of the particular world order it imperils: the context imaginatively mapped out and disrupted by the narrative sequence. Iurii Lotman's description of event structure in spatial terms perhaps captures this most vividly. According to his topographical model, the narrative text establishes its powerful status quo in the form of disjunct and opposing semantic fields. Depending on the values and concerns that inform the text, these antithetical realms may reflect a juxtaposition of the "native" and the "foreign," for instance, or vice may be constructed to inhabit a realm separate from that of virtue. Characters are normally fixed in one sphere or the other, and their behavior within their respective domains is largely "predictable"; it embodies a norm. The boundary between these distinct realms is seemingly impenetrable, securely separating the world of friend from that of foe, the artist from the philistine, the living from the dead. But this pat array of classifications does not remain intact. When one of the figures proves mobile enough to violate that "inviolable" boundary—the most important topographical feature in Lotman's model—then something significant has happened: an *event* has occurred. Leaving the known world for the unknown, falling from virtue to vice, dying, or, for that matter, returning from the grave, might entail the transgression of such an apparently impenetrable textual boundary. But so might sneezing, if the textual norms of decorum strictly proscribe it. The more difficult, unlikely, or unexpected the infraction within the context of the normal spatial configurations established by the text, the more "eventful" the story.[11]

Here it becomes clear why Lotman's notion of event is important for my purposes: by vividly figuring the event as a *departure* from a textually inscribed norm, it emphasizes the connection between change—disruption of the status quo—and narrative tellability, and it locates the significance and poignancy of an event not in its objective magnitude but in the magnitude of its disruption of an established context. If the dead returned to life routinely, their comings and goings would excite little narrative interest. But even "trivial" occurrences are newsworthy if they undermine a stable norm. If "food in a bowl" were encountered after prolonged deprivation rather than at regular mealtimes, if it were handed across the "boundary" that separates the starving from the well fed, it would make a tellable event indeed.

In his book on *War and Peace*, Gary Saul Morson elaborates a theory of "prosaics— . . . the infinitesimal, . . . the accidental, . . . the trifling incidents on which everything ultimately depends." Although this valorization of the trivial is in some ways consonant with the conclusions facilitated by Lotman's notion of the event, the thrust of Morson's understanding of eventfulness differs from Lotman's. Prosaics (which Morson presents as fundamentally Tolstoyan) views ordinary and unsensational incidents as not only potentially, but presumably important. In Tolstoy's view, in fact, they are the *only* important events. Moreover, these significant events are "hidden in plain view," *imperceptible* and absolutely *normal*, not a function of disruption and unlikeliness at all. If Tolstoy is correct, then exceptional events, departures from the norm, *cannot* be genuinely important—not historically, psychologically, or ethically. Novels and histories that feature big events and perceptible changes lie about what life is really about, imposing structure and meaning that are false. Narratable (I might say "tellable") stories are *not true*.[12]

But if, as Morson reminds us, Tolstoy's hero was "truth," must truth necessarily be our criterion in considering narrative worth? Especially if, as Tolstoy believed, "narratives—all of them—are lies"?[13] Might not such "false" accounts be worth telling if they engage the kind of contemplation, evaluation, and interpretation that are the hallmark of the tellable? Some of the aspects of storytelling that Tolstoy condemns as falsifying are those that have produced the most enjoyable stories. Morson agrees that perceptible and disruptive events may be interesting—narratable or tellable—but in Tolstoy's prosaics, their very visibility vitiates their real importance. "Prosaically" speaking, what is important is by definition imperceptible; the deeds of real saints, we are told, are unnarratable.[14]

Significance here somehow has a moralistic ring. Prosaics—perhaps in response to Tolstoy, in whose honor it has been defined—seems to wield "significance" as an index of mimetic and ethical integrity.[15] A "pragmatics" of insignificance is rather more inclined to consider significance in terms of tellability and interest value. I am less concerned with the representational probity of stories than with their production and consumption. And while I am more than willing to join Morson in discarding the prerequisite that an event be *big* in order to be important (indeed, it is part of the purpose of this study to do so), because of the most basic requirements of interest I am still unable to eliminate from the notion of eventfulness the quality of perceptible *difference* from the norm. It is certainly central to Chekhov's and Zoshchenko's manipulation of the "insignificant" event, as we will see in Chapters 1–3, and it is arguably crucial to all successful storytelling. As Morson himself acknowledges in detail, Tolstoy's experiment with the unnoticeable, his refusal to cater to the persistent "desire for narratable stories," is part of what made *War and Peace* so disconcerting and irritating to its first readers.[16]

Lotman's notion of "eventfulness" thus remains a useful criterion for calibrating a story's "tellability": the less likely something is to occur—the more abnormal and disruptive it is in the given context—the more noticeable it is and the more significant and worth telling it is likely to seem. The status quo mapped by the narrative text in its fields and boundaries creates a *context* as surely as the profile of the listeners around my dinner table. As in natural narrative, what is tellable is what is unusual, contrary to expectations, or problematic—only it is the textually established status quo rather than the status of the interlocutors that determines the content of those expectations and the magnitude of their violation.

Nevertheless, the ultimate index of whether something can be considered "worth telling" is whether it is perceived as "worth reading." The prerogative of readers to disengage at any time makes them the final arbiter (if not the determiner) of tellability; hence the attention in the present inquiry to the *pragmatic* dimension of textual significance.[17] In the chapters that follow, I examine the reader's predicament in negotiating flagrantly insignificant material, texts that confound their readers' sense of proportion and import and tempt them to quit. Because well-educated, retrospective readers are trained to respond with relative ease to canonical works, those aspects of these works that complicated their original reception become less palpably problematic. The "reader" referred to here, for the most part, is perhaps a less indoctrinated one, one for whom the story of a galosh may be a genuine affront.

Rainer Warning argues in his own treatment of Lotman that the "eventful disorder" at the heart of every narrative ensures that reception will always be confrontational. By thematizing the norms of order and disorder, the world model constructed by the narrative text confronts "the usual with the unusual, the normal with the abnormal, the positivity of the allowed with the negativity of the excluded, the construction of a world with its destruction." The addressee must decide which to applaud, the reigning order or its disruption, the norm or its subversion.[18] Which is more valid? And which is more interesting? Lotman himself conceives of reception as a "struggle between perceiver and author," an ongoing contest in which the reader strives at each stage of reading to project the structure of the whole, only to be repeatedly undone by the successful author, who "triumphs" over the reader's literary competence, aesthetic norms, and preconceptions, enforcing instead his or her own model of the world. When the reader's expectations are repeatedly confirmed by a text, it is unnecessary to continue; the discomfiture of the unexpected, on the other hand, makes the engagement seem more "worth it." "Thus, the victory of the artist brings joy to the defeated reader."[19]

It is true that the first official readers of Chekhov's stories did not always experience unadulterated joy at the defeat of their expectations. The Russian critical arena of the 1880s reacted rather violently, accusing Chekhov of all manner of triviality, a total inability to distinguish between the significant and the incidental, and a general dearth of "larger ideas." The attack is not unmotivated: Chekhov's tiny stories were indeed boldly diminutive, and if newspaper headlines are any index at all, there is a strong tendency to associate size with significance.[20] Even more provocative than the brevity, though, was the subject matter: a man sneezes, or a cockroach runs across a desk. Chekhov presents the reader with incidents ostensibly too trivial to constitute an event and too minute to reflect important issues. Nevertheless the *general* readership of Chekhov's short stories was enrapt by what it discovered: Chekhov's public was able to perceive the cataclysms in the "pinpricks" of experience around which he constructed his narratives.[21] In his hands, the most "trivial" incident has profound consequences, or conversely, the anticipated "major event" is shown to be utterly inconsequential. In either case, it is the sociocultural norms of classification that bear the brunt of the jolt: "A text can take on norms given by society and shake them up by means of event. It can also however merely cite such norms, in order to interpret as non-events those things which would be considered as events under such norms. Or vice versa, it can take as valid [certain] norms which in the societal context have lost all validity, in order to make social non-events into events."[22]

Chekhov himself contended that the norms upheld by a society become palpable only when they are violated, and he adopted as a kind of goal the displaying of such infractions. "My goal," he wrote to Pleshcheev, "is to kill two birds with one stone: to depict life truthfully and, in the process, to show how much this life deviates from the norm. The norm is not known to me, just as it is not known to any of us. We all know a dishonorable deed when we see one, but just what honor is we do not know."[23]

It is the very nature of the normal, the ordinary, the "hidden in plain view," that it goes unremarked. "It does not require comment (one doesn't write news stories about it) because it is obvious, right there on the surface; anyone can see it."[24] But just as obviously, Stanley Fish continues, what one sees is a product of the tacitly accepted verbal and mental categories that locate significance. It is Chekhov's achievement that he makes these norms of significant and tellable action manifest. He does so by manipulating the dimensions of the narrative event, leaving the reader with a fresh perception of the prevailing order and a need to reevaluate what might actually constitute a "significant" event in that context. What I undertake to explore in Chapter 1 is the way in which, by exploding the inferences we make about significance and insignificance in terms of both our ordinary coded knowledge of the world and our literary experience, the ostensibly "trivial" can be subtly but powerfully subversive, and the process of reading it very worth our while.

By the 1920s in the Soviet Union, new ideological and imaginative urgencies had emerged, but the most interesting prose of this period, too, is characterized by a heightened attention to the very small. In an era that officially privileges monumentality, Mikhail Zoshchenko's stories in particular focused stubbornly on such crises as accidentally stepping on someone's foot or trying to hang up a coat. Why, then, did the reading public regard his little pieces as so profoundly worth reading?

While ostensibly the most harmless "drivel," Zoshchenko's little two-paged trifles about life's most trifling incidents blatantly flout the demands of the party critics for grandeur of both form and content. More provocatively still, Zoshchenko develops an ingenious poetics of "noticing" to assert the importance of the problems officially designated too trivial to merit attention, and, conversely, to trivialize the larger-than-life icons of Soviet power. By reversing the regime's determinations of what is and is not important; by replacing the Revolution with "big events" of his own (problems with coats and feet); by structurally reversing crisis and norm, figure and ground; and by thematizing the relationship between noticing and storytelling, between perceptibility and tellability, Zoshchenko foregrounds the reading not only of textual events, but also of historical ones. As Chapters 2 and 3 will suggest, his rereadings are not only humorous; they are inflammatory.

The chapters on Chekhov and Zoshchenko, then, address the issue of *story* construction in order to examine the ways in which incidents normally considered small and unimportant can be reinterpreted as events of enormous significance and tellability; or, conversely, how institutionalized significance can be unmasked as petty and inconsequential. In either case, the reader is made to reexamine his or her criteria for evaluating both experience and text.

The question of what is worth telling reasserts itself at the level of the *discourse* in terms of the deployment of detail. Although the items, qualities, and incidents invoked by narrative detail may belong fundamentally to the *story* in that they are all part of the potentially infinite continuum of facts and attributes of the *inventio*, the arrangement of these details in the actual text—as well as the determination of which to make explicit and which to omit—is performed by the *discourse*.[25] Just as extreme reticence in disclosing the details of a story must be seen as the function of a particular discursive manner, so too must the superabundance of textual detail be treated as a result of discursive strategies. To explore the "tellability" of the discourse, then, I consider the prose of Nikolai Gogol for its extravagant use of detail, much of which seems to be insignificant or extraneous. Gogol's distended discourse violates the principle of prose economy, that maxim which prompts the speaker/narrator to "get to the point" and gives the reader some hope of getting there too.

Not every "small" detail automatically gets in the way of our reading; a violation of the threshold of tellability is most likely to be felt only with *excess* minute detail. Much has been written, for instance, about Chekhov's use of minutiae. His characters and settings are often described by a single obscure and ostensibly haphazard detail.[26] And yet Chekhov's prose is a model of economy—his particulars are of the pregnant, pithy sort that epitomize in a single stroke what a drawn-out descriptive passage would have accomplished less felicitously. Chekhov is not opposed to specificity, but he is a fierce opponent of superfluity of specification: this is an important feature of his poetics. If a gun is reported to be hanging on the wall in chapter one, stipulates his oft-quoted imperative, then it must be fired by the end or it ought never to have been mentioned.[27] Thus, though he serves us well in the examination of story-level "insignificance," provocatively casting a sneeze in the role of event, Chekhov will have little to offer in the way of audaciously superfluous detail. Zoshchenko, too, decries prolixity in telling, and although his language is certainly idiosyncratic, it gets quickly to the matter at hand and then just as rapidly terminates the performance. Gogol, by contrast, indulges in much more elaboration than we really want, and certainly more than we really need.

Superfluity of detail is admittedly a slippery proposition, since most descriptive detail is not logically essential to the continued progress of the events. Thus, there are no clear limits as to what is enough and how much can be tolerated. Instead, the reader's standards seem to accommodate the particular exigencies of an author's period or individual style.[28]

In the context of realist aesthetics, for example, where detail is deployed quite generously, reality itself—"l'*avoir-été-là* des choses"— justifies the enumeration and description of things in a text: they are invoked to create the effect of the real.[29] Thus, Barthes contends, sometimes it is not the objects themselves that are important, but rather the fact of their inclusion in the narrative. In the name of referential specificity, oddly enough, it is the *category* of the real, rather than any specific member of that category, that is signified. The reader perceives not so much that there is a barometer on the wall, for example, as that the narrator has undertaken to reproduce faithfully "every" aspect of the room's decor.[30]

The realist enterprise has been described as the transmission of as much information as possible and the concomitant reduction of "noise."[31] But can what purports to be information be "noisy" itself if provided in excess? How, for instance, are we to account for—or even tolerate— the glut of "data" in Gogol's prose, detail that is neither informative nor "realistic" but rather ostentatiously trivial and excessive? At every juncture Gogol elaborates and enumerates ad nauseam and digresses beyond the purview of any imaginable descriptive purpose. Gogol's discourse goes off on excursions of its own, leaving the story matter far behind, while we require correspondingly prodigious mental dexterity to recall the "point" of departure and even more patience to get to any point at all.

Gogol's violation of the norms of significance, in other words, is played out at the level of his discourse rather than in his construction of story. Unlike Chekhov and Zoshchenko, who contrive to engage our attention with a story of immoderately small proportions, Gogol conspires to delay the unfolding of the story, whatever its relative magnitude, by overloading his account of it with such a barrage of extraneous detail that the "point" is infinitely deferred, if not obscured altogether. The story, the "what," may well be big news—a detached nose roams Petersburg, a scoundrel devises an ingenious scheme for trafficking in deceased servants—but the relentlessly elaborative discourse, the "how," seems mired in trivia. If only we *could* interrupt him now and again and urge him to get to the point.

Barthes tells us that the narrative text "ne connaît pas le bruit": everything, regardless of its apparent obscurity, has its effect.[32] What, then, is achieved by such overly specific and overabundant verbal matter that violates not only all of Grice's maxims of quantity, relation, and manner, but all recognizable standards of tellability as well? What makes such extraneous detail worth reading? Whether or not, as Robert Crosman would have it, "readers make meaning,"[33] they do at least attempt to make sense of what they read. What operations must a reader perform to assimilate or structure the verbal chaos presented by prose such as Gogol's?

If, as I will observe in the chapters on Chekhov and Zoshchenko, the strategic use of insignificance at the level of the story can delight by exploding both tacit assumptions about and explicit demands for significance, what, if anything, does the *discursive* use of trivia explode, and how delightful is the eruption? Does Gogol's ongoing deflection of our desire for sense and significance actually bring "joy to the defeated reader"? Chapters 4 and 5 explore the pragmatic repercussions of a discourse distended with apparently insignificant and irrelevant detail and digression. As I consider the types of "irrelevancies" Gogol looses on his reader (both suspecting and unsuspecting), I will be concerned principally with the function of this stylistic excess in the context of the narrative transaction, performing not a stylistic analysis, but rather asking what this persistent characteristic—which may be considered stylistic—does to the text and its reception. I will explore what the text requires of the reader, what the reader desires from the text, and how these desires fare in the face of Gogol's infinitely elaborative prose, treating his writing as a kind of test case for the pleasures and pitfalls of discourse-level insignificance.

Because discursive insignificance obstructs narrative progress, the discourse overwhelms and obscures the story, presenting almost insurmountable difficulties for the reader who had hoped to contemplate, evaluate, and respond to a "state of affairs" or a "series of events," or even to discover "what happens next." If this primeval hunger for *story* is, as E. M. Forster argues, the most fundamental, indeed indispensable, aspect of the narrative transaction,[34] what happens to the reading process when our access to the story is thwarted by the very medium that purports to present it? This phenomenon occasions a consideration of the relationship of discourse to story, which in turn accounts for Gogol's position at the end of this book in spite of his chronological priority. For although Gogol is clearly a precursor of the other two authors in ways that have been amply elucidated—in terms of their humor, for instance, and the stature of their heroes—still, his manipulation of the insignificant is a phenomenon of a different order. It involves the veritable sandbagging of story by discourse, the problematization of what is logically anterior by what, in theory, exists in its service.[35] By considering discourse second, I provisionally accept the apparent logic of the story/discourse relation, but go on to examine theoretically the implications of the distinction.

In addition to the chronological deformation, the reader of the present study will discern a certain archaeology of critical approaches and concerns as I progress from chapter to chapter. This does, in part, reflect the chronology of my own engagement with the material, but it arises more fundamentally from the idiosyncrasies of the writers in question. Chekhov's manipulation of the reader's sense of proportion is most palpable in structural terms, Zoshchenko wields his trivia almost deconstructively, and Gogol's great discursive orgy works both with and against an economy of narrative desire. Each suggests its own most appropriate model of text production. It is the book's enduring concern with text reception, however—the reader's project in confronting the "insignificant"—that is meant to unite the individual considerations.

ONE

Anton Chekhov: Reinventing Events

"MINNEAPOLIS (AP)—Georgia O'Keeffe's 'Oriental Poppies' looks great hanging just as it has for nearly 30 years, say officials of the University of Minnesota Art Museum."—News story (in its entirety) from the *Tulsa World*. *New Yorker*, Dec. 1, 1986

"*Honey, I'm home.*"

© 1988 Mick Stevens
originally in The New Yorker Magazine, Inc.
All Rights Reserved.

The Myth of Eventlessness

In one of Chekhov's stories there is a character by the name of Ippolit Ippolitych who has the dubious distinction of saying only what is already well known to everyone. "Summer is not the same as winter," proffers Ippolit Ippolitych. "In the summer it is warm and there is no need to heat. In the winter it is cold and heating is necessary." During the day it is light, at night it is dark. Horses eat oats. People sleep in beds. And so on.[1] In short, Ippolit Ippolitych contributes nothing that could be regarded as "assertible" or even remotely "tellable." His speech epitomizes uneventful narrative: it contains no disruption, no violation, no surprise—rather it *fixes* the prevailing order. Like a telephone book or a calendar—or the Associated Press dispatch on Georgia O'Keeffe's "Poppies"—it simply retraces the map of the known world. (This final image is not just a metaphor. As the teacher of geography, Ippolit Ippolitych reproduces maps day in and day out, year after year, fixing and reaffirming the abiding order of things, rehearsing as doggedly in colored pencil on paper as he does in conversation only the eminently obvious.) What is well known and unchanged typically "goes without saying"—"one doesn't write news stories about it."[2] But Chekhov's geographer makes a career out of just such reports.

In Ippolit Ippolitych, Chekhov has created a preposterous character, but not a gratuitous one. By emphasizing Ippolit Ippolitych's absurdity, by ridiculing what is fundamentally unacceptable in natural narrative, Chekhov exposes the inadequacy of *any* narrative that communicates nothing new, significant, or "worth telling." The writer's business, Chekhov wrote to his editor, is not only "to depict truthfully," but also "to be able to distinguish between important testimony and trivia." This, continues Chekhov, is the sign of real talent.[3]

And yet, in apparent non-compliance with his own dictum, Chekhov generated an entire corpus of stories of the most minute dimensions (frequently of no more than five pages) and with subject matter of the most unspectacular sort: a sneeze, a stray cockroach, a slight fever, a boring conversationalist. This display of minutiae not only seemed to challenge Chekhov's own feelings about "important testimony," but also conflicted with a vast body of realist precedent. The paradigm of the realist novel, which, while attentive to detail, had postulated a certain standard for the magnitude of a work as a whole and the events portrayed therein, and which continued to inform the expectations of the Russian reader, appeared to be lost on Anton Chekhov.

The critics were not slow to object. From the most varied ideological camps came the reproach that Mr. Chekhov was "preoccupied with absolute trivia [*melochi*]." Couldn't he think of anything more important to apply himself to?[4] His earliest critics lamented the "waste of a great talent" on such "insignificant incidents"[5] (though we might ask where they discerned this "great talent" if not in the very form they were militating against). Worse than the "excessive brevity" of Chekhov's prose,[6] it seems, was his apparent inability to distinguish between the "significant" and the "insignificant": "To Chekhov it's all the same: a man, or just his shadow, a little bell, or a suicide," declared the prominent populist critic N. K. Mikhailovskii in a formulation that came to be the canonical explanation for Chekhov's undiscriminating choice of subject matter.[7] Chekhov, it was said, simply "went out for a walk in life," and whatever happened to cross his path, whether serious or frivolous, major or minor, portentous or ordinary, was recorded in the same casual tone; his stories consisted of nothing more than impressions that were merely accidental.[8] Thus, they were frequently "without content" (*bessoderzhatel'nyi*), and they were always "devoid of ideals" (*bezydeinyi*).[9] Saltykov-Shchedrin had called for an unmistakable commitment to strong ideals to combat the encroaching and pernicious "trifles of life" (*Melochi zhizni*, 1886–87). Much as he admired the older writer, though, Chekhov spurned this tendentious route and ambled aimlessly, apparently eager to embrace any and all of life's trifles.[10]

"Chekhov operates like a photographer," complained P. Pertsov, echoing and further developing Mikhailovskii's earlier accusation. He takes snapshots of everything "with exactly the same impartiality": "His camera does not distinguish between a lovely landscape . . . , the thoughtful face of a young girl, the disheveled figure of an unsuccessful intellectual . . . , an obtuse merchant, or the disgraceful social order. . . . Chekhov really is indifferent as to whether the bells are ringing, or someone is being murdered, or champagne is being served."[11]

This was a "pure artist," it was noted with scorn, one who recorded his observations directly and without purpose, unmediated and unglossed, like so many beads on a string—or more often than not, just beads with no string at all.[12] Chekhov, it was said, provided no "artistic cement" to unify his haphazard observations.[13] Thus, while A. P. Chudakov, in his ambitious study of Chekhov's poetics, emphasizes the importance of "chance" (*sluchainost'*) as a *positive* structural principle for Chekhov,[14] most of Chekhov's contemporaries saw the "randomness" very differently. His stories, characterized as they were by "a complete absence of ideas,"[15] lacked the unity and purpose that would give these light and airy little pieces substance and make them worthwhile.

With hindsight comes the temptation, now that we know that Chekhov is a "great writer," to ridicule these initial reactions, cite the most outrageous ones and confidently overrule them, congratulating ourselves on our ability to recognize true genius. Still, they are too revealing to be dismissed so summarily. While later criticism had the project of integrating Chekhov into the literary canon, the early reviews of Mikhailovskii, Skabichevskii, Pertsov, and others are eloquent testimony for the prosecution: they document the extent to which Chekhov's works differed from what preceded them, and they illustrate vividly the reigning assumptions about literature that made Chekhov's manipulation of the public's sense of proportion so disconcerting.[16]

Jeffrey Brooks, in his study of "Readers and Reading at the End of the Tsarist Era," demonstrates the overwhelming prevalence of that era's expectation that a literary work evidence not only "social verisimilitude," but also "inherent moral value."[17] This implicit demand for didacticism no doubt had much to do with the negative response to Chekhov's somewhat skimpy stories. What could one possibly hope to glean from such trifles? Not only did Chekhov ignore "significant issues"; he also assiduously refrained from adopting an explicit stand, formulating a moral, or extolling or condemning his characters and their actions. This was a principle Chekhov defended repeatedly. "My task," he wrote to Suvorin, is "not to solve problems . . . but to depict them," to pose questions, not to answer them. Let the readers act as jurors. And is it really necessary to *say* that a horse thief is "bad" when (like the testimony of Ippolit Ippolitych) "this is already long since well known to everyone"?[18]

This strategy, however, tended to support the complaint of "social indifference" already provoked by Chekhov's marginally significant subject matter. Socially indifferent material was by definition trivial; thus this was an accusation not easily dismissed. Soviet criticism, with its special burden of confirming the social significance of an undertaking, went to some lengths to overturn whatever remained of this charge.[19] The ideological obligation to discern great social import in the negligible "events" of Chekhov's prose, for instance, led the early Soviet critics to take great care in distinguishing the by then canonized Chekhov from other devotees of the *mig* (brief moment), the notoriously decadent Symbolists.[20] A similar demand for social relevance and commitment led the critics of Chekhov's own time to diagnose his fixation on the "insignificant" as a product of a defective or even nonexistent world view. Chekhov's prose, complained M. A. Protopopov, presents "sort of a disorderly pile of material." "What his world view consists of, no one can say, because Mr. Chekhov doesn't have one—period."[21]

Some critics did attempt to account for Chekhov's utter "inability to write as literary theory demands."[22] What appeared to be "a deliberate violation of the rules" may have actually been due to Chekhov's "literary inexperience," or more precisely, to his "humoristic past."[23] Disterlo refers here to Chekhov's affiliation in the years from 1880 to 1886 with the comic papers *Budil'nik* (*Alarm Clock*), *Strekoza* (*Dragonfly*), *Zritel'* (*Spectator*), and *Oskolki* (*Splinters*). During this time, even Chekhov with his credo of brevity complained repeatedly about the 100-line limit and the pressing deadlines that resulted in the production of what he himself termed "trifles."[24] Even when his first collection, *Multi-Colored Stories* (*Pestrye rasskazy*) appeared in 1886, it was still as a "Grub Street hack" that Chekhov was discussed.[25]

But while some of his contemporaries underscored Chekhov's journalistic connections as an alibi for his minimalist enterprise, most dwelt on his apparent indifference and purposelessness. He is so noncommittal, ran the argument, that his stories do not conclude: they simply stop. They are no more than excerpts, time segments that end arbitrarily rather than logical sequences culminating in an *event*, the presumptive backbone of narrative.[26] In Chekhov's world, summarizes Merezhkovskii, "there is only daily routine without any event."[27]

Thus we have a view of Chekhov that regards his prose as trivial in scope, plagued by an inability to separate significant material from insignificant, and consequently devoid of ideals, purpose, and even proper events. The tone of vehement condemnation diminished as Chekhov's popularity increased, but the gist of the complaints persisted. Even after he was awarded the Pushkin prize for excellent literary achievement in 1888, Chekhov was still attacked frequently in the press for his "trivial" and "indifferent" works.[28] It was impossible to identify an ideological affiliation, for instance, from either the text of his stories or the journals that published them: Chekhov continued to publish regularly in Suvorin's conservative *Novoe vremia* (*New Times*), while also contributing to the more progressive monthlies.[29] And in neither did Chekhov demonstrate an explicit commitment to any "important" goals, or even to his heroes, whom he abandoned after a few "uneventful" pages. Chekhov was clearly indifferent.

Why, then, was the reading public not indifferent to Chekhov? Even Skabichevskii, one of Chekhov's harshest critics, had to concede:

Chekhov is a writer devoid of ideals and principles—that we know as a fact, signed, sealed, and delivered. Nevertheless, whenever a new story of his appears in a journal, its pages are the first to be slit in that issue, that story is read before anything else, and it makes an incredibly strong impression on the reader, powerfully affecting his mood, inspiring a whole range of new ideas and notions, in a way that most so-called "ideological" works never manage to do.[30]

How was it that Chekhov's reputed "trivia" was so affective and so worth reading?

The fact is that Chekhov does not simply say anything that comes into his mind, as Ippolit Ippolitych does, nor does he indiscriminately reproduce anything that crosses his path, whether in a little book, like Trigorin,[31] or photographically, as Mikhailovskii and his colleagues claimed (as if photography were without its own principles of composition and selection). Chekhov's own account of his method refutes the snapshot theory anyway: "I can write *only* from memory—I've never written directly from observation. The subject must be filtered through my memory so that there remains on it, as on a filter, only what is important."[32]

In fact, for someone who was constantly being accused of indifference to "important" issues, and whose stories really do evidence a certain predilection for smaller, less monumental matters, Chekhov was tremendously concerned with the significance of the things he depicted. I would suggest that his selection of ostensibly trivial material is not accidental, but is rather a deliberate principle of story construction; further, that he proceeds in this fashion *not* out of disregard for that all-important distinction between significant and insignificant, but rather out of an intense preoccupation with those very categories, a preoccupation that is induced in turn in the reader; and finally, that the resulting texts, far from being unconcerned, are subtly but acutely critical.

In Chekhov's stories, this preoccupation is expressed in his constant play with reigning notions about what is and is not significant enough to merit telling. The tremendous appeal of Chekhov's "trifles" acknowledged by Skabichevskii reflects the public's display of delight at the defeat of its expectations.[33] Chekhov's story "At Home" ("Doma," 1887) proposes a tentative model for the production and reception of stories. It depicts a lawyer who must tell his young son Serezha stories, but not really knowing any, is forced to improvise. "Serezha loved these improvisations, and the lawyer noticed that the more modest and unpretentious the plot turned out to be, the more powerfully it affected the boy" (6:104). Chekhov's own results were not dissimilar. The less pretentious his stories appeared and the more infinitesimal the "pinprick" seemed at first glance, the more interesting it was for his readers to confront unexpectedly that incident's unanticipated significance and be forced to revise their original assumptions.

How does Chekhov violate the conventional thresholds of tellability? Certainly by the late nineteenth century it was no longer a major transgression to select a character of sub-kingly stature. Wordsworth had defended the "lowly subject" as worthy of poetry by the end of the eighteenth century, and Goethe had effected a certain democratization of classically "heroic" forms when he cast the bourgeoisie in hexameters in *Hermann und Dorothea*. Nor had the Russian tradition lagged behind the European Romantic movement in this regard. The golden age of Russian literature showcased the "little man"—from Gogol's impoverished and inarticulate clerks to Dostoevsky's psychologically complex "poor folk"; from Turgenev's enterprising peasants to Tolstoy's low-born moral exemplars; and in the works of writers such as Pleshcheev, Pisemskii, Kokorev, Khvoshchinskaia, and Mikhailov—Russian literature gave the "insulted and the injured" a voice and a plot of their own. In this illustrious company, Chekhov's "ordinary people" were not strikingly undersized. Many of his characters were, in fact, culturally significant figures: professors, doctors, magistrates, teachers, bishops, bureaucrats, artists, writers, and so on.

But the exigencies of the short-story genre relate less to who is in the starring role anyway than to what *befalls* that character, or in other words, WHAT HAPPENS. The short story, as its name suggests, is brief. Not all languages are as explicit as English in this matter, but nonetheless, the *rasskaz*, the *Erzählung*, the *conte* are all characterized by relative brevity. So while the expectation has been that the novel provides "a full and authentic report of human experience," the short story's more limited dimensions make the portrayal of a whole life problematic.[34] The short story's brevity, it was argued by Chekhov's contemporary Arsen'ev, restricts the range of appropriate subject matter, making many topics too ambitious, too extravagant, too unwieldy:

A short story should be neither a simple snapshot of some arbitrary fact, nor an excursion into the sphere of complex psychical and emotional developments which do not lend themselves . . . to radical condensation. There are limits to the elasticity of a plot; some projects are impossible to carry out in the course of a few pages, matters which cannot be compressed beyond a certain point, even with the help of the most powerful artistic vise.[35]

This does not imply, however, that the short story is nothing more than a receptacle for trivia or a forum for Ippolit Ippolitych to rehearse the obvious. What it has come to mean is that a *highlight* of a life is displayed, a "moment of truth," often *the* significant event of that life.[36] In fact, though there have been numerous attempts to characterize the genre by such determinations as unity of tone, or how long it takes to read, the most consistent expectation (whether tacit or explicit) in the countless discussions of the short story has been that an "extraordinary event" occur.[37]

No doubt this consensus is partly a legacy of the earliest practitioners of the genre—Irving, Poe, Hawthorne, Pushkin, and Gogol—who recounted events that were not only extraordinary, but often downright supernatural. But the "extraordinary event" has persisted, albeit in less dramatic form, as an integral component of the short-story paradigm. It is the decisive shaper of the familiar diagram,

the schematic representation of what has come to be recognized as typical short-story structure: exposition, rising action, climax, denouement—with the climax, the turning point, supplied by the celebrated "extraordinary event."

An "event," I have said, is the disruption of the reigning order, the crossing of a seemingly inviolable boundary between opposing semantic fields, and hence represents a challenge to the norms of classification that deemed that feat impossible or intolerable. The more unlikely, the more unanticipated the infraction within the context of the particular sociocultural system of values that informs that map of the world and establishes its boundaries, the more eventful the story. Uneventful narrative, such as the "Diary of a Cat" or the *Tulsa World*'s piece on Georgia O'Keeffe's painting, simply chronicles an unchanging world or, like Ippolit Ippolitych's announcement that summer will follow spring, merely documents a change that is in no sense unpredictable and in no sense tellable. Eventful narrative reports an extraordinary deviation.

An event, then, is by definition something "unlikely to occur." The curious thing about Chekhov's events is that they are composed of incidents unlikely to be perceived as eventful—matters ostensibly too trivial to constitute a major disruption. Chekhov was amply criticized for this throughout his career. "All his attention is directed to trifling detail and none at all is paid to the essential," griped one critic.[38] In the world of Chekhov's stories, however, the "trifling detail" is shown to *be* the essential. When the philosopher-critic Lev Shestov used the phrase "creation out of nothing" to describe Chekhov's work, he was referring to Chekhov's alleged pessimism, his hopelessness, the existential void that Shestov felt caused Chekhov to withhold every possible consolation in his work.[39] But the formulation could alternatively be applied to Chekhov's fondness for portraying the "pinprick" as ultimately cataclysmic, making the proverbial mountain out of a molehill, creating "something" out of "nothing."

This is one of Chekhov's four basic strategies, each of which targets the notion of the requisite "significant event" in order to render problematic the usual assumptions about what is significant. The first of these strategies experiments with a seemingly minor incident that emerges in the end as extremely significant, eventful, even cataclysmic; the second reverses this revelation, staging an ostensibly "significant" event but going on to expose its fundamental unimportance; the third confronts two contradictory perspectives on a single event, one of which views the incident as inconsequential, while the other is overwhelmed by its importance; and the final strategy generates strong expectations that a significant event will occur, but ultimately withholds it altogether.

If typically a significant event "surprises" the reader by happening (since unlikeliness to occur is the earmark of eventfulness), Chekhov's assault on the event either reverses this—as in the fourth strategy where the expected event surprisingly fails to occur—or displaces the astonishment from what *occurs* to what it turns out to be worth—as in the first two strategies, which recalibrate an event's significance, and the third, which even more explicitly makes eventfulness a matter of interpretation. In each case, in spite of (but obviously related to) the critics' complaints about Chekhov's disregard for eventfulness, the *event* is clearly central.

The four-part typology elaborated below derives from a large sample of Chekhov's stories and accounts fairly completely for the many works with this agenda of exploring significance and insignificance. The strategies do not apply to all of Chekhov's works, nor do they pretend to exhaust the possibilities of the stories they do describe. They are meant, rather, to facilitate an exploration of one important aspect of Chekhov's poetics and to allow us to consider otherwise unrelated stories as diverse reflections of one of Chekhov's most enduring concerns.

Without attempting anything like a real periodization on the basis of these types, I will simply note that the first category is dominated by Chekhov's earlier, shorter, and more explicitly humorous works, while the second strategy, the logical complement of the first, includes more of his later, longer, more "serious" stories. In stories that feature the third strategy, Chekhov most often creates the disparate perspectives by providing both adult and childhood points of view. Since his narrative interest in children seems to be concentrated in the mid-1880s, the third strategy is fairly localized temporally. The final strategy, by contrast, extends throughout the central years of Chekhov's career. The chronological regularities, however, are not consistent—there are plenty of later stories in the first category and many early ones in the second. Moreover, the last thing I want to do is to contribute to the already overblown mythology of the "two Chekhovs," one callow, one mature; one silly, one somber. While his strategies clearly evolved over time, Chekhov's preoccupation with significance, insignificance, and tellability was abiding and not easily exorcised. If anything, I am left with a renewed sense of continuity.

Strategies of Eventfulness

The First Strategy: Maximizing the Minimum

The first strategy involves staging an ostensibly insignificant incident that turns out, on the contrary, to have major consequences, to be truly *eventful*, thus forcing a reevaluation of the original categories for classifying experience. Probably the most memorable example of this (though far from the only one) is the story "Death of a Clerk" ("Smert' chinovnika," 1883), which opens with an insignificant clerk at the opera.

Cherviakov sits comfortably in the second row of the stalls, watching the action on stage and experiencing the height of contentment, satisfaction, bliss. "But suddenly... [and Chekhov underlines that "suddenly," the conventional here-comes-the-event signal to the reader:][40] We often find this 'but suddenly' in stories. Authors are right: life is so full of unexpected surprises! But suddenly," the narrator continues, our blessed hero sneezes (2:164).

Not that this is so unusual—peasants sneeze, presidents sneeze, everybody sneezes—and Cherviakov is not in the least disconcerted. But lo and behold, from his seat in the second row, Cherviakov notices that just ahead of him, in the first row, a dignified older man is delicately wiping his bald pate. And he recognizes that this elderly gentleman is a general, a person of superior rank.

Suddenly Cherviakov becomes terribly upset. He has failed to keep his sphere of activity in the second row befitting his own rank, and though it may not be unusual to sneeze, it is an infraction to sneeze across class and rank boundaries. He has figuratively violated the "inviolable" boundary in Lotman's sense: he has sneezed on a member of the first row. This is the beginning of the end. He tries to rectify things by apologizing during the performance, but the general just hushes him. Cherviakov's former bliss has now been lost forever: he is overcome with distress. He then makes a series of earnest attempts to apologize properly—first during intermission and later on subsequent days at the general's office—until at last the general, who had quite forgotten the incident and who finds the unremitting repentance more irritating than the original "sin," explodes with a resounding "Get out of here!!" (*Poshel von!!* [2:166]). Cherviakov backs away, blindly makes his way home, and without taking off his new coat, lies down on the couch and dies.

What has happened here, and how can a sneeze be an event? It may be an overstatement to say that Cherviakov sneezed and died of it, but only a slight one. This is a figure who oversteps the bounds of his rank (albeit with nothing more serious than a sneeze), and then once on this foreign and shaky ground, proceeds to do himself in by *escalating* the proscribed contact that can only be fatal to him (even though our general is, ironically, an illustrious official of the department of communication). First, Cherviakov disturbs the general with a sneeze; then he pesters him with apologies during the performance; next he approaches the general during intermission; then he appears in the general's outer office; next he penetrates into his inner rooms; finally, he succeeds in being enough of a nuisance to provoke the wrath of a superior (and one of the only multiple exclamation points in all of Chekhov's works, aside from the one associated with the sneeze itself).

What we actually have here is a model of an order conceived as so rigid that even to sneeze is to break rank, and to break rank is unforgivable. The rigidity of conception here is clearly Cherviakov's own; the general tolerates substantially more provocation than a simple sneeze before he flies off the handle. But the clerk has only perfectly internalized the dehumanizing table of ranks and its abhorrence of insubordination. Hence Cherviakov's frantic and all-consuming efforts to reestablish the proper boundaries. His efforts are doomed, however, because each time he tries, he transgresses the boundary that he wants so desperately to reinstate. He succeeds only in aggravating the situation beyond hope.

As in mathematical catastrophe theory, the tiniest alteration in the "order of things" is amplified to overall chaos. Or to express the phenomenon in Jakobsonian terms, Chekhov, in his perusal of the axis of selection, chooses an element from the paradigm "small and insignificant" and situates it on the axis of combination in the position (function) of something "big and important."⁴¹ But what does this manipulation do for the validity of the "world model" constructed by a narrative? Isn't this a distortion of reality rather than a meaningful representation? Can this absurd disproportionality of cause and effect be anything but farcical?

To begin with, the episode is not as absurd as it might appear. Chekhov's correspondence includes an 1882 letter from a Taganrog acquaintance who writes of a similar event in Chekhov's hometown. It seems a pedantic local postmaster had threatened punitive action against a clerk for an alleged "violation of discipline" consisting in a "personal insult." After his repeated attempts to apologize were rebuffed, the clerk finally fled in despair to the public gardens and hanged himself.⁴²

Whether that incident is actually the source of "Death of a Clerk" is not the point. What is crucial is that both stories picture the logical (if extreme) conclusion of consistently viewing a dignitary as a higher creature, and someone of a lower rank as inferior. Notably, this is not a portrait of the big bad general flexing his muscles like his Gogolian predecessor.⁴³ Here, as in "Fatty and Skinny" ("Tolstyi i tonkii," also 1883), it is the little man who insists perversely on his own inferiority. Cherviakov's name, derived from the Russian word for "worm" (*cherviak*), speaks eloquently enough for his pathetic sense of self-worth, invoking the traditional endorsement of meekness as a cardinal virtue.⁴⁴ Cherviakov's sneeze is an explicit violation of the prescribed pious posture.

Nor are the spatial arrangements of the story arbitrary: they model and incorporate specific cultural norms and ethical values. The theater, for instance, where the original transgression occurs, is a place of strictly codified decorum. As an enclosed public space, it is a locus of potential encounters, but it is also a place in which separation is enforced and lines are drawn. The proscenium came into being to separate the actors from the audience (there is traditionally no interaction; the action on stage is viewed from afar, through the mediation of binoculars). The system of seating, with its strict rows and discrete levels and classes of seats, emphasizes and preserves class distinctions. Instead of interaction, *appearances* assume paramount importance.⁴⁵ Even in the prison theater in Dostoevsky's *House of the Dead*, where a real sense of community is established, strict configurations and demarcations reign: the sense of community is predicated upon a strong sense of "who belongs where." The exceptional occasion when real contact *is* made in the theater represents a terrible removal of the usual barriers, such as Natasha experiences in her meeting with Anatol' Kuragin in *War and Peace*. And Cherviakov's sneeze has even more dire consequences than Natasha's "infidelity."

Sneezing is actually not such an improbable form for symbolic transgression. It is, in a sense, eventful pollution. Russian canon law, as it has come down to us from the Novgorodian priests of the twelfth century (in particular in the hundred and one questions of Kirik) is adamant on the point of the impurity of bodily secretions.[46] In Gogol's *Taras Bul'ba* we are told it is the distasteful habit of the "enemy of Christendom" to "sneeze right in your face." The folkloric significance of the sneeze is the exit of the soul from the body, or the entrance of the "evil one," either of which, if unchecked by a "God bless you," can have fateful consequences. And the Freudian sneeze represents the ultimate penetration into the space of the "other." So while Cherviakov's overreaction is ridiculous, his fundamental anxiety is not.

And while to sneeze on someone is just generally offensive, the action also brings into play the colloquial meaning of the phrase *nachikhat' na chto-libo, kogo-libo* (not to give two shakes about them, not to accord them the respect expected or required). We find this usage explicitly elsewhere in Chekhov's works;[47] in this story, the double entendre is underlined by Cherviakov's eagerness to explain "lest [the general] think I was trying to spit" (2:165). (*Pliunut'*—to spit—has the same colloquial thrust as to sneeze, i.e., not to give a damn.)

The story thus presents a challenge to the dehumanizing principle of subordination and to the social structures that foster it: more joy for the defeated reader, who never would have expected a sneeze to have such a powerfully agitational effect, but who can certainly relate to "sneezing" on it all. The triviality of Cherviakov's consequence-laden transgression undercuts the social norms that determine and uphold the boundary between ranks. Any event challenges the inviolability of the boundary, but an absurdly small one challenges that boundary's very validity. The distinction in rank turns out to be an untenable position if applied consistently. And a sneeze turns out to be eminently tellable. In fact, discussion of the sneeze is itself transgressive. It is Cherviakov's unflagging insistence on mentioning what the general deems trivial (*pustiaki* [2:165]) that gets him in irreversible trouble; and it is Chekhov's insistence on mentioning it that not only addresses an ossified system of social protocol, but challenges as well a well-ensconced set of literary norms and expectations. Significantly, far from abandoning their reading, Chekhov's public clamored for more.

"You do tremendous things with your little short stories, arousing in people an aversion to this sleepy, half-dead life—I swear you do!" exclaimed Gorky in a letter to Chekhov.[48] He discerned in Chekhov's "little bottles" (as he dubbed Chekhov's stories) "that subtle, pungent, and healthy smell" of critique, just as Zoshchenko pointed out years later that the laughter of Chekhov's stories is far from neutral: "Each smile, even the most seemingly indifferent smile, is already an evaluation, already criticism, already interference."[49] It is not for nothing that Simon Karlinsky entitled the introduction to his volume of Chekhov's letters "The Gentle Subversive."[50] "Death of a Clerk" may be a story about a sneeze, but it is also a subtle critique of a social hierarchy in which a sneeze can be viewed as a mortal offense. As Viktor Shklovskii contends, nothing is ever "small" or "commonplace" in Chekhov's work: "A high court is present in any story by Chekhov."[51]

G. N. Pospelov argues that the "drama in the lives of Chekhov's heroes is produced not by their personal fates but by the general conditions of their environment and the general atmosphere of civic life in Russia which these reflect."[52] But while it certainly is true in Chekhov's stories that "trivial" individual fates are the deviations that show up the societal norms as such, still it would be a mistake to demote these "personal fates" too far. Chekhov's somewhat hyperbolic attention to an apparently small and insignificant turn in a character's fortune (or even lunch menu) is important not only for what it tells us about the "general atmosphere of civic life in Russia"—it also moves toward a central modern psychological insight as to what can really *matter* in a person's life. Individual discomfort, slight as it may appear to an observer, assumes a new force and power. Chekhov's is a quiet psychology, an alternative to the breast-beating—or "finger sawing"—customarily associated with psychological portraiture.[53] His stories bring into focus the minute alterations that can make all the difference.

In "Small-Fry" ("Meliuzga," 1885), for instance, we encounter another insignificant clerk. This one, however, far from sitting contentedly at the opera, finds himself on duty on Easter eve, as he has been every Easter for as long as he can remember. The setting is the epitome of gloom: the deserted duty room is dark, the kerosene lamp flickers and threatens to go out, the ceiling is smoky, the cornices dusty, the walls are blue-brown with age, and our hero, Nevyrazimov, sits dejectedly at a table, composing a letter to a man he despises, his superior, to whom he has been applying for ten years for a two-ruble raise. A cockroach runs across the belabored page.

Outside—in the opposing "semantic field"—it is Easter. The church bells are ringing, the air is fresh, carriages rumble past, and people are alive with laughter, food, drink, conversation, and the warmth of their family circle. It is a world of light and renewal, a world he desperately longs to join, but which he can perceive only, like some Platonic cave dweller, from the shadows of the passing people and carriages and the muffled sounds that reach him through the tiny *fortochka* (small ventilation window). He is utterly separated from that world by the dark walls that surround him and embody his DUTY.

Nevyrazimov is miserable. He has no education, no hope, and no answer. The walls get even darker, the lamp flickers more weakly, the cockroach reasserts itself. Nevyrazimov casts about for solutions to what is truly a "no-exit situation" (*polozhenie bezvykhodnoe* [3:210]), but each idea is more useless than the last, and by the end of the story he is *still* sitting in the same gloomy room, still in the company of the same cockroach, still trying to compose the same letter to the same hated superior. Finally—suddenly—in a fit of rage, our hero curses and crushes the unfortunate cockroach and tosses it into the kerosene lamp, which flares up brightly for a moment.

And he feels better.

It is a small thing, the elimination of a cockroach, but of incomparable significance to the man who, moments before, had been without hope. Suddenly he has mustered enough wrath to take action—an action that alters the prevailing order (since the cockroach is no longer bothering him, and, at least momentarily, the darkness has been dispersed), an action that relieves the sense of unbearable confinement, and returns to the hero a modicum of control over his life (and his light source). The flame in Nevyrazimov's lamp "flared up and flickered" (*vspykhnulo i zatreschalo* [3:212]) in the same words Tolstoy uses to describe the flame that "illuminates" Anna Karenina's final moments—only Nevyrazimov's does not go on to complete the quotation, to be "extinguished forever." Chekhov's hero is rather *saved* from despair and suicide.[54] Nevyrazimov, whose very name seems to preclude tellability,[55] may not have managed to finish his letter, but he has engendered a real story that is supremely tellable. Whereas in "Death of a Clerk" the insignificant incident precipitates a tale of woe, in "Small-Fry" it produces an inspirational Easter parable of resurrection and enlightenment.

Not that Nevyrazimov's solution is unambiguous. His destruction of a creature weaker than himself is ultimately only an extension of the abusive hierarchical power structure he himself longs to escape. Above all, his act does nothing to get him out of the duty room and out on the street. Is it his satisfaction with so little that keeps him down? It could be argued that deriving such gratification from something of so little consequence prevents the downtrodden from undertaking any truly significant action.

The value of the "split second of felicity" is avowedly problematic and is explored in several of Chekhov's stories that expose the "insignificant" as unexpectedly meaningful. Does the student Velikopol'skii's sudden recognition of truth and beauty in the world ("The Student" ["Student"], 1894) represent a genuine change of heart, as the critics hastened to believe? (They congratulated Chekhov on his own long overdue "conversion," not doubting for a minute that Velikopol'skii's words of faith were an expression of Chekhov's own feelings.)[56] Or is the student's surge of faith simply a transitory result of his youthful impetuosity, a phase of no lasting significance?

Or when Mar'ia Vasil'evna ("In the Cart" ["Na podvode"], 1897) rides home from town on a journey she has made thousands of times, feeling that her life always has been and always will be the same, with no mission, no love, no friendships, no acquaintances, and she happens to catch sight of a woman on a passing train who reminds her of her mother, has the trip been an eventful one? Suddenly she remembers the family life she had long forgotten, and is filled with unsurpassable happiness. Life had hardened her beyond feeling, but now, suddenly, she is overwhelmed by emotion. But is the felicity destined to pass as quickly as the train had vanished from sight? Has anything significant really occurred?

This ambiguity is never entirely resolved, but in focusing on the oxymoronic "insignificant event," Chekhov manages to demonstrate several things. First, it becomes clear that what is ostensibly the most infinitesimal incident can in fact prove to have monumental significance. Second, it is this slight deviation from the norm (whether societal or personal) that reveals the contours of the order from which it departed and challenges the inviolability of those confines. Also, by foregrounding the criteria for assessing "significance," the strategy demonstrates how tied these standards are to a given worldview and consequently shows the categories of "significant" and "insignificant" to be supremely value-laden and contingent. Finally, by presenting ostensible trivia in the form of a narrative event, Chekhov quietly but pointedly forces the issue of what is worth telling in the literary context.

The Second Strategy: Minimizing the Maximum

Such play with significance and insignificance is a provocation that continued, in various forms, throughout Chekhov's career, perhaps most recognizably in what I call his second strategy. Here, he reverses the revelation of the first strategy. These stories build toward a climax, a significant event that comes vividly to pass—but then turns out to be singularly non-eventful. It has no news value whatsoever, representing simply the fulfillment of the inevitable. The *really* significant event occurs only subsequently, and consists of breaking out of the strictures of inevitability. This is the shape of the narrative in "The Teacher of Literature" (1889–94).

The story opens with a portrait of philistine domesticity, featuring the Shelestov family, complete with whistling samovar, petty jealousy, and idiotic complaints. Nikitin, the local literature teacher and aspiring romantic hero, is passionately in love with Masha Shelestova and consequently is infatuated with everything about her family, including their narrowly conventional views. He is stupendously happy to be riding horseback alongside of Masha and wants desperately to secure his position beside her on a permanent basis. He is bitterly insulted when someone assumes he is a student in town for the holidays, and he angrily protests that he is employed, firmly rooted, indeed *permanently* there. He resolves to declare his love and propose marriage, in hopes of cleaving forever to this most perfect and wondrous existence. One slight twinge of dissatisfaction makes itself felt momentarily: here he is, a teacher of literature, and he has never read Lessing—but, ah well, all in good time. When Nikitin finally does summon up his courage to propose, he is accepted without much fuss. He then begins to anticipate his wedding day, the culmination of his hopes, and the ultimate event of his life.

Part II opens with an account of the wedding taken from Nikitin's diary. In this privileged text-within-a-text position, the extraordinary event is portrayed as the attainment of impossible bliss: "How my life has blossomed," writes Nikitin, "how poetically it has unfolded! . . . The happiness which once seemed to me possible only in novels and stories, I was now experiencing in reality" (8:324).

But at that moment, in pipes our friend Ippolit Ippolitych, Nikitin's colleague at the school, with his own account of what has transpired: "Until now you have been unmarried and have lived alone, and now you are married and no longer single" (8:325). In short, Ippolit Ippolitych, in his inimitable way, gives us an index of just how eventful and significant this supposedly ultimate event is—namely, not at all. This marriage represents the realization of the inevitable, the most ordinary and least tellable outcome. As Masha herself later tells the surprised Nikitin (who regards his marriage as a monumental conquest), it was simply taken for granted that they would be wed. "Once you start hanging around," she shrugs, "it's your obligation to marry" (8:330).

The happy couple settles down in the two-story house allotted to them as part of Masha's dowry, and Nikitin feels comfortable and cozy.

Best of all are Sundays and holidays, when he can stay home all day, basking in the warm glow of the icon lamp, and watching Masha's household activities. Their life is a veritable domestic idyll.

But one night, while outside his secure circle of domestic bliss, out on the dark and rainy street with only the feeble light of a street lamp and no glowing icon lamp to soothe him, Nikitin arrives at the realization that things are not good at all. "Foo, how awful!" (8:329), he exclaims in distaste. Had he been struggling for his existence, harassed by anxiety and uncertainty, a snug home would be truly significant. But as it is, he has simply gone from the glow of one icon lamp to another, and nothing has really changed. Furthermore, he *still* has not read Lessing. How dare he be content? He knows that there is another world, less safe and secure than the one he inhabits, and he passionately wants to escape the small-mindedness (*poshlost'*) that surrounds him. The illusion has run out, and his former peace and contentment are banished forever. For Nikitin, a new nervous, conscious life has begun.

It has often been noted that Nikitin's change is unmotivated.[57] This may be so, but it is hardly the point. The important thing is that it does represent a change, whereas his marriage did not. In almost no respect was his marriage a bold crossing of boundaries, a changing of states. Nikitin had only become more and more encircled by the narrowly conventional system of values that he had come to accept. His marriage is more trivial, less eventful (and certainly less disruptive) than a sneeze. This second Chekhovian strategy presents an apt counterpart to the first, which selected an incident out of the "small and insignificant" paradigm and assigned it a highly consequential role. Here, something ordinarily regarded as major (i.e., marriage) is shown to be, on the contrary, a non-event, newsworthy only to Ippolit Ippolitych. The *extraordinary* event, that which is most difficult, least likely to occur, and which makes the whole story worth reading, comes when Nikitin resolves to escape. The emergence of Nikitin's new sense of disquiet coincides, not incidentally, with the death of Ippolit Ippolitych, indefatigable mapmaker and chronicler of the status quo.

Perhaps most critically lacking in the "apparent" events Chekhov exposes as null and void (such as Nikitin's nuptial triumph) is any discernible impact on the character's way of thinking and knowing the world. Events, after all, can demonstrably disrupt the external order; but if these concrete changes effect no change of heart, no alteration in a character's consciousness, then they have failed to disrupt the most powerful status quo of all.[58]

This concern becomes abundantly clear in the event structure of

"The Nightmare" ("Koshmar," 1886). When Kunin, the permanent council member for peasant affairs, summons the priest from the neighboring village to his estate and officiously expresses his readiness to make funds available for the church's proposed educational program, he is as pleased with his own magnanimity as he is displeased with the priest's slovenliness, undignified demeanor, and apparent lack of interest in the new school. We follow Kunin through a series of increasingly disheartening interactions with Father Iakov, who conducts worship services inexpertly in soiled garments and responds ungraciously and even unintelligently to Kunin's ministrations. Finally, Kunin's distaste and righteous disapproval impel him to act decisively: he submits a complaint to the church hierarchy requesting the immediate removal of this disgraceful excuse for a priest.

But though the action will carry indisputably severe consequences for the errant Father Iakov, even as a "last straw" this denunciation, composed in Kunin's customary spirit of self-satisfied efficiency, represents nothing new or different for the councilman. The ostensible event, the removal of Father Iakov, primarily enables a *continuity* of Kunin's way of life, rather than a change of either awareness or relative position. The map of the world and its population will not have shifted in any appreciable way until much later—lamentably much too late—when Kunin finally discovers the reasons (abject poverty and misery) behind the cleric's "intolerable" lapses. In fact, the impoverished priest, who in spite of his own affliction gives most of his meager income away, is not a failure but a shining example, embodying in his actions *real* generosity—in distinct contrast to the ostentatious variety indulged in by Kunin. Only after Kunin has recognized this fact and his own reprehensible complacency, only when he finally understands how he might help genuinely and discreetly, has something really occurred. That the realization comes entirely too late to be of much use to poor Father Iakov only underscores the essential bankruptcy of Kunin's earlier activity, philanthropic as it pretended to be, and the unswerving sameness of its spirit.

Similarly, in "The Lady with the Little Dog" ("Dama s sobachkoi," 1899), when the hero Gurov seduces a woman in Yalta, as virtuous as she may have been, it is hardly surprising. This is what Gurov *always* does—it is his way of life. Moreover, it is perceived as the usual business of Yalta, the turn-of-the-century version of the singles' bar. A seduction might be reported by Ippolit Ippolitych, but scarcely by anyone with a sense of news. When Gurov's involvement becomes more than just a fling for him, however, when he feels he is actually in love with Anna Sergeevna, then a real departure from the norm has occurred. Gurov is no longer on familiar ground; he has no map, none of his usual certainty, and no answers. The man himself has changed irrevocably—and the story becomes eminently tellable.

This displacement of the plot from an expected trajectory to a very different line of development has often been noted as a typically Chekhovian ploy: Mirsky refers to Chekhov's "curves," his habit of indicating a "straight line" of action and then veering away from that course, at first imperceptibly, but finally quite radically.[59] It is precisely this divergence, rather than the more conventional "event," that is so eventful.

We see this vividly in "The Betrothed" ("Nevesta," 1903), whose very title promises a certain course of action. Nadia, age twenty-three, who has been longing ardently for marriage since her sixteenth birthday, is about to have her dream realized. But though she is now being groomed and feted for her impending marriage, "and it seemed as if life would always be like this, without change, and without end" (10:202), she suddenly departs from the designated route and accepts the challenge of her grandmother's ward Sasha "to turn her life upside down" (*perevernut' zhizn'* [10:214]). She leaves for Petersburg, where she enrolls in the university and begins a radically new and uncharted existence. This, and not the long-awaited wedding, is the event.

But the story is an endorsement less of the actual content of her new life than of the fact that it is new. Sasha, for instance, though the catalyst for Nadia's personal revolution and a living representative of the enlightened cosmopolitanism she adopts, is himself mired in a repetitive, predictable pattern of existence. "For years, Sasha had been repeating the same thing over and over again, like a script" (10:206), advocating a life-affirming transformation for others, but never effecting one himself. When Nadia encounters him subsequently, he is still saying the same old thing, adding nothing new, and is busily convincing the wife of a friend to turn *her* life upside down. This is conservative; Sasha is conducting his business as usual, growing older and more settled in his ways even as a young man until he literally withers away and dies. Nadia alone has taken a bold and decisive step in a new direction, a step for which Chekhov was roundly congratulated, even by the Social Democratic critics for whom a personal revolution could only be a first step.[60] This story was widely heralded as the *author's* first step in a commendable new direction, his move toward a world of active heroes who would finally be able to effect meaningful changes and bring to Chekhov's narratives, at long last, some properly significant and extraordinary events.

But Chekhov, who had rarely complied with his critics' enthusiastic urgings, was to let them down on this occasion as well: he never published another story, and thus neither confirmed nor refuted their theory about a new direction. Nevertheless, we scarcely need to hazard predictions about Chekhov's unwritten stories to discern a commitment to the "significant event" in his prose. Whether he is maximizing trivial incidents or minimizing five-star occasions, Chekhov relies heavily on the structurally entailed, institutionalized force of the event for the effects he achieves. Far from disregarding the significant event, he exploits it and our expectations of it.

By inscribing in this crucial position a traditional event of some magnitude (a wedding, denunciation, seduction, or even death) that stubbornly fails to alter anything, the stories of the second strategy rattle the reader's tacit and conventionally conditioned sense of consequence. Such an "event" surprises not by occurring, but by occurring so inconsequentially, by carrying so little impact and import. In exposing these ostensibly "extraordinary" occurrences as little more than grist for Ippolit Ippolitych's mill, as "long since well known to everyone" and hence fundamentally untellable, Chekhov offers a subtle critique of what is commonly told—in both social and literary contexts. And by redirecting the reader's attention from the garish but empty headlines to the small print that follows, where the real story is told, these texts require a revisionary act on the part of the "defeated" reader—a reassessment of news value and general value—and a renewed responsibility to attribute significance well.

The Third Strategy: Maximal vs. Minimal

That the categories of significance/insignificance are ascribed rather than absolute, that they reflect and inflict a whole set of values, is precisely the thrust of Chekhov's third strategy. Here he stages an incident and then provides two separate perspectives on it, one that regards the incident as utterly trivial, barely worth mentioning, while the other discerns the maximal degree of catastrophe in the same event. One of the best examples is a story actually entitled "The Event" ("Sobytie," 1886).

As it opens, Vania (age six) and Nina (age four) have awakened to sensational news: their cat has had kittens! The children's habitual games and pursuits are pushed aside, and their "prosaic duties" are forgotten (5:426). They are utterly consumed by the tiny mewing things. The box of kittens is their whole world and they devote their full attention to it, constructing cardboard houses for the newcomers, and making plans for their respective futures. The children's joy is "boundless" (5:427).

Their parents, oddly enough, do not seem to share this fascination. Parental "habitual pursuits" (5:426) are not abandoned in favor of the new arrivals: mother is impatient when her conversation with the strange gentleman is interrupted by her kitten-bearing children; father is irate when a kitten turns up amidst his papers; an angry scene ensues when the children, unable to tear themselves away, smuggle a kitten to the dinner table.

The title-event occurs after dinner when Uncle Petrusha arrives with his tremendous black dog, Nero, who unceremoniously *eats* the kittens. The children are naturally beside themselves with shock, rage, and profound grief; after all, their new world has been demolished. And they expect everyone to be aghast.

The adults, however, display only mild amusement at the dog's appetite, then resume business as usual: "Nine o'clock, bedtime," calls mother, observing the usual schedule (5:428). In the adult world, the "event" goes unacknowledged. For them, essentially nothing has happened. These are separate and antithetical realms, the world of the kittens (who had been exiled to the kitchen) and the world of the big black dog (who has free roam of the family's social rooms and never pays the remotest attention to the children). The attempt to fuse them (for the children had hoped to conscript the dog as a surrogate father cat) means annihilation for the kittens. Nero, the destructive dog, emerges unscathed from his exploits in the kitchen, oblivious as usual to the children and their trauma, returning to the dining room and the adult world, which he represents—a world unperturbed by the other world's tragedy. The story derives its power from the disparity of the two perspectives, from the fact that what is momentous from one point of view can be utterly insignificant from another. Such assessments as to the significance or insignificance of life's occurrences reveal much about the values that underlie those appraisals.

It is true that Chekhov's play with perspective here is not the most impartial; the dice are heavily loaded on the side of the children and their sense of eventfulness. This privileging of the child's point of view is later developed more fully by such writers as Olesha and Pasternak, who utilize children's perceptions as a means of de-automatizing observations and reactions to the world.[61] These twentieth-century writers provide the child's point of view exclusively (though it necessarily operates on the principle of *difference*, relying on an implicit "normal" point of view). Chekhov's interest in the child's vantage point, as evident in several stories, seems to emphasize its role as *alternative*: the punch lies almost always in the striking disparity between the adult and the juvenile perspective.

The story "A Trifle from Everyday Life" ("Zhiteiskaia meloch'," 1886) capitalizes on the contrasting interpretations by adult and child of the "trifle" cited in the title. It involves an encounter between the serious Petersburg property owner Nikolai Il'ich Beliaev and the young son of his lady-friend Ol'ga Ivanovna, the eight-year-old Alesha. When the trusting Alesha divulges a deep secret to Beliaev and then earnestly entreats him never to reveal the matter to his mama, the elder interlocutor gives his solemn word of honor as requested. No sooner does Ol'ga Ivanovna arrive, however, than Beliaev, thoroughly caught up in his own considerations, discloses the confidence with not a thought about his promise. Alesha, on the other hand, pales with disbelief, and trembles and cries with profound hurt at the betrayal. For him the slight indiscretion, already forgotten (or never even registered) by the adult, is the ultimate disillusionment, his first encounter with a lie. Similarly, in "Grisha" (1886), which is presented almost exclusively from the child's bewildered point of view, when the impressionable two-and-a-half-year-old burns with fever in response to the day's upsetting sensations and discoveries, his reaction to the momentous day is dismissed by his practical mother as a slight case of indigestion. (Mama is a narrowly conventional reader.) And with that assessment, the story concludes.

These stories work by juxtaposing the contrasting interpretations of an event. Has something significant transpired or not? Given the choice, the reader adopts the "deviant" evaluative stance of the child and thus the first interpretation. But this hardly represents a real choice, since the texts themselves overwhelmingly endorse that perspective and its underlying values, which are shown to have lost their validity in the adult world, the "normal" context established by the narrative. The advantage of this strategy is that it affords us a view of the norm by forcing it into relief from the textually privileged perspective. It forces an articulation—and a recognition—of the "business as usual" position, which presumably would otherwise remain unperceived because of its very status as a norm (though, admittedly, the hyperbolic insensitivity portrayed here seems anything but imperceptible).

The Fourth Strategy: Event Withheld

Chekhov's fourth assault on traditional event structure rests less on interpretation than on the binary logic of occurrence and non-occurrence of the significant event in question. An impending cataclysm is prepared, expectations run high, but the event fails to occur. In fact, nothing occurs.[62]

As "The Wife" ("Supruga," 1895) opens, Nikolai Evgrafych, an older man in somewhat poor health, sits waiting for his attractive young spouse to return. Their marriage has been anything but blissful; it has consisted of a steady diet of lies, reprimands, threats, hysterics— in short, it has been "a kind of hell" (9:95). Now things are really beginning to look a little suspicious: someone keeps sending hyacinths every day, there is a young foreigner who turns up frequently, and Ol'ga Dmitrievna herself never comes home before four or five A.M. and repeatedly requests a foreign passport. Lately she has even been receiving love letters. On this particular evening, the wronged husband has located and laboriously translated a very incriminating telegram addressed to his wife. This is finally too much. The crisis begins. Nikolai Evgrafych decides to stay up and wait for Ol'ga Dmitrievna, and prepares a tremendous confrontation. The tension mounts during his all-night vigil, until he nobly decides to grant her a divorce to put an end to this insufferable arrangement at last.

As it turns out when she finally arrives, however, she doesn't want a divorce. He then tries to kick her out, but she doesn't go. The "crisis" turns out to be just one more scene like so many others, more standard fare. It belongs to the protocol of their marriage just as "The captain has illuminated the no-smoking sign" belongs to a commercial airline flight. The confrontation does not end in her eviction, no boundaries are crossed or redrawn. Her institutional affiliation is still the home, and life in that home is still insufferable.

For Ol'ga Dmitrievna, as for the man in the *New Yorker* cartoon, "Honey, I'm home!" describes stasis rather than reporting news—and the next morning she is literally conducting business as usual, demanding the twenty-five rubles her husband had promised her. At eleven o'clock the husband puts on his tie to go to work as usual. And, in a favorite Chekhovian device, we find a word-for-word repetition of the beginning at the end to demonstrate how little has transpired in the intervening pages: Nikolai Evgrafych is still sitting at his desk, still writing "mechanically," as he was before the "confrontation," and once again formulates the same question in exactly the same words: "How is it that he, the son of a village priest, a simple and direct man, could have surrendered himself to such a worthless, false, venal, petty creature?" (9:94, 99).

That nothing significant has happened is bad enough, but to have to reread the exposition at the end is an extremely frustrating reading experience. It is deft of Chekhov that he should model his fictional reality to reflect the social malaise of "nothing happening" in this way, so that it is perceived first as a flagrant violation of *artistic* principles;

it is an apt challenge to a despondent and torpid society that makes more stringent demands on its literary forms than on its forms of life. Tellability, we realize, is not just an aesthetic index, but also an ethical one. A significant narrative event resounds with meaningful change and action. When these are missing from a narrative, the reader is rightfully annoyed. And when they are missing from a life story?

In the eighteenth century, Lotman submits, Russians had turned to the theater and to literature in general for the spectacular "events" lacking in everyday life, where "events and happenings . . . either did not take place at all, or were rare exceptions to the norm. Hundreds of people could live their lives through without experiencing a single 'event.'" In the early part of the nineteenth century, the gentry had actively modeled its behavior on the grandeur and daring of literature's momentous events.[63] In the stories of the fourth strategy, Chekhov counters by withholding the expected "significant event" from the one sure source of eventfulness: literature.

"An Unpleasant Incident" ("Nepriatnost'," 1888) uses this strategy to expose an order that maintains itself at all costs.[64] It opens with another situation sorely in need of alleviation: Grigorii Ivanovich Ovchinnikov, a country doctor of some academic and social standing, is forced to run his deplorable hospital with the help (if not hindrance) of an incompetent and unreliable staff, embodied most notably in the figure of his drunken assistant, Mikhail Zakharovich. The assistant, it is well known, steals medications from the clinic, takes bribes from the patients, performs unauthorized medical procedures on his own (with unwashed hands!), and gets away with it all because of an aunt in high places. And unlike the sloppy priest in "The Nightmare," Mikhail Zakharovich has no hidden redeeming features, no surprise enlightenment to bestow upon the doctor. That these hygienic lapses are the norm is emphasized by the story's frequent repetition of *kak vsegda* and *po obyknoveniiu* (as usual [7:141–42]).

On this particular morning, while making his usual rounds, followed, as usual, by Mikhail Zakharovich, the doctor is so angered by his assistant's slovenliness that he strikes him, precipitating a "crisis" that presumably will resolve the intolerable situation once and for all. Clearly the professional relationship between the two men has been irrevocably damaged, and the affair must end with either the doctor's resignation or the assistant's dismissal. The moment of truth—the event—has arrived.

The act was so decisive, the doctor feels, that it is doubly unbearable to him that his staff should carry on as if nothing had happened. Neither will the assistant's apology satisfy him. A genuine change is needed. After numerous abortive attempts of his own to draft an appropriate letter requesting official action on the incident, the doctor finally manages to provoke his assistant into taking the matter to court. There—or rather, in the judge's adjoining quarters—the whole matter is summarily dismissed by the chairman and the judge on the grounds that "one must simply reconcile oneself to such evils" (7:154); a new assistant would undoubtedly prove to be just as bad as, if not worse than, Mikhail Zakharovich anyway. Between glasses of vodka and bites of radish, the officials admonish Mikhail Zakharovich to watch his step, and congratulate themselves on having avoided the fuss of a needless trial.

The doctor returns to the hospital, and the story ends exactly as it began, with the doctor making his usual rounds, followed, as usual, by Mikhail Zakharovich. And they all—the assistant, the nurses, and even the doctor—assiduously pretend that nothing has happened and that everything is in order. But there is really no need to pretend, because everything is "in order": in exactly the same order they started with. Nothing has changed. And this time the phenomenon and the torpid existence it typifies receive explicit comment: "Stupid, stupid, stupid" (7:158).[65]

By persuasively preparing an event and then withholding it, Chekhov poignantly models the failures to take action, the missed opportunities that pervade life (or rather empty it of meaningful content) and that are repeatedly the target of his critical portrayal. Again and again we are shown the ineffectualness of mouthing platitudes rather than acting decisively ("Misfortune" ["Neschast'e"], 1888); the immorality of "justifying" inactivity with philosophy ("Ward Six"); the perpetuation of misery by repeatedly duplicating a lamentable arrangement ("Aniuta," 1886); the passivity that comes from abandoning hope ("In Exile" ["V ssylke"], 1892); and the tragedy of idleness ("The House with the Mansard" ["Dom s mezoninom"], 1896).

In this final story (subtitled "An Artist's Story"), the phenomenon is presented in markedly social (rather than purely individual) terms, and provides a pointed critique of the (unchanging) configuration depicted. Monsieur N. is an artist, the prototypical *flâneur*, idle and self-indulgent. Moreover, he is a landscape painter: even his paintings are the very antithesis of the *engagé*. Like Chekhov's stories in the minds of his early critics, Monsieur N.'s paintings evince no social awareness; they are absolutely uncritical, they do not militate for change. On the contrary, they are eventless, they reproduce a static scene, and (much like Ippolit Ippolitych's maps) they fix and support the status quo. The artist's life is passing in complete idleness, and he especially delights in Sundays, when "healthy, well-fed, good-looking people will do nothing all day long," and he longs for life "to be like this always" (9:179).

When on one of his beloved aimless rambles through the countryside he comes upon a neighboring estate, he is presented with a very different kind of existence in the person of Lida, the elder daughter. She is committed to a life of activity, even activism, in the zemstvo. She is an impassioned believer in that institution, the initiative it implies, and the changes for which it works. She is perpetually occupied, and speaks heatedly and constantly of the need to establish a medical post for the peasants, or to improve their opportunities for education. And she *always* prefaces her remarks on such practical matters in Monsieur N.'s presence with a caustic "This won't interest *you*," directed at him (9:183). For all her humanistic enterprises, Lida is impersonal and cold in her interactions.

Fortunately for Monsieur N., though, there is a younger sister, Zhenia, who because of her youth is not expected to participate in zemstvo efforts or discussions, and "having not a care in the world, spends her time in total idleness" (9:178). It is she, and not the harsh and self-righteous Lida, who keeps him coming every day, and who eventually captures his heart.[66] Zhenia, in turn, is utterly taken with Monsieur N.

Thus, the big "love affair" is prepared (though it is noteworthy that even the big "event" smacks of conventionality—a typical summer romance, born of nothing better to do, with the sweet young thing on the neighboring estate). The artist's agitation is extreme as he reveals his love to Zhenia (in kisses, if not in words), and he at once feels the urge to paint again. (Even as a painter, it appears, he has been inactive.) Suddenly, life is exquisite and filled with hope.

But, as fate (or rather, Lida) would have it, Zhenia is immediately whisked away from his decadent grasp to another province. The artist himself is in the habit of attributing the vicissitudes of his life to "fate." At the beginning he blames even his own idleness on *sud'ba* (9:174). At the end, too, he is mistaken. Not destiny, but Lida—decisive, if heartless, human engagement—is responsible for the removal of Zhenia, and his own inactivity is to blame for his lack of intervention. Again we have a study of what could have but does *not* come to pass. The story closes chiastically, with Monsieur N. retreating along the same path by which he had originally approached, describing the fir trees, lime trees, orchard, gate, courtyard, and willows in reverse order from the original description. He withdraws after visiting a landscape, and the story paints one: there is no motion, no eventful disorder, just life as it has always been. He makes no effort to overtake his love, who has, after all, only just departed, a "prosaic everyday mood took over . . . , and once again life became a boring prospect" (9:190–91). He never sees Zhenia again.

Beyond Monsieur N.'s individual "tragedy" looms the larger issue, underlined repeatedly in Chekhov's story, of the viability of the artist who (in Monsieur N.'s own words) "works for the entertainment of a predatory unclean animal by supporting the existing order of things" (9:187). This consummately private role, this unwillingness to become involved in social change (the charge, not incidentally, so often leveled at Chekhov), can hardly be said to emerge triumphant from "The House with the Mansard." And yet the alternative, Madame Zemstvo herself, is a pedantic and unpleasant character. (Typical of Chekhov, lamented his critics, to make the only character capable of any socially useful action unsympathetic.[67] Clever of him, I would submit, to refute in this way the critics' assumption that social engagement is necessarily significant, or even interesting.) Chekhov, whose own career spanned both spheres of endeavor (writer and zemstvo physician), endorses here neither bullheaded activity nor chronic inactivity—the artist just resumes his life of unproductive tedium, and even Lida's continued zemstvo activism "years later," as reported in the epilogue, is ambiguous in terms of social productivity and benefit. Neither the artist nor the activist comes even remotely close to reconsidering his or her own perfectly self-satisfied position. In the case of Monsieur N., this failure is reinforced by his prodigious physical inertness. In Lida, this blind certainty helps demonstrate how the counterexample to inactivity can be equally unacceptable. Ultimately both inertia and momentum are ways of maintaining the status quo. *Significant* change, it seems, is not effected at any level: not politically, not personally, and not structurally. The "event" is conspicuously absent. Therein lies the critique and, paradoxically, the tellability.

Thus, even the non-occurrence of an expected event can be worth telling. Moreover, the telling itself can sometimes override the non-occurrence, as in the case of Miguev's erroneous confession in "Transgression" ("Bezzakonie," 1887). Though the expected event (first prepared by the maid's threat in the opening paragraph: "I'll leave the baby at your door!" [6:248]) never materializes, the hero's great terror and shame in anticipation of being accused impel him to plead guilty at the first sight of an unaccompanied infant. Once he has dramatically confessed to his wife that he has an illegitimate child, even when the crisis turns out to be a false alarm (the child is someone else's), the confession stands: his *discourse* about a presumptive event is as disruptive and devastating as the actual occurrence would have been. Miguev's subsequent denial when he discovers his mistake, his ineffectual "Ha ha, just kidding" (6:252), cannot reverse his wife's anguish.

Granted, in this particular situation, the very possibility of having fathered an illegitimate child entails infidelity—in other words, a transgression has indeed occurred, even if it is not the specific one attested to by the bundle on the doorstep. The confession is not entirely unfounded. But it does vividly reflect the force of expectations on the human imagination: the possible becomes the probable, the probable—the inevitable, and Miguev proceeds to report the "necessary event" even as Chekhov withholds it.

The Arbiters of Significance

The four strategies I have examined—(1) the recasting of an ostensibly trivial incident as a major, consequential event; (2) the exposure of a "big" event as simply normal and inevitable and hence not particularly tellable; (3) the staging of a single incident with two disparate perspectives on its significance; and (4) the preparation of a major cataclysmic event that dismally fails to occur—all demonstrate Chekhov's intense concern with the textual moment associated with the significant event.

These basic strategies recur persistently throughout Chekhov's work; still, the categories are neither all-inclusive nor mutually exclusive. "Death of a Clerk," for instance, which served as an example of the first strategy (the sneeze as the ultimate disruption of the status quo) could also have been discussed usefully under the third strategy, since the general cannot grasp Cherviakov's anxiety over what seemed to him so trivial an occurrence. "The Nightmare," considered here in terms of displaced eventfulness (the second strategy), might also represent the final strategy, the study of what does not come to pass, in that its hero's revolutionary realization is so delayed that it remains without practical effect. In fact, the irony of the story's conclusion suggests that a change that comes too late is an unaffordable luxury and that, in effect, nothing *has* come to pass here, even in displaced form. Other stories, such as "The Kiss" ("Potselui," 1887), in which a shy officer's imaginative life is transformed by a fleeting kiss bestowed by mistake in a darkened room, combine all of the questions posed by these strategies: has something happened, or not? Was it extraordinary, or not? And do you tell it, or not?

There are numerous other ways, too, in which Chekhov evinces a keen interest in the issue of what is significant and tellable. In "The Darling" ("Dushechka," 1899), for example, the repetition ad infinitum of Olen'ka's pattern of attachment and bereavement demotes life's normally singular and traumatic events (marriage, death of a spouse) to the status of mere "variations that give us nothing new."[68] This is a view of a *state* of being, sustained by a cycle as regular as inhaling and exhaling, and never disrupted.[69] The repetition makes a travesty of Olen'ka's "events," for they clearly perpetuate rather than upset the order of things, and Olen'ka's life is shown to be unswervingly resistant to authentic change.

Elsewhere, Chekhov leads the reader up to the most dramatic moment and then provocatively "skips a line" in the narration, reporting only the results of the drastic action while maintaining silence on the event itself. The murder of the perpetually crying baby in "Sleepy" ("Spat' khochetsia," 1888) takes place in the lacuna between two sentences: "Laughing, winking and wagging her fingers at the green patch, Var'ka steals up to the cradle and bends over the baby. Having strangled him, she quickly lies down on the floor [and] laughs with joy that she can sleep" (7:12). In "The Murder" ("Ubiistvo," 1895), Iakov points to an iron and then stops feeling angry only when the blood is already running through his fingers (9:153). Between those two phrases he has smashed his cousin's skull. And we learn in "Gusev" (1890) that the hero has a dream, then is carried out of sick bay and sewn up in sailcloth for his burial (7:338). We can only assume that he has managed to die in the meantime. Chekhov playfully leaves the most momentous announcement unspoken.

And everywhere, Chekhov's stories are peppered with characters who have the opposite tendency, who are unable to distinguish the great from the small, who leave *nothing* unsaid, or who say the same thing day after day, "as if reporting some interesting news" ("A Boring Story" ["Skuchnaia istoriia"], 1889). They are shown to be ridiculous—but they too demonstrate Chekhov's deep and abiding concern with what is worth telling. Nikolai Stepanovich's wife ("A Boring Story"), the host who bores his guest to death with incessant talk ("The Pecheneg," 1897), Ippolit Ippolitych, and even Olen'ka, who repeats verbatim every word uttered by her current "love" (including his geography lessons, as if she were an understudy to the notorious teacher of geography: "An island is a piece of land surrounded by water" [10:111]), reflect Chekhov's dim view of indiscriminate chatter about any old thing.

"A Boring Story" may be a study in tedium, but it is also a self-conscious exploration of what is tellable. Some items are rejected: "To describe our dinner nowadays is as unpalatable as to eat it" (7:277); others are selected judiciously: "The rings of the bell may follow one another endlessly, but I will limit myself here to describing four of them" (7:268). And when Nikolai Stepanovich reflects on the art of lecturing, his comments simultaneously address the perennial Chekhovian concern of how to compose a story:

> To lecture well—that is, without being boring, and with profit to the listeners—one must have, besides talent, a special knack, and one must have an exceedingly clear conception. . . . Every moment I must be adroit enough to snatch out of that vast material what is most important and necessary, and . . . clothe my thoughts in a form that may be accessible to the monster's understanding, and may arouse its attention. At the same time I must be on the alert that my thoughts are presented, not just as they come, but in a certain order, essential for the correct composition of that picture I wish to sketch. (7:261–62)

The indispensable principles of storytelling, important testimony and scrupulous composition, are explored thematically as well as strategically in "A Boring Story."

Not incidentally, the passage from "A Boring Story" locates the index of a narrative's success in its *reception*; a lecture or story is constructed well if it does not "bore" the audience, but rather "arouses" its attention and brings "profit to the listeners." Stories such as this that include an explicit teller (whether a character who, in the course of the tale, ventures a narrative of his or her own, or, less frequently, an actual first-person narrator) most often inscribe as well an exacting listener who scrutinizes the performance and determines its worth, intent on that "profit" he or she is entitled to expect and ready to object if it is not forthcoming. These responses run the gamut—from the enthrallment of Vasilisa and Luker'ia, who are transformed by the student's retelling of the Gospel story (and whose reactions, in turn, inspire the teller in "The Student"), to the kibitzing of the critical Burkin, whose rebukes ("Stick to the subject!") constrain the narrator, and who remains, in the end, dissatisfied with the story ("Gooseberries" ["Kryzhovnik"], 1898, 10:59); from the skepticism of Mariia Timofeevna's friends that stifles her shy stories ("The Bishop" ["Arkhierei"], 1902), to the *amused* disbelief of Father Savka, which only encourages his son's "inventions" ("Sancta Simplicitas" ["Sviataia prostota"], 1885); from the alternating yawns and rapt attention of the little girl that show her father she prefers his stories to his prayers ("The Requiem" ["Panikhida"], 1886), to the rude dismissal by the other officers in "The Kiss," that makes the man with the kiss-and-tell story feel how trivial his indiscretions—both kiss *and* story—really are. The audience's presence is daunting; "A Boring Story" figures the professor's listeners as a collective "monster." But its absence is worse: nothing is more heartrending than the grief-stricken father whose listeners either fall asleep or walk away, leaving him with no one but his horse to tell of his sorrow ("Misery" ["Toska"], 1886).

If falling asleep is an effective, albeit passive-aggressive, way to interrupt a speaker whose story is a letdown, staying awake through a nocturnal storytelling session must be construed as active approval of the proffered tale. In several stories, in fact, Chekhov develops a whole sleep-or-story economy to calibrate narrative worthiness.[70] Stories that are delivered nocturnally must represent adequate reimbursement for the listener's forfeited sleep. Eventful stories make for a night well spent awake; less-than-tellable tales are curtailed in favor of "bedtime!" (a more emphatic version of Labov's "so what?"). When the vigilant Burkin, the inscribed listener in the "Man in Case" trilogy, rules more than once that it is time to turn in (*pora spat'*), he echoes exactly the peremptory adult dismissal of the children's "insignificant" horror story of the neatly digested kittens ("The Event"). If it's not worth telling, it's not worth the sacrificed sleep. We need only recall the agony and exasperation of the beleaguered guest in "The Pecheneg" when he is kept awake all night by the narrative exertions of his excruciatingly boring host. In Chekhov's world, people have even been known to kill the source of the noise that keeps them awake ("Sleepy").

In emphasizing repeatedly the need for an audience, and more specifically for its approbation, Chekhov reinforces thematically what he accomplishes structurally in his strategic manipulations of the event: he forces the issue of what is worth telling and maintains, correctly, that this is one of the most pressing questions of all. Additionally, in his textual inscriptions of a responding audience, he reminds us who has the final word in this matter, and who thus bears the responsibility for recognizing and embracing significant activity, narrative or otherwise.

As Labov found in his study of natural narrative, most narrators not only represent a sequence of events but also actively attempt to persuade the listener that the tale is worthwhile, hoping to forestall a dismissive rejoinder.[71] Wayne Booth has demonstrated the rhetorical resources available to writers of fiction to heighten persuasively the significance of their events, both by explicit and by more furtive means.[72] Chekhov, however, contrives not to convince but to provoke.

The provocation has been an effective one. Initially, as we have seen, Chekhov's critics were amply disconcerted by his unlikely events;

later, once his popularity was assured, critics moved to account for his provocational "pinpricks" as the "form of the times" rather than as a quirk—as the "fashionable form of fiction," responsive to the needs of mass literacy and in tune with the "modern rhythm" of life.[73] But whatever social and historical urgencies may have influenced the *production* of Chekhov's "trifles," the most enduring exigency has been the *recognition* by readers of textual significance in the form of the event. The apparent eventlessness (or the mythology of eventlessness) of Chekhov's stories continues to plague critics to this day. Krystyna Pomorska gives "eventlessness" a positive twist by identifying it as a Chekhovian innovation to present an eventless model of life.[74] For Andrew Durkin, Chekhov's "elimination" of plot and events facilitates the author's more pressing concern with psychological experience; the only changes and "results" in Chekhov's stories occur at the level of insights, and even these are often achieved only by the reader.[75] Chudakov resurrects the event in his consideration of Chekhov's story structure by arguing for a new Chekhovian definition of "event," one that no longer includes the notion of result. Events do occur in Chekhov's stories, he claims, but they do not change anything—the order remains intact.[76]

To divest the event of its consequences, though, seems an unwarranted impoverishment of the notion. By doing away with this textual index of eventfulness, Chudakov is left to identify events by their extratextual magnitude, rather than by their role in a given artistic system (in spite of his original disclaimer to the effect that in fiction, the purchase of a pencil is potentially as significant as the purchase of a pistol).[77] Nor are Chekhov's stories in need of such an apologia.

The reader is left not with "the impression of a continuous stream,"[78] but rather with a sense of surprise at what, oddly enough, disrupted that stream, or dismay at what failed to. The focus is on the event, especially when it is a peculiar one, and even in the stories that implement the fourth strategy, where the event is withheld. It takes shape in the reader's mind, informed by the familiar requirements of storytelling, the demand for significance, and by Chekhov's own conspiratorial preparations; its absence in the actual text is a glaring inadequacy, one which is felt. The reader is forced to look again: at what should have happened, but did not; at what should have been disruptive, but was not; or at what did upset the order, in spite of its apparent insignificance.

To classify something as eventful and significant when it is ordinarily regarded as unimportant (and vice versa) is to subvert the priorities of a system of values. It is this intrigue that confronts Chekhov's reader (rather than any so-called Chekhovian despondency[79]) and that forces a reexamination of categories. This is what makes Chekhov's stories worth reading as well as worth telling and distinguishes them unequivocally from the "works" of Ippolit Ippolitych.

TWO

Mikhail Zoshchenko: Great Strides and Trivial Indiscretions

© 1989 Robert Mankoff
originally in The New Yorker Magazine, Inc.
All Rights Reserved.

The Big Picture: Context and Criticism

Usually we conceive of restrictions placed on literary subject matter in terms of excess and *upper* limits. Something that is too racy, too critical, too sensitive, too explosive, too subversive, too provocative—whatever the particular term of condemnation, something that is "too x" risks exclusion, or at least some clash with the guardians of order and propriety, whether these authorities are political, religious, or literary. Depending on the degree of overt repressiveness of a given society, this may mean actual sanctions against the author, suppression or censorship of the work, literary-critical disapproval, public indignation, or even heightened curiosity (and increased sales, for that matter).[1]

At the other extreme of the forbidden, however, operates the criterion that, while substantially less dramatic, nevertheless exerts the most consistent power of veto over prospective subject matter, namely: IS IT WORTH TELLING? That is, is it "x enough"? Is it racy, critical, sensitive, explosive, subversive, provocative, or interesting *enough* to engage the attention? The constraints on subject matter operate like the thresholds that govern our responses to sensory stimuli: any light, sound, or sensation too intense is intolerable, while a stimulus too slight is simply not noticed. No external agency is required to enforce the latter exclusion; when a contribution falls below the "x-enough" threshold, the audience disperses quite on its own.[2]

And yet we have seen how Chekhov's "trivia" becomes supremely worth reading: not by disregarding the interest threshold, but by manipulating it, by playing on its exigencies, Chekhov forces a reassessment of the very category of significance. Mikhail Zoshchenko, another inveterate challenger of the "lower boundary," produced hundreds of "trifles" about galoshes and coat hooks that nevertheless excited the unwavering attention—enthusiastic and censorious, respectively—of the reading public and the literary-critical establishment of the 1920s. But unlike Chekhov, whose inimitable Ippolit Ippolitych was always undiscerning but never indiscreet, Zoshchenko wields his trivia in a way that is less potentially boring than inflammatory. In an era that privileges monumentality, Zoshchenko's stubborn use of subject matter that seems "not x enough" is itself provocational. Paradoxically, it is the very triviality of his material that raises eyebrows and thus risks exclusion under the terms of the "too-x" stipulation.

The audacity of this "trivia" derives, in large measure, from the circumstances of its production. Zoshchenko began publishing during the politically charged 1920s, when the new Soviet state was making earnest efforts to define the role of the new revolutionary literature it fervently hoped would soon emerge. Though there was lively debate as to exactly what form this literature would take, the exclusionary upper limits were clear: works of literature should not be too negative, too critical, or in any way opposed to the goals of the October Revolution. This is only logical; counterrevolutionary texts are patently "too x."

Such prohibitions were not new in the Russian literary tradition; censorship was hardly a Soviet invention. But Soviet control in the field of literature was innovative. It not only forbade undesirable topics, it also prescribed desirable ones.[3] Literature had long been viewed in Russia as a sphere of significant social action; now, especially with its more recently acquired Marxist underpinnings, it bore a renewed responsibility. Envisioned as an enterprise of utilitarian value to the state, an indispensable "weapon" in the class war, literature was expected not merely to refrain from hostile critiques, but actively to support the Bolshevik project. This meant that not only must a work of literature not be "too x," but it must embody a specific, "appropriate" content as well.

Appropriate content meant, most immediately, contemporary, fraught with the events and aspirations of the period.[4] This dictate ensured literature's relevance and facilitated its immediate engagement with the goals of the present. But contemporaneity did not legitimize indiscriminate portraiture of any random fragments of everyday life; what it came to refer to above all was scale. Genuinely "contemporary" works of literature would be BIG; commensurate—in dimension, in scope, and especially in subject matter—with the era's momentous achievements.[5] Little stories about little things may have been appropriate for Chekhov's times, but that had been an era resigned to zemstvos and small deeds. "It is no accident that Chekhov was a master of the miniature short story, even though he had always dreamed of writing a novel," ran the logic. "The era was such that people were small, emotions were petty, and Chekhov's novel just plain would not materialize."[6]

The assumptions here are clear: small forms reflect a social and political malaise, not an artistic inclination; they are less significant than large forms; and they embody only "petty" emotions. Little stories, it was concluded, are manifestly not for us. Today, the argument went, we are still reeling from earth-shattering events (most notably the cataclysmic October Revolution), we are taking massive steps, our progress is on a grand scale, and our loftiest hopes are being realized. "We are living in un-Chekhovian times. Our dynamic, tempestuous epoch demands the epic, the novel."[7] Literature, in other words, was to be infused with the greatness of the Revolution, both in its content and in its form. "The time has come," proclaimed Voronskii, for *bol'shaia literatura* (big literature); it is imperative that today's art be "equal to" and "worthy of its great epoch."[8]

The operative criterion, then, was *masshtabnost'*: literary dimensions were to be *proportional* to the immensity of the era's historical ones. This monumentality could be attained by embracing (1) capacious genres (the novel, the epic); (2) extraordinary literary forebears for emulation (ideally, Tolstoy; above all, not Chekhov); and (3) sensational (revolutionary!) events.

Genre became an issue for the Marxist critics not only as a concrete manifestation of magnitude, but also for its role in defining subject matter. Just as a lecture treats different problems than does a marriage proposal or a job interview, a major novel, it was reasoned, would most naturally and effectively embody the epochal events of 1917.[9] Moreover, the monumental forms of literature (in particular the realist novel) had always been regarded as a sign of cultural health. Shorter forms were associated, by contrast, with decline.[10]

Since a downward trend was naturally inadmissible, writers were encouraged to hark back to the classics for their models. The great novelists of the nineteenth century were "giants" whose stature allowed them the elevated vantage point from which to assess their whole era and beyond; they were steeped in *important* ideas, and their works were founded on *great* emotions—clearly the very language chosen to recommend them celebrates monumentality. Writers like Tolstoy and Gogol "never got helplessly mired in their material, *their* works never deteriorated into trivia, however topical, they never simply recorded didactic and tantalizing little incidents or anecdotes, but rather created monumental works, distilled from their material gigantic, generally valid conclusions, opened the broadest perspectives and horizons, and became life's teachers, preachers, and prophets."[11]

While it is difficult to concur with the remarkable contention that Gogol never descended into trivia (see Chapters 4 and 5), it is not hard to see why Chekhov is not among the list of exemplars, given the preference for "gigantic, generally valid conclusions" delivered in monumental forms. The call went out specifically for a "Red Lev Tolstoy," who was to create the modern-day *War and Peace*, the epic to confirm and celebrate the new order by focusing on the larger project rather than on the trivial and inconsequential specifics of everyday life.¹² This latter-day view of Tolstoy's novel as a majestic tribute to order and monumentality is largely misguided, as Morson has argued. In fact, *War and Peace* celebrates precisely the trivial and inconsequential specifics of everyday life so abhorrent to the Soviet critics, as well as disconcerting to Tolstoy's own earliest readers.¹³ In what follows I will suggest that insofar as Zoshchenko echoes the Tolstoyan obsession with the "prosaic," he complies much more graciously with the request for a Red Tolstoy than his critics imagined. From their perspective, however, the sheer magnitude of Tolstoyan form seemed to vouchsafe the gigantic truths they so earnestly sought. It is in this spirit that F. Zhits could assert with complete confidence that "from the point of view of craftsmanship, any little ten-line miniature can be as fine as Tolstoy's *War and Peace*; but in significance, in artistic and ideological influence, there is as much difference between them as between a shallow, clear stream and a deep, navigable river."¹⁴

Thus, though the themes, heroes, and events of Soviet literature were to be programmatically new (contemporary), the preference for voluminous genres reveals a predilection for more traditional forms. The modernist experiments in literary form (Symbolism, Acmeism, Futurism) and in criticism (Opoiaz) of the years immediately preceding the revolution were "out of step" with the new age, while the nineteenth-century literary tradition was considered "up to scale."¹⁵

As for content itself, literature was exhorted to reflect the *events* of the present. Since the era in question boasted the event par excellence—Revolution (radical change, big news, unprecedented results)—the narrative event had an imposing paradigm to embody. Literary texts were envisioned as the "artistic incarnation of the Revolution," "the artistic echo of revolutionary reality"; they were to beat with the "pulse of the Revolution," burn with the "flame of the Revolution," embody "revolutionary heroism," "revolutionary will," and "revolutionary action." Even non-Party writers, whose works rarely followed the adumbrated paradigm, were extolled by as party-line a critic as Pereverzev, providing their events somehow reflected the event of the century; such reflections were celebrations—if not necessarily conscious ones—of the elemental, even cosmic, importance of the Revolution.¹⁶

Essentially, in thus dictating the dimensions of literary form and content, in mandating what is "great" enough to register in the literary text, in decreeing that only the "sensational" is "sensible" (available to the senses, perceptible), the Party took it upon itself to legislate—and substantially elevate—the lower "x-enough" boundary that ordinarily calibrates itself with no help at all.

The impulse is not frivolous. That lower boundary is the arbiter of perceived importance; it reflects the standards of what is sensed to be worthy of mention. It divides the imperceptible, the unnewsworthy, the "so what?" from the noticeable, the interesting, the tellable, the eventful. And since the literary event, as we have seen, is the textual inscription of important change and, consequently, real news, what occupies that position is of genuine concern to a regime whose stake in its own revolutionary status is great: to confirm its own newness, its newsworthiness, and the magnitude and importance of the change it had wrought, the Soviet state demanded literary corroboration that a significant event, in Lotman's sense, had indeed taken place in 1917. Once the state has asked literature to record history (insofar as it has been urged to deal with contemporary events), literature had best recognize what's worth telling in that context. In a certain sense, this represents an astute (if not entirely conscious) recognition that even the official story needs to be a good *story*.

At the same time, it would be misleading to represent this artificially imposed lower threshold, or even the upper exclusionary limit, as unyieldingly restrictive. In fact, though the Party quickly established a "temporary" organ of censorship that it never dissolved, during most of the 1920s the constraints were more readily articulated than strictly enforced.[17] The period was marked by a proliferation of literary groups with visions and programs as diverse as they were exuberant, ranging in orientation from the militant Proletkul't and the Octobrists, who promoted literature as a proletarian, propagandistic enterprise, to the emphatically apolitical Serapion Brothers (including Zoshchenko), who valued above all complete ideological freedom, individual expression, and good writing.[18] The Proletkul't, the Octobrists, Lef, the Pass, the Smithy, and the Serapion Brotherhood engaged each other in verbal battle and produced fiery manifestos formulating their competing positions, but no single group could yet claim to represent the "authorized" platform; no strictly codified program for literature had as yet emerged in the early 1920s. While Marxist critics encouraged literature to mind its dimensional p's and q's, and proletarian writers' organizations pressured writers to produce works that would contribute significantly to the building of socialism, the heavy-handed prohibitions and recriminations that would be legislated at the end of the decade were still to come.[19] Thus, when the Serapion Brothers and other "Fellow Travelers" dominated the literary market with their fragments, sketches, vignettes, anecdotes, and very short stories about "trifling" incidents, these works were permitted, if not exactly sanctioned.[20] In response to these challenges, though, the Party articulated even more forcefully a lower boundary more to its own specifications.

If these "trifles" (which weighed in well below the proposed minimum standard) were not thrown back like so many undersized fish, they owe their grudging publication at least in part to the embarrassing dearth of anything else that showed much promise. A disturbing number of the best writers had emigrated after the Revolution, and most of the talented ones who remained not only had not joined the Party, but had failed to demonstrate any enthusiasm at all over the new state of affairs. The so-called proletarian writers, who did produce according to Soviet prescription, had yet to write anything of any recognizable merit; throughout the first half of the 1920s, the small, inconsequential forms remained uncontestably "more alive than monumental art."[21] Understandably, the authorities were uneasy: Soviet cultural prestige was sinking desperately low in the West. Why couldn't this new state produce a worthy paean to its "magnificent" achievements?[22] Moreover, literature was simply important to the Soviets, as it had always been to the Russians. Despite all the rhetoric of change, there was never any question that literature *had* to continue to exist, that it could not be allowed to waste away from diminutive to ever-more-diminished form.

To encourage renewed growth, a policy of relative leniency was implemented in the hope of eliciting the support of the non-committed writers, or at least of preventing further emigration and the exportation of works to Western publishers.[23] This initiative produced one of the few periods of Soviet literary history in which explicit demands were articulated, but not strictly enforced.[24] As a result, multiple sides of a complex debate are represented in the literature of the 1920s: the demands of the authorities, the resistance to these demands on the part of many writers, and the dismayed response of the Party's literary critics.

On the subject of trivial subject matter, this dismay was ample: "Our writers have given us thousands of small trifles," lamented Voronskii, "they have crept into all the most remote, little corners, they have told us about amazing and unheard-of things, and they have constantly left out, forgotten something important."[25] "Something important" was missing; indeed, "the most important thing" was perpetually being omitted.[26] Even by Pereverzev's accommodating definition of "revolutionary reality," the October Revolution was disturbingly difficult to detect in many of the works of the period. Reviewing Zoshchenko's *Tales of Nazar Il'ich, Mr. Sinebriukhov* (*Rasskazy Nazara Il'icha gospodina Sinebriukhova*, 1922), Voronskii was indignant at this lapse: "This is supposed to be Revolution? Here we get backyards, little crumbs, and tiny anecdotes. But that which shook all of Russia from end to end, the loud rumble that was heard around the world, . . . where is the *echo* of all this?"²⁷

Some critics, it is true, attempted to account for the writers' prodigious production of "crumbs" and avoidance of larger-scale undertakings. M. Gorky cited the "destabilizing effects of the revolutionary period," which obviously made it difficult to sustain the concentration necessary to produce a longer, monumental work.²⁸ L. N. Seifullina echoed Gorky's feeling that "life is teeming all around; one would like to write volumes, but there's no time."²⁹ Others pointed to the "bourgeois" aesthetics of the Serapion Brothers, which unfortunately continued to exert an unhealthy influence on the as-yet unformed Soviet writers. However they chose to account for the fragmentary nature of early Soviet prose, many critics were also quick to point out that the smaller forms prevailed in the West as well at that time. Literary "crumbs" were not a specifically Soviet malaise.³⁰ Still, when Fedor Gladkov's novel *Cement* appeared in 1925, the ecstatic reviews made it clear that diminutive literature, however understandable it might have been, was not welcome. Gladkov had produced a masterpiece "on a large scale" which presented "large problems in all their magnitude," thereby once and for all "sweeping away the traditions of small literature."³¹

The Little Pictures: Indecent Exposure

Zoshchenko, for one, was not swept away; but neither was he oblivious to the demands of the Party critics for genres, literary models, and events of stature. He defied them quite consciously, as his own tongue-in-cheek proclamations and manifestos make clear:

> Some are of the opinion that what is needed is a Red Lev Tolstoy.
>
> This order [*zakaz*] must have been placed by some misguided publishing house. For all of life, the entire public domain, and the whole environment that a writer lives in today demands anything but a Red Lev Tolstoy. If anything is "commanded," then it's a work in that disrespected small form that, at least in the past, has been associated with the worst literary tradition.
>
> I've decided to fulfill that command.
>
> I don't think I'm mistaken.
>
> I don't plan to get into high literature. In high literature there are enough writers as it is.³²

So much for the faithful imitation of nineteenth-century giants. So much, as well, for the mandated generic amplitude. Although Zoshchenko's earliest works were written in a more traditional style, he quickly abandoned the "old forms" as a "mistake" in favor of the "sheer nonsense" (*sobach'ia erunda*) that became his trademark.[33] Ideally, according to Zoshchenko, the whole plot should fit easily into fifty to one hundred lines.[34] "Everything short. Three seconds' worth. . . . All in three pages,"[35] he explained, in his characteristically compressed style of "short sentences. Accessible to the poor."[36] Indeed, even this three-page allotment is less generous than it sounds, given the 15-centimeter publication format (including wide margins and large print) commonly used in the 1920s. Most of Zoshchenko's stories are under 600 words. The most notable exceptions in the 1920s are the lengthier early stories, *Tales of Nazar Il'ich, Mr. Sinebriukhov*, the form of which the author renounced shortly thereafter, and the ostensibly revivalist *Sentimental Tales* (*Sentimental'nye povesti*, 1927), which take up the question of trivia more thematically than compositionally. Interestingly, the only stories of any formal magnitude belong to this "sentimental" collection, billed explicitly as "nostalgic," not of the present or proportional to it.

But more refractory perhaps than the dimensions of Zoshchenko's stories was his subject matter. In terms of tellable content, Zoshchenko's work became a direct polemic with literature that was obediently *masshtabnaia* (up to scale), as well as against the critics who agitated for it. In the preface to his *Sentimental Tales*, Zoshchenko anticipates the discrepancy between expectations and product: "This book was written at the height of NEP and Revolution. The reader, of course, has the right to demand of the author genuine revolutionary content, large-scale themes, planetary tasks and heroic pathos—in a word, full and high ideology."

Not wishing to mislead the low-income buyer into wasting hard-earned cash on *this* book only to be disappointed, Zoshchenko comes clean. This work, he acknowledges, treats instead a "trivial theme": "The author admits that in these stormy years of ours he's downright ashamed, it's positively embarrassing, to come out with such insignificant ideas, such humdrum conversations about individual people." But, he concedes, I can only do what I can. I'm a trivial sort of guy. "From each according to his abilities." Not incidentally, here, Zoshchenko enlists socialism's own rhetoric in a context it did not mean to address and in defense of a kind of literature it would not eagerly embrace.[37]

The plea of "I can't help it" that one meets so often in the public Zoshchenko is plainly a ruse; it contrasts sharply with Zoshchenko's own work notes and admissions made in confidence. "I went over to this type of writing in the full consciousness that it is just what is needed, and expecting all sorts of unpleasantness as a result," he wrote to Gorky.³⁸ Zoshchenko's posturing (and its function in his fiction, which I will examine in greater detail) was cleverly designed to forestall some of that "unpleasantness." And though the artful dodge was effective and generally made it difficult to say with any certainty what Zoshchenko *really* thought, the criticism of his choice of trivial subject matter never went away. "Zoshchenko has gotten so mired in trivia that it's terrifying," remarked one of his contemporaries, in horror.³⁹ Others, such as V. Vishnev, felt compelled to try to educate the errant trivialist. In his 1927 article "Heart-to-Heart Talk," Vishnev expressed the fervent desire to have just such a tête-à-tête with the writer in order to ask him directly, "Hey, Comrade Zoshchenko, what are you wasting your talent on?"⁴⁰

Indeed, Zoshchenko's stories dwell almost exclusively on such inconsequential matters as losing a boot, hanging up a coat, switching on a light, or accidentally stepping on someone's foot in a crowd. Nor do such items belong to the level of descriptive detail: these commonplace pursuits constitute the actual subject matter—the substance of the story—not its discursive treatment. The titles themselves unabashedly proclaim Zoshchenko's preoccupation with "trivia"—"The Trifles of Life" ("Melochi zhizni"), "A Trivial Occurrence" ("Melkoe proisshestvie"), "Small-Fry" ("Melkota"), or "A Trivial Incident" ("Melkii sluchai"). Even in the illustrious company of the era's other talented miniaturists, Zoshchenko's obsession with trifles was unparalleled. Vishnev was not entirely unjustified when he sneered, after an exhaustive survey of Zoshchenko's works of the 1920s, that "themes of any greater significance are not to be found."⁴¹

Inflated Soviet standards of importance aside, material this unequivocally marginal would appear to present a formidable problem to even the most organic lower boundary (except, perhaps, in the *New Yorker* cartoon's "era of reduced expectations"). What could possibly be the appeal of two-page stories about trying to buy a lamp shade or forgetting to change one's socks? "Little episodes again!" anticipates one of Zoshchenko's own narrators. "Who, on a cosmic scale, cares about your little episodes?" ("What the Nightingale Sang" ["O chem pel solovei"], 1925, 2:108). Who, indeed, short of Ippolit Ippolitych, would find this trivia interesting?

Evidently Zoshchenko's readership did, because his so-called "trifles" met with enormous success. The response to his stories in the satirical journals was tremendous. An issue of *Begemot* (*The Hippo*), *Buzoter* (*The Roughneck*), or *Mukhomor* (*The Toadstool*) containing a Zoshchenko title could sell as many as 200,000 copies. When Zoshchenko's stories began to appear in collections, they were published in large (usually inexpensive) editions, and always sold out immediately.[42] One million volumes were sold between 1922 and 1927; in 1926 and 1927 alone the editions ran to 700,000 copies.[43] Admittedly, publication figures do not always give a true picture, particularly in the Soviet Union, where the production of books, like most things, proceeded more by plan than by demand. But in this case the figures are eloquent. Zoshchenko was one of the most widely read writers in the 1920s—his name had become one of those proverbial household words, regularly occasioning the exclamation that this or that real-life scenario was "just like in Zoshchenko!"[44]

Zoshchenko's immense popularity was surely related to the fact that his stories were hilarious. His success was also due, no doubt, to the familiarity of his material, its accessibility to a broad segment of the population. His little episodes typically transpired in the streetcar, the bathhouse, the communal kitchen—loci of encounter and collision on a daily basis and the source of plenty of incidents in real life.

I would like to suggest, though, that Zoshchenko's stories were felt to be so "worth reading" at least in part as a result of the paradox I alluded to at the outset: his subject matter, which barely registers on any objective scale of tellability and which seems to be "not x enough," at the same time challenges the prohibitions of the *upper* boundary. It threatens to transgress the limits of the tolerable, even in the relatively tolerant 1920s, not only by criticizing, albeit surreptitiously, on a pseudo-innocuous small scale, but by daring on all fronts—fictional, historical, and political—to thematize, and ultimately to reject, the canonical determination of what is *important*. By reversing the regime's designations of event and norm, figure and ground, perceptible and imperceptible, tellable and not tellable, Zoshchenko transforms the untellable ("not x enough" to tell) into the unmentionable (with the attendant thrill of the "far-too-x"). The imperceptible becomes intolerable (to return to the analogy of sensory stimulation), the insensible too great a sensation for the official Soviet sensibility.

At the most superficial level, this provocation exploits the fact that by adopting proportions too minute to attract attention, Zoshchenko has positioned himself masterfully to volley inconspicuous pot shots at a conspicuous political power structure. His "humorous little anecdotes" pointedly expose the many so-called "minor" inconveniences of Soviet life. Each miniature saga is an insistent display of some negative: how *hard* it is to find a bucket in the bathhouse ("The Bathhouse" ["Bania"], 1925), how every lost boot precipitates an insufferable ordeal of red tape ("The Galosh" ["Galosha"], 1927), how little the seamier side of human nature has been changed by the Revolution ("The Merry-Go-Round" ["Karusel' "], 1923), how life in the communal kitchen is fraught with quarrels, greed, and constant unpleasantness ("Nervous People" ["Nervnye liudi"], 1925), and how everywhere people's feet are getting stepped on ("Absence of Malice" ["Dushevnaia prostota"], 1927).[45] None of this is openly counterrevolutionary, but it is unrelentingly critical. It betrays an irreverence that on a larger scale would be far "too x," way beyond the allowable limits.

In this sense, then, as is often noted, the use of ostensibly insignificant subject matter operates as an evasion: criticism on a small scale is less flagrant. But Zoshchenko has devised more than just a way of sneaking past the censorship, limited as it was. As we have seen in Chekhov's manipulation of event structure, the presentation of unlikely material in the position of narrative event thematizes the very significance of that content. It is the ongoing enterprise of Zoshchenko's stories to demonstrate in this textual way not only that such little glitches in the mechanism do exist, but that these minor "technical difficulties" are extremely important, that they have real consequences in the life of the average citizen. One was not supposed to notice these things, and given the newly adumbrated lower boundary circumscribing literary attention, one certainly was not supposed to write about them. But these "little problems" that went publicly unacknowledged and were officially disregarded as too trivial to merit attention emerge under Zoshchenko's literary scrutiny as significant and tellable events.

Thus, not only does each literary indiscretion belie the myth that everything is optimal under the new system, but more insidiously makes the point that these difficulties, these so-called trifles of life, *cannot* be overlooked. The result is an indictment not only of specific social problems, but also of the system of priorities that contrives not to notice them.

But as pointed as Zoshchenko's social criticism is, it is still less globally subversive than the underlying dynamic it reveals. Ultimately, what is paramount is not the social import of what is or isn't noticed (a number of Zoshchenko's stories in fact treat quirky individual "trifles" with little societal resonance), but rather the very fact that the institutional thresholds of tellability, the specifications for observable data, are routinely and flagrantly disregarded (or, more precisely, flouted) by his stories and their narrators: to gaze below the threshold is to aim below the belt. Zoshchenko thus has less to fear in the way of a Labovian "so what?" than an indignant "how dare you?" Noticing and failing to notice—as an index for what is *important* enough to attract attention—functions as one of the central oppositions in Zoshchenko's poetics and one of the chief means of opposition in his work to the preposterous notion of "designated significance." His dalliance on the frontiers of perceptibility works to destabilize the opposition of "significant" and "insignificant" as handed down from above.

In what follows, I will consider Zoshchenko's idiosyncratic deployment of "insignificant" material and the sensations it produces. Like Chekhov, Zoshchenko capitalizes on (in order to violate) the operative norms of eventfulness—norms that in Zoshchenko's time are both more explicit and more exigent. To a certain extent, he does so in ways similar to the earlier writer by maximizing, minimizing, and staging events of equivocal status. Since events are by definition *noticeable* (and noticeability is his particular hobbyhorse), Zoshchenko, as we might expect, conducts his play with perceptibility by staging (1) "insignificant" incidents that are nevertheless noticed; (2) ostensibly significant ones that are not; (3) events that are simultaneously heeded and overlooked; and (4) "events" with no perceptible impact at all. While Zoshchenko's strategies can thus be articulated to fall neatly into Chekhov's four categories, in practice they subdivide and overlap so many times that ultimately this typology is more artificial and constraining than elucidating. I will note the points of resonance with Chekhov's structural designs where it is useful to do so, but I will be guided overall by Zoshchenko's own more associative logic.

Whereas Chekhov developed a particular *grammar* of eventfulness, arranging incidents and consequences in unexpected and disproportionate *combinations*, Zoshchenko elaborates most insistently a *vocabulary* of events (a lexicon less verbal than compositional), a set of recurrent elements that he wields in a play of paradigmatic *substitutions*, replacing sanctioned material with components from his own repertoire. In canvassing Zoshchenko's stories for characteristic procedures, I discern most consistently, beyond the structural regularities Zoshchenko shares with Chekhov, a barrage of reiterative trifles—both events and "existents"[46]—that become functionally significant both because of their position in the individual text and their obsessive repetition in Zoshchenko's oeuvre as a whole. My approach here will consequently be less typological (as in Chapter 1) than "topological," locating the *topoi*, the "common places" scattered throughout Zoshchenko's landscape (or, more precisely, his cityscape). And since Zoshchenko's patterns emerge more readily in a review of a large sample of works, I will consider numerous stories in varying degrees of depth. If, as a result, my inquiry appears at first to reproduce the fragmentation (and disarray) of its object,[47] this reflects the particular pragmatic force of the stories themselves. By establishing the coordinates in Zoshchenko's compositional "chaos," though, by pinpointing his characteristic little things, I propose to show how they work to integrate the apparent disorder of his oeuvre, while they dis-integrate the established order and hierarchy of his world.

In rooting Zoshchenko's force and originality firmly in his story-level strategies rather than in his discursive mannerisms (such as the famous verbal tics of his narrators), I depart somewhat from the usual presentation of Zoshchenko's work. Chudakova, for instance, believes that the plot is secondary, even difficult to discern. Because the first-person narrator occupies the foreground, "the real event takes place not at the level of the story, but at the level of the discourse"; the story itself offers little insight into Zoshchenko's poetics.[48] I distinguish myself most sharply from the recent project of Mikhail Kreps, who dismisses the composition of Zoshchenko's plots as "almost always obvious, superficial, and universally comprehensible," and requiring no elucidation from the literary critic (in stark contrast to Zoshchenko's subtle and complex linguistic strategies, which demand the scrutiny Kreps proposes to give them).[49] Both Chudakova and Kreps support their claims for the ascendancy of the discourse by asserting that it is nearly impossible to paraphrase a Zoshchenko story (Chudakova because the narrator lacks the logic and coherence to present a distinct and reproducible structure, Kreps because all the humor resides in the language). Since I will be retelling and paraphrasing these stories extensively, I can only hope that the critics are mistaken both about the futility of the enterprise and about its value. I will consider Zoshchenko's language as well, later, but from a different perspective.

Proportions and Paradigms

Zoshchenko's project of repudiation proceeds by declining the Party's generous "suggestions" for how to produce great works of literature. Instead of adopting the mandated large genres, monumental nineteenth-century models, and revolutionary events, he *reduces* length to a bare minimum, *refracts* parodically the classical models he has been urged to embrace, and *rereads* events in such a way that makes eventfulness itself the issue.

One particular strategy that accomplishes all three at once is his adoption of epic *form* without epic proportions. In this wry "acceptance" of the Party's generic specifications, Zoshchenko simultaneously overturns the imperative to compose on a grand scale, to imitate his predecessors, and to embody the era's most dramatic events in prose.

His "shrunken epics" are perfect condensations: full formal execution in a page and a half, with exclamatory passion and imperceptible trifles set as high drama, mayhem in miniature.

"Absence of Malice," for instance, introduces the big, strong pedestrian whose excellence seems to consist in his ability to walk down the street smoothly and evenly, without bumping into his fellow pedestrians or rudely interfering with their progress. The narrator happens to be walking behind this exemplary Soviet citizen, and devotes nearly half of the actual narrative to a step-by-step panegyric to his gait:

> He's walking and walking. And I'm walking behind him. And he's walking along ahead. No more than one step ahead of me.
> And so, you know, we're walking along nicely. Real orderly. We're not stepping on each other's feet. We're not flinging our arms around. You could say we're not touching each other a bit. In a word, we're walking in perfect harmony. It makes your heart sing.
> And I thought:
> "How gloriously this pedestrian is walking! Smoothly. He doesn't kick. Anyone else would get all tangled up in his own legs, but not this guy—he places his feet so calmly." ("Dushevnaia prostota," 1:392)

The narrator's hyperbolic glee is short-lived, however, as he himself becomes distracted and treads "with all [his] might" on the good pedestrian's foot ("on his heel. And a little above it," we are informed with the degree of specificity appropriate to an event of such "magnitude" [1:392]). The perfect harmony has been destroyed. The heart stops singing, and the narrator freezes in terror in his tracks.

How could he fail to be distraught? His misstep is the major, irrevocable event that thoroughly disrupts the harmony of his immediate world. Yet in the context of society's "giant strides," a few faltering baby steps were not supposed to be noteworthy. Zoshchenko *does* deign to notice, however, and he notices relentlessly. In real life, he implies (unlike in the world of Party rhetoric), the man who just stepped on your toe is a more tangible foe than all the enemies of socialism put together. History may be coming to fruition and all that, but the pain of a stubbed toe is still suffering, and suffering is still eminently perceptible and problematic. Zoshchenko's scenario recalls Ivan Karamazov's hypothesis that just such an inadvertent misstep on someone else's foot might permanently inure a man to another's suffering.[50]

Zoshchenko's evocation of Dostoevsky, we will see, is not an isolated reference. It is part of a complex network of parodic allusions to the literary tradition he had been urged to recapitulate, a set of evocations that serve (like the epic form) both to flout the demand for reverent imitation and to render his own "trifles" that much more fraught with hidden significance. Zoshchenko made a practice, too, of adopting well-known titles only to depart markedly from his prominently displayed "models": "Opasnye sviazi" (Laclos's *Liaisons dangereuses*); "Stradanie molodogo Vertera" (Goethe's *Leiden des jungen Werthers*); "Bednaia Liza" (Karamzin's "Poor Liza"); "Zhivoi trup" (Tolstoy's *Living Corpse*). The chapter headings in Zoshchenko's later autobiographical work *Before Sunrise* (*Pered voskhodom solntsa*, 1943) reflect the same compulsion to reuse preexisting titles. The story about the foot, "Dushevnaia prostota," itself recalls Chekhov's "Sviataia prostota," and both evoke the "holy simplicity" (*sancta simplicitas*) of St. Francis. Thus, we must laugh when, at the end of the decade in the preface to *Michel Siniagin*, Zoshchenko apologizes for his unimaginative title, necessitated by his unfortunate discovery that "all the good titles have already been used" (*Mishel' Siniagin*, 1930, 2:177).

"Absence of Malice" first appeared in *Begemot*, but it was widely read in the popular 1927 collection of eleven stories, *Melochi zhizni* (*The Trifles of Life*), which derives its title from Saltykov-Shchedrin's collection of that name, while manifestly rejecting its strategies. The earlier work, if projected onto a scale of eventfulness, would find its place dangerously close to the telephone-book (or kitty-diary) end of the spectrum. It is written almost entirely in the imperfective, recording what usually happens in the spring, what is normally done in the summer, describing life as it has always been and as it "ought to be." The life portrayed is as cyclical and about as eventful as a calendar.[51] In "Absence of Malice," by contrast, the narrator's little "feat" is presented explicitly in terms of *eventfulness*, as exception and disruption. Zoshchenko charges the trifles of his own reality with great import and poignancy by casting them in his shrunken epics as not only perceptible, but downright catastrophic events. It is a strategy that allows him to expose as crises those insignificant "minor" inconveniences of Soviet life, as well as to travesty the "desirable" literary form he felt to be so inappropriate for his time.

Edward Brown has noted that Zoshchenko's shrunken epics tend to follow a rather formal structural scheme, beginning with an "exordium," proceeding to "epic narration," and closing with a "moral conclusion," all, naturally, on a diminutive scale.[52] To compose story after story about "life's trifles" is defiant enough. To enshrine them in such a pompously epic mode actually thematizes the purported triviality of these little incidents.

"A Trivial Incident" ("Melkii sluchai," 1927), for instance, opens with a lofty preamble (the exordium described by Brown) on the subject of who will and who will not appreciate the forthcoming narrative.[53] Since the occurrence in question is "trivial, not of worldwide significance," not everyone will understand "what the big deal is all about. A Nepman, for example, with silver jingling in every vest pocket, will hardly be able to comprehend this incident" (1:370–71). The simple working man, on the other hand, will not only understand, but will sympathize warmly with the hero, Vasilii Ivanovich. Enter the hero, begin the epic narration.

Vasilii Ivanovich's adventure begins with the purchase of a theater ticket. Lest we fail to appreciate the magnitude of the occasion, the narrator tells us that Vasilii Ivanovich made a special trip to the theater to ensure his admission, spent a whole ruble, and didn't even blink (though his tongue did wag a little) when the cashier grabbed the money. Already we can see that the expenditure of a ruble is itself noteworthy to Vasilii Ivanovich.

> And Vasilii Ivanovich took his preparations for this play very seriously. He washed, shaved, and put on a tie.
>
> Oh, oh, Vasilii Ivanovich, Vasilii Ivanovich! Did your noble heart sense a worldly pitfall? Did you foresee all the trifles of life? Did your steel hand perhaps tremble as you tied your tie?
>
> Oh, oh, sad things, depressing things happen in this world. (1:371)

The major complication (the "pitfall" hinted at above) arises when Vasilii Ivanovich arrives at the theater a well-considered twenty minutes in advance (to allow plenty of time to hang up his coat, casually readjust his tie, and so on), only to discover that an additional twenty kopecks are required for the privilege of hanging up one's coat. He has eight kopecks, maximum. Or maybe six.

Deciding to try anyway, Vasilii Ivanovich approaches a cloakroom attendant, places his coat and galoshes on the counter, presses his meager change into the man's hand, and asks him to accept it, insufficient as it is, without counting. The attendant, a "cynic," counts the six kopecks with great precision, initiates an exchange of screaming insults, and refuses to take the things. Vasilii Ivanovich must fight back tears.

Meanwhile, the leisurely twenty minutes have elapsed. Vasilii Ivanovich puts his coat back on, stuffs his boots into his hat, and rushes toward the entrance: no admittance in coats. Vasilii Ivanovich despairs. He has a ticket, the play has begun, and they won't let him in. He tries taking off his coat, wrapping his boots and hat inside, and carrying it as a small bundle: no good. No bundles allowed in the theater.

Finally, an older, somewhat kindlier attendant takes pity on the hero and agrees to hang up his things (if Vasilii Ivanovich promises to bring the twenty kopecks the next day). But by then the second act is well under way, and the defeated hero declines, commenting that he won't understand anything, as he is not accustomed to watching the end of plays without the beginning. He barely manages to sell his one-ruble ticket to some poor waif for ten kopecks, spits in the direction of the disagreeable cloakroom attendant, and leaves. The story ends there, without Zoshchenko's characteristic "moral conclusion."

The mockery of the epic mode is especially apparent in the pseudo-high-style apostrophe and the hyperbolic warnings of impending disaster. Going to the theater is shown to be of great significance to Vasilii Ivanovich by the account of his preparations, consciously modeled after the epic hero's donning of his armor in anticipation of a great battle (though this hero's "solemn" preparations consist only of washing and shaving for the occasion). The "battle" in which our hero must engage is cruel, to be sure, and bitter enough to bring tears to the warrior's eyes. But the stakes are low (fourteen kopecks in all) and the ammunition crude: a barrage of choice epithets ("dog's blood," "plague," "black personality," "old snout," "oaf," "parasite") and a threat or two ("I'll pull your beard out"; "I'll smash your face with your own galoshes"[1:372]). Still, Vasilii Ivanovich's big day is ruined, and if going to the theater was a big event, then having the (paid for!) privilege rescinded and humiliation heaped on to boot is indeed a memorable occurrence.

This is a trivial incident, as the title suggests, and since the narrative ends as Vasilii Ivanovich leaves the theater, we do not see its effect on the rest of his life. But it is one of many such encumbrances of daily existence, the *melochi zhizni* (trifles of life) that pervade and overwhelm. And the *cumulative* effect of Zoshchenko's stories is precisely one of overwhelming oppressiveness; it appears there is no end to the unpleasantness. Yet we are not called upon to shed tears for the hero. Zoshchenko is less concerned with upholding the significance of a particular incident than with relativizing and personalizing eventfulness—with flouting the exclusionary boundaries that would eliminate all such small-scale phenomena from view and from text.

We recognize in both these shrunken epics (the coat snafu and the pedestrian misstep) a structural challenge to the norms of tellability analogous to Chekhov's first strategy, which presented an "insignificant" incident as a significant event. More interesting, though, and more critical, are the terms these two texts introduce, most notably the foot and coat complex that figures prominently in Zoshchenko's almost fixed inventory of story elements resistant to the prescribed epochal paradigms. If later in his *Light-Blue Book* Zoshchenko identifies exactly five forces that produce stories—money, love, perfidy, failure, and "surprising events" (3:163–64)—in the 1920s, all of his stories seem to be born instead from outer garments and lower extremities (and their respective appurtenances). Insofar as feet and coats in particular acquire a kind of paradigmatic status in Zoshchenko's oeuvre, I will return to these two stories (both so closely associated with Zoshchenko's trademark title "The Trifles of Life") as paradigms of my own.

Coat Capers

That the hero's trial in "A Trivial Incident" should take the form of taking off his coat is particularly trenchant. As a glaringly trivial but stubbornly recurrent event in Zoshchenko's stories, it "dismantles" the more official pantheon of momentous matters by audaciously seizing that canonical status for itself. The apparently uncomplex act of taking off one's coat regularly precipitates serious trouble in Zoshchenko's stories. It is grounds for divorce in "The Wedding" ("Svad'ba," 1927).[54] Young Volod'ka cannot recognize his new bride after she removes her coat at their wedding reception. Because they met in a streetcar and spent their entire three-day acquaintance on the street, he has never seen her without her coat and hat. Even the official registration of the marriage is performed "on the run" (*na khodu*), without the fuss of removing outer garments. The "main event" unfolds afterward when she finally does take off her overcoat in the crowd of guests. "Nothing like this had ever happened to [Volod'ka] before," and to identify his bride, the bewildered groom resorts to trying out his charms on each of the young women present. Since this is viewed as radically unacceptable behavior for a newlywed, he is cast out by the bride's family. The divorce is finalized the next day. Neither the marriage ceremony nor the divorce proceedings occasion much fuss (or much narrative attention), and the more potentially climactic act of bridal "disrobing" is deferred forever because the coat usurps our attention. This apotheosis of the everyday is invested with cataclysmic importance (while remaining resolutely trivial).

But this is hardly the first featured coat in Russian literature; even the association of garment and wife resonates with the plight of poor Akakii Akakievich. But if Gogol's "Overcoat" presents certain obstacles to an unreservedly empathic reading, Zoshchenko's coat capers nearly preclude it, foregrounding instead the insistence on articulating the trivial, refuting, while appearing to accept, the injunction to adopt the "important themes" both of the present and of Russian literature's great nineteenth-century literary forebears.

Zoshchenko, in fact, adopts the traumatic loss of a coat as one of his quintessential plots, but each time he rewrites Gogol's "Overcoat" it is with little compassion and less obeisance. "Love" ("Liubov'," 1924) gives us Vasia Chesnokov escorting (albeit somewhat reluctantly) his date home after a very late party. All is in place—the cavalier, his lady, and their respective coats (and, I might note, in anticipation of the foot complex, their galoshes)—and in spite of the extreme chill, Vasia waxes expansive, boasting about all the death-defying exploits he is prepared to perform for Mashen'ka should the need arise. When, however, the couple is accosted by a shadowy figure who demands Vasia's coat and boots, the gallant escort urges the thief to consider Mashen'ka's things instead. The ensuing loss of his overcoat (and, as a direct consequence of the episode, of his lady) can scarcely be read as too tragic. Zoshchenko's "Misfortune" ("Beda," 1923), which parallels "The Overcoat" most closely, effects a similar diminution of Akakii Akakievich's pathos. Here, an impoverished hero scrimps and saves for years, starving and undergoing untold deprivations in order to acquire the one thing that would become—in fact had long since become—the center of his life. In Zoshchenko's story, though, the hero is relieved of his treasure more stupidly than tragically by drinking it away as soon as he acquires it.

As I will argue in Chapter 4, the practice of viewing Gogol's work as fraught with accessible significance (of the sort Zoshchenko and his contemporaries were urged to recapitulate) may well be as much a learned response as the one that reads *War and Peace* as supremely novelistic. Be that as it may, Zoshchenko, for his part, dutifully borrowed the most ludicrous aspects of Gogol's "important concerns." In "Administrative Ecstasy" ("Administrativnyi vostorg," 1927), for instance, an incident involving a pig and the law is one of a complex of references to the Gogolian sow who absconds with the court proceedings in the story of the "Two Ivans" ("Povest' o tom, kak possorilsia Ivan Ivanovich s Ivanom Nikiforovichem"), and possibly to the demonic snout that pokes its way into the windows of Dikan'ka. This association is underscored by several other stories with either figurative or actual pigs. "Swinishness" ("Svinsto," 1923) makes the connection to Gogol's story in both the substance of its title and the form of its subtitle: "Rasskaz o tom, kak Ivan Petrovich khotel po-novomu nazvat' svoego mladentsa" ("The Story of How Ivan Petrovich Wanted to Name His Son in an All-New Way"). The saga of naming a new child itself recalls the story of how Akakii Akakievich got *his* name (with the patronymic playing a similarly determining role). "A Swine Affair" ("Svinoe delo," 1923), too, invokes both the Gogolian pig and the coatless hero. The self-important official who turns up to investigate the matter of the disappearing pig echoes Akakii Akakievich's verbal tormentor in his thunderous "Do you know who I am?" (1:125). As usual, in Zoshchenko's versions the stakes are much lower. After all his careful deliberations, the new father in "Swinishness" simply gives up and goes drinking, and his wife gives the twins the first names that come to mind; and no one in "A Swine Affair" dies of fright from the attempted verbal terrorism of Zoshchenko's "significant" personage.

If "Comrade Gogol" ("Tovarishch Gogol'," 1926) had lived in our humble times, writes Zoshchenko, his "big works" like *Dead Souls* (*Mertvye dushi*) would be inadequate. He would find himself writing instead *raznye melochishki* (various little trifles [1:499]). In the physical absence of the "master," Zoshchenko effects this reduction on his behalf, often in Gogol's own terms. If Petr Bitsilli, in his early article "Zoshchenko i Gogol'," undertakes to defend Zoshchenko from his critics by detailing his affinity with Gogol (demonstrating thereby the later writer's universality and high tragedy), Zoshchenko has already performed the reverse operation, offering up a hypothetical 1920s Gogol to the same critics who, he shows in a fictional review, would tear the good Nikolai Vasil'evich to shreds. That there is a connection between Zoshchenko and Gogol is well established; Chudakova even speaks of a "dependence," at least in Zoshchenko's earliest work.[55] But the relationship may be more complex, more ambivalent, than most of these observations suggest. The most flagrant borrowing—and shrinkage—of Gogolian material takes the form of the recurrently problematic coat.

The purloined coat motif reappears in the story of "The Thief" ("Vor," 1923), who doesn't steal jackets (or anything else) very successfully, but ineptly loses his own. (Not incidentally, he becomes an attenuated Raskol'nikov when he stops on his way to the caper to pick up an axe he encounters and when he steals, instead of the anticipated silver, only a child's toys, and then loses even them.) The stolen coat comes to stand for afflictions of any kind, from house guests—they'll run off with your coat if you don't keep an eye on them ("Guests" ["Gosti"], 1927, 1:363)[56]—to romantic disappointments. In "A Trivial Incident from Private Life" ("Melkii sluchai iz lichnoi zhizni," 1933), the fellow who exerts a supreme effort to change his life by changing his clothes procures secondhand a miraculous coat that is guaranteed to attract female attention.[57] When an elegant lady is indeed transfixed by his new acquisition, the man swells with pleasure. Unfortunately, the coat has caught her eye solely because she recognizes it as the garment recently stolen from her husband, and our hero ultimately succeeds in exciting only police attention. Again, in this association of coat and wife, erotic possibilities are ironically foreclosed by the removal of body covering.

Zoshchenko, like his unfortunate hero, uses the coat to attract attention and, similarly, manages in the process to bring down on himself the displeasure of the authorities; but he maintains his reader's interest by playing on the coat as an object not only of desire, but of narrative attention. In "The Hero" ("Geroi," 1922),[58] coat removal is the mark of "heroic deeds" in the making. Even if the most exalted hero Zoshchenko can deliver is the bystander who refuses to remove his coat (in preparation for saving a drowning man) until he is assured that a medal will be forthcoming, coat removal facilitates action; it produces story.[59]

The theft motif, even of something as commonplace as a coat, under circumstances substantially less heartrending than Akakii Akakievich's, still introduces a dynamic of loss, a presence-turned-absence that disrupts the status quo and functions within the textual context as event. But coat removal also mirrors the function of the stories themselves: exposure. In "Dog Scent" ("Sobachii niukh," 1924), for instance, the theft of a coat not only precipitates the action, but literally *uncovers* rampant corruption. When a dog with a remarkable sense of smell is brought in to sniff out the thief, he uncovers a lot of dirty linen, eliciting with his formidable nose and impressive teeth a confession of wrongdoing from each of the "innocent bystanders." Everyone, it turns out, is concealing some offense, all of which are mercilessly exposed. Finally the infallible dog attaches himself to the original complainant, who is forced to concede that *he* had pinched the coat from his brother-in-law in the first place. This forced confessional mode, this airing of dirty laundry, is not unlike what Zoshchenko himself accomplishes in his stories by doggedly removing coats, his own *sobach'ia erunda* ("dog drivel") bearing a strong resemblance to the fabled *sobachii niukh* (dog scent) that exposes the undersides of things.

Zoshchenko's own "Confession" ("Ispoved'," 1924) exposes the worst thing possible: the confessor's lack of faith. The specific skepticism here is religious, but the act of questioning authority, of doubting the canonical version, is both striking and familiar. Zoshchenko's exposure—of skepticism, of difficulties, of bodies, of what's worth telling in spite of its legislated triviality, of what is beneath the surface and below the line—is *indiscretion*; Zoshchenko uncovers what (as the narrator of "A Trivial Incident from Private Life" comments in reference to his own attire) "one musn't really talk about in literature" (3:257). To tell is by its very nature to disclose and expose; in the context that calls for keeping things discreetly "under wraps," Zoshchenko specializes in indecent exposure, exposés that are emphatically "too x."

High Drama

If, in Zoshchenko's oeuvre, the removal of coats replaces the removal of czars as the event of record, in the context of the theater, where so many of his stories are set, that bodily exposure is translated into laying bare the norms of decorum. In "The Charms of Culture" ("Prelesti kul'tury," 1926), for instance, we encounter another citizen who, like Vasilii Ivanovich in "A Trivial Incident," experiences coat removal problems at the theater. Having just stepped out to make a quick purchase—something to wet his throat, it seems—Vasilii Mitrofanovich happens to encounter two acquaintances on the street. They are on their way to the theater and convince him to join them. The happy threesome purchases its tickets at a ruble thirty each, and begins to mount the stairs to the balcony. Unfortunately, they are called back: no coats (of course!) in the theater. Vasilii Mitrofanovich's two companions comply without a second thought, but he himself is in a bind. He had simply thrown his coat on over his nightshirt. His trial has begun. After numerous attempts to get by undetected, he is forcibly removed and will be brought to court for indecent exposure.

Wearing a coat in the theater is more casual, less rigid, and perhaps even a little slovenly, but it had been permissible (if we are to believe Zoshchenko's narrators) during the hectic period of War Communism. The pretensions of NEP will not permit it, however. What is good and reasonable in bourgeois countries sometimes goes awry here, muses the narrator of "The Charms of Culture." There the populace is well dressed and refined and naturally people look even more so without their wraps. But, the story seems to argue, the Russians are still in their nightshirts, so why the affectation?

The theater figures recurrently in Zoshchenko's works as a place of codified decorum, a locus governed by a certain protocol that must be observed. You don't wear your coat in the theater; you don't even carry it over your arm ("You might as well have brought your feather bed too" ["A Trivial Incident," 1:372]). You don't express your approval by standing up for the duration of the performance (at least until they start seating spectators by height—"Theater Life" ["Teatral'naia zhizn'," 1922]). And you certainly don't attend in your nightshirt (let alone do isometrics during the performance to keep warm, because it's chilly when you're only in your nightshirt). But Zoshchenko's heroes do all these things, and no matter how "trivial" the "incident," each violation is disruptive enough to constitute a story.

Precisely because the theater dictates a certain propriety, it is a perfect setting for the disruption of that decorum, a place to "stage" events, a field of action, a veritable theater of war. The reclusive hero of "Wisdom" ("Mudrost'," 1924), for instance, who has lived an isolated and eventless existence for eleven years, nevertheless *must* have a story, for one element of his prehistory is known: he once punched somebody in the nose—in a theater lobby, naturally. In the theater, particularly in its margins, dramas unfold, disruptions occur, problems arise, stories worth telling are born.

Often the theatrical adventure (in keeping with a rich fund of literary precedent) is erotic in nature (though like most of Zoshchenko's nods to precedent, the stakes are greatly reduced and the results are parodic). The questing hero of "A Trivial Incident from Private Life," whose new coat is his ticket, begins his pursuit of feminine "spectators" by attending the theater. One (former) husband forbids his wife to go anywhere near the place because it is equated in his mind with adultery ("Liaisons dangereuses," 1936). "The Lady Aristocrat" ("Aristokratka," 1923), in fact, reproduces the seating arrangements of the loving but adulterous couple of Chekhov's "Lady with the Little Dog"; when Zoshchenko's couple reunites during intermission, however, it is not to pledge their everlasting love, but to terminate their budding romance over the price of a cream puff. In the theater, comments the bitter hero, his *dama* exposed her true colors (1:170).

Normally, people who are cultured go to the theater; those who do not go to the theater "go to beer halls, or in a drunken stupor beat each others' mugs into the curb" ("A Trivial Incident," 1:371). Or they are on their way to wet their whistles ("The Charms of Culture"). The hero of "Strong Medicine" ("Sil'noe sredstvo," 1925), too, is an inveterate alcoholic until someone gives him a ticket to a performance one Sunday. Art, it seems, makes such a strong impression on him that he actually becomes the most prominent theatergoer of the district: he attends the show every Sunday. Not really having mastered the conventions, he has a tendency to keep his seat once he has taken it, remaining long after the conclusion of the performance. But he is a convert! Culture prevails over *nekul'turnost'* (coarse, uncultured behavior). Of course he still drinks like a fish on Saturdays, and when he injures himself during his Saturday bouts he is forced to forgo his more refined Sunday activities.

With such threats to order and decorum about (patrons who drink or appear in various stages of undress), it is no wonder that access to the theater must be limited and guards posted to keep the uninitiated from entering in their coats. As Iu. Shcheglov has observed, Zoshchenko's theatergoers invariably prove themselves incapable of rising to the "cultural challenge" (*kul'turnyi vyzov*) of the theater.[60] It is not insignificant (though it is coincidental) that I began my consideration of Chekhov with his character's capital offense in a theatrical setting; the clear delineation of the permissible there makes any aberration at once palpable and inadmissible. Most often in Zoshchenko this lapse is figured in terms of a violation of the dress code, and most frequently the result is forced exclusion.

But as I have suggested, it is the artificial norms of behavior that are exposed as reactionary and gratuitous. Aleksandr Zholkovskii, in fact, sees in the distress of Zoshchenko's heroes an explicit parody of the confusion experienced by Natasha at the opera in *War and Peace*, Tolstoy's classic exposé, via *ostranenie* (defamiliarization), of the hyperbolic conventionality of opera, as seen through the naive eyes of a young country girl. And if Natasha, not knowing the code, cannot see the play, Zoshchenko's characters, similarly untutored, cannot even get in to see the stage;[61] again, Zoshchenko out-Tolstoys Tolstoy in ways not exactly envisioned in the demand for the "red" incarnation of the novelist.

Zoshchenko's characters, like his stories, remain resolutely at the snack bar, box office, and coat check—literalizing Stanislavsky's injunction that theater begin "right at the coat hook" (*s veshalki*);[62] they remain outside the sphere of high drama, out of sight of "the main thing." The snack bar deflects attention from the play, the margin usurps the function of the main attraction, *byt* (daily life) receives the scrutiny reserved for *sobytie* (event). Zoshchenko follows the noncompliant principle of theatrical illumination of his own "Electrician" ("Monter," 1926): the lighting technician steals the lead role from the tenor by fiddling with the spotlights to demonstrate his own backstage and marginal importance. And Zoshchenko, like his ill-attired theatergoers, fails to meet the cultural challenge issued by the guardians of public order of his own time, the enforcers of artificial norms, who would rather keep such things as coats out of the theatrical and literary spotlight.

That so many of life's traumatic "trifles" seem to be played out in the theater and involve acting out of line suggests that the lives of Zoshchenko's heroes—and Zoshchenko's contemporaries—are governed by the sort of theatricality Lotman has described as an aspect of everyday life in the eighteenth century. Zoshchenko's typical theatergoer lacks the requisite "ability to renounce his own system of behavior and switch into the conventionally traditional behavior prescribed for the given type of character"[63] or, I might add, a given type of scene. For while Zoshchenko's character is not *on* stage, and in fact comes nowhere near the stage, "theatrical space" extends beyond the boundaries of the proscenium and the footlights. Life is divided into different "scenic areas"; each setting is a scene, demanding not only a different costume, but a different genre of behavior.[64]

Thus even the events that occur outside the theater proper reflect the theatricality of Soviet life; the confusion that produces story frequently derives from appearance out of costume or behavior out of character. Mothers carrying packages, for instance, may be mistaken for exploited servants ("NEP Grimace" ["Grimasa nepa"], 1927).[65] Students without uniforms may be expected to work for a living ("The Incident" ["Sluchai"], 1925).[66] The injunction to see everything in terms of its public significance, its role on the stage of history, leads husbands to arrest their wives, reading small private gestures as "obstructions of justice" ("Administrative Ecstasy," 1:507); or it incites passengers to withhold carfare from their conductor-relatives. The poor berated conductor, who is being asked by his "Comrade Uncle" to play the private role on the public stage, cannot figure out how to satisfy both audiences at once ("Who Needs Relatives?" ["Ne nado imet' rodstvennikov"], 1924).

Thus it is not merely rhetorical flair, but a keen sense of the need to define the setting, to set the scene, that inspires Zoshchenko's characteristic *recusatio*: "This is not 1919," they scream at the coat-bearing theatergoer ("The Charms of Culture," 1:359). "This is not a theater!" they retort repeatedly at the bathhouse cloakroom ("The Bathhouse," 1:278–79). "This is not a hotel," objects the doctor when the patient begins to remove his jacket in the operating room ("Operation" ["Operatsiia"], 1927, 1:398). The lavatory is "not a living room" ("The Economy Campaign" ["Rezhim ekonomii"], 1926, 1:343). And it is more than just a proverb when the well-respected Dereviashkin of "The Dictaphone" ("Diktafon," 1924), who might well be speaking for all the stories, concludes most emphatically of all, "This is not America!" (1:205). The "comrades" are being exhorted repeatedly to learn their new lines, to stay in character (no matter how contrived), and to dress the part.

Costumes

Zoshchenko's spotlighting of the "incidental" details of dress exposes not only the indecorous bodies underneath, but also the perils of artifice and sugar "coating." The scripting of attire and behavior—the costuming and acting demanded of Zoshchenko's "citizens"—is, after all, a type of fraudulence. Acting the part can be nefarious.

When, during a robbery scene in "The Actor" ("Akter," 1925), the performer is victimized by a real criminal in full view of the cheering public, his calls for help are interpreted as appropriate to his role—as are the machinations of the thief. In fact, it is not clear in the end to which professional the title applies, the thief or the thespian.

For traditionally in Russian culture masquerading of any kind is in principle sinister, a kind of "anti-behavior" associated with black magic. "Pretending" came to be something of a theme with the phenomenon of royal imposture (*samozvanchestvo*), and "by forcing his people to wear 'German,' i.e. European, clothes, Peter [the Great] had in the eyes of his contemporaries transformed his entourage into mummers. . . . It was said he had 'dressed people up as devils.' "[67] In Zoshchenko's scrutiny of contemporary costuming we begin to sense the shadier implications of enforcing norms of behavior in terms of dress codes. Impostors should be unmasked, not cloaked in splendor.

Zoshchenko is especially daunted by the image of the *transformator*, the quick-change artist whose identity changes with his clothing. "An Incident in the Provinces" ("Sluchai v provintsii," 1924) turns on the public's *over*valuation of costume. When four performers (three men of diverse appearance and one woman) appear on stage in quick succession, the audience is transported not by their performances but by what they believe is the remarkable ability of a single actor to "transform" himself. They listen patiently to the recitations (if not all the way through), but are really interested in how the subject is arrayed and how that changes, how different roles can be assumed. Appearance itself is performance.

Zoshchenko exposes a world in which all elements of wardrobe are aspects of behavior (carrying, accordingly, a heavier than average semiotic load). In Zoshchenko's fictional universe, clothing thus functions less as a descriptive flourish for readers than as a well-articulated sign system among the citizen-players (anticipating Barthes's insights on the semiotics of fashion).[68] In "The Lady Aristocrat," for instance, the narrator/character has only to sneer "I don't like women in hats" to reveal the class of his lost *dama* (1:170). Not incidentally, Zoshchenko's invocation of the semiotics of clothing refers at the same time to Gogol's story of a nose masquerading as a civil councillor, and a collegiate assessor who is self-conscious about being noseless in uniform ("The Nose"). Zoshchenko's narrator describes ladies in hats in the same words Gogol's noseless officer uses to characterize the spot on his own countenance whence this indispensable element of his uniform—his nose—has dematerialized: *gladkoe mesto* (a big blank; literally, "a flat place" [1:170]).[69] Gogol's characters take off their noses,

Zoshchenko's only their coats, boots, and hats. But the effects of these costume changes involve a comparable alteration of identity and fate.

In "Philistines" ("Meshchane," 1928) we see that costume is every bit as significant in streetcar scenes as in the theater.[70] A painter in his splotchy overalls (thus clearly not a Party member!) is ejected from public transport because the Nepmen are offended by his paint-spattered garments. Much more offensive than his attire, though, are the self-appointed guardians of decorum who enforce this arbitrary code at the expense of the working man who had come as he was, in his nightshirt, so to speak. The gatekeeper figure so prominent in the theatrical episodes also reappears in "Work Clothes" ("Rabochii kostium," 1925) at the entry to a restaurant, apparently with much the same task: to uphold arbitrary rules, to keep people in character. One customer in work clothes becomes belligerent when he is forbidden entry. " 'What, my suit isn't to your taste? ... My *kostium* leaves something to be desired [*neinteresnyi*]? ... OK, so I don't have French cuffs, and there are no ties,' he says, 'swinging around my neck. And OK, maybe,' he says, 'I haven't washed my face for three months. But,' he says, 'maybe I'm knocking myself out in industry! Maybe I don't have time to keep changing outfits' " (1:302). Finally, he works himself up into such a state of righteous indignation about how it's criminal that a man is not allowed to eat without French cuffs that he is arrested "on grounds of costume" (1:303). Upon his release the following morning, he discovers he has misread the event—it was his drunkenness that was objectionable. Intoxicated patrons are prohibited by law to enter restaurants, and even Vasilii Stepanych has to agree that this is reasonable. But in misidentifying the violation he has proved himself an outstanding reader of Zoshchenko, in whose world outer garments are the trappings of permissibility, the figurative index of inclusion and exclusion.

The most formidable guardians of the threshold may well be the checkroom staff at Zoshchenko's famous "Bathhouse," who collect and dispense (and thus regulate) not only coats, but all of the bathers' nether-layers of clothing as well at the entrance to what seems to be the "netherworld"—the bathhouse proper—creating insuperable obstacles for the patrons who pass through (or on). What does one do, for example, with one's several garment checks in a state of complete dishabille, when one is "all legs and belly"? (1:278). You tie one *nomerok* to each ankle. But they're only paper and string and tend to dissolve under moist conditions. So after countless frustrations inside the bathhouse, when the bather turns to leave, the problems become even more intractable. First, he is given the wrong pants. "Mine had a hole here—this hole is there"; "We're not responsible for watching the holes," they reply, adding what by now has become a refrain at each roadblock: "This is not a theater!" (1:279). So he puts on the costume he has been assigned. Then the coatroom attendant demands the second check for his coat. Off come the pants again, the other leg is searched, but the paper check has been lost in the ordeal of bathing, the string alone is insufficient collateral. After more disclaimers about it's not being a theater, the man reclaims his coat. But he's forgotten his soap, and turns to fetch it—no admission in coats! Perhaps it is a theater after all. "Please," he implores them. "I can't get undressed a third time! This isn't a theater!" (1:279). But the entry is closed to him; he must abandon his soap, like the hope of all who enter there.

The comparison suggested by these Dantean overtones is not frivolous. Dostoevsky had created the archetypal infernal bathhouse in his *House of the Dead*,[71] and Zoshchenko's "ordinary" (*obyknovennaia*) bathhouse resurrects it, as usual, in diminished and parodic form. If Dostoevsky's dramatic rendition of exile in terms of the lower reaches of hell is an exposé of the extreme horrors of czarist imprisonment, Zoshchenko's reductio ad absurdum of the same setting, his own reduction to nakedness, is the ultimate exposure of everyday Soviet existence as a kind of inferno. In exposing the bodies of its citizens, he has exposed the body of the state to scrutiny, and this squalid tableau is a grim revelation. We are told for good measure, in classic Zoshchenko form, that not only is this not a theater, but it is "not the czarist regime" and also not America (1:278). It is explicitly here and now, and somehow we seem to have died and gone to hell. The gatekeeper, too, is every bit as formidable as one would expect in the nether regions. Bathhouses have carried sinister associations since early Christian times when they were characterized as demonic, evil spaces (thereby imaginatively reversing the valence of holiness attributed to them by pre-Christian culture). The bathhouse figured as a kind of alternative to sacred places—those who didn't go to church were said to go instead to the bathhouse,[72] just as in Zoshchenko's stories, those who don't go to the theater go to beer halls. Zoshchenko seems to confirm, if humorously, this connotation of blasphemy in his peripatetic invocation at each new torment of the conversational *grekh odin* (it's a sin).

More striking than its function as counterweight to the sacred, however, is the bathhouse's role as counterweight to the *living*. The association of bathhouse and death suggested by Dostoevsky's title and Dantean allusions is strengthened by Zoshchenko's own contrivances. In this story, waiting for a fellow bather to relinquish his bucket is like "keeping watch over his soul" (for three days, no less [1:278]). Even after three whole days of bathing here, where getting clean is not among the options, release offers a poor sort of "resurrection from the dead," with no cleansing of soul or body.

The connection of bathhouse to dead house is made most forcefully in Zoshchenko's explicit use in the 1925 "Bathhouse" of the same elements he had established shortly before in "The Living Corpse— A True Story" ("Zhivoi trup—Istinnoe proisshestvie," 1924). A man in the morgue (mistakenly delivered to those grim lodgings by hospital personnel unable to distinguish death from a drunken stupor) finds himself in a bathhouse-like enclosure, on similar wooden benches, in the same state of undress, and surrounded by others just as naked, without pockets, just long legs. He has a number tied around one ankle that, like a coat check, flops around uncomfortably with every step, and a vigilant guard stands at the gate of what is truly the other world. The story, ostensibly about the perils of heavy drinking, is a great deal more damning to the shoddy practitioners of public health, the careless and incompetent classifiers of vital and non-vital signs, and presents, like "The Bathhouse" but more poignantly, the trifles of life as potentially devastating, as not only bad news but big news, as a matter of life and death.

In addition, Zoshchenko manages to invoke simultaneously all three of his suggested models. He alludes to Dostoevsky by linking bathhouses and death. He cites Tolstoy by borrowing not only the title of his play, but also his association of bathing and mortality. The spectacle of all those naked bodies crowded into an unappealing bathing spot calls to mind Prince Andrei's disgust in *War and Peace* at the bodies of his soldiers splashing about in a dirty pond and his vision of their naked white flesh as "cannon fodder."[73] Zoshchenko even evokes Gogol in "The Living Corpse" by essentially reversing the title of *Dead Souls*, the monolithic epic that was reputed to include "all of Russia."

As we must begin to realize, Zoshchenko's treatment of his esteemed models is always complex. Irina Reyfman shows in forceful detail the extent to which even the "Sixth Tale of Belkin," presented as an earnest effort to "imitate" Pushkin on the occasion of the 100th anniversary of the master's death, engages in an infinitely more complicated transformation of sources.[74] But if Zoshchenko deforms his sources rather than imitating them, the gesture need not be interpreted as an expression of hostility toward the nineteenth-century pantheon. Reyfman suggests that what Zoshchenko esteems in Pushkin, well beyond his pristine style, is his protean playfulness, Pushkin's own transformation of precedent. Such play is fundamental to the poetics of

Pushkin's composition and is arguably indispensable for all creative work.[75] Zoshchenko's diminution of his predecessors' various bathhouses and theatrical traumas—like his retailoring and shrinkage of their coats or his parodic repetition of their titles and episodes—does far less to denigrate them than to sneer at the demand (*zakaz*) for straight imitation that can only be antithetical to real writing; it strikes a blow for the inalienable need to play with what looms large, rather than to revere it more or less verbatim. Zoshchenko adopts recognizably Dostoevskian, Tolstoyan, and Gogolian elements to model a world that is pointedly reformatted.

In Zoshchenko's universe, where a naked man is a dead man and all the world's a stage, costume is the great admission ticket to life. As we have seen, clothing not only signifies, identifying and legitimizing its bearer, but insofar as only designated costumes are acceptable, the presence or absence of attire motivates and thematizes exclusion: from theater, from bathhouse, from streetcar, from restaurant, from text. Coats come to stand for all those unwritten, but familiar, interdictions; the various gatekeepers allude to the enforcers of that arbitrary order; and the failure to comply with the coat code represents deviation as such. The theft motif associates the coat even more strongly with violation (whether it involves the perpetrator or the victim).

Each coat removal is also an act of exposure: of the "hellish" torments to which citizens are regularly subjected; of real identities beneath scripted roles (even husband and wife cannot identify each other out of costume); of bogus heroics (the empty boasting of "Love"); of unsavory behavior (sniffed out by the *sobachii niukh/sobach'ia erunda*); of pajama-clad drunks masquerading as men of culture; and, most poignantly, of the arbitrary norms that circumscribe that culture and the gatekeepers who enforce those (upper and lower) boundaries. Zoshchenko operates as a kind of cultural gatecrasher—underdressed, undersized, out of bounds. By wearing the coat repeatedly into the spotlight, by keeping coats and the like firmly center stage (at the expense of more socially "significant" phenomena), he not only violates the threshold that seeks to exclude subject matter not "x-enough," but exposes the exclusionary limits themselves. It is telling that all of Zoshchenko's *garderobshchiki* (cloakroom attendants), the symbolic watchdogs of decorum, are themselves grossly indecorous and offensive.[76] The business of dictating a uniform (or a uniform index of tellability) is effectively disparaged. The coat is the mufti battle garb of Zoshchenko's guerrilla warfare against the official norms of what is worth telling, an anti-uniform that becomes recognizable as the strength of this attack force becomes perceptible.

Great Strides

Zoshchenko plays with his own persistent overvaluation of coat transactions in "Operation," where the hero (like the contentious drunk in "Work Clothes," who views all prohibitions as the effect of his suit) can only conceive of any eventuality—troublesome or erotic—in terms of removing his jacket. Petiushka Iashikov, who has been suffering from an abscess on his eyelid for three years, has finally scheduled the minor surgical procedure that will correct the problem. On the day of the event, he makes a special point of dashing home between work and surgery to change his undershirt. Even though the operation is to be an external one, he reasons, still, you never know with medicine. It might be necessary to remove his jacket, and the doctor *is* an attractive young woman. . . . He even rubs his neck with gasoline and rinses his hands.

Alas, poor Petiushka is called upon not to disrobe (this is, after all, not a hotel), but simply to remove his boots before lying down on the operating table. This is an eventuality he had not foreseen. And it is a genuine event because his socks are in sorry shape.[77] Zoshchenko's story pivots here from one paradigm to another. Petiushka had performed his preparatory ablutions like a veritable understudy to Vasilii Ivanovich ("A Trivial Incident"), only, dressing to undress, he has anticipated the "pitfall" that the theatergoer had failed to foresee. Unlike Vasilii Ivanovich, who is unable to leave his coat, and Vasilii Mitrofanovich, who sports an unseemly nightshirt underneath, Petuishka is perfectly arrayed to shed his outer garment. But Zoshchenko displaces the catastrophe from coat to footwear, and in doing so enacts an exposure that spells both humiliation for his hero and expository mileage for himself.

If by removing his coat Petia has hoped to *attract* the feminine gaze of his *doktorsha* (the outer garment may be shabby, but the undershirt! Ah, the undershirt!), he is desperate to divert her attention from what has become the main attraction. He begs her to take no notice of his feet, but in vain. She can hardly control her guffaws, and the operation proceeds with her laughing and cutting away at his eyelid, trembling hand and all. She could have killed him!

As luck would have it, she does no such thing. "The operation, by the way, was a smashing success" (1:399). No more spots before Petia's eyes, and no tragic accidents. But by baring the foot (the operation of *real* consequence to the hero and to the story), Zoshchenko again reveals the unpreparedness of the Russians who, even if they've replaced their nightshirts, still have socks full of holes; and he activates the terms that he embraces almost fetishistically in his work to thematize both eventfulness and tellability.

The drama of Petiushka's foot, which is termed initially "a small sad story" is reevaluated: "But how can it be called small! A man was nearly slaughtered." There follows another immediate reassessment: "Of course it didn't really come anywhere near that. It was even extremely far from a slaughter." The narrator concludes, however, that it's still a sad story. "Although, actually," he continues, "nothing sad really happened" (1:397). But that "nothing" unfolds as narrative nonetheless, complete with traumatic event. "Operation" asks anxiously whether anything worth telling has occurred and answers emphatically in the affirmative by unveiling in the well-illuminated surgical glare of the operating room the one thing in Zoshchenko's world that commands notice: a man's foot.

The foot is ubiquitous in Zoshchenko's stories, primarily as a central element of plot, secondarily as rhetorical flourish. The intrusive misstep, we have seen, is at the center of "Absence of Malice," where the model pedestrian gets his foot stomped on in Zoshchenko's model story. It is the final solution to the cockroach problem ("Cockroaches" ["Tarakany"], 1925). And it reappears in "Casting Bait" ("Na zhivtsa," 1925), where the first car of the tram is shunned in favor of the second one because the first one is boring—nothing ever happens there. "You can't even find anyone's foot to step on" (1:280). And it is, in fact, in the second car that the noticeable and tellable event occurs; the second car produces a story. In Zoshchenko's fiction, the violated foot perversely usurps the Revolution's narrative function as source and center of all stories.

In Zoshchenko's only story that complies with the demand that fiction depict the era's most monumental event, the Revolution itself goes unnoticed (and unreported)—that is, until the main character, deeply involved in his own private business, happens to get in the way of a revolutionary vehicle, which very indelicately runs over his foot ("Victim of the Revolution" ["Zhertva revoliutsii"], 1923). The story this citizen has to tell is set into motion each time he takes off his boot to reveal the revolutionary scar on his heel. In all his stories of the 1920s, and in this one most dramatically, Zoshchenko emphatically refuses to notice, let alone recapitulate and celebrate, the event of the century as prescribed by the Soviet critics, focusing instead on the individual feet that get stepped on.

And exposed. Feet, like the bodies they support, are repeatedly left vulnerable and uncovered because of theft and loss. We have already seen the depths to which a man can sink when relieved all at once of his coat and galoshes ("Love"). Consider as well the anguish of the bootmaker who sleeps right through a major earthquake, but notices immediately that his shoes and clothes have been stolen ("The Earthquake" ["Zemletriasenie"], 1929). Footwear becomes the quintessential object of desire (and, like the coat, of narrative attention). The famous "Galosh" lost in the streetcar is the object of a feverish quest (and passionate ejaculations) as well as the subject of an entire story. In the later children's story "Galoshes and Ice Cream" ("Kaloshi i morozhenoe," 1939[78]), the plot is built on the illicit acquisition and fencing of galoshes by two children in order to finance their passionate appetite for dessert. Their plot is well conceived and well executed, but parental authority mercilessly interferes, issuing a two-year punitive ban on ice cream. As currency, the galoshes stolen by the children displace the true object of their juvenile desire. When the sentence is up and ice cream reappears, it brings with it the aftertaste of the rubbers and their object lesson. The galoshes are the enduring presence.

In "The Power of Talent" ("Sila talanta," 1923), footwear is shown to represent, contrary to appearances, the *primary* object of desire rather than just a mediated form of adoration. A theatergoer, ostensibly overwhelmed by an actress's performance, makes his way to her dressing room to kiss her feet, or, at a more respectful distance, her shoes. Only the cathexis is to the shoes themselves, and they disappear into the night with the stealthy fan, his adoration staged (this *is* a theater, after all) to facilitate the burglary. Appropriately, as in most of Zoshchenko's theater pieces, the violation occurs in the margins (backstage), in this case even in a prohibited zone.

Shoes are the object of extended quest and ultimate theft (another shrunken epic) in "Slippers" ("Baretki," 1927).[79] And galoshes even acquire mystical powers in "A Scientific Phenomenon" ("Nauchnoe iavlenie," 1927), where the booted policeman is mysteriously immune to the twitching caused by some inexplicable underground force (presumably electricity, another of Zoshchenko's favorite targets[80]).

Zoshchenko supplements his foot-based plots with a generous use of idiomatic expressions that invoke the foot or leg—*noga*[81]—and a readiness to translate other turns of phrase into foot terms. His theater audiences invariably express their approval (or the opposite) by stamping their feet—*publika bila nogami*—marked as a reference to the formulaic Soviet "applause" ("The Power of Talent," 1:145). The strutting hero of "A Trivial Incident from Private Life" reinforces his campaign for attention (featuring the coat unlike all other coats) by doing a little two-step (*delaiu pa nogami*) and otherwise cutting capers with his feet (*igraia nogami*), a sexier version of *igraia glazami* (casting one's eyes about)—all this pussyfooting around the Pushkin monument, no less (3:258). Try, for that matter, the narrator of "Theater for Oneself" laments, to attract any audiences at all these days: you have to drag them there by the foot—*Priamo khot' za nogu voloki zritelia!* ("Teatr dlia sebia," 1926, 1:353). A hero taken seriously ill collapses as if his "hind" legs had been shot out from under him—*sleg bez zadnikh nog* (a play on *spal bez zadnikh nog*, to have slept soundly). The same hero is introduced with reluctance by the narrator who bewails the fact that these days there are no real heroes, nothing but peons underfoot—*Vse bol'she nastoiashchaia melkota pod nogami putalas'* ("Small-Fry" ["Melkota"], 1927, 1:369). There is plenty of interesting material in our Soviet reality, exclaims another narrator, *ne govoria uzhe o nogakh* (not to mention feet) ("Casting Bait," 1:280).

So why mention feet? Why focus so intently on an aspect of existence literally below the line of vision and significantly below the lower threshold of tellability? Why dwell on "the lower extremities, which one musn't describe in literature" ("A Trivial Incident from Private Life," 3:257)? Perhaps this is Zoshchenko's "utilitarian" gesture in the spirit of Pisarev, who claimed to prefer a good pair of galoshes to any work of art. Alternatively, "talking about boots" might be seen as a figure for admitting trivia into one's reportage—Chernyshevsky, for instance, had made a point of reporting the details of his footwear as part of his program of all-inclusiveness, and Bunin had cited galoshes as the essential element of concrete visual detail.[82] Or, judging by some of the other prose of Zoshchenko's period, the "triviality" of boots might not have been such a foregone conclusion: as a deficit item, the galosh became a problematic absence (as unnoticeable as such difficulties were supposed to be) and thus a real focus of desire and attention.[83]

Shoes are also an effective image for problems that cannot be ignored—when they pinch (*zhmut*) they are insistently perceptible. But Zoshchenko, a man who clearly conceived of problems in images of footwear, also observes that shoes stretch out; their difficulties are perhaps not insoluble. Vera Vladimirovna Zoshchenko, the writer's wife, has commented in a conversation with M. Chudakova that Zoshchenko frequently concluded his discussions of the problems of carrying out social reform in a "backward" country like Russia with the refrain: "That's OK. Shoes stretch to fit your feet if you wear them enough" (*Nichego! Obuv' stopchetsia po noge*).[84] Moreover, feet evoke for Zoshchenko the questionable hygienic practices he regarded as an index of his fellow citizens' lamentable cultural level. "Why do people wash their hands and not their feet?" (*Pochemu ruki moiut, a ne nogi?*), explodes the exasperated father (in the anecdote widely known in the 1920s) in "answer" to his son's indefatigable "why?"

Shoes also mark the threshold between public and private realms—footwear is traditionally removed and left at the doorway, marking the retreat into the domestic sphere.[85] Thus shoe removal makes an apt vehicle for an insistence on individual, private "thresholds" of eventfulness; and shoe removal in public places represents a rude violation of privacy (as well as a jab at the demand that all events resonate with greater public—social and historical—significance). In fact, the ceremonial removal of boots (the groom's by the bride) marks the consummately private and first-order event of the wedding night in the nineteenth-century Ukrainian marriage ceremony (following the groom's contribution of stomping on the bride's foot until it bled, a sign of the bride's submission).[86]

Zoshchenko's foot fetish also reprises fairly patently Pushkin's famous fondness for little feet (as always, in a lower key), evoking in the process Dostoevsky's spoofs on Pushkin's parodists as well.[87] The association of foot-related products and literary productivity is persistent and strong throughout Zoshchenko's oeuvre. In several of his little self-portraits, he lists "shoemaker" among his numerous and diverse professions; and though cobbling is a good deal less sensational than most of his other former callings (as gambler, big game hunter, flyer, policeman, criminal investigator, doctor, and even instructor of rabbit breeding), he singles it out for special affection and a little anecdote presenting himself as a writer/shoemaker making shoes for writers.[88] Even Zoshchenko's "Literator" ("Man of Literature," 1927) turns out to be, in truth, not a writer, but a manufacturer of shoe polish. Perhaps, considering Tolstoy's repudiation of his fiction in favor of bootmaking, Zoshchenko's conflation of cobbling and writing can be seen as yet another attenuation of Tolstoyan precedent.[89]

But as literary as Zoshchenko's featured feet may be (and as bared and trampled as they unambiguously are), they resonate most loudly (and most provocatively) with the era's rhetoric of "great strides" and "giant steps." *Revoliutsiia idet vpered bol'shimi shagami!* (the Revolution marches forward in great strides!), proclaim the era's propaganda posters. Revolutionary progress was figured as a "victorious march" (*pobednoe shestvie*); Lenin himself had urged the revolutionaries to take a decisive step forward (*shag vpered*) and cautioned against the potential *dva shaga nazad* (two steps back).[90] And Mayakovsky's proclamatory verse adopts the idiom in its celebration of the "Levyi marsh" ("Left March"), in its depiction of the era's magnitude in terms of "a million boots," and, especially in the epic poem "150,000,000," in its convulsive incantation of *Idem! / Idemidem! Go, go. / go, go, go, go, / go, go! and Ide-e-e-e-m!*[91]

Zoshchenko, recognizing the need to "keep in step with the times" (*popast' v nogu so vremenem* [2:180]), picks up on these inspiring lyrics, extolling his epoch's capacity to "go far" (*daleko shagnut'* [2:184]). But for Zoshchenko, "not lagging behind" (*idushchii noga v nogu* [1:474]) refers to the "technology" of pest control, and a firm stride is merely the best way of eliminating a cockroach.

Moreover, Zoshchenko takes aim at the kind of motion implied by the official version of postrevolutionary progress as a great forward march. In Zoshchenko's fiction, motion is typically indiscriminate rather than purposeful (conveyed by his characteristic use of *khodit'* rather than the *idti* favored by Mayakovsky[92]). His people spend a lot of time milling around rather than striding purposefully forward. And this indiscriminate motion is every bit as constant as the official, progressive sort. If Zoshchenko's citizens do anything, they walk around: the city is the place where citizens walk. Backward and forward. All around. There and back. In full consciousness of their human grandeur. *Nu, khodiat*, he concludes ("A Terrible Night" ["Strashnaia noch'"], 1925, 2:91). Not only do they marry "on the run" (*na khodu*), they "go" (*khodiat*) to the theater; they "go" (*khodiat*) in coats; they go to the theater in coats ("Theater for Oneself," 1:353). (Because Russian regularly expresses the notion of wearing an article of clothing as "going about in" it, this is hardly a marked formulation, but given his overarching concern with questions of wardrobe, it does create ample opportunity for Zoshchenko to emphasize perpetual, random motion with no sense of progress attached.)

He also makes fun of revolutionary momentum more directly. How far we have managed to stride forward (*shagnut' vpered*) in ten years, he exclaims! It used to be that even locomotives would constantly grind to a halt, or even move backward. Once, he recalls—and this is the substance of the narrative—an engineer's cap blew off (the inevitable loss of an article of clothing) and delayed everything. The passengers were justly outraged: "Why are we stopping? Why do we keep moving in reverse?" But now, in our progressive era, he assures the contemporary reader, even if a *passenger* blows off we won't stop for more than a second. "Gotta keep moving" ("The Cap" ["Shapka"], 1927, 1:408).

Thus Zoshchenko not only manipulates the era's vocabulary of strides and rechoreographs its movements, but he literalizes its metaphors, translating its rhetoric into actual subject matter, into the very event. It is in terms of feet—their regular motion and the jarring injuries that interrupt it—that eventfulness is measured. *Rovno* (smoothly, evenly) is the operative term to describe regular, unimpeded motion, and Zoshchenko uses it compulsively throughout his fiction to refer to the movement of life in its normal, uneventful, unremarkable course. Motion (interestingly) is the status quo; the problematic footfall that disrupts that smooth, even progress represents an event.

Just as coat removal is tellable in Zoshchenko's stories because it is "indiscreet," so blocking someone's way, stepping on someone's foot, or having one's foot bared or stepped on (or otherwise violated) comes to function as the paradigmatic event in Zoshchenko's works because it is supremely *noticeable*. As I will argue in the next chapter, it functions as a figure for something truly important and worth noticing, and hence worth telling—in stark contrast to the events of October 1917, which, in Zoshchenko's fiction, pass more or less imperceptibly.

THREE

Zoshchenko and the Politics of Perceptibility

© 1988 Lee Lorenz
originally in The New Yorker Magazine, Inc.
All Rights Reserved.

Stop-and-Go Traffic

Noticeability becomes for Zoshchenko the index of eventfulness and tellability. Thus it is especially salient that the model pedestrian, whose foot has been stepped on by the distraught narrator in our model story ("Absence of Malice") takes no notice and continues on as if nothing had happened. The narrator keeps waiting for his fellow walker to "turn around and clobber" him. But no. "Nope. Kept going. Didn't notice," the story concludes. "What is there to talk about?" (1:393). This phenomenon of not noticing the "quintessentially" noticeable is the source of tremendous mileage and manipulation by Zoshchenko.

To begin with, this story does "notice" and "talk about" the incident. The story contrives to notice what ordinarily just "passes," restaging in reduced form Dostoevsky's famous pedestrian "duel" on Nevskii Prospekt—the underground man's existential battle for recognition, his obsessional quest to be noticed by bumping into an officer and thus to stand "on equal footing" (*na ravnoi noge*) with his fellow pedestrian.[1] Like Zoshchenko's pedestrian, Dostoevsky's officer does not notice the affront—or, in the underground man's interpretation, only pretends not to notice. But in Zoshchenko's version, the narrator is unconcerned about his consciousness and dignity; he revels in the utter "absence of malice" that makes such missteps "unimportant" in Soviet life: "You step on someone, they step on you—so what? Cruise on through" (1:393). Zoshchenko's story itself, however, does in effect stop walking and take notice, suggesting that the stakes of such an encounter are perhaps higher than the Soviet sensibility would have it, that such "pedestrian concerns" must, in fact, be articulated, that they are in the end as existential as the underground man's confrontation. They demand our attention.

"What is there to talk about?" There is evidently a great deal to be said not only about such events, but also about the failure to perceive them. Given the context he has established in which to stumble, to sustain a blow to the foot, is the prototype of the significant event, Zoshchenko aptly figures the failure to notice an incident as motion maintained. Not to acknowledge event, disruption, violation, is, like the response of Dostoevsky's haughty officer or Zoshchenko's inured pedestrian, to keep walking.

Thus Zoshchenko not only makes a point of noticing, articulating, and dignifying the ostensibly insignificant and imperceptible by defining event in terms of and on the scale of a single foot; he thematizes especially the *failure* to register these mishaps. By noticing the failure to notice, Zoshchenko accomplishes several things: (1) he exposes the contrivance of this artificially set lower boundary that rules that individual foot problems are "not x enough" to engage the attention, thus excluding them on grounds of imperceptibility; (2) he exposes the violated foot as, lamentably, the normal state of affairs, which renders it (and the many problematic disruptions it stands for) naturally imperceptible (the model pedestrian of "Absence of Malice" does not notice his injury precisely because it happens all the time); (3) he thematizes the connection between noticing and telling (thereby putting his own foot in his mouth); and (4) by failing (refusing!) himself to notice (and tell) what the regime defines as noticeable, he enacts a radical trivialization of his own.

Keep Moving

Zoshchenko's stop-and-go principle of eventfulness is confirmed by another "Street Incident" ("Ulichnoe proisshestvie," 1925). People stop walking, and an unruly crowd accumulates, keeping other passersby from passing by, to gawk at a big "event": a policeman is leading a female suspect out of a building. Speculations about her crime range from moonshining to murder, and everyone is excited about this genuine "happening." But the pedestrians have misread this street scene. They have stopped needlessly, because the policeman is *not* arresting, detaining, or otherwise disrupting the life of this woman. On the contrary; he is simply taking a walk (*guliaet*) with his girlfriend, and walking is precisely the norm, "just the ordinary thing" (*delo obychnoe*). "So," the story concludes, "everyone just walked off" (1:304). Motion is resumed because nothing was happening.

But in accordance with these same laws of motion (to pause is to perceive, to perceive is to acknowledge a problem), one citizen vows never to stop again—no matter what is happening—having once during a walk gotten himself in trouble with the law for noticing a crowd, the wringing of hands, "in short, an event" ("The Downfall of a Man" ["Gibel' cheloveka"], 1926, 1:352). Indeed, a fellow citizen lies immobilized (*idti teper' ne mozhet*) with a fractured leg (*noga*). Unfortunately, our solicitous hero's call for an ambulance is inauspicious, for the "broken" leg is a prosthetic device, and the unwarranted summoning of emergency medical equipment is a punishable offense. Never again, he promises himself, will he interrupt his walk. Let them kill a man before my very eyes! I'll just keep walking.[2]

There emerges a veritable conspiracy not to notice the stumbles, not to acknowledge the small obstacles to smooth progress. Hence, the loss of an individual passenger in "The Cap" gives no pause to today's speeding trains. "A Trivial Occurrence" ("Melkoe proisshestvie," 1927), too, assures the reader that there was no delay as a result of the title occurrence, that the engineer managed to make up for lost time. The passengers had been alarmed, but none fell out of their seats. And when they looked out the window, they saw that nothing had really happened. The entire story is told in this self-effacing apologetic tone, as if to excuse its very existence in light of its own triviality. Still, the train has made a sudden, unscheduled stop, because the switchman's flag is too dirty to convey the necessary information (red or green? stop or go?). The train finally proceeds, making up for lost time, and the schedule remains unaffected. But meanwhile we have been afforded a glance not only at the slovenliness of the supposedly smoothly running mechanism, but of the system that suppresses its slipups.

Similarly, in "A Trick of Nature" ("Igra prirody," 1927), a resident of a small village goes out walking one fine spring day to enjoy the glorious air and the song of the birds. Spring being what it is (wet) and the roads being what they are in the provinces (terrible), he walks along the railroad tracks, stepping carefully from tie to tie to avoid the puddles. Suddenly, distracted by the sweet song of the birds (who are fortunate enough not to have to rely on such miserable footpaths), he accidentally steps too far to one side and lands, knee-deep, in a ditch full of water. His outing has been ruined, as have his pants, his left shoe, and even his undergarments.

Outraged that such conditions should prevail on government roads, he composes a complaint and sends it in to the *Red Newspaper* (one of Zoshchenko's own publishers). His letter appears in print by the end of April, at which point, the narrator remarks sarcastically, things proceeded "at breakneck speed. By the time the complaint was read, discussed by those in charge, and a commission was formed to investigate the matter, fourteen years had passed" (1:509). Well, the narrator concedes, perhaps it was less than that, but ours is such a "tempestuous" period and so much of such magnitude is occurring, that each day is practically equivalent to a year.

In any case, by the time the commission arrives in the village in June to investigate the mishap, there is no mud, and no water to be seen anywhere (not even in the water pitcher). The road is even dusty. In early July, the commission's findings are released: no such event has occurred. The citizen made it up.

Granted, to have fallen into a mud puddle is not a major catastrophe, and perhaps the citizen's reaction was a trifle strong (as is the narrator's zeal in reporting the details of the deterioration of the unfortunate man's left trouser leg). But that the incident is deemed not to have happened—this absurdity is a real dig at precisely those sorts of official determinations that fail to acknowledge traumatic insults to little feet (not to mention the formidable obstacles to progress presented by public thoroughfares). Individual (and especially provincial) distress clearly does not qualify as worthy of attention. This is a perfect example of the operation of that artificially set lower boundary; things that are deemed "not x enough"—not significant enough to register—never even happened. Obviously, therefore, they are not worthy of mention. Zoshchenko, however, like his hero, not only notices the event, but writes it up for publication.

Norms and Notices (Pedestrian Perceptions)

By setting up this opposition of noticing and not noticing, staged as an ongoing conflict between tripping up and walking on, Zoshchenko, as we have seen, exposes the mechanism through which unwelcome news is suppressed: it is simply deemed too trivial to notice. But he also exposes something perhaps even more pernicious than this intentional disregard: the conditions that make stubbed toes the norm, and as such, inherently imperceptible. The pedestrian who strides blithely on following his rude stomping does so because there is nothing extraordinary about such treatment. On the contrary, it is normal.

Gestalt theory holds that the perception of any figure has everything to do with the ground on which that figure is located.[3] As Catherine Chvany points out, this perception of an object as the figure against a ground is not a function of that item's "importance" in an absolute sense. A hair or piece of lint on a precious fur is still the "figure" to the fur's "ground."[4] It is the disruptiveness, the contrast, the difference, the not-belonging to its surroundings that highlights the figure (and causes it to be perceived as such). And while the properties of the ground are never determined by the figure,[5] we can still learn something about the ground if we know, for instance, that a certain item is luminescent orange and its ground still manages to obscure it; we can conclude that the ground must be of approximately the same hue. Or, conversely, if a notice goes up announcing that the copy machine *is* working, we can surmise that the normal state of affairs must be the opposite (see the *New Yorker* cartoon that opens this chapter).

When one of Zoshchenko's characters triumphantly reports several hours of abstinence (*Ne p'iu i ne p'iu. Chas ne p'iu, dva ne p'iu*), we may safely assume that the norm has a substantially higher alcohol content ("Lemonade" ["Limonad"], 1926, 1:362). Similarly, the assertion that "no fleas have bitten me this month!" carries strong implications about the remainder of the calendar year ("The Quality of the Production" ["Kachestvo produktsii"], 1927, 1:367). And we can only speculate about the normal behavior of the man who begins his story with the proud announcement that he has never killed a doctor (nor even hit one!) ("Hypnosis" ["Gipnoz"], 1926, 1:341). Conversely, when a "fortune teller" exacts payment for her accurate prediction of a big fight in the future of Tovarishch Iashikov (who participates in at least one such brawl per day), it is as comical as Ippolit Ippolitych charging for his wisdom ("Fortunetelling" ["Khiromantiia"], 1927). Ordinarily the normal course of affairs goes unarticulated.

In Zoshchenko's writing, however, we are shown precisely such "figures" that, in their usual context, remain unperceived due to their status as norm, their lack of contrast with the ground behind them. These invisible footfalls afford us a view of the ground that obscures them. The ground, the general context of Zoshchenko's stories established so persistently by his periodic *recusatio* exclamations, is emphatically "not 1919," "not the czarist regime," and "not America": it is Soviet society in the 1920s, and when a seemingly newsworthy item is dismissed against this ground as "ho-hum," this is at least some indication that the supposedly "extraordinary" item is really just par for the course.

Since bad manners are all-pervasive, since a crude "lack of culture" (*nekul'turnost'*) has become the normal state of affairs, the most outrageous behavior is accepted by the inhabitants of Zoshchenko's world with absolute equanimity (and presented by the narrator almost as if in passing). Theft is not noteworthy because it is automatic—it is self-evident that given the opportunity, people will help themselves. What *is* worth telling, on the other hand, is when a character actually *pays* for a streetcar ride. "Normal" civilized behavior is shown to be the exception.[6]

If the decorum of the theater makes it a perfect ground for disruption, Soviet reality is definitely not a theater.[7] Disorder and violation are the norm here; no wonder the narrator of "Absence of Malice" carries on at such length about a smooth, unmolested passage—this, rather than being stomped on, is unusual. When a character in "Administrative Ecstasy" speaks of the "disruption of *dis*order" (*narushaet obshchestvennyi besporiadok*, 1:506) it is more than just a comical grammatical error. Figure and ground are reversed. The bystanders, the ostensible "background" against which the culprit will be unmasked ("Dog Scent"), become the objects of investigation themselves. And in "Street Incident," it is the passersby who become rowdy; the "criminal" they gawk at is just someone out for a walk.

Thus the nature of each exception forces the nature of the norm into view. When someone drops a bottle on a public sidewalk and keeps walking (*poshel dal'she*), all the other pedestrians follow suit, undeterred and undelayed by the broken glass that crunches beneath their feet—*narod khodit po steklam*, taking no notice (with the single exception of the hooligans who wish someone would come by barefoot). It remains there all afternoon until a policeman finally has it removed; "the most amazing thing in this story is the fact that the policeman ordered the glass to be cleaned up at all" ("The Bottle" ["Butylka"], 1927, 1:390). And the fact that Vaniushka Ledentsov is a veritable hero simply for getting a job without resorting to connections or bribes is an eloquent statement about the norms of finding employment ("It Happens" ["Byvaet," 1927).[8] The postal service in this world has even instituted norms indicating what percentage of the letters, telegrams, and money orders may be lost rather than delivered ("It's Bearable" ["Terpet' mozhno"], 1929). In this context, a purloined letter would hardly constitute a noticeable event or occasion a story: "It's not like taking off a coat, if you'll pardon the expression!" (1:519). Neither do the officials blink an eye when the newlywed who was unable to recognize his coatless bride stops in on his way home from work the next day for his no-fuss divorce. " 'It's nothing,' they say, 'it happens. These days,' they say, 'longer-lasting marriages are rare.' "[9] The divorce is much less noteworthy and tellable than the removal of the bride's coat.

And lest we assume that the bathhouse from hell is in some sense extraordinary or extreme, it is identified in closing as emphatically *obyknovennaia* (usual, ordinary, commonplace [1:279]). So too the much sought-after galosh with the toe torn off and the heel worn out and the holes all around (*obyknovenno kakaia* [Priboi, 2:135]). And the useless colorless train signal (*obyknovenno kakim* [1:383]). And all that infernal walking on (*delo obychnoe* [1:304]). It's all absolutely normal.

Nor are the protagonists exceptional beings. Clearly this panorama of peons comes from the tradition of the "little man" mined by both Chekhov and Gogol with their poor pathetic clerks. But Zoshchenko's characters—these crude, illiterate, petty creatures that are like some kind of lower organism, "made up mainly of water," like "a mushroom or a berry," with "an unseemly hole in the front [the mouth]" and "ears hanging off the sides"—are anything but a dignification of the little man ("The Lilacs Are Blooming" ["Siren' tsvetet"], 1930, 2:145–46). Petiushka in his smelly socks is no hero. Neither is Vasilii Ivanovich, who doesn't normally wash ("A Trivial Incident"). In fact, as scholars have noted, the contortions of Zoshchenko's plots function, if anything, to discredit the hero/narrator.[10]

Zoshchenko's low-life cast represents not only a refusal to deliver the "positive hero" as ordered up for the prescribed plot of heroic feats and great deeds[11]—it works even more palpably to complicate an already thorny pragmatic dilemma. Since none of the characters are really developed enough for us to care about them as psychologically complex and emotionally viable individuals, they function in the texts as bearers of a certain posture, as representatives of an attitudinal norm that we must either accept or reject. Their outrage, and especially their lack of outrage, presents us most poignantly with the problem of how to react.

In this world where *nekultur'nost'* (lack of culture, boorishness) is the norm, evaluative categories have necessarily become very skewed. Since the given attitudes are suspect, the reader is forced to decide for him- or herself what is noteworthy and significant, often adopting an evaluative attitude at odds with that of the vulgar narrator, or exasperated with the passive victims. Behavior or events that might be noticed (i.e., considered in some way significant) by a "normal" civilized person in that they are unacceptable simply fade into the background for the inhabitants of the fictional world. The characters take no heed. Yet the reader does—either because he or she *is* more cultured, less inured to bad treatment, than the admittedly exaggerated "water creatures" of Zoshchenko's universe; or because of a literary competence that teaches that an event told must be worth telling (or else why bother?). Identification with the characters and their perceptions is clearly problematic. In stories where the delegates of authority decline to notice events, the reader comes to question the official determinations of what is important; but here, where the victims themselves are oblivious to their plight, the reader is called upon to reverse as well the criteria applied by the general population.

What these adaptive criteria reveal is that in Zoshchenko's world the crisis has become the norm, and people have simply gotten used to it. Shoes, after all, no matter how constraining, eventually become a perfect fit. (Is Zoshchenko's comment to his wife confidently optimistic or deeply cynical?) By establishing the foot as the consummate object of violation, then demonstrating how little notice these tramplings occasion, Zoshchenko shows that encroachments such as these have indeed become the norm, that people's feet are getting stepped on routinely, and that they really can't take for granted that "that old left foot should be coming into view soon" (see the cartoon that opens Chapter 2). And like the good pedestrian of "Absence of Malice," they take it in stride.

That epic tale of foot stomping is itself only motivated by the visiting "negroes" who turn up in the exordium and who, as cultural aliens, are unaccustomed (*s neprivychki*) to the traffic (*dvizhenie*) and find the going hard (*Priamo, govoriat, khodit' trudno: pikhaiutsia i na nogi nastupaiut*). "But give them a year or two," the narrator assures us, "and they'll be stomping up a storm themselves. Guaranteed" (1:392). Just as aristocratic ladies are "used to" excesses in cream puff consumption (1:172). Or as factory workers, who no longer fuss when a colleague reports for work too intoxicated to sign the duty roster, have gotten used to chronic alcoholism (*privykli*) ("A Little Mistake" ["Oshibochka"], 1925, 1:277). Problems are only perceptible when one is *neprivykshii*—like Petiushka Iashikov, "unaccustomed" to the protocol of the operating room (i.e., boot removal [1:397]); or Vasilii Ivanovich, who is "not used to" spending the whole first act dealing with his *own* costume (1:373); or the fainthearted hero who "deviates" from his heroic course in his own death scene because he is still "unaccustomed" to the idea of cremation ("Small-Fry," 1:370); or the poet who still "has not gotten used to" his audience—*ne svyksia* ("An Incident in the Provinces," 1:251); or the audience "not accustomed" to reading about trivia ("Cockroaches," 1:473).[12]

Zoshchenko's exposure of the failures to notice explores one of the chief exigencies of Soviet life: the need to adapt, to get used to it, to not notice the glaring difficulties. One citizen must get used to the poisonous fumes emitted by his defective stove, because the representatives of the housing cooperative insist that they notice nothing wrong with the air in his apartment (as they are being carried out on stretchers, overcome by the gas, their legs having given way). The stove, they say, is "normal"; the air quality is "regular" (*rovnyi*). The *niukh* (sense of smell) of officialdom is obviously less sensitive than the olfactory agency of either the famous sniffing dog ("Sobachii niukh") or the nosey reporter of *sobach'ia erunda* (Zoshchenko's own "dog drivel"). "One can live with it," is their repeated pronouncement. They cite the fact that the kitten, as impartial an observer as they come, evidences little or no discomfort. Alas, the cat, who had only recently been vomiting at the bucket from the noxious fumes, appears to have gotten accustomed to the tainted air. As the story closes, the citizen, too, is mastering his nausea. "*Privykaiu*," he says—I'm getting used to it. "Man is not a flea—he can get used to anything" ("Kitten and People" ["Koshka i liudi"], 1927, 1:406–8).[13] The stories cast people in this perverse adaptive posture of not noticing everything from the officially sanctioned extortion of their funds to the fumes that asphyxiate them.

The 1927 collection of stories *The Trifles of Life*, a cycle that focuses on the pervasive daily difficulties (both noticed and "imperceptible"), closes with a retrospective verdict: "No problem. Not noticeable. It passed" (1:387). The assessment is made by the hero/narrator of the final story ("The Fantasy Shirt" ["Rubashka-fantazi"], 1927), whose fantastic new shirt had been purchased for the purpose of *attracting* (female) attention. After another set of elaborate preparations of the Vasilii Ivanovich sort, the hero's wondrous shirt has tragically shrunk beyond repair before the occasion for which it is needed. But this is "normal [*obyknovenno*]. It's nothing. New shirts always shrink nowadays" (1:386). So he wears his old shirt over his new but tiny acquisition for decency's sake. He has adapted—successfully. Thus his closing remark. But both in content and in its marked position as the final words of the collection about "life's trifles," the verdict appears to have a wider relevance, or at least poses a more general question. If you put on more layers, become more inured, as it were (the alternative, perhaps, to taking *off* your coat and exposing your nightshirt), you notice (and are noticed) less. But does that really mean there is "no problem"? Some of the characters in this cycle kick up a fuss (e.g., the provincial walker who *publishes* his complaint in the *Red Newspaper*— the very publisher of this collection). Most of them, however, (like the pedestrian in "Absence of Malice") just keep walking.

The narrator of "The Light Fixture" ("Kolpak," 1927) keeps walking from store to store—to thirteen or fourteen of them—in an attempt to replace the fixture that has been broken in his communal apartment. When there are no light fixtures to be had, he good-naturedly buys an umbrella stand instead (and not, interestingly enough, the chandelier suggested by one salesman, from which "you can always hang yourself" [1:399]). This customer is not suicidal. He is not even surprised, outraged, or frustrated, even though he and his fellow tenants have been saving for a year for this purchase. Unavailability is the norm (underscored by the fact that the clerks greet the customer with a confident "We don't have any" before he even manages to formulate the question [1:400]). The folks at home are delighted with the umbrella stand, by the way. " 'It's all for the best,' they say. 'A light fixture is a fragile thing. It would just get broken again' " (1:400). Prone to fracture, neither fixture nor foot (*noga—veshch' neprochnaia* [1:352]) is awarded much attention when shattered.

Thus, not only do the problems remain unprotested, insofar as they go essentially unnoticed, but they are greeted with a kind of forced optimism that is parodied mercilessly in Zoshchenko's stories. How wonderful that we have no skyscrapers! (since we have no working elevators—"Hard Labor" ["Katorga"], 1927[14]). How enviable to live in a communal bathroom! (the children can bathe without threat of catching cold—"The Crisis" ["Krizis"], 1925, 1:321). How ingenious that paint ("the usual kind") never dries, comes off on your clothes, and eventually just evaporates! ("Green Production" ["Zelenaia produktsiia"], 1927, 1:394–95). It doesn't leave stains and is "accessible to the poor" (*dostupnaia nebogatym*), the same formulation Zoshchenko uses to describe his own prose.[15]

Unlike the colorless paint that "hides the dirt," however, Zoshchenko's stories present a vibrant array of stains, spots, and other blemishes that defy oversight. And Zoshchenko's portrayals of the gleeful acceptance of a bad deal that has become the norm make perceptible not only the blotches, but also the conditions and contrivances that conceal them. For adaptation is ultimately a kind of de facto self-censorship. If you acclimate yourself, you cease to notice, and if you cease to notice, you cease to tell. To adapt is thus to obliterate story.

Telling Tales

"Happiness" ("Schast'e," 1924) turns on precisely this relationship between *noticing* and *telling*. It is the story of a glazier who never noticed his marriage, the birth of his child, the death of his wife, or even the death of his child. Yet he has the most vivid recollection of once acquiring 35 rubles in one incredible stroke of luck (the *schast'e* invoked by the title). The story sets up an opposition between what, on the one hand, has been etched on the memory for life (*na vsiu zhizn' zapomnilos'*) and what, on the other hand, is not even noticed (*nezametno, ne zametil*). The memorable windfall occurred 20 to 25 years earlier, when Ivan Fomich, who tells his own tale, was young and handsome and "waiting for happiness to arrive. But meanwhile, the years were passing imperceptibly and nothing particular was happening. I didn't notice getting married, or how I fought with my in-laws at the wedding, or that my wife had a baby. And that my wife died. And that the baby also died. Everything proceeded quietly and smoothly. And there was no particular happiness in all that" (1:212). Until that unforgettable November 27th (and none of the other anniversaries are memorable or important enough to be dated), when the glazier hit it big.

Most immediately striking here is that Ivan Fomich regards the traditionally "significant" events as so unnoteworthy. In this he closely resembles Chekhov's Iakov of "Rothschild's Fiddle," who exhibits a comparable memory lapse about the birth and death of his child and a marked inattentiveness to his dying wife.[16] But Ivan Fomich's description of these "milestones" as *rovno* is apt. They really do only describe a kind of ebb and flow, a regular cycle of pluses and minuses that add up to zero. For each gain there is an answering loss, and even the positive experiences are flawed, much as Chekhov's Iakov had tallied up his own life as a series of profits and inevitable losses. But Zoshchenko is less concerned with his character's truly awful values than with the tellability of experience in an existence whose greatest joy comes in the form of 35 rubles. The grayness is so unremitting that the slightest departure from the norm constitutes a tremendous *schast'e* (happiness, good fortune). The reader is encouraged to question the real value of this magnificent luck: it brought Ivan Fomich two months of drunken stupor, one silver ring, and a pair of warm socks. It was not enough, we are told, to buy him the shirt and pair of trousers he needed.

But it is part of the point that such a paltry gain should register as the happiest and most memorable event of Ivan Fomich's life. When the narrator of the *frame* story (for Ivan Fomich's account is a story within a story) asks him whether his was a *great* happiness, or just a small one, Ivan Fomich can't even answer the question: "Big or little? I don't know. All I know is that it was unforgettable" (*na vsiu zhizn' zapomnilos'* [1:212]). The stroke of luck was memorable not in its rewards, but in its function as difference, as exception to the flat, even, unnoticeable everyday he had experienced otherwise. Its "eventfulness quotient" is what makes it worth noting, and, in response to the frame narrator's question, worth telling.

It is in the relationship of the inner story to the frame narrative that noticing is associated with telling. The whole text is introduced by a narrator who, since the onset of his catarrh of the stomach, has the irrepressible need to ask everyone he encounters whether they have ever experienced happiness. Significantly, he does not ask, "Have you ever had any disasters in your life?" Crisis, bad fortune, is presupposed as norm, while happiness is assumed to be the exception. The assumption reverses Tolstoy's affirmation that "all happy families are alike," that there is no story in happiness. Here, where unhappiness is the norm, the story is born of a single piece of *good* news. The question the narrator has posed asks: Do you have anything unusual (noteworthy) to report? His "Have you ever known happiness?" (1:211) is essentially a request for a story.

Even though the respondent's tale is bracketed by an opening and closing wink at the narrator, the mark of apparent fictionality, the first-person narrator of the frame is satisfied with Ivan Fomich's story. It has provided him with something worth passing on, something worth telling. In his own life, he admits enviously, he has had no such "luck." He is a storyteller with no story of his own,[17] an inveterate framing device doomed to elicit stories from other characters because he has nothing to tell. "Or maybe," he concludes, "I just haven't noticed" (1:214).

Trivialization

The norm is unutterable—because it is imperceptible (one cannot articulate what one does not notice); because it is uninteresting (it does not make a good story); and because, in the Soviet context, its manifestations are deemed too trivial to warrant attention. Like the flawed tooth in "Wisdom," the unnoticeable will remain unnoticed if one keeps one's mouth shut. But Zoshchenko opens his mouth again and again.

And because telling is contingent upon noticing, and noticing is a function of attributing importance to something, it is doubly poignant that the Revolution is so flagrantly absent in Zoshchenko's fiction. We have seen it come to the attention of the characters (and readers) only as a result of the inevitable foot violation (the political upheaval representing even then only background, not figure). By replacing Revolution as the paradigmatic event with his own prototype of the eventful (individual problems with coats and feet), Zoshchenko trivializes matters that by Soviet standards ought to be accorded the highest respect.

This trivialization proceeds in several ways: directly, by lampooning the most hallowed revolutionary concerns; passive-aggressively, by failing to notice and report the era's large-scale events; and most pointedly of all, by presenting the event of the century as a narrative failure.

The direct strikes are familiar; they take aim at the momentous "achievements" of the new regime. One of the major ambitions of Soviet Communism, for instance, was to bring electric power to all regions of the USSR. ("Communism equals Soviet power plus the electrification of the whole country," runs the famous slogan that long dominated one portion of the Moscow skyline.) Zoshchenko celebrates this monumental achievement by showing us the benefits electricity brings to one communal apartment: when the lights go on, the tenants actually *see* their bedbugs for the first time ("Poverty"[18]).

The vaunted Soviet campaign against illiteracy receives similar treatment. We are shown the triumphant factory that has achieved complete success in its quest to "liquidate literacy" (sic) in its workers (in the words of those newly "liquidated" employees themselves ["A Little Mistake," 1:276–77]). The benefits of the widely publicized campaign to encourage workers and consumers to economize on deficit items are likewise reduced to the level of absurdity. By not heating the lavatory one winter, the employees of a certain Borisov institution manage to save 50 feet of firewood. Never mind that the plumbing froze and the pipe burst—it was a czarist pipe, and "such pipes should be torn out by their very roots." Heady with success, the zealous employees curse the warm spring weather that eliminates the need to economize further ("The Economy Campaign," 1:342). Here, as in the accounts of literacy and electrification, the discrepancy between the great successes claimed in capital letters in headlines and on banners, and the actual magnitude of the progress, is sorely apparent.

But the trivialization also proceeds more subtly. In addition to deflating pomposity of all kinds, Zoshchenko also maintains virtual silence on the events of 1917, an absence that is perhaps more eloquent than any specific commentary on the successes or failures of the Bolshevik objectives. Not that Zoshchenko was necessarily opposed to the Revolution and its goals. But he did have certain problems with its fixity of vision, its fixing of the thresholds of tellability, its determination to see everything in terms of one master plot with one master event, and its view of the writer as a priest of the holy writ that issues from that gospel. His great blasphemy is not to recite the litany. Withholding comment is definitely not an act of discretion.

What his reticence reflects, beyond a stubborn refusal to deliver what has been ordered up, is Zoshchenko's understanding of the *impact* of the Revolution. Even the most unimpeachable ideals can encounter difficulty in a society unprepared for their implementation, plagued by material difficulties and cultural shortcomings. Being a good storyteller, Zoshchenko cannot portray the October Revolution as the great narrative climax it is cracked up to be. Its omission from consideration and text reflects what, in a narrative sense, can only be called its lack of significance.

Where Revolution is taken explicitly into account, its eventfulness quotient is zero: the hero of "People" ("Liudi," 1924), for example, who had begun a book on revolutionary possibilities in Russia, must abandon the project once the big event has become a reality—the real

Revolution reveals his possibility-laden manuscript to be full of "nonsense" (2:64–65). More poignantly still, the hero of "A Terrible Night" has a life "story" as untellable as the pre-event existence of the hero of "Happiness"—another *rovnaia liniia* (smooth, even trajectory), this time encompassing not only marriage and career, but explicitly the Revolution as well, which did nothing to disrupt the even flow: "All of this faded, it all flowed together into a continuous, unbroken, even line"; "his life passed quietly and peacefully."[19]

Interestingly, in later editions the Revolution is given considerably more attention, both by the even-tempered protagonist and by the narrator (2:94–96). And Revolution is actually inserted in other spots where a character's life has undergone some cataclysmic change: in "Wisdom," for instance, the hero's eleven years of static existence are recast as explicitly *pre*-revolutionary in the 1935 and subsequent publications. In the original 1924 version, those eleven eventless years seem to encompass 1917 and reach well into the 1920s.[20]

Most inimical to the official Soviet sensibility, in other words, are the narrative strategies that deny the Revolution's potency and strip it of its impact, rendering it a non-event (hence trivial and untellable, background at best) and greeting it with an ingenuous Labovian "so what?" instead of with the usual fanfare. When, in *Michel Siniagin*, Zoshchenko "exonerates" the Revolution, absolving it of all guilt for the hero's downfall, he is in effect emasculating it, eliminating its consequences. "People are ready to blame everything on the Revolution," explains the narrator. "But the Revolution doesn't explain everything!" The narrator's neighbor, for instance, would have come to the same dire straits "Revolution or no Revolution" (2:181–82). This object of customarily extensive rhetorical treatment in terms of *perceptibility* and *consequence*—ten days of resonant world-shaking, and all that—is reduced to making no difference at all.

This refusal to concede that something has happened, that a meaningful change has occurred as a result of the Revolution, is reflected in the stories as a flagrant lack of results—not that the *stories'* events have no impact, but the stories are set explicitly *after* the big historical cataclysm and reveal that it has not made the world an all-new place. The story-internal events, by contrast—the "trivial" coat and foot incidents that Zoshchenko spotlights so tirelessly—have major repercussions. The coat offenders are all ousted from their respective theaters or divorced. And in "Nervous People" we are shown the results of mere "trifles": a housewives' scrap over a wire brush leaves the one-legged veteran Gavrilych on the floor with his skull bashed in. But in the larger setting, things have changed little if at all. The Communist ideal has not altered human nature. A policy that allows each citizen to take "according to his needs" cannot work: if there is no charge to ride the carousel, people will ride it in definite excess of their needs, until they vomit—and then some ("The Merry-Go-Round").

The birth of the communal apartment had not miraculously spawned cooperation, as the antagonistic behavior in "Nervous People" and "A Summer Breather," among other stories, eloquently demonstrates. Nor had any of the corrupt practices of the czarist era been eradicated. No amount of exclaiming by the narrator of "Weak Packaging" ("Slabaia tara," 1932) on the subject of how character has now changed for the better can convince us that bribes are no longer taken. They are simply administered under the cover of self-righteous "unbribability."

"How history has changed!" cries the narrator of "The Czar's Boots" ("Tsarskie sapogi," 1927, 1:378). Now even a common man can wear the boots of a czar! But, alas, things are still shabby for this common man, for the imperial boots fall apart a mere three days after he has purchased them at an auction. The threads are old, of course, so it's not surprising that they don't hold up, he reasons. After all, it's been ten years since the Revolution! Zoshchenko has cleverly provided an artifact of the old regime (footwear, naturally, the ultimate index of eventfulness) to occasion the realization that "ten whole years have passed!" (1:379). The reader understands the tacit question: It's been ten years now. What have we got to show for it? Has history changed? This citizen still has no decent boots; his feet are just as vulnerable as ever. The narrator of "The Chinese Ceremony" repeats a similar refrain of how different everything is now, how much history has altered everything in our lives—everything, that is, except what we do to each other on Nevskii Prospekt (1:206). He refers, actually, to the anachronism of shaking hands, but the story suggests more generally that the fundamentals of pedestrian interaction have remained unaffected by the grander movements of "history."

By placing his stories explicitly in the dismaying denouement of a big fizzle, Zoshchenko suggests that in the larger historical story, the "significant event" has failed to disrupt the status quo in any palpable and significant way. This works like one gigantic application of Chekhov's second strategy, where the big event turns out to be singularly non-eventful. But the "events" Zoshchenko reads are historical ones, or, more precisely, the canonical accounts of these historical events. Zoshchenko sketches a critique not only of reality, but of the stories told about it, most notably the "official" story. Zoshchenko dismantles the big story by casting the event of the century as unnoticeable at the time of its occurrence, inconsequential in terms of significant changes wrought, and hence, not even remotely "x enough" to tell.

Perceptibility and Pragmatics

Zoshchenko thus creates his own policy of exclusion and inclusion somewhat at odds with the imposed indices. The basic criterion of both systems, official and anti-official, is *significance*—both determine what is worth telling according to some measure of importance. But in his personal calibration of "too x" and "not x enough," Zoshchenko relies more consistently on perceptibility as both index and goal of tellability. He takes perceptibility as his subject and his guideline, and he makes perceptible the perversions of perceptibility.

Art in general, as understood by Zoshchenko's Formalist contemporaries, has the mission of de-automatizing perception. But Zoshchenko's maneuvers make ordinary things palpable less through the kind of deformation and estrangement described by Shklovskii and Tomashevskii than by lingering on the thresholds of noticeability; not by making things weirdly unrecognizable, but by reversing their valences, presenting (Chekhov style) the ostensibly trivial as revolutionary, the revolutionary as virtually invisible (Chekhov style number two), figure as ground, violation as norm, and hence the officially noticeable/tellable/significant as just the opposite (and vice versa).

In this, Zoshchenko once again recalls Tolstoy (though again, not in the spirit the Party critics would have liked). The very question of noticeability and significance links the two authors, for as Morson demonstrates in his book on *War and Peace*, Tolstoy conceives of the truly important as "hidden in plain view." What is noticed *cannot* be important; anything ostentatiously historic is by definition insignificant. What *is* important for Tolstoy is the small-scale, unexceptional, imperceptible flow of everyday life. Thus his work embodies what Morson calls Tolstoy's predilection for *prosaics*.[21]

But although for Zoshchenko, as for Tolstoy, "life begins where the tiny bit [*chut'-chut'*] begins,"[22] Zoshchenko nevertheless sticks to a *poetics*, as miniature and as "trivia"-based as it may be, in which noticing is the key. Whereas for Tolstoy perceptibility always invalidates something's importance, Zoshchenko seems to regard noticeability as an imperative. For Tolstoy the important is by nature imperceptible; for Zoshchenko it is only a legislative perversion that keeps the important "unperceived." Tolstoy, Morson comments, makes the mediocre interesting; Zoshchenko makes it noticeable. He tacks the sign up by the copy machine, labeling both norm and exception in big letters. And if, as Morson shows, we must recognize the radical insignificance of many of the incidents Tolstoy includes in his novel, in Zoshchenko's work we are invited to concede the unimportance of what he explicitly leaves out (the Revolution). Zoshchenko is thus surprisingly traditional in terms of narrative structure: the important is *precisely* narratable (unlike for Tolstoy, who sees good stories as inherently unable to encompass the truly significant, which is unstructured, unpatterned, and unnarratable). For Zoshchenko, the official story is a bad one, not because it is untrue, but because it lacks a significant—perceptible—event.

The Question of the Discourse

As we have seen, Zoshchenko counters by recording the unofficial stories of the era, crises of coats and feet and the like that *are* noticeable, consequential, and tellable. In fact, the *skaz* narration, Zoshchenko's famous "broken intonation," sees to it that not just the subject matter, but the act of telling itself attracts attention.[23]

There is no question that this illiterate, uncultured narrative voice, with its abominable grammar and absurd "logic," continues in a fairly direct way Zoshchenko's project of trivialization of what was held in official esteem. The damage dealt to the "authoritative word"—the slogans, the proclamations, the neologisms, the state's new vocabulary and chief propaganda tool—by this inept, inarticulate narrator is immense. When the word, that ultimate weapon in the class war, is wielded by a speaker with incomplete mastery of the idiom, when "embracing your class enemy" is explicated as one of the hazards of heavy drinking ("The Earthquake," 1:444), the effect is anything but reverent.[24] No objection is made to these terms and principles—on the contrary, they are adopted with zeal—only the credentials of the convert are so poor that his support is of dubious value. This Bakhtinian hidden polemic is particularly effective in that it borrows the language of the "oppressor" in order to undermine the oppressive structure from within, on its own terms. It allows the rhetoric to show *itself* to be inappropriate or false. Zoshchenko's parody of an authorial voice parodies authority itself.

Certainly the narrator's misuse of language has a comic force as well. Although Zoshchenko claimed his stories were not deliberately humorous,[25] the laughter they elicit is an important feature of their reception. And as Zoshchenko himself was quick to point out, "laughter can never be neutral."[26] Laughter is irreverent.

It is also clear that the *skaz* narration, insofar as it creates a distance between the "straight" authorial voice and the linguistically marked discourse of the narrator, serves as a kind of mask. The "fool" can express opinions about the Soviet state that would be far too offensive from a more serious and respectable speaker. He can also utter judgments too absurd to be taken seriously and thus imply the opposite. As I have said, this discrediting of the narrator confronts the reader with a rather complex decision about what happens, who notices it, what he says about it, and how reliable that perceptual stance is.

But it is not necessary to pinpoint Zoshchenko's real voice, if that were even possible, to sense the most powerful effect of Zoshchenko's *skaz*: what the *skaz* does above all is to make the telling itself noticeable by simulating a voice that is as irritating and indiscreet as Chekhov's sneezer who perpetually apologizes. The *skaz* is important not only as a discursive measure. The idiosyncratic speech makes apparent not just *how* the story is being told, but also *that* it is being told. It makes the unbelievable indiscretion of mentioning the unmentionable all the more conspicuous. Chekhov anticipated this to some degree by inscribing tellers of tales, but in Zoshchenko, the illusion of oral performance is overpowering. Zoshchenko replaces Chekhov's indiscriminately talkative but stylistically bland Ippolit Ippolitych with a narrator who foregrounds the act (and audacity) of telling itself. Noticing, in Zoshchenko's work, is a story-level phenomenon. That characters and narrators notice or fail to notice is their plot function; that they tell or do not tell is equally eloquent for the plot.[27] *How* Zoshchenko's narrator tells is not unimportant, but paramount is *that* he tells what he does, and that he does it in such a high-profile fashion makes his violation of the threshold of tellability undeniably palpable.

Interestingly, as bizarre as his language is, and although Zoshchenko has often been said to resemble Gogol stylistically, Zoshchenko's violation of the threshold of significance and tellability is very much in terms of the *what* rather than the *how*. Whereas Gogol provokes by distending his discourse with apparently extraneous and insignificant elaborative detail (as the next chapters will show), Zoshchenko exhibits a distinct restraint at the level of discourse.

"Speak briefly and leave," reads the sign in "Americans" ("Amerikantsy," 1923).[28] To get carried away and talk voluminously, to "detain" (*zaderzhivat'*) unnecessarily, is irritating and perhaps should even be punishable with a "fine for each extraneous word."[29] Odd as the speech of Zoshchenko's narrators is, it *is* brief; it does comply. It does not *zaderzhivat'* inordinately. "We won't tax your attention for too long" (*Vniman'ia dolgo ne zaderzhim*), promises (truthfully) the narrative persona in "Cockroaches," particularly on such a "small" topic (1:473). The object is to *get* the attention, not to monopolize it. Extravagant "ornamental prose" is inappropriate ("The Lilacs Are Blooming," 2:158); too much information is ludicrous (see "The Prayer" ["Molitva," 1923], in which the speaker provides painstakingly exact personal data to her interlocutor—God!);[30] repetition, vocalizing without saying anything new, is a waste of everybody's time (see "Capital Item" ["Stolichnaia stuchka," 1925], in which an interpreter provides a "literal" translation by simply repeating everything verbatim); and digression is infuriating (see "The Patient" ["Patsientka," 1924], who exhausts her doctor with her "talking cure").

Zoshchenko's stories, on the contrary, evince a distinct hesitancy to describe extensively, to "gossip unnecessarily in belles lettres" ("What the Nightingale Sang," 2:112). To tell good stories one must know "what to pass over," how to *select* carefully;[31] and one must avoid the rambling of the old woman in "Wisdom," who, "though she remembered the beginnings [of stories], could never reconstruct the endings, and having gotten irrevocably confused, would simply stop speaking, trying not to annoy Ivan Alekseevich any further" (2:52). Zoshchenko's narrators keep it rather short and sweet. "We won't go into detail and vex the nerves" ("Guests," 1:364). That's the story, they say, "and anyone who wants the details can come see me" ("A Historic Tale" ["Istoricheskii rasskaz"], 1924, 1:211).

In fact, even in *Michel Siniagin*, which has been likened to a novel in range and breadth, and which crowns the decade in 1930, the so-called "digressions on all sorts of irrelevant topics" that are used to "offset" the plot are anything but irrelevant or extraneous in Zoshchenko's fictional world: walking as a norm, socks, feet, stolen coats, stolen titles, and a demoted Revolution are topologically resonant and thematically eloquent.[32] As we have already seen, what is not important is simply left out.

Zoshchenko's discursive procedure, then, while it ruthlessly deforms standard literary diction, does less to violate any principle of verbal economy (Chudakova's insistence on Zoshchenko's "prolixity" notwithstanding[33]). His discourse is not profligate; rather, in its own offbeat way, it is discerning and selective. By articulating explicitly trivial concerns and telling these tales in a loud and conspicuous voice, Zoshchenko makes a rather constant and undismissable issue of what's worth telling. "Notice me noticing," is his challenge.

Zoshchenko highlights this provocation most persistently by opening his stories with self-deprecating acknowledgments that "warn" the reader of what is to come, "concede" triviality, and "anticipate" objections. "Of course this incident is trivial, not of worldwide significance," begins the narrator of "A Trivial Incident" (1:370). "Of course this is not the time to write about petty things," admits the man about to launch into a tale about "Cockroaches" (1:473). "Of course this is a trivial matter," acknowledges the narrative persona of "Something Special" ("Chto-nibud' osobennoe," 1927, 1:405), "so trivial that some of our readers'll probably even take offense or pick a fight." Disclaimers of this sort abound in Zoshchenko's work; rarely a story escapes without an initial mea culpa or scattered apologetic references to the "insignificant occurrence" ("A Little Mistake," 1:276) or "tiny incident" ("Guests," 1:363) at its center. The "of course" tag itself emphasizes the question of what's worth telling. What does it mean to begin story after story with a formula that introduces a matter of course, something that "goes without saying" (*konechno* and *konechno, ob chem govorit'*)?[34]

These ubiquitous concessions that "everything is small change and small-fries—it's downright revolting" ("Small-Fry," 1:369) do less to identify the stature of the obviously small-scale content than to emphasize the interactive nature of the literary enterprise, evoking graphically all the players and making manifest the uneasy face-off between the "author" who chooses to tell certain things and the belligerent readers who might indeed "pick a fight" (yet another form of interruption). Just because something has been written, we learn in "Fog" ("Tuman," 1925) does not imply that it can or will be read.[35]

In emphasizing the decision to tell in spite of, indeed because of, a matter's alleged insignificance ("Admittedly this event is rather petty, ... but still, allow me to tell you" ["Fortunetelling," 1:367]), Zoshchenko explicitly *declines* the canonical reading of eventfulness offered by the Soviet mythmakers. In embodying in newsprint ("A Trick of Nature") all the news that's "unfit to print" ("Administrative Ecstasy"), Zoshchenko not only declines official readings, but actively *issues* readings of his own. To articulate an event is to wield enormous power. In "Fortunetelling" we see that *ukazyvat' sobytiia* means to determine events in the sense of both recognizing and making them happen. The man with the destiny who thinks it will make no difference whether or not his future/story is told ("Let her tell! I won't lose weight from it!") is shown to be mistaken (1:367). And even if storytelling does not actually make things happen, it does acknowledge them as events. "A Historic Tale" articulates the principle: "If you saw Lenin, say so. If you didn't, shut up" (1:210). Make your contribution (as Grice might say) one that is worthy of note. And if you saw something important (the example of Vladimir Il'ich is particularly funny given the marked absence of such historical giants in Zoshchenko's work), stand up and say so. Do it *dlia istorii* (for history's sake [1:210]); *dlia informatsii* (for information's sake); or *prosto tak* (just because) ("Home Remedy," 1:516).

Public Readings

But not only the teller is so empowered. Zoshchenko inscribes determinedly in his stories a vocal and responsive *publika* that not only "gathers" reliably at the first hint of a trivial episode (*Tut publika, konechno, sobralas'* [1:302]; *Nu, narod, konechno, sobralsia* [1:172]), "watches" with interest (1:302), and "oohs and ahs" as appropriate (*Nu, narod, konechno, akhnul* [1:181]), but also "speaks up" (*Tut publika stala vyrazhat'sia* [1:332]), offers cartloads of unsolicited advice (*Tut narod stal sovetovat'* [1:383]), and, most assertively, attacks (*Tut publika stala nasedat'* [1:332, 302]). The public aggressively issues rulings: has there been a theft, or not? Has the citizen left a toothmark in the cream puff, or not? *They* are the "experts," the arbiters of whether a violation is discernible—in other words, whether or not something worth telling has occurred.

That everyone's intimate dilemmas occur so consistently before spectators exposes the public incursion into domestic space (even the events that play out "at home" are attended and interpreted at length by meddlesome neighbors in the communal apartment). But more importantly, the palpable presence of this Greek chorus–like body of citizens, before whom all is enacted in this extended theatrical space and who call out interpretations of the footfall they have witnessed, has a particular pragmatic force.[36] In this arbitration by the audience, Zoshchenko not only *declines* established measures of magnitude and *proposes* unofficial ones, but actually *invites* alternative readings of eventfulness as well. The "people" have the final word. And when nothing interesting is afoot, they disperse: *Tak i razoshlis'*.[37] This is Zoshchenko's way of putting the lower boundary back in the hands (and feet) of the reading public (as opposed to Soviet officialdom) and allowing it to calibrate naturally what's worth telling. Zoshchenko's own *publika*, we notice, has done anything but walk away. Zoshchenko, who declined an early offer from Gosizdat to issue an official three-volume "collected works" in order to "roam freely—to cavort with the wild reader,"[38] gives that untutored reader a voice: that year he publishes (instead of the Gosizdat collection) his *Letters to the Writer*, a collection of actual letters from his actual readers. Their sanction is both more valid and more valued.

The power of the public not only to approve or dismiss a presentation, but to rule on its very nature is most apparent in "An Incident in the Provinces," where the audience evaluates the undistinguished performances of four artists as the work of one skilled *transformator*. Although Barmin claims that Zoshchenko's real hero is the author-figure he has devised,[39] it becomes clear how important the receiver function is as well. Deciding what to tell is defiant and heroic; evaluating what is seen and told is equally crucial. The particular audience in "An Incident in the Provinces," in ruling that it has seen a sensation, is mistaken. Possibly this can be seen as a reminder not to fall prey to preconceptions that obstruct one's ability to see the world clearly—master plots, for example, that organize all data according to a preconceived pattern. In any case, it demonstrates that reality is complex and difficult to read—like the color of the flag in "A Trivial Occurrence" or the color of the paint in "Green Production," life is ambiguous, and signs, even red banners, require critical decoding. Things are not as black and white (or red and white) as their designations would imply.

In fact, the almighty *publika* produces its share of misreadings. The self-seeking residents of one communal apartment, for instance, must pay a high price when they choose to read a neighbor's cries for help as not worthy of their attention. They interpret the commotion as "merely" a robbery attempt on someone else rather than the imperatively noticeable "rather grandiose event" it in fact turns out to be—a raging fire that destroys *everyone's* possessions ("The Event" ["Sobytie"], 1927, 1:395). As the concerned citizen who calls an ambulance rather than a repairman for a wooden leg learns, falling down is not the only downfall. An interpretive misstep, too, can have serious consequences ("The Downfall of a Man"). And "times are such" that you can never really tell what's happening; you think you're witnessing something big, but maybe they're just filming a movie (1:353). Sometimes an error is not so serious—the citizens who mistake the position of the woman in police "custody" ("Street Incident") can (and do) just keep walking when it is revealed that there has been "no event." They themselves, in fact, have created the only disruption. To *respond*, to *notice* is itself eventful.

And when the other passengers in "NEP Grimace" misidentify the overloaded mother as a servant ("you figure it out!"), they misread a family affair as a "certified violation of the official code of labor" (1:401). But there is more truth in this misreading than in the official interpretation. Only in official terms has a violation of the old woman *not* taken place. If it all depends on how the situation is interpreted—as in "Woman's Happiness" ("Bab'e schast'e," 1926), where a minor-key interpretation of events (catastrophic pregnancy) is transposed into a major-key response (an opportunity to extort money from the putative father)—the act of judging becomes that much more urgent and complex. Interestingly, Zoshchenko's stories often end in court where a determination is made. The judge in "Nervous People" reads the wire-brush incident as a violation of great magnitude and seriousness and gives the participants, accordingly, "a real whopping" (1:324). The judiciary scene at the end of "The Glass," conversely, rules the cracked vessel a trifle. Only the defendent contests the outcome and moves to file countersuit, hoping to make a federal case out of it after all. The brother-in-law of his adversary seems rather to share the judge's interpretation; he calmly eats watermelon in the face of the hysterics.[40]

All this emphasizes not only the pivotal role of judgment, but also the prerogative of the final arbiter—audience or reader—to "pick a fight," or worse still, *naplevat'* (spit, not give a damn) when presented with something uninteresting (*Vy zaderzhivaete. . . . A nam naplevat'*).[41] The narrator of *Michel Siniagin* expresses profound anxiety over the present and future reception of his work. Acknowledging "the grandeur of our times," he finds himself (like so many of Zoshchenko's narrators) unequal to the task of producing a work commensurate with the epoch and offers "trivia" instead. In light of his contribution, when he imagines his *future* readers picking up such trifles he becomes so flustered that he drops his pen. No, there is nothing to interest "future respected readers." Better just to give in and compose for today's audience (2:178–79). The enterprise of writing *for*—or rather writing *to*—an audience is emphasized both in his colloquial declamation and his formal forms of address. Having chosen not to worry about the future "respected readers," he addresses his contemporary "respected citizens." *Uvazhaemye grazhdane*, one of Zoshchenko's most popular collections of the 1920s, takes this form of address as its very title, an apt opening of its interaction with its reader, an appeal to its judge. We sense in these stories the extent to which considerations of their reception are built into their conception.

By stressing the discriminating role of the receiver, the stories raise again and again, explicitly and implicitly, the question of what makes something worth the reader's effort. In "Pelegeia" (1924) we get one answer.[42] The simple country woman, whose ambitious husband is embarrassed by her illiteracy, regularly dismisses all requests and enticements to learn to read. She is unmoved by the great campaign to liquidate illiteracy and remains equally unaffected by the materials her husband brings home to "enlighten" her—until she finds a suspicious letter in her husband's pocket. This personal artifact, which touches her life and her heart, is finally worth reading. (Here the "future reader" envisioned with such apprehension by the narrator of *Michel Siniagin* might indeed comment, "Honey, it's interesting—they had, she'll say, some kind of personal life back then!" [2:179].) Though the going is rough, the faint trace of perfume and the small feminine script on the envelope motivate her to persevere for months until at last she can decipher the secret letter. She devours the text voraciously and then weeps—from relief that it is not a love letter, from humiliation, and from other more ambiguous feelings.

In the end, the letter turns out to be merely a "please find enclosed" accompaniment to the elementary reader her husband has requested for her edification (though it *is* from a woman and it does refer to Pelegeia deprecatingly), addressed to Comrade Kuchkin and containing a lot of empty slogans. Interestingly, the *Golubaia kniga* version co-opts Pelegeia's story as "an astounding case in the history of the liquidation of illiteracy" (3:247). But it emphatically does not belong to this public discourse. Perhaps Pelegeia "felt secretly hurt and began to cry" because she had gone to so much trouble to read what amounted to only vacuous slogans that did not touch or interest her. Unlike Gorky's famous mother, whose secret reading lessons bring her enlightened reverence for the revolutionary Word, Pelegeia (who, not incidentally, bears the same name as Gorky's inspired heroine) finds emptiness, disappointment, and vague despair in reading the Party's discursive products.

The Assault on the Reigning Order

What's worth telling?—this is the constant provocation presented by Zoshchenko's eminently visible and audible narrators. What's worth reading?—the issue is forced by Zoshchenko's constant inscription of quick-tongued (and quick-fisted) readers of street scenes and other texts. But these strategic inscriptions simply *focus* the same two questions raised over and over by the content itself. The story-level events and existents—present and absent—are the most provocative aspect of Zoshchenko's production, more unsettling, in the end, than the faulty grammar of his narrators. What is finally accomplished by Zoshchenko's coats and feet, these programmatic marginalia, these determined footnotes to history's "great" events? Ultimately, the small subject matter not only challenges (and foregrounds) the superstructure's boundaries and prohibitions, but works to destabilize the very foundations on which it stands. Noticing, telling, appreciating, and inviting evaluations of the very small both thematizes relative size and importance, and disturbs the logic of "lesser" and "greater," of part and whole—thus undercutting the very principles of order and coherence.

Both foot care (and abuse) and the October Revolution were real features of Zoshchenko's world, but as literary alternatives they reflect radically divergent ways of incorporating the raw material of that reality into narrative. The wide-angle lens (Revolution and all that) gives a picture of a coherent and purposeful whole. It presents an intact body, with lower extremities nicely in proportion. A fixation on random, individual incidents (or body parts), on the other hand, gives a more chaotic, less integrated view. Zoshchenko's supporters contended that this latter technique gives the truer picture of reality, free from idealization and illusory heroics. His critics maintained that Zoshchenko's portrayal maligned reality by violating its morphological and ideological integrity.

Zoshchenko's portraiture was "vile," for it depicted only "the most preposterous aspects of Soviet reality."[43] The problem with this writer, summarized Gorky, is not a lack of talent, but an inability to choose his material properly. He has no sense of the *typical*, the generally true.[44] Zoshchenko systematically refused to discern any coherence whatsoever and persisted in simply registering what appeared to be stray particulars, and not the most pleasant ones at that. Even if these things did occasionally occur, the critics held, such episodes were atypical and purely accidental, and therefore extraneous and external (and hostile!) to the real reality, which was harmonious, orderly, and governed by the laws that propel all life and history.[45]

The common concern of all these criticisms is Zoshchenko's use of data. Most of the attacks are based on the assumption that his stories are only a "chaotic sequence of impressions, disconnected dots," with the author "swimming in a sea of raw material . . . without a compass."[46] But Zoshchenko was not in the habit of simply going out for a swim any more than Chekhov went strolling with his camera. Zoshchenko himself, in one of his only non-satirical commentaries on his own work, emphasizes what he regards as an artistic imperative: the "ability to select out of the chaos," to be discerning, to choose the "detail that means a lot," and then to construct out of the raw facts an artistic whole.[47] We have seen how his stories ridicule speakers who recount randomly and at too great a length. Zoshchenko's choices are deliberate and each story is a complete artistic unit. Even the letters of his early period evidence this concern with artistic unity. They are all titled, as if to point out the thematic unity of the no-doubt carefully selected data.[48] The simplicity and casualness are deceptive.

Where the Soviet critics were correct, however, is in recognizing that Zoshchenko's choices are hardly calculated to prove the laws of dialectical materialism. The overall impression created by the stories is one of a life that is "essentially purposeless and resistant to interpretation."[49] Zoshchenko's raw material is manipulated not to confirm any inherent order, but rather to reveal chaos. If Morson is correct that the fundamental insight and innovation of *War and Peace* is to acknowledge the irreducible randomness of life and to expose structure and pattern as imposed and false,[50] then the Soviet critics got what they were asking for in ordering up a Red Tolstoy: an unsettling, destabilizing picture of fundamental disorder, a refusal to see laws and structure and direction in life and history. In Zoshchenko's work, history, like his pedestrians, rather than advancing purposefully, does a lot of shuffling around. No matter how much resonance we discern in each little item, no matter how much Zoshchenko's network of coat hooks and galoshes works to unify his own apparently disjunctive oeuvre, the effect of these "little episodes," these programatically minuscule events and existents, on the larger picture is disruptive, disunifying, dis-integrating. Instead of the "grand synthesis," the "single powerful, integral, harmonious picture" envisioned by Voronskii,[51] Zoshchenko produced sketch after irritating sketch of the pesky trifles of life that distort that sublime image.

To Zoshchenko's critics, a certain amount of attention to *byt* (the mundane details of daily life) was defensible and could even be valuable if employed as the field of investigation for fundamental problems and general truths (as in Saltykov-Shchedrin), as long as it did not overflow its channel and obscure the contours of that field.[52] The "small" was tolerable, even in this monumental epoch, as long as it was made in the image of the large—as long as the "part" stood in synecdochic relationship to the "whole," as long as it corroborated the larger picture rather than deforming it. A "midget" is acceptable; a "dwarf" is not. The midget is diminutive, but perfectly formed. The dwarf is a grotesque distortion.[53] And in the contest between the "grotesque" and the "model" as a subject for representation, the Soviet critics overwhelmingly favored the latter. Soviet literature, as a modeling system in a model society, was to fashion representations of exquisite order. Literature should "organize in fiction what is unorganized . . . in life."[54] No dwarfs allowed.

What the Soviet critics were after, in effect, was what Bakhtin calls an epic worldview, one that would suppress the imperfections and deviations of historical, present-day reality in favor of the more perfect patterns of myth and legend[55] (a perspective diametrically opposed to the Tolstoyan project). This demand for a continual reenactment of the Bolshevik myth led to the "legislation" of a new literary tradition in 1932: socialist realism. The officially compiled canon of works to emulate comprised novels that imparted meaning to present-day reality by rendering it to fit the patterns of one master plot: the coming to fruition of history.[56] Notoriously absent from the prescribed list are accounts of taking off coats and accidentally stomping on passersby. Obviously such activities did little to legitimize the Bolshevik project. They were dwarfish distortions of the perfect body of the state.

The failure to glorify the body, to verify actively its coherence and well-wrought form, was correctly regarded as a political affront, and although Zoshchenko issued numerous "proclamations" disavowing any ideological agenda behind his "little episodes,"[57] and though he kept his sights firmly fixed on such trifles as dissolving coat checks and rubber boots, nobody *really* felt that his little stories were innocuous. As some of Zoshchenko's contemporaries noted, "this very rejection of tendentiousness is itself tendentious."[58] A spate of articles began to appear with titles like "Whose Side Is Mikhail Zoshchenko On?"[59] The official literary paper published caricatures of Zoshchenko as a street vendor hawking the lifeless bodies of "respected citizens" priced by the kilo.[60] At the first Congress of Soviet Writers in 1934, one of the speakers opened with an anecdote involving the need to devise a particularly severe punishment, and the most merciless variant anybody could come up with was to send the offender to Zoshchenko for the latter to write a story about him.[61]

Soviet criticism dealt with Zoshchenko's venom by identifying an appropriate object for it: Zoshchenko's satire, it was said, was directed not at the Soviet system, not at the New Soviet Man, but at petit bourgeois and philistine survivals of the *old* regime.[62] If Zoshchenko was busily exposing enemies of socialism, he could even be co-opted for the Soviets' own purposes. After all, satire was useful and necessary in unmasking the enemies of the proletariat.[63] Still, it was noted uneasily in regard to Zoshchenko's satire, it would be nice to sense an unmistakable commitment to socialism behind his attack. There was a certain "indefiniteness" in his ideological foundations. Where exactly was the great revolutionary spirit of the epoch that should be discernible in every story, on every page?[64]

The Revolution and its glorious achievements are, as ever, imperceptible. The overarching meaning and movement of history are indiscernible. Noticeable—and adamantly noticed—are only isolated steps. This career of wholesale *recusatio*—the refusal to be and say what was mandated (Zoshchenko is "not a Communist," not Tolstoy, not Dostoevsky, not Gogol, not a novelist, and emphatically not a purveyor of large-scale "significant" events)—is, in fact, an act of insurrection on every count:

1. It rejects the regime's literary authority by parodying in a rich network of hidden allusions those classical exemplars it was exhorted to emulate.
2. It flatly defies the imperative to write on a grand scale.
3. It reveals under its microscope the small-scale but all-pervasive deficiencies in the system.
4. It adamantly asserts the real significance and centrality of these minor inconveniences in people's lives.
5. It trivializes matters officially accorded the highest respect by making them less noticeable than an overcoat or a stubbed toe.
6. It reveals in its insistent poetics of "perceptibility" the perversity of both the self-censorship born of adaptation and the artificially imposed boundaries of tellability.
7. It flouts authority per se by impudently rejecting the regime's determinations of what is important and what is not, transferring that power, in effect, to the *people* (the readers themselves).
8. And by problematizing the relationship of small to large, of part to whole, it glaringly fails to reveal the overall order and organization of contemporary reality, and thus refuses to glorify the larger project. On the contrary, it *undermines* any larger sense of coherence.[65]

To anatomize, to dissect the body of the state or of its citizens into parts that assume a magnitude and importance beyond their usual accessory function, is to break down the hierarchical logic that orders the world and subordinates low to high, insignificant to significant, margin to center. Zoshchenko's multitudinous feet, the product of his ongoing entrenchment below the established "x-enough" periphery, thus endanger not only standards of size, but also relations of order, the principles on which hierarchy conceptually depends.

Does hyperbolic attention to the very small *inherently* undermine the integrity of the larger picture? Voronskii had claimed, in bemoaning the work of the Fellow Travelers, that the enormity of the epoch demanded an elevated vantage point: you can't see the whole Revolution through a narrow chink in the fence.[66] Order is discernible only from what Morson has called an "absolute perspective."[67] Zoshchenko, gazing fixedly through his numerous little cracks in the fence, produced instead a lot of isolated scenes that do not add up to the "bright future" featured by the state. Chekhov, too, used the most infinitesimal "pinpricks" of experience to explode the sociocultural categories for assessing significance. Granted, both Chekhov and Zoshchenko had clearly iconoclastic motivations.

But even from the most pious of postures, the subversive potential of insignificant subject matter is considerable. The nineteenth-century Biedermeier ethic, for instance—espoused most famously by Adalbert Stifter—embraced subject matter of the smallest proportions, but justified its apparent violation of the threshold of tellability by invoking the principle of the macrocosm in the microcosm, the whole world in every grain of sand. Stifter claimed that his subject matter was not trivial at all, but simply a series of particulars viewed as representative of a totality, conforming to a greater order, and revealing the essential goodness of this organization. There is an implicit faith in the order of the universe and the "gentle law" that governs it. This universal harmony is meant to be *confirmed* at the level of the small particular.[68] In intention, anyway, the project is clearly very different from Zoshchenko's.

Despite all these reverent protestations about order and goodness, however, Stifter's microscopic world is frighteningly fragile.[69] It is perpetually threatened by destructive forces and destabilized by the crushing weight of the rampant details themselves, almost as if the scrutiny of too small an aspect of the order is more than the order can stand up to—much as holding up a magnifying glass to one small corner of a painting grossly distorts the surface and upsets the unity, rather than revealing at the level of the detail the artistry of the whole.[70]

The most minuscule "insignificant" subject matter, then, has the potential for tremendous power. A trivial detail can wield an authority of its own, not necessarily consistent with, and possibly hostile to, the ideology it may have even been intended to serve (at least until the full triumph of Communism, the "final synthesis," when the interests of the individual will coincide perfectly with the goals of the state, when any small corner of society will be a perfect mirror of the whole).[71]

Deconstructive criticism seizes precisely this explosive potential of the single, ostensibly peripheral detail to dismantle the superstructure of a text, to subvert its logic and abrogate its authority. Zoshchenko anticipates this poststructuralist insight in his reading of Soviet reality of the 1920s and the larger-than-life story that was told about it. By magnifying the marginalia that fall outside the purview of the big picture, he undermines the integrity of the official portrait, erases the center that gives it meaning, and fragments the desired Great Soviet Novel into a proliferation of tiny vignettes—not consecutive chapters—that are disorderly and indecorous, but eminently eventful, perceptible, tellable, and readable. They are also profoundly political, not only because by decree every literary act was a political gesture;[72] and not because, as Frederic Jameson would have it, "everything is 'in the last analysis' political";[73] but because at every level they implicitly undermine the very authority that would exclude them. "Not x enough" is "too x" in the extreme. Zoshchenko's proto-deconstructive project—to undercut the imposed hierarchy of significance and insignificance, to embarrass the logic of "too x" and "not x enough"—focuses precisely on the minuscule to destabilize the authorized version, dismantle its oppositions, and re-empower its readers.

FOUR

Nikolai Gogol: Distended Discourse and the Pragmatics of Elaboration

DOONESBURY copyright 1989 G. B. Trudeau. Reprinted with permission of UNIVERSAL PRESS SYNDICATE. All rights reserved.

Gogol Gabs

To get to the point: Gogol has a tendency to run on. Or, to put it more politely, Gogol exhibits an almost limitless capacity for elaboration. He seems unable to introduce even the most peripheral character without expatiating at length on his trousers, the material from which they were made, where that material was purchased, who is the richest man in that fabric-producing town, what kind of fence this affluent gentleman has built, who paints it, how regularly, whether oil-based paint is used, why or why not, and so on. He regales us with page-long catalogues of carriage types, veritable inventories of food and drink, and extended similes of unsurpassed extravagance.

Whatever the point is, Gogol is not one to get straight to it. His prose is grotesquely distended with digressions and details of no apparent relevance or significance to the story he purports to relate. Story line, point, and significance are all but lost in the limitless volubility of the discourse. If Ippolit Ippolitych articulates what everyone already knows, Gogol's narrators elaborate chiefly on what no one has any interest in finding out.

When, for instance, Gogol spends the entire first page of "The Story About How Ivan Ivanovich Quarreled with Ivan Nikiforovich" extolling the qualities of the (still-unintroduced) hero's marvelous coat, it is not because that much-touted garment will play the remotest role in the dramatic events to come.[1] Whereas Zoshchenko's eminently perceptible coat occupies center stage, Gogol's elaborately delineated wrap obstructs our view of the main events, delaying almost indefinitely the account of how one Ivan quarreled with another Ivan. Far from focal point, this coat is pure verbal obstacle.[2]

Similarly, when we are informed at length about the shoe fetish of an otherwise unknown lieutenant from Riazan'—"apparently a great lover of boots"—how he had, for some reason, ordered four new pairs and repeatedly tried on a fifth; how he examined in great detail the construction of that fine footwear, raising his leg again and again and again to inspect the shape of the beautifully built heel; how he kept approaching the bed to end his interminable strutting, to remove the boots and retire for the night, only to shun sleep once again and resume that absorbed contemplation of his feet . . . (6:153)—the real characters and plot of *Dead Souls* (1842) are fast asleep.[3] All action is suspended while something of unaccountable relevance is rehearsed in detail. Here, as elsewhere in Gogol, disquisitions on shoes are absurd rather than meaningful.[4] Thus, while in Zoshchenko's work the foot acquires significance from its textual role as the carrier of the narrative event, in Gogol's narrative it figures principally as a means to get "carried away," to digress from the linear path of the account. The police captain of Mirgorod, whose gait parallels his digressive speech patterns (he is constitutionally unable to get to the point), is propelled by a defiant left leg that keeps him from advancing purposefully and in a straight line (2:256); each time he tries to move forward, he (like the narration) "lurches off a long way in the opposite direction" (2:272). In Chekhov, this lack of control would likely provoke an immediate cautionary "You're losing the thread" ("Gooseberries"). But Gogol's narrators proceed unchecked.[5]

In other words, as I emphasized in the introduction, in contrast to the machinations of Chekhov and Zoshchenko, Gogol's most flagrant challenge to tellability occurs at the level of his *discourse* rather than in the event structure of his *stories*.[6] There is nothing trivial about losing a nose or perpetrating massive fraud throughout the countryside or succumbing tragically to an act of urban crime—as the title page of the next chapter makes grimly clear, this is precisely the stuff of headlines. But the profusion of apparently extraneous, insignificant detail and digression the reader must negotiate in order to follow Gogol's story is nearly prohibitive.

Thus it seems to me that Belinsky (along with those who have since echoed his assessment) misses the boat when he characterizes the substance of Gogol's plots as "simple" or "petty" occurrences and the "ordinariness of everyday life," especially given the extraordinary events of such works as "The Nose" (1836), "The Portrait" ("Portret," 1835; 1842), or the supernatural Dikan'ka stories (1831–32).[7] It is not that Gogol chooses such humdrum topics, but that he includes so much incidental material along the way. I would suggest that this imbalanced economy of detail is the real source of the myth that Gogol deals in only the most ordinary incidents. Often cited in support of Belinsky's view is Gogol's own claim that the greatest artistry consists in making the "usual" (*obyknovennoe*) "unusual" (*neobyknovennoe*). We must remember, though, that Gogol is applauding Pushkin in these remarks, not himself.[8] Gogol's trademark is not the *meloch' i ogranichennost'* (triviality and limitedness) of his material,[9] but rather the limitlessness of his trivial detail.

This observation about boundless detail is hardly new—it reflects what we have come to recognize as Gogol's style. And ever since the first reviewers of *Dead Souls* derided Gogol for his compulsive stockpiling of things and his equally pathological deployment of irrelevant detail about them,[10] critics have had to contend with this stylistic peculiarity in one way or another. The morass of minutiae has been read variously as Gogol's commitment to "naturalistic" representation, as a clever way of including "all of Russia," as a rich source of humor, as an artifact of an earlier attraction to the fantastic, as a network of symbols pointing to something greater, as a general celebration of "plenitude," as an exhaustive catalogue of human vices, as a ruse to distract the czarist censors from his searing social commentary, as evidence of a propensity for the carnivalistic, as a reflection of widespread linguistic upheaval, or as plain old stylistic excess.[11] Whatever explanation or complaint it has occasioned, Gogol's gift of gab has rarely gone unnoticed.

It is the task of these next two chapters to consider both Gogol's verbal extravaganzas themselves and the reader's urge to account for them, to identify what makes all this apparently gratuitous and unconnected data worth telling and, more to the point, worth reading. I will examine, in other words, both the confounding and the sense-making operations involved in the interaction between Gogolian text and reader.

Readers React

Robert Maguire has commented that recent scholarship seems to follow one of two general critical tendencies to contend with Gogol's characteristic excesses.[12] The first, to which Maguire himself subscribes, views each detail, no matter how petty, as inherently meaningful. Although Gogol's fervor for "data" is seldom regarded as an index of his realism anymore,[13] his energetic invocation of things and names for things, according to this first point of view, establishes each one "as a solid and unforgettable presence" and conditions us to "assume that any detail, however small, is potentially important." The now famous detail of the bronze pin from Tula (6:7), for instance, teaches us "that we must sharpen our eyes lest we miss important clues."[14] Reading Gogol, then, becomes a challenge to interpret these abundant "clues," to discern the order and logic in the apparent untidiness, to urge the text to reveal its "secrets."[15]

Hence many of the ingenious sense-making ventures of current Gogol criticism; hence Carl Proffer's contention that the apparently gratuitous detail of Gogol's similes is actually scrupulously selected and exceedingly pertinent; hence James Woodward's insistence on the absolute expressiveness of each element and the coherence of the whole; hence, also, while very different in approach, Daniel Rancour-Laferriere's psychoanalytic attributions.[16] For the orthodox Freudian there are no accidents and no superfluous details.[17] As Michel Foucault comments in reference to narrative specificity and another kind of orthodoxy, "for the true believer no detail is unimportant."[18] It must be seen precisely as a testimony of faith when Setchkarev declares, in awestruck wonder, that in Gogol, "every little episode, every descriptive stroke, every ever-so-tiny detail has a critical significance for the work as a whole."[19]

But, as Naomi Schor points out, to read in detail in this way is, "however tacitly, to invest the detail with a truth-bearing function, and yet . . . the truth value of the detail is anything but assured."[20] Or, leaving "truth" aside, we might say that the "significance" or even the "substance" of the details—the "solidity" and "presence" averred by Maguire and others—is anything but assured. If we persist in "sharpening our eyes" on every Gogolian bronze pin that appears only to disappear, we are likely to go blind. Thus, proponents of the *second* inclination, who might criticize the first as a kind of "semiotic totalitarianism,"[21] take the opposite tack. Rather than parsing for hidden meaning, these critics hesitate to interpret the verbal clutter, even allowing the details to stand as rampant signifiers whose exuberance is quite independent of their well-bracketed signifieds.[22]

Donald Fanger, for instance, has posited a "verbal counterreality" that occasions not exegetical engagement, but rather delight in the performance.[23] For Victor Erlich, "language is the only active protagonist" in the Gogolian oeuvre.[24] Sergei Bocharov, too, has pointed to Gogolian "expression without corresponding content," like the many items featured on Soviet menus that were inevitably unavailable.[25] A. P. Chudakov as well insists on the radical unmotivatedness of so much of Gogol's material by pointing to the innumerable things that get crowded into the *fabula* with only the flimsiest connection to the story.[26] But even more extreme, he contends, is the swelling of the *discourse*, most notably in Gogol's famous extended similes. Chudakov compares the path of Gogol's prose to the trajectory of a multistage rocket ship, hurtling ever farther from the center of gravity—the story—and becoming progressively lighter as it discharges each verbal stage. He cites the fabulous example of Chichikov's approach to the Sobakevich estate, identifying numerically each successive stage of remoteness from the original object that prompted the comparison:

As he drove up to the front porch he noticed two faces that peeped out the window at almost the same time: a female one in a house cap, long and narrow like a cucumber, and a male one, round and broad like (1) Moldavian pumpkins, (2) known as "calabashes," (3) which in Russia are made into balalaikas, (4) two-stringed, light balalaikas, the pride and joy of (5) the spirited twenty-year-old lad, (6) a flirt and a dandy, winking and whistling at (8) the white-bosomed and white-necked (7) maidens who (9) gather around to listen to (10) his soft strumming. (6:94)

The pumpkins, Chudakov remarks, which have themselves only been called up as a term of comparison, take on a life of their own, metamorphosing into a balalaika, which in turn prompts all sorts of information, first about its construction, then about who plays such instruments, namely the foppish youth, who then acquires multiple characteristics and eventually even an entourage of admiring young lasses with specifications of their own. Chichikov, like the earth the rocket has left behind, has utterly disappeared from view; the descriptive detail we have been treated to has nothing to tell us about his activities or even his perceptions.[27] And the face that launched the thousand details (and the rocket) has long since vanished from the window and from our minds. "No sooner had the two faces peeped out than they disappeared," the text itself reports, as if commenting on its own discursive procedure.

Potebnia had conjectured that this diversion of our attention from the "main thing" has an important *calming* effect, since the main thing is a fairly harrowing story.[28] Bely, too, suggested that the digressions provide a welcome "lyrical relief."[29] Chudakov restores some of the tension of the digressive trajectory, but suggests that this joyride on the rocket ship is intensely pleasurable; this aspect of Gogol's narration "excites in the reader an especially burning and irresistible fascination."[30] Fanger, too, regards the flights of verbal prodigality as "occasions of delight,"[31] as sorties into pure pleasure.

But is all this enforced detouring really so inherently pleasurable? How diverting is all this diversion? From the terms of their descriptions, both the semiotic "totalitarians" and "anarchists" seem to consider Gogolian prose great fun. In fact, in a recent informal survey in which Slavists were asked to complete the sentence "It is [blank] to read Gogol," all but one responded that "it is FUN to read Gogol." The exception, on the other hand, who requested with some urgency that he/she remain anonymous, responded, "It is [audible sigh] *necessary* to read Gogol." I suspect this is less a matter of liking or not liking Gogol than of learning how to like him. Slonimskii's documentation of Gogol's funniness notwithstanding, the "fun" answer is now so axiomatic that it sounds suspiciously like a learned response. Mirsky, that inveterate purveyor of axioms, affirms that "fun" is what has attracted readers to Gogol "above all," fun which is "simple and unadulterated."[32]

But untutored reactions to Gogol have been less than unanimous on this point.

Among Gogol's contemporaries, for example, the consensus was considerably less overwhelming: the extended similes that were praised by Aksakov horrified Senkovskii,[33] and while Belinsky rejoiced in the expansiveness of the procedure and its potential to provide extensive information, Masal'skii found the detail extraneous and irritating. Zhukovskii called the experience of the Gogolian text *both* "fun" and "painful" (*zabavno i bol'no*).[34] Earlier in this century, I. Mandel'shtam, too, complained of the "prolixity, irrelevancy, and distraction" of the ubiquitous and endless similes.[35] And though Proffer found the apparent obscurity of the simile material hilarious, Bely maintained that he failed to understand what was so funny.[36] Now, in our apparent unanimity on the joys of reading Gogol, we may have become one of Fish's "interpretive communities" with shared explanations, institutionalized procedures, several "usual and customary" ways of characterizing Gogol's excesses that render them tolerable and even self-evident.[37] Iu. Mann notes (with some amusement at the earlier misunderstanding) that many of the excesses we now cite as proof of Gogol's genius were originally adduced with a "minus sign."[38] We might profitably consider our own reversal of that valence.

Perhaps we should try to reconstruct the greatest challenge in reading Gogol, whether we choose to decipher him or not, namely, to keep reading. It is frustrating to read Gogol. It is annoying to be perpetually derailed by diversions of no apparent significance. And if we read the opening of "The Overcoat" with no sense of impatience and only a knowing smile at the characteristically Gogolian digression when we are left in the lurch after the first two words (*V departamente* [In a certain department], 3:141), if our immense erudition obscures that disorientation, then we have lost something to the distortion of *Nachträglichkeit*;[39] we have impoverished the experience of reading Gogol. I am not suggesting that we necessarily read Gogol for the plot, but only that we should not lose sight of the sensation of being *unable* to do so, of being thwarted by the digressions, by the endless elaboration, by the exhaustiveness which is, after all, exhausting, by a narrative syntax that exhibits about as much connectivity as the items on Ivan Nikiforovich's clothesline or the objects ("whatever comes into anyone's head" [2:244]) hung out to dry on the incomparable Mirgorod fences.[40] Plot is an issue not only for pulp fiction ("why we read *Jaws*, but not Henry James"); it is "the principle of interconnectedness and intention which we cannot do without in moving through the discrete elements . . . of narrative."[41] Charles Bernheimer suggests that Gogol's prose challenges this by celebrating literature's prerogative to be discontinuous;[42] but what about the reader's prerogative to discontinue, to throw the thing over in despair?

Barthes, in discussing the very issue of textual pleasure, posits two kinds of reading, a directed one that goes straight to the point (to the *story*), and another that revels in the *discourse*. The first, hungry for answers, says Barthes (in terms singularly appropriate to Gogol), devours; the second is content to graze.[43] Gogol himself attributed his critics' inability to appreciate *Dead Souls* to their greediness for plot, the rapidity and avidity of their reading—their essentially consumerist mentality.[44] The alternative, non-directed mode of reading is suggested by his portrayals of Chichikov's man, Petrushka, who reads "without troubling too much about content" (6:20), enjoying the phenomenon of reading itself; of Chichikov, who indulges in a thorough perusal of random notices, the contents of which have nothing relevant or significant to offer (6:12); of Shpon'ka, whose fortune-telling book does little to elucidate his puzzling dream, but who contemplates it "just as a clerk reads a directory of addresses with great delight several times a day with no ulterior motive, but enormously entertained by the printed roster of names" (1:289).

Even a directory, the telephone book par excellence, the epitome of plotless prose, it seems, can occasion prodigious amounts of pleasure.[45] Surely this grazing, this reading "without ulterior motive," is in some measure the only hope of negotiating the trivia-laden Gogolian text. But even Gogol cannot quite recommend it with a straight face, and perhaps the consummate inscription of this Kantian *ästhetische Anschauung*, this placid "aesthetic contemplation" *ohne alles Interesse* (without any vested interest), is the image of the spectator on Ivan Nikiforovich's porch who stands by, tranquilly picking his nose (2:238).[46]

Thus, when Ivan Ivanovich exhibits an urgent "inquisitiveness" to match his acquisitiveness ("God forbid you should start to tell him about something and not finish the story!" [*da ne doskazhesh'*; 2:227]), and when his heart throbs with impatience at the police captain's digressions and slowness to "come to the point" (2:257), we cannot help but sympathize.

For while narrative, as Barthes reminds us, is by nature dilatory (contriving to keep the enigma open in spite of the reader's craving for closure); and while it never takes the shortest, most direct route between point A and point B (plot being "a kind of arabesque or squiggle toward the end"); still, that detour is "irritation," or, as Peter Brooks claims, a state of appetite and arousal that is tolerable only because it looks forward to its satisfaction.[47] "We are all like Scheherazade's husband," E. M. Forster concedes. We submit to narrative proliferation primarily because of our primitive, atavistic drive to find out "what happens next."[48] And while we can tolerate a certain amount of delay in having our curiosity satisfied, and while deferred gratification has its own rewards, our desires—for sense, for significance, for plot, for end—reassert themselves persistently. Narratives, Brooks tells us, are doubly inhabited by desire: they both tell of desire—for a new coat, or a neighbor's gun, for a lost nose, or a roster of dead serfs—and they "arouse and make use of desire as a dynamic of signification."[49] They excite what Barthes refers to as a reader's "passion for meaning."[50] Gogol, however, goes to well-documented lengths to frustrate the requiting of our passion for sense, signification, and relevance by perpetually derailing us with wildly irrelevant elaboration.

Nevertheless, it is not clear that we read Gogol more sensibly by renouncing our desire for what he dangles provocatively beyond our reach. In other words, while I concur absolutely with those critics who refuse to posit a hidden meaning everywhere in Gogol's clutter, I would defend at the same time the other camp's passion for relevance. Can we really read "without ulterior motive?" Can we really achieve the equanimity of Gogol's idle nosepicker?

The fact is, we crave a degree of organization and structure in our lives and above all in our texts. Indeed, comments Morson, "a large part of the pleasure of reading literature derives from the identification of that structure";[51] we strive to uncover the configuring principle that establishes the relevance of each element of material, thereby making it *tellable* rather than gratuitous. What has kept readers of Gogol reading when, like Maguire's first camp, they crave discernible significance but, like the proponents of camp number two, find that it is not necessarily forthcoming is a readiness to structure and account for the discursive excess *themselves*. In what follows, I will consider what makes Gogol's verbal morass problematic and what kinds of reading strategies make it tolerable. I will ask both how the text motivates its abundant material and how readers' moves—my own included—are attempts to motivate it retrospectively.

"Historical" Accounting: Ulterior Motives / A Posteriori Motivations

Gogol's Own Purposes

One temptation is to locate a source of significance and coherence in Gogol's own professed motivations for writing the way he did. This promising resource must be abandoned, however, for Gogol's many pronouncements on the subject of superabundant detail are wildly inconsistent. On the one hand, he denounced Dostoevsky's unbearable "verbosity" in *Poor Folk* and preached that, though much can be spoken, "only what is necessary should be written down—this is the source of significance in literature."[52] On the other hand, he announced with pride his determination to consider "all the most prosaic rubbish, . . . every shred of material down to the smallest pin that surrounds a person every day . . . , everything from the tiniest thing to the largest, omitting nothing."[53] On the one hand, Gogol warned that the epic inclination to "go into particulars," to attempt "to grasp and encompass much," almost invariably produces a work of lesser significance (8:478). On the other hand, while pathologically concerned with the significance of his own undertaking,[54] he himself was unsurpassed as a creator of Homeric similes of the most unwieldy proportions, locutions that seem to attempt to "grasp and encompass" *everything*. In his own handbook on literature, Gogol elaborates a code of relevance as stringent as that of Chekhov's gun that must be fired if it is to be mentioned at all. In the novel, Gogol explains, any person, place, or thing that enters the text must be integrally related to the fate of the hero. There is no room for "just anything that happens to fly by"— any *proletaiushchikh mimo iavlenii* are strictly prohibited (8:481). We can only surmise that the anomalous generic designation of the "epic" *Dead Souls*, a work that explicitly embraces all the "rubbish and nonsense that flies by on all sides" (6:21), exempts it from these strictures. And even while celebrating the fact that "all of Russia" will go into his *poema*, Gogol privately regards his text in progress (in the part of the letter less often cited) as a "jumbled heap!"[55]

In the very act of praising Pushkin's ability to render perfectly in a few deft strokes what it might take someone of lesser talent whole paragraphs to convey ("laconism," he declares, "is pure poetry"), Gogol summarily betrays his own stated ideal. While paying apparent tribute to this laudable spareness in the title of his remarks ("Neskol'ko slov" ["A Few Words"]), Gogol celebrates the economy of Pushkin's prose, the refreshing absence of "that cascade of eloquence that fascinates only by its verbosity" in the most cascading verbal outbursts of his own: Pushkin's simplicity and clarity, for instance, reflect nature, "as vividly as the stream of some silver river, in which suddenly and brilliantly there appear flashes of dazzling shoulders, or white hands, or an alabaster neck, on which dark curls play, loosened by the night, or translucent grapes of the vine, or myrtles and a canopy of trees that have been created for life" (8:54–55). Clearly Gogol's programmatic statements do little to constrict his own prodigality.

If anything, his remarks—like his fiction—are a provocation. This is nowhere more apparent than in *Arabesques* (*Arabeski*, 1835), the miscellany whose very name implies the baroque and fanciful, referring explicitly to Schlegel's Romantic conception of prose as squiggle. It is in this collection, interestingly, that we find Gogol's lavish praise of Pushkin's spareness, selectivity, and precision. Yet his own volume was composed by cleaning out his desk, he writes to Pogodin (8:748); instead of consigning old scraps to the trash, he has them typeset.[56] In the preface he refers to his own failure to select, his decision to indulge in absolute inclusiveness—his "finders keepers" mentality. His disclaimer cites an unspecified "inability" to exercise care in composition, to eliminate substandard work, to edit, to refine (8:7). We are to get it all, without regard to relevance, connectivity, or quality. He disavows, in effect, all standards of any kind.

We need not take Gogol seriously about his mode of compilation, which is probably as much persona-construction as anything else.[57] What is of interest here is the invocation of the hoarding instinct (which I will cite in Chapter 5 as a kind of motivating fiction for the indiscriminate accumulation of material) and the awareness of the burden of arrangement, selection, and sense-making this shifts to the *publika* (which threatens, as a result, to dwindle to single digits).[58] But the apologetic tone could not be less disingenuous. The assumption of this kind of editorial policy is more of an affront.

Gogol and the Tradition

If Gogol is less than absolutely serious about exonerating himself for his dereliction of editorial duty, literary precedent, too, offers little to extenuate his discursive transgressions. Certainly as much as he admired Pushkin, Gogol did anything but follow the example set by his most illustrious predecessor. Occupying opposite ends of the spectrum in terms of economy of presentation, Pushkin and Gogol have come, in fact, to define opposing paradigms for the tradition. Mirsky celebrates both "great" but antithetical styles of Russian literature, contrasting Gogol's "rhetorical, swollen" discourse with the austerity of Pushkin's "terse, precise, economical" prose, "pruned of all irrelevant ornament."[59] Others have been more openly partisan. Leont'ev bewailed what he saw as Tolstoy's affinity with Gogol, noting with regret that Pushkin's *kratkost'* and *prostota* (brevity and simplicity) would have embodied Tolstoy's great themes much more effectively.[60] Zoshchenko follows suit in the introduction to his "Sixth Tale of Belkin," extolling the line of development initiated by Pushkin and bemoaning the sloppier departures from that trajectory.[61] In accordance with this imaginative division of the tradition, Rozanov takes issue with Dostoevsky's apocryphal but universally cited observation that all subsequent Russian literature had emerged from Gogol's overcoat; Rozanov reminds us that much of Russian literature reflects an anti-Gogolian urge rather than a continuation of his discursive excesses.[62] Gorky seems to concur: "Beginning with Pushkin," he claimed, "our great writers have extracted from the verbal chaos only the most exact, clear, weighty word."[63] We can only surmise that he was mentally excluding Gogol, for, as Proffer succinctly sums it up, "where Pushkin pruned, Gogol fertilized."[64]

But if Gogol differentiated himself radically from the Russian national poet, situating himself squarely across the stylistic table, he was hardly the first writer ever to revel in descriptive plenitude. The compulsive cataloguing of many things in his prose constitutes, like his generous use of the Homeric simile, a powerful evocation of the classical epic tradition (particularly in the context of *Dead Souls*, his own self-styled epic). If this is a ploy by Gogol to magnify his own project by association with classical masterpieces, it might help explain his deployment of detail. Gogolian excess recalls as well Rabelais's celebration of superabundance, the Renaissance humorist's spirit of "more is more," and more is more fun. Gogol's own comic aspirations suggest this as another possible incentive for his extravagance. Or perhaps Gogol sought, like Laurence Sterne, to demonstrate his authorial virtuosity by embracing digression as a kind of stylistic virtue.[65]

Perhaps most strikingly, though, Gogol's generous use of detail evokes the European realist commitment to circumstantiality, the imperative inclusion of things in the text simply because they were there. This impulse to recreate the real, or to achieve the "effect of the real" by invoking many objects, lent a certain weight and credibility to the nineteenth-century text, just as the encyclopedic prose of the eighteenth-century novelists had celebrated the very possibility of knowledge about the world and the communicability of that knowledge.[66] In Defoe's exhaustive list of Robinson Crusoe's possessions, the "circumstantial realism, elaborate detail, careful enumeration" are all "island substitutes" for mastery—of world, of material, of a situation (shipwreck) that represents a loss of control.[67]

But while Gogol's strategy may recall Defoe's hoarding instinct, it does not reproduce its effect. The Gogolian explosion of words and things, as we will see, does little to authenticate and less to inspire authority, suggesting, if anything, a rather serious lack of control. While the narrative showcasing of apparently insignificant details has its source in the rhetorical genre of the "epideictic" ("discourse for pomp or show, the set-piece to inspire admiration for the orator"[68]), Gogol's verbal embroidery seems more destined, if not calculated, to raise a few doubts about the orator's mastery. In the seventeenth and eighteenth centuries, digression may have been enlisted to establish authority (by demonstrating the speaker's ability to elaborate knowledgeably on this or that subject), but Gogol's lengthy asides on "a certain department" can only be seen as a travesty of this credential building.[69]

Interestingly, Gogol exhibits a keen awareness of his own authorial malfeasance in these matters. In a letter to M. P. Balabina bearing the title "Journey from Lausanne to Vevey," for instance, Gogol devotes a full page to the meal he had before his departure, dwells interminably on the most absurd details associated only by contiguity to the announced topic, and then, declining to describe the passage itself, since "the road from Faucon to the post station is completely well known to you," proceeds directly to the subtleties of disembarkation. The mockery of his own narrative idiosyncrasies and the problems they present is unmistakable:

> But to your very great regret (because I know you love details) I don't remember which spoke of the wheel I stepped onto with my foot—the third or the fourth. If I recall all of the circumstances well, I think it was the third; but again, if I examine it from another angle, it seems to have been the fourth. However, I advise you to send for the conductor immediately, right now; he surely should know—and the sooner the better, because once he gets a good night's sleep he'll forget.

Everything else that happened, Gogol concludes, was not worth mentioning.[70] Hardly calculated to demonstrate authority, this passage about a passage makes fun of the ability to command or communicate knowledge; it lampoons exhaustiveness, plays with conventions of inclusion and exclusion, and forces the already vexed issue of what's worth telling. It also confounds fairly explicitly, as his fiction does throughout, the attempt to read Gogol into a tradition of information-laden prose.

This distinguishes Gogol from his contemporaries in Russia, whose lavish use of minute detail was precisely freighted. In the transitional years between the end of the neo-classical tradition and the appearance of the great works of Russian realism later in the century, under the influence of Balzac in particular, some Russian writers had begun to experiment with more microscopic units of material. Aspiring realists wrote detailed "physiologies" of urban life, and practitioners of the "society tale" succumbed to a veritable mania for *les petits faits*—for infinitesimal detail and barely perceptible inner events. But again, the

Gogol: The Pragmatics of Elaboration 139

primary concern of these writers in increasing the amount of detail was to augment the verisimilitude of their representation, to approximate the "really real," most particularly in the world of domestic, everyday life.[71] Although Gogol's ubiquitous dinner menus are undeniably domestic, their value as an index of the real is dubious.[72] Nor does Gogol's scrutiny have the same analytic pretensions of disclosing psychological motivations or other intimate secrets of the heart. Gogol's deployment of detail is unconstrained by such commissions.

It was this flagrant gratuitousness that unnerved Gogol's earliest readers, and even those reviews that celebrated the "amazing verisimilitude" and the "liveliness" of the material demanded, uneasily, "What is the purpose?" "Why paint this picture," they wondered again and again, "to no purpose at all?"[73] Some critics have found, to their satisfaction, that Gogol's enumeration of many things "helps in the achievement of truthfulness." The hyperbolic inclusiveness does indeed "serve a purpose," one not alien to realism.[74] Alternatively, the many things enumerated may be read as attributes of the characters: they testify to the "moral and mental characteristics" of their owners.[75] But in Gogol things do not always enjoy such a functional relationship to their bearers, and, more often than not, the things have no "bearers" at all.

Still, the inclination to see Gogol's distended discourse as somehow purposeful, as something that, in one way or another, "goes to show," has been a persistent one. The long-lasting identification of Gogol as a realist, an earnest purveyor of social facts, is eloquent testimony to this urge. He had, after all, undertaken to fill his works with "data," and full they were. There remained some disagreement about the accuracy of Gogol's details, but despite these differences of opinion, and despite the frequent intrusion of the supernatural into Gogol's fictional world, the fundamental assumption that Gogol's works were mimetic and at least *sought* to reflect reality went essentially unchallenged by critics for the first 30 years (1830–60).[76]

Not surprisingly, Gogol resisted this stubborn association of his work with the naturalist school. More curious is that he should disavow the connection on the grounds of the latter's "superfluity, verbosity, and lack of simplicity in style,"[77] considering both his own expansiveness and his cavalier attitude toward it. Plainly, if we seek Gogol's purpose in forsaking the compactness (*kratkost'*) of Pushkin and adopting instead the hoarding instinct of Robinson Crusoe while nevertheless scorning Defoe's stern management, placid proctorship, and composure, Gogol's equivocation and obfuscation on the subject do little to sort out the "jumbled heap." Equally unsatisfying are the attempts to account for Gogol's eccentric prose by recourse to literary-historical precedent. No wonder we retreat to the self-congratulatory recognitions of erudition ("ah, how Gogolian!") or cling to the conviction that such loopdy-loops are fun.

If we cannot reliably identify the reasons behind this stylistic idiosyncrasy, we can at least examine its effects. Perhaps Maguire is right: Gogol's explosionary tactics force us to read like the adherents of one of the two camps he identifies—either ingeniously (collecting the disparate and explaining the inexplicable) or permissively (reveling in the bedlam without undue impatience). But even the most tolerant readers have purposes, if only their own desire to read "pleasurably and profitably."[78] Aren't most readings of Gogol in fact largely attempts by readers to make the problematic tolerable (and with luck even pleasurable), to account to their own satisfaction for the discursive overload, to motivate it for themselves, if not in literary-historical terms, then on more text-internal grounds? For whatever *Gogol's* purposes were for writing the way he did, readers do have an ulterior motive of their own, a vested interest in remaining interested and ensuring that the reading process is worth the effort.

One strategy for accommodating the barrage of detail has been the alibi, the recourse to the special "circumstances" of the work's context to identify the relevance of the irrelevant, to make the insignificant signify. Gogol's first major work inspired particularly imaginative explanations. (Maybe the "fun" it occasioned was not nearly as "pure and unadulterated" as Mirsky would like to believe.)

Alibis: The Specifics of Dikan'ka

"I must remind you again that our conversations are never about trifles," reports Rudyi Pan'ko, narrator-in-chief of Gogol's *Evenings on a Farm Near Dikan'ka*.[79] And yet this "reminder" introduces one more of his numerous parenthetical excursuses, this time informing us of his own preference for "decent conversations" before proceeding to the conversation he purports to recount: apple pickling is the issue, and with his usual reluctance to omit anything that might prove to be of significance (after all, Dikan'ka conversations are "never about trifles"), Pan'ko dutifully reports in full all techniques suggested, with an appropriate measure of editorial indignation at "inferior" methods.

In short, Rudyi Pan'ko's claim is a remarkable one, for it is difficult to imagine more trivial concerns than those discussed at length by the residents of Dikan'ka. At least we feel we can pin the responsibility for the interminable chatter on the undiscerning townsfolk. But the citizenry is not alone in expatiating indefinitely on such weighty matters as the protocol of melon eating; the dauntless narrators, too, insist on squandering their verbal energies in detailed descriptions of such gastronomical "events" (from the careful cleaning of the fruit, to the holes poked in the rind by eager fingers, to the sucking of the juice, the cutting of smaller pieces, and the popping of the pieces into awaiting mouths ["The Enchanted Place," 1:310–11]). The narration is as distended with trivia as the local conversations are. It presents a discourse glutted with things, with names of things, and with details about them. What is the significance of all this insignificance?

What is the reader to make, for instance, of the paragraph after paragraph of immaterial facts about Stepan Ivanovich, a minor figure who plays no role in the plot? Is the rash of "information"—about where he lives, where he shops, what he buys, whom he chats with while shopping, what he usually wears to market, and so forth— informative, or even tellable within the given context ("Shpon'ka," 1:284)? Or does it shed any light on the incident Pan'ko is ostensibly "narrating" (i.e., Foma Grigor'evich preparing to tell a story) to qualify what begins as a valid plot element—"Foma Grigor'evich . . . handed me the book"—with a superfluous explanation: he did so because his glasses were broken; he had unfortunately forgotten to repair them; his usual method of repair (obviously not forgotten enough to escape mention) is to tie them with string and secure them with wax ("Saint John's Eve," 1:137)? If we are moved to shake our heads it is more likely to lament Rudyi Pan'ko's loquaciousness than to bewail either Foma Grigor'evich's myopia or his forgetfulness.

Thus, the Dikan'ka cycle, with the quirky Rudyi Pan'ko at the helm, offers the possibility of glossing some of the verbal clutter as characterization of the narrator who sees fit to include it, and readers have hastened to seize upon this explanation. But Pan'ko is only the *frame* narrator of the Dikan'ka tales (the actual stories are "told" by others). More importantly, the colorful Pan'ko owes his very existence to an afterthought on the part of Gogol's editor, who obviously felt the need, like many readers, to motivate the disproportionate gab retroactively.[80] Rudyi Pan'ko is a consequence of Gogolian discourse, not its source. Gogol himself does not typically provide perceiving characters to motivate the unwieldy descriptions and digressions;[81] the Mirgorod and Petersburg stories sport a discourse every bit as swollen as Pan'ko's without any developed narrative persona. Characterization, then, cannot finally account for or justify the extreme accretion of nonsignificant detail. Bernheimer even refers to the "absent sender,"[82] a ventriloquistic free play that makes the elaborate detours as mysterious in origin as they are in destination.

An alternative "explanation" has been found in the folkloric affinities of the Dikan'ka cycle. Rich in Ukrainian folklore and folk motifs, the stories *are* consciously presented as extravaganzas of "local color" in contrast to the highfalutin cultural artifacts of the "great world" (*bol'shoi svet* [1:103]), in which, Pan'ko tells us, he wouldn't dare show his face. Mukařovský argues that it is really only in products of "high art" ("artificial poetry") that strict relevance is expected, that every detail is assumed to be "significant." Folk art, on the contrary, consists of more loosely connected elements that enter the text irrespective of their significance for the work as a "whole."[83] Ukrainian popular tradition in particular, N. A. Polevoi declared, is notoriously disinclined to differentiate significant from insignificant material.[84] Indeed, *Evenings* was initially dismissed as "too Ukrainian"; but many of the grounds for this objection remained long after Gogol moved his cast out of Ukraine to provincial Russia and even to the capital city itself. The prodigality in telling persists far beyond the borders of "Little Russia."[85]

The verbal exuberance in the Dikan'ka stories can alternatively be seen as representational—motivated by the very situations on display. Many of the Dikan'ka tales ("The Fair at Sorochintsy," "Saint John's Eve," "Christmas Eve," "The Enchanted Place") revolve around fairs, enchanted places, and enchanted times—*topoi* of life wrenched from its routine order and plunged into the eccentricity and "merry relativity" associated with the carnival tradition.[86] Decorum is suspended, hierarchies of importance are abrogated, and structures collapse. Thus, when Gogol explodes conventional syntax by opting for lengthy lists of the myriad things at a fair, or affixes a medley of predicates to each of these objects, his overzealousness is in effect mimetic: it reproduces the chaos of things in the "whirlwind of the village fair,"

> when all the people merge into a single enormous monster and move as one huge body onto the square and along the narrow streets, shouting, laughing, thundering. Noise, swearing, bellowing, bleating, roaring—everything blends together into a piercing clamor. Oxen, sacks, hay, gypsies, pots, peasant women, gingerbread, hats—everything is bright, colorful, clashing; it piles up in heaps and flies around before your eyes. Discordant voices drown one another out, and not a single word can be caught, can be saved from the deluge; not one cry can be distinguished clearly. (1:115)

It is this world of the carnival that Bakhtin argues is at the basis of Gogol's early stories and that inevitably infects the style, not only lifting Gogol's own injunction against *proletaiushchikh mimo iavlenii* (whatever flies by), but also making more demure description inappropriate.[87]

In the portrayal of dancing, laughing, drinking, carousing, and celebrating, the prose mimics the characters' intoxication.

Even without the rationale of carnivalization, however, Gogol's texts unloose a plethora of words to evoke a plethora of things. The artist's dismal room in the later "Nevskii Prospekt" (1835) contains "all kinds of artistic nonsense," and the many things, as disconnected as folk motifs and as topsy-turvy as "carnival," are enumerated every bit as expansively (3:17). Even the tomb-like Pliushkin mansion, as far as imaginable from the revelry of the carnival square, is besieged by things whose disorder is complete and whose dominion is uncontested. There, cotton-wool quilting "crawls" out of Pliushkin's gown; bits, scraps, objects, mounds, and piles accumulate, lean, lie, cover, hang, dry out, and acquire bewildering shapes obscured by dust (6:115–17), and, again, the narrator undertakes to reproduce the jumbled heap word for thing.

If Pliushkin didn't exist (so to speak), Gogol would have had to invent him. Collectors such as this notorious Gogolian pack rat serve the writer well as a motivating device, as a hook on which to hang the many things he loves to list, and a node of relevance for the reader who is more disposed to plow through an interminable list if it is attached to a "he had"—if, in other words, it is earmarked as personal inventory rather than just random or even associative proliferation. In fact, had Gogol not invented Pliushkin, no doubt his readers would have. Though such alibis ultimately fall short, the numerous explanations readers have advanced to make the verbal proliferation comprehensible or even necessary testify to the strength of their desire to identify the significance of the material they wade through.

Theoretical Considerations

What *do* readers want? And what gets in their way? Why, theoretically speaking, should a richly detailed discourse necessitate such readerly ingenuity or permissiveness, either sending us into interpretive contortions or forcing us to capitulate? What do we need to make reading "worth it," pleasurable, or, as the operative expression has it, "fun"? My goal here is not to elaborate a theory of reading or to establish universals, but rather only to consider the conditions that make reading Gogol problematic and, in the process, to outline the terms and distinctions that will become important in Chapter 5.

Desire: "Readers Just Wanna Have Fun"

Much has already been made of the role of desire in narrative. And whether the object of that desire is "just" fun (or pleasure, or satisfaction) or something more specific that the text ought to "provide," I would contend that such vested interest is neither venal nor lowbrow. It is an integral part of the reading process. And it is especially germane to the project of reading Gogol—not only because the text so systematically derails all attempts to read directedly, toward some goal, some "object," but also because, as I will point out in the next chapter, the text's own generative strategies encode human appetites and inscribe various forms of desire.

Peter Brooks, in his provocative study of desire and narrative, begins where Gogol does: by recognizing a human *need* to tell (and be told) and, thus, a desire to do so.[88] This compulsion to tell, with its correspondingly urgent desire to hear, is, as the narrator of *Dead Souls* tells us (just as urgently) an invariable trait of "mortals": "No matter how stupid a piece of news is, as long as it is news, the mortal will without fail communicate it to another mortal" (6:173). Hence the avidity of the lady (agreeable in all respects), who needs to travel what seems an interminable distance to impart her news and the reciprocal eagerness of her counterpart (slightly less agreeable, but no less eager) to *get* the story (6:178); hence the urgent proliferation of stories about the enigmatic Chichikov and the equally insatiable desire of the townsfolk to *get* the truth; hence, as I have mentioned, the impatience of Ivan Ivanovich when faced with the unrestrained digressions of the police chief. Hence, also, the desire readers bring to Gogol's text and the frustration they experience in the face of his proliferative prose. For even if Lacan has overstated the case when he claims that "texts have in them that which we most *want*, that which we desire and are in need of,"[89] surely we read for something. What do we want? And do Gogol's texts provide it?

Certainly we do not typically read literary narrative for assertible *information* in the way that we may pick up an instruction manual, a textbook, or a newspaper. But we do seek the *sense* that makes the material tellable. The significant "information" that a literary text provides is whatever contributes to that sense-making project. Brooks, as we have seen, equates the sense-making urgency of reading narrative with the endeavor to follow the plot, the desire to move "from beginning to end in a significant way." Plot, and the corresponding inclination to proceed along its trajectory, satisfies a basic human longing for progression forward—through life, through time, through text. In this sense, reading is goal oriented and intentional. It involves a drive to get somewhere, to get something, even if just to "get it," to make sense of the itinerary.[90] So when Barbara Herrnstein Smith posits an itch to "learn," her "epistemic hunger" is for directions, for the kind of "information" that enables a reader to follow the organizing line of the plot.[91] Even Gogol in his often-cited request to Pushkin for a plot claims to be "hungering" for one.[92]

Plot is not the only organizing principle in narrative, but as a figure for interconnectedness and purposefulness, it is emblematic of the sense we need and the sense of direction we crave when we read. The longing to "get somewhere," we will see in Chapter 5, is of particular relevance to Gogol, whose oeuvre is dominated by the image of traveling along a road. To enjoy *our* trip, we need a road map, a structuring, sense-making, organizing impulse in order to identify the "place"—and hence the significance—of the details we encounter in the work's design.

"When we have in this way 'explained' (identified the structural place of) a hitherto unexplained detail," comments the pre-prosaics Morson, "we say we have understood the work better and we take pleasure in that increased understanding. . . . So long as the work is read as literature at all, readers will seek an integral design and postulate a structure to reward their search."[93] In fact, avers Frank Kermode, it requires "a more strenuous effort to believe that a narrative lacks coherence than to believe that somehow, if we could only find out, it doesn't." We are loath to dismiss extraneous detail as "muddle" when it might be a deliberately plotted, significance-laden "enigma." Interpretation craves the functional and "abhors the random."[94] We have seen in the ingenious ways readers have scurried to tidy up Gogol's jumbled heap that pleasure-seeking in reading is truly "purpose-seeking."

Indeed, structure and design are among the great advantages literature has over life. Even those of us who can accept the muddle of the real world expect a far greater degree of purposefulness and significance in the data of fictional texts. Gripped by what Martin Price refers to as the "impulse . . . to convert all content to form" (or, in the language of information theory, to convert "noise" to "information"), we want details to be relevant rather than accidental, we expect events to be meaningful rather than random, and we assume that "a pattern of significance will emerge by the end that reveals the implicit connectedness of the material."[95] When it comes to structure and the sense it bestows, readers *are* greedy, covetous, desirous. "*Form* in literature is an arousing and fulfillment of desires," and reading is a quest to be "gratified by the sequence."⁹⁶ Must we simply renounce these desires when we encounter Gogol's clutter? Must we follow the path of the traveler through Mirgorod, who by the end of the "Two Ivans," as Hugh McLean suggests, leaves a world with all libido dissolved?⁹⁷

More to the point: is it really in our power to relinquish our desire for sense and a sense of purpose and, bowing to the sheer prodigality of Gogolian detail, simply revel in the excess? "The hypertrophy of information . . . tends to interfere with our enjoyment," Burke puts it mildly.⁹⁸ Chichikov may relish playbills full of useless information (6:12), but our needs and expectations persist with greater vigor.

And Gogol resists just as resolutely. To read him for the plot, as Dr. Johnson quipped about Richardson, "your impatience would be so much fretted that you would hang yourself."⁹⁹ Naturally, resisting desire is part of what narrative does—it depends on meaning "delayed, partially filled in, stretched out."¹⁰⁰ At the same time, though, a text must sustain the interest it has aroused.¹⁰¹ We keep reading because "we read the incidents of narrative as 'promises and annunciations' of final coherence."¹⁰² Maguire's imaginative division of readers' responses to Gogol suggests that this coveted coherence is either discovered in a text or the desire for it is renounced. I think rather it is either discovered or *supplied*. It is easier to create order than to give up the desire for it.

For desire is the motor force of reading, whether or not one chooses to adopt Brooks's erotic metaphors to describe it; it is essential to the workings (or failings) of narrative. Even aesthetic pleasure is still pleasure, and seeking and obtaining pleasure is something reading and passion have in common. Moreover, this impassioned search for sense is not misguided, even when the text blocks it, because it is desirous reading that enables us to feel what the text does. A strong desire for significance produces a more powerful, if not necessarily more pleasureful, experience of Gogolian irrelevance.

When we are deflected from the introduction of the main character of *Dead Souls* by the profile of the now famous young man with the Tula pin, for instance, or when Chichikov's business is suspended for an in-depth consideration of the respective physiques, ranks, names, and serial numbers of the obscure Greek generals depicted in the incidental paintings in the Sobakevich home (6:95), it is perfectly legitimate to wonder what all this "information" is doing there. The only illegitimate reaction may be to become so inured that we are no longer put out by such intrusions. William Paulson hypothesizes that "before we have read a work of literature, we do not know how to read what is most literary in it. . . . Only by reading it can we become its reader"; in other words, the desires we bring need to be educated.¹⁰³

If, however, the upshot of this education is that we just acquiesce and become adept, scholarly, and well-mannered, then I think a loss has occurred—a loss not only of self, but of the work's power to disturb. Gogol's fascination with Russian society and its "polite talk" notwithstanding,[104] his own verbal onslaughts are anything but courteous. Why, then, should discursive rudeness evoke a polite response? Irritation is an eminently legitimate reaction to the obstruction of desire.

Nor is there anything illegitimate about desirous reading. Gogol himself speaks of being driven, about the "burning desire" to read even in reference to the Gospels.[105] And although Chizhevsky claims that the indictment of drives and passions is integral to Gogol's moral philosophy, and Karlinsky speaks of the punishment of desire,[106] the Gogolian oeuvre is predicated upon desire of the most feverish pitch.

"Diary of a Madman" ("Zapiski sumasshedshego," 1835), which exaggerates but also exemplifies the standard Gogolian breakdown of sense, is a record of the clerk's unfulfilled longing. So is "The Nose," at the center of which are the want ads (3:58–63). The fictional plot of *Dead Souls* is generated by the money-making one of Chichikov, and the reader is every bit as eager to get a grip on the dead souls as Chichikov is to get his hands on them. Miserliness (which has "a wolfish appetite, and the more it devours, the more insatiable it becomes" [6:119]) may be most focused in the figure of Pliushkin, but it has left its trace all around, in character and narratorial acquisitiveness alike.

In "Two Ivans," for instance, the greedy characters and narrator outdo each other in turn. The story opens with the narrator's expansive exposition so full of possessions and exclamations about them (most notably expressions of *desire*: why oh why don't I have a coat like that? [2:223]) that it obscures rather than introduces the characters. Chapter 2, "From Which One May Learn What Ivan Ivanovich Desired . . ." (2:228), features the unsurpassed, indeed rapacious, inquisitiveness of the title character (who asks all the peasants where they are going [and how, when, and why] and practically succumbs to heart failure with the impatience of hearing the police captain digress) as well as his equally extreme acquisitiveness. "What is there I have not got?" he muses. Ivan Ivanovich, having surveyed his kingdom and finding that it includes everything he could imagine ("birds, buildings, barns, every possible whim, an inexhaustible supply of distilled vodka; in the orchard, pears and plums; in the garden, poppies, cabbage, peas") simply "lets his eyes go roaming around in search of new objects" (2:228)—and so does the narrator, whose optical search mission produces another whopper of a simile before Ivan Ivanovich lights upon his "indispensable thing" (2:234).[107]

Noses, carriages, overcoats, and other "indispensable things" are the objects not only of desire, but of epic quests. Desire is paramount. Even on the Tolstogubov estate, the peaceful home of the "Old-World Landowners" ("Starosvetskie pomeshchiki," 1835), where there are supposedly no passions, urges, or restlessness of any kind (2:13), everyone is touched by desire—even Pul'kheriia Ivanovna's docile little cat is seduced and returns wild and hungry (2:28–30). The hunger in this "idyll" is, in fact, insatiable.[108] And though this old-world estate is portrayed as a locus of absolute plenty,[109] desire survives to the very end, not only in the figure of the thieving steward, but in a persistent sense of lack and longing. The larger tale of loss of passion digresses easily into a tale of the most passionate loss (2:33–34). Pul'kheriia Ivanovna herself becomes a conspicuous *absence*; the major event is her death and Afanasii Ivanovich's bereavement. Even before his loss, Afanasii Ivanovich's indefatigable appetite signals desire: he liked to watch the girls, then go inside ravenous (2:22–23). And what about the inexplicable pregnancies among the maids? (2:18–19). The sedate and settled relationship of Afanasii Ivanovich and Pul'kheriia Ivanovna is contrasted to the "ardent pursuit of some brunette" assumed to preoccupy younger men (2:17), but even these two old folks once felt enough urgency to elope over the objections of their relatives (2:16). The narrator declares that one has but to see this old couple to renounce all desire (2:14), but his nostalgia presents a kind of longing of its own. As "naive" as the protagonists are presumed to be, we, the readership, are forever "sentimental"—separated and desirous.[110]

Perhaps the most "devilish urgency" of all is the desire to hear a good story ("A May Night," 1:156). But given the obfuscations of Gogolian discourse, "Do we ever get what we desire?" ("Nevskii Prospekt," 3:45).

Reception

Thus, readers have wants, and readers have needs, and when it comes to Gogol, readers have a problem. Gogol's provocation of and assault on directed, desirous reading plays out in the tension between infinite elaboration and finite patience. Dying of curiosity about the puzzling dead soul scheme, readers find their "epistemic hunger" acknowledged, only to be mocked by extensive descriptions of things that are utterly beside the point: "The author is certain that there are readers so curious that they would even like to be informed of the plan and internal arrangement of the box. Well, I suppose, why not satisfy them?" (6:55). The rhetoric of satisfaction is particularly excruciating given the real result, namely obstruction and delay, for, as promised, the ridiculous box is unpacked in full. Confronting Gogol's prose is like his description of dealing with servants: if you ask them about something directly, they don't remember and won't answer. Ask them something else and they will answer the original question in so much detail that you don't want to hear anymore (*Dead Souls*, 6: 196). Even Chizhevsky acknowledges that "on certain pages a reader who has not grasped the author's intention sometimes feels some irritation"—as if the problem can be isolated to "certain pages."[111] As for grasping the author's intention, we have already seen how dicey that is.

Smith sums up the reader's plight in the face of prose such as Gogol's: "In a situation where structural relations are elusive or fragmentary, where we encounter mostly clutter and noise or discontinuity, unpredictability and irregularity, where the objects of perception resist classification and offer no readily graspable principles of order . . . we will feel radical discomfort, disorientation, alienation."[112] Chekhov gives us a perfect portrait of this exasperation in "The Pecheneg"; Zoshchenko's public walks rapidly away from displays that are not worth their while.

But if Zoshchenko activates his readers to make another choice about what's worth reading (a choice that rejects *official* determinations), Gogol provokes his readers quite possibly to do so at his *own* expense. Unless readers can find a way to convert frustration to content, to make that experience of resisted desire part of the "organizing line" of the narrative, a functional part of the "plot," in Brooks's sense—unless, in other words, they can make the insignificant signify—they might well vote with their feet as summarily as Zoshchenko's *publika*.

Robert Belknap proposes a process by which the "real" reader of Gogol's clutter regards the fictional one (the "narratee") as an illustration of the position the real reader should *not* take. Gogol, he suggests, provides in his imaginary addressee a negative example of readerly taste. The real reader, in turn, who *does* in fact find the glut of indiscriminate detail trying, feels comfortably superior to the narratee, who presumably enjoys the discursive deluge.[113] If this is true, though, what are we to make of all the actual readers who have signed on to the position that the rocket ship ride is fun?

Or perhaps readers manage by undertaking the process of selection that the writer himself shuns: no one really reads every word of any text, and it is especially tempting to cut to the chase when the author shows no signs of doing so. In our quest for pleasure, owns Barthes, we are impatient: "Our very avidity for knowledge impels us to skim or to skip certain passages (anticipated as 'boring') in order to get more quickly to the warmer parts of the anecdote (. . . whatever furthers the solution of the riddle, the revelation of fate): we boldly skip (no one is watching) descriptions, explanations, analyses, conversations."[114] Skipping, to be sure, is a mitigated form of interruption resorted to when what is being told seems temporarily not worth telling. But this, as Barthes would acknowledge, assumes an ability to distinguish between "purposeful" and "purposeless" material. How can a reader of Gogol identify what may *not* be skipped? Our attempts to exercise such discretion in Gogol's effusion are every bit as ludicrous as the determinations of the mayor in "A May Night," who "can't hear a thing" and finds everything "incomprehensible," but still pronounces authoritatively that "that's not the important part" (1:178). If isolating a hierarchy of significance is part of what makes reading pleasurable, reading Gogol can't be much fun.

In fact, our own chronic problems of reception—the radical discomfort, disorientation, and alienation diagnosed by Smith—find corroboration in the numerous instances of non-comprehension, boredom, and associated distress inscribed in Gogol's text.[115] No one in "The Nose" can understand anything. "I can't figure it out," says Ivan Iakovlevich in desperation (3:50); "Excuse me, I can't make any sense of what you're talking about," says the nose, impatiently. "I can't understand a thing," it reprises, becoming increasingly irritated (3:56). Maguire cites the story of Captain Kopeikin in *Dead Souls* as an inscription of universal non-comprehension. No one understands: not Chichikov, not the characters, not the narrator, not the reader.[116] And is it any wonder, given the volubility of Chichikov's exposition, that poor Manilov "couldn't explain" the dead soul scheme, even to himself (6:39)? Korobochka, too, "just can't make any sense of it" (6:51). And yet they cannot reasonably be expected to "read" like Petrushka, caring not a whit for the content but delighting in the pure verbality of Chichikov's proposal; they are interested in every sense. But no meaningful exchange is possible.[117]

In "Two Ivans," even the most "interested" listener, the person whose case is being tried in court, routinely falls asleep because the delivery is so excruciatingly boring and long-winded. The judge only forfends himself from dozing off by keeping up a lively conversation during the proceedings (2:245). By the time we've plowed through the story, we have discovered on our own and had confirmed by the text that discourse can be not only unclear and dull, but downright unpleasant. "Two Ivans" is explicit about this, associating too much jabber with flatulence, the only possible response to which is to wash well and fumigate (2:236).

In short, we begin to get the impression that whatever "pleasure" is engendered by all this discourse is distinctly one-sided. Mirsky claims that Gogol wrote the way he did not for the acoustic effect on his listeners, but for the "sensuous effect on the vocal apparatus of the reciter."[118] His self-indulgent narrators are perfectly indifferent to their listeners' needs: "Do not interrupt!" they warn, in folktale formula, suspending interlocutor privilege on the pain of discontinuation of the tale—either you accept my getting to the point in my own good time, or I won't proceed at all (1:181–82). If our interests as readers are so systematically disregarded, indeed flouted, by Gogol's texts, what's in it for us?

The Narrative Transaction: A Fair Exchange?

Barbara Herrnstein Smith argues that narrative is precisely a kind of "transaction" and, as such, is ultimately "subject to the economics of the marketplace."[119] A reader has desires and demands that finally must be fulfilled in order for the customer to go away satisfied rather than just go away. While a consumer may be willing to sacrifice some ease of access to the "point" in exchange for "the pleasure of getting there," the degree of pleasure experienced in the face of elaborative excess is determined by the extent to which readers feel they have been compensated for their trouble.[120] What is the payoff with Gogol? With Chekhov, it seems, it is the "joy" of discovering that something is unexpectedly important. With Zoshchenko we recognize a certain subversive thrill in declining the official determination of what is significant and deciding instead for oneself. But when Gogol's narrators say too much, go into too much detail, or dwell on the irrelevant, we are bored and annoyed because "the amount of interesting information we receive from such utterances is quite minimal—and thus out of proportion to, or insufficient payment for, the time and attention we have been constrained to donate."[121]

Smith's assertion that how much elaboration readers can tolerate depends on how well their *interests* are served emphasizes once again the desirous nature of reading, the active quest for gratification at work in the reading process.[122] Aesthetic interest, often imagined as somehow purer than the financial or erotic sort, is itself subject to Brooks's "libidinal economy,"[123] and although both Horace and the garrulous Pan'ko posit the complementarity of *dulce et utile* (Preface 2, 1:196), reading for "pleasure and profit" may well be the same thing.

Smith's formulation also stresses that reading takes place in the context of an *exchange*. Readers give up their turn-taking privileges in exchange for something that makes the sacrifice "worth it"—they trade their time and undivided attention for some kind of sense (whether "meaning" or pleasurable "sensation"). Just as readers long to "get somewhere," they want just as urgently to "get something" for their effort. The exchange metaphor (as will become apparent in Chapter 5) is as fundamental to the project of reading Gogol as is his famous metaphorical road, especially because the reader is perpetually short-changed by the transaction.

The profitability of text *production*, on the other hand, is underscored by Gogol's legal "scribblers" who are financed with silver rubles (2:274); in "The Nose," letters counted up and words printed for money introduce the notion of advantage (3:60–62) (in fact, the story closes with the question of *why* authors should choose to print something *without* advantage [3:75]). "Saint John's Eve" conveys anxiety about the ownership of stories and about filchers who appropriate them and publish them for financial gain (1:137–38). Stories are also conflated with money insofar as both wind up baked into dough.

But readers have their profit motive too. Granddad the storyteller has little luck getting the attention of his audience until he begins to talk about money. *Then* his listeners are all ears (1:187). Not that money is literally the point; like Chichikov, we crave not the money but the pleasures it can buy (6:228). What this financial angle emphasizes, though, is that readers are demanding customers: they want the narrative transaction to be worth their while. But if readers are greedy in this sense, why is Gogol's splurging so problematic? Why is more not necessarily more?

Superfluity: More Is Not More

Even the covetous Chichikov does not want more than he needs. "Why on earth should I acquire something that is of absolutely no use to me?" he protests to Nozdrev, who wants to sell him all manner of dogs, carriages, and, most notably, a broken hurdy-gurdy that plays only incomprehensible snatches of songs. *Zachem?* he keeps asking the overzealous vendor: "To what purpose?" (6:80–81). This is precisely the question of even the greediest reader. More is not necessarily more, and when it comes to superabundant detail, prodigality is not necessarily generous. Martin Price reminds us that details have a dual power: they are revelatory, insofar as they supply information and specification and "give us the air of reality"; but they can also cover, obscure, *get in the way* of important matters if they are "irrelevant."[124]

This is an old point: Aristotle warns that elaborate diction obscures action, character, and thought, and should be reserved for points of minimal action.[125] Whatever the specific purposes of a given text—from explicitly didactic to simply mimetic—excessive information attenuates these purposes.

Admittedly, even avowedly excessive information can serve purposes of its own. It can be perversely representational, characterizing the speaker or situation on display. It may be the sign, for instance, of a particular type of narrator, such as a child, who has not mastered the categories of hierarchical significance, or an adult who is either in a peculiar mental state or is simply loquacious, like Pan'ko. Or, as is often maintained about the digressive, wandering, chattering narrator of Dostoevsky's feuilletons, a disordered discourse "approximates" the disordered life it sets out to describe. (This, we have seen, is the mimetic argument advanced about Gogol and his fairs.) Alternatively, superabundant detail can function as a rhetorical device, a signal that, for instance, something is being adduced with some irony.[126] Or, as is most commonly claimed in the case of Gogol, discursive overkill can be harnessed to get a laugh. It can also be a clue that a particularly cryptic code is in effect, one that requires special scrutiny to decipher its hidden (and thus heightened) significance; often "insignificant" detail screams out this way in detective fiction.[127] Or, because extended description stops story time, overspecification can be exploited to generate suspense.

With the exception of such "directed" deviations, though, what we commonly accept as description, specification, or enumeration is what is "demanded by" or "essential to" an appreciation of the events and existents, rather than some gratuitous collection of qualities, facts, and things.[128] Normally we neither provide nor accommodate more information than is necessary.[129] While the guarantee that "nothing is left out" is a claim that sells tell-all biographies,[130] the promise is grossly hyperbolic. Even the most graphic, "unexpurgated" sexual detail is produced by a scrupulous process of selection; the Marquis de Sade spends as much time in his most pornographic work agonizing about what sort of detail is affective and worth telling as he does describing his lurid pleasures. Maximal titillation comes even for Sade from not saying too *much*.[131] Chekhov, for related, if less prurient reasons, asks again and again in the construction of his stories, "What's worth telling?" But Gogol seems to refuse to screen his material—or worse, casts about for more and more, asking only, like Ivan Ivanovich, "What is there that I have not got?"

Even if we allow (in the language of information theory) that literature simply is a noisy transmission channel, and what is best avoided as a "surplus of information" in regular speech may well be "necessary surplus" in a literary text, nevertheless, the "hypertrophy of information" is a "disease" of narrative form.[132] How much "surplus" are we likely to accept as "necessary"? When Gogol's narrator, like his wheeling and dealing Chichikov, "omits nothing" (6:63), it is positively mortifying.

We can only thank our lucky stars that the narrator of *Dead Souls* did not undertake his project "in former days," when, as he claims, *everything* captured his attention. He devotes several whole pages to what he formerly "would have" noticed, but no longer does—every building, every window, every architectural feature, even every "local dandy who turned up in the middle of town" (with a bronze pin in the shape of a gun, perchance?). Back then, he claims, he would have been moved to provide each passerby with an imaginary destination, and, while he was at it, a point of origin, and another whole life history would have been written (along with the stories of all his relatives and colleagues) (6:110–11). Nowadays, by contrast, "it is with indifference that I drive up to every unknown village"—and what formerly would have inspired "an unceasing torrent of speech, now slides right by me, and my motionless lips maintain an apathetic silence" (6:111).

Well scarcely. Moreover, his spurious pretermission is difficult to accept as "necessary surplus." More material is not necessarily more informative; it is not even more fun, and it certainly isn't more tellable. While Nozdrev considers the "subtly superflues" to be the very "height of perfection" (6:75), Gogol's readers may have somewhat more stringent criteria for their attention.

When we pray for Gogol to "cut the cackle and come to the 'osses,"[133] it is that irrepressible desire for *relevance* asserting itself; our goal is to identify the purpose of the material we encounter. But what finally makes us feel that something in the narrative text is *relevant* and something else is not?

Relevance/Irrelevance

Before he developed his notion of prosaics, Morson once wrote, "If a work is assumed to be complete, we are justified in hypothesizing the thematic and formal relevance of all its details."[134] Morson has since abandoned this approach to reading, and indeed, even to the non-prosaic reader it seems an extreme position. Chatman, somewhat more moderately, allows that "certain events or existents that are not *immediately* relevant may be brought in. But at some point their relevance must emerge, otherwise we object that the narrative is 'ill-formed.'"¹³⁵ Reading is not infinitely tolerant. "If the reader feels insufficient connection between a given complex of motifs and the work as a whole, then that complex is 'superfluous.' If all the parts of the work fit together poorly, the work is 'incoherent.' Thus, the introduction of each separate motif or complex of motifs must be *motivated*."¹³⁶ When textual material is thus "extraneous" or "superfluous," we feel our attention has been abused. But determinations of irrelevance and superfluity presuppose a hierarchy of importance. What defines this scale?

Tomashevskii distinguishes between bound and free motifs, bound motifs being the elements one would include in any paraphrase. One can determine the "relative importance" of a motif, says Tomashevskii, "by retelling the *story* in condensed form" and seeing whether or not that particular motif survived the cut.¹³⁷ Gerald Prince, too, understands relevance as what allows us to extract a story line; the "irrelevant" is, by contrast, what may be omitted.¹³⁸

Two things are suggested by these definitions of relevance: one is that readers can and do accommodate a certain amount of material that is "not immediately relevant." Literary texts inevitably include a great deal more than what is necessary to an adequate paraphrase. It becomes part of normal readerly activity and enjoyment to exercise the "intolerance" that is the reader's prerogative. This is what readings do, as Culler would say—they separate the text into "marginal and essential elements."¹³⁹ Normally readers can rely on the relevance/irrelevance opposition to locate the essential; with Gogol, who privileges the irrelevant, the hierarchy is toppled.

The second thing underlined by these formulations that link relevance to story line is that relevant and irrelevant are relational terms. Something can only be relevant *to* something else. Tomashevksii and Prince propose *story line* as the basic index of what feels "relevant" in a narrative text. For readers as well as for theorists, I would argue, *story* functions as a primary index of relevance for the material spun out by the *discourse*. Readers look to the story line for the sense of purpose they crave; discursive elaboration feels most purposeful when it relates palpably to the story.

How much of a story's continuum of events and existents to make explicit, I have said, is always a function of discursive discrimination. If "story" (*inventio*) is a set of designs, then "discourse" (*elocutio* and *dispositio*) is a set of decisions. But Gogol invents at least as much in the discourse. His principle of selection is apparently *not* relevance to the story, and if there is any principle of exclusion, it is not evident. Gogol's discourse is overloaded not because he makes too much of the story-stuff explicit, but because he includes massive amounts of material with no connection whatsoever to the story at all. If Price is correct that irrelevant details get in the way of important matters, what is Gogol's reader to *do* with a discourse that impedes access to the story it is ostensibly there to tell? If we crave relevance, and story is its touchstone, how is Gogolian discourse to be tolerated at all?

Story/Discourse

Story, as I said in the introduction, is the "what" of narrative. Discourse is the "how." Chatman, probably the chief champion of the distinction, contends that the transposability of a given story from genre to genre, from medium to medium, demonstrates the independent existence of story structure, which is logically anterior to any particular discursive manifestation.[140] Smith, probably the distinction's chief antagonist, argues that "basic" story is itself constructed only after the fact according to "hierarchies of relevance and centrality" that *we* create, "and it is in terms of these hierarchies that we will distinguish certain elements and relations as being central or peripheral, more important or less important, more basic or less basic." Accordingly, there are always many possible basic stories for any given narrative.[141]

In her staunch opposition to the story/discourse distinction, Smith nevertheless confirms two important aspects of my own position. First, that "relevance" and "significance" are the defining criteria of the story/discourse relation. Second, when Smith rejects the notion of underlying story because narrative is a *transaction* rather than the *representation* of events and existents, her very language undercuts her argument. Even her "minimalist" formulation (proposed as an alternative to Chatman's dualistic one) has two verbs and two time frames: narrative discourse is "someone telling someone else that something happened."[142] Conceiving of it as "part of a social transaction" does not obscure the fact that the "happening" and the "telling" of it are two operations, one logically anterior to the other (note the tenses), and that when we encounter a narrative text, we read it "as if" this were so.

Even if it is not actually the case, it matters less what narrative *is* than how readers imagine it and what they *want* from it. Culler holds that the analysis of narrative always depends on the story/discourse distinction and that "this distinction always involves a relation of dependency." There is an assumption (at least in the reader's mind) that a "nontextual substratum"—the story—exists prior to and independent of discursive treatment. "Understanding" a narrative, says

Gogol: The Pragmatics of Elaboration 157

Culler, means following this story which bestows the sense we so fundamentally desire.[143] Thus, even when the relationship between story and its discursive treatment is a vexed one, we make a valiant attempt to get behind the words to the matter at hand. We sift through the discursive detail to reconstruct the story and its world, its logic and its implications, preferring what contributes to "sense" to what obstructs it. We may enjoy some levity, but we rely on gravity[144]—the force countered so powerfully by Chudakov's imaginary rocket as it moves out and away from the story—to satisfy our desire to move forward purposefully through the text.

The problem with Gogol is that the discourse hampers this operation rather than facilitating it. We sympathize with the Lucinda ridiculed by Kermode:

> Lucinda can't read poetry. She's good
> Sort of, at novels, though. The words, you know,
> Don't sort of get in like Lucinda's way.
> And then the story, well, you know, about
> Real people, fall in love, like that, and all.
> Sort of makes you think, Lucinda thinks.[145]

My question will be what to do when the words do "sort of like get in the way"—when it is not the "plot" that thickens, but the discourse.

This dialectic of excess and access will occasion a discussion of the problematic relationship of discourse to story in Gogol's swollen texts. Is the story "behind" the discourse in the sense of being logically prior to it, generating, in effect, its many words?[146] Or is Gogol's story "behind" his discourse more in terms of obscurement, lost behind a verbal smokescreen? Or is story *paradoxically* "behind," coming later, temporally and logically posterior? For while Gogol's extreme verbal prodigality may not be news (literary-critically assertible), what may be less generally recognized is the extent to which his discursive procedure itself is inscribed concretely and metaphorically as story content. One strategy for embracing Gogol's irrelevancies, in other words, is to read the story as an expression of the discourse rather than the other way around.

FIVE

Gogol's Coats and Clutter: Content and Its Discontents

From the *New York Post*, copyright 1990 New York Post Co, Inc. Reprinted with permission. Photograph by Susan Farley from *New York Newsday*, copyright 1990. Reprinted with permission of *Los Angeles Times* Syndicate.

Confronted with what linguists refer to as "excessive generative capacity,"[1] readers face the problem of access, in Gogol's excess, to what's behind it, the story, the "point," the object of their desire—whatever might make reading it worth the trouble at the very least, pleasurable at best. The discussion that follows reflects my own particular method of wreaking order in Gogolian havoc, of identifying significance and purpose in the aimless chatter—and thus of making the whole enterprise of reading Gogol more tolerable to me. I propose a mode of reading that identifies Gogol's strategies for generating prodigious amounts of text, then recognizes that these generative strategies serve not only to produce discourse, but also to comment on that over-production (as well as its reception), that they inscribe as *story* the text's own discursive strategies. What makes Gogol worth reading (and maybe even fun) for me is to read the story as being in some measure *about* the discourse.

In the opening section of this chapter, I survey briefly the different types of verbal obstacles that get in the reader's way and the impatience they breed. In the interest of ordering my own "jumbled heap" of material, a set of examples that might well include "all of Gogol," if not quite all of Russia, I distinguish several categories of textual excess, noting how, in each instance, the formal problem—whether the expansiveness (saying too much) or the illogic (making no sense)—acquires a certain contentual status. I then turn to some of Gogol's favorite "subjects"—the road, the devil, food, and hoarding—to suggest that, even in terms of its most prominent story elements, Gogol's prose is somehow about its own discursive dilemmas. In fact, as I will argue, in these stories about discourse the apparently infinite material may be as immaterial as Chichikov's "dead souls," and the substance we crave as chimerical as the bodiless objects of Chichikov's desire.

Excess and Access: The Problem of the Material

Expansiveness: Too Much

Gogol not only elaborates indefinitely himself; he embodies his own discursive practices in Chichikov, who begins "somehow very remotely" when broaching his prospective suppliers about the dead souls, touching on Roman history, the Russian empire, and everything in between (as a result of which, we recall, his addressees fail to understand his proposition [6:100]). In perfect imitation of his own inability or unwillingness to set the sort of limits on scope that have long been understood as the delimiting gesture of narrative, "the arbitrary drawing of a boundary line establishing an edge beyond which the writer will not allow himself to go,"[2] Gogol gives us Nozdrev, who has a similarly hard time with the concept of boundaries ("everything on this side of the boundary is mine, and everything on that side too" [6:74]). From the exasperating Pan'ko, who mercifully resists including one of his own stories in the Dikan'ka collection, since he would need "at least three books this size" (1:197) to accommodate it, to Nozdrev, whose skill at prevarication is matched only by his volubility (6:82), to Shpon'ka's neighbor, Ivan Ivanovich, who could (and given half a chance, would) talk about "anything and everything that one could possibly talk about" (1:301), Gogol's characters exhibit a garrulous streak matched only by his narrators. For character speech in Gogol does more than just characterize the speaker; it reproduces the excesses of the narrative voice and foregrounds its problems. Although Chizhevsky observes that Gogol fashioned his narrators after his characters,[3] it seems to me just as apt to say that he creates his bizarre characters in the (verbal) image of his narrative persona.

And since at the level of character the *addressees* are actually present, the dilemmas of those listeners—the impossible "exchanges" that result—demonstrate the difficulty of being on the receiving end of such a deluge and the pressing need to devise ingenious ways of interrupting the torrent. Beleaguered husbands resort to tuning out the "verbal onslaughts" of their wives' "inexhaustible tongues" ("The Fair at Sorochintsy," 1:115). Townsfolk grow restive when their mayor indulges in his favorite (and too often repeated) long story ("Why do you have to tell us?" they moan ["A May Night," 1:171]). After all this jabber, Gogol's famous mute scenes offer more than *comic* relief. Considering that the characters routinely pretend to be deaf when they have heard enough (1:161), the mute scenes may be the most eloquent testimony to the difficulty of hearing any more.

While even Rudyi Pan'ko finally evinces some anxiety about producing another volume lest he wear out his narrative welcome (1:195), Gogol's principal narrators proceed unabashed. Their two basic modes of expansion—describing and informing—are elaborate diversions from the task of narrating and are ultimately neither descriptive nor informative. They are ploys for generating more material.

Describing

In his descriptive passages, Gogol typically either only *pretends* to describe his object by expanding indefinitely on matters far removed, or he disingenuously *declines* to describe what he then proceeds to delineate extensively. The first he accomplishes in his famous extended similes, which have been amply elucidated.[4] I wish only to emphasize here that the similes represent a travesty of the descriptive function they ostensibly serve. Clearly when the narrator of *Dead Souls* tells us that "the day was neither clear nor cloudy, but of some sort of light gray color such as one finds only on old uniforms of garrison soldiers, basically peaceful troops, some of whom, however, are not sober on Sundays" (6:23), this bit of intelligence about the weekend sobriety of military personnel offers little insight into the color of the sky as Chichikov sets off to locate Manilov, any more than the balalaikas made out of pumpkins and the young men who learn to strum them help us to visualize Chichikov's approach to Sobakevich's. Insofar as they describe everything *but* the object at hand, the similes may well be, as Proffer suggests, Gogol's strategy for cramming in all of Russia by hook or by crook.

Gogol's other great descriptive ploy is his version of preterition, claiming to omit what, by virtue of his elaboration on the omission, he includes with a vengeance: "I assume that it is absolutely superfluous to describe how Ivan Nikiforovich put on his trousers, how his tie was knotted for him, and how, finally, he was helped into his coat which split under the left sleeve" (2:269), the narrator contends, getting in a good measure of detail nonetheless; or

> I don't intend to describe all the dishes that were on the table! I will make no mention of the cheese cakes in sour cream, nor of the sweetbread served with the borscht, nor of the turkey with plums and raisins, nor of the dish that looked a lot like boots soaked in kvass, nor of that sauce that is the swansong of the ancient cook, the sauce that was served flambé, which very much entertained but also alarmed the ladies. I do not intend to talk about these dishes because I much prefer eating them to expatiating upon them in conversation. (2:271)

And despite the claim that it is unnecessary to prove to the enlightened reader that Ivan Nikiforovich was not born with a tail, the narrator proceeds to do just that, enlarging upon the dorsal features of witches, although he allows that this, too, is wholly unnecessary, since witches are female and Ivan Nikiforovich is not (2:226). In each case of preterition, the disclaimer becomes its own refutation.[5]

By expatiating on what he has "no intention of describing," Gogol mocks the necessary intentionality of verbal description. In visual art, after all, whatever appears automatically has an appearance. In written narrative, on the other hand, descriptive detail must be explicitly asserted. Thus, extended description is normally not perceived as especially intrusive, even though it necessarily stops the action, because it is verbal narrative's only way of conveying sensory detail. By describing at length what he assumes is "superfluous to describe," however, Gogol foregrounds his own abuses of these acknowledged "exigencies of the medium."[6] His frequent renderings of what he "would" describe "if only" he were a painter (elaborating, as a consequence, quite substantively on what he claims to be utterly unable to address in prose) accomplish much the same thing. Gogol also motivates many of his more motley assemblages of things ("Indian pigeons that Ivan Nikiforovich fed himself, melon rinds, greens here, a broken wheel there, or a hoop from a barrel, or a boy lying around in a soiled shirt") by invoking the painter ("the sort of picture painters love!" [2:231]). Given this obsession with alternative media, I find it difficult to concur with Maguire's contention that Gogol means painting to stand for all art, verbal art in particular, and that icon and word are identical and easily interchanged.[7] Gogol seems to capitalize precisely on the inherent limitations of verbal art to indulge in his own form of limitlessness.

Informing

If Gogol cultivates similes and preteritions to produce and comment on the "unnecessary surplus" that masquerades as description, his arsenal of "informative" practices is even more diversified, every bit as expansive, and equally self-referential.

Diachrony. Gogol exhibits a "diachronic urge" to account historically for any object that comes into range. The notorious painting of the nymph with enormous breasts in the first chapter of *Dead Souls*, for instance, is not only described intricately—it triggers extensive speculation by the narrator on where the painting came from, who brought it to Russia, on whose advice it was imported, and so on. Then, as the still unintroduced hero stands marooned in front of this very canvas while we wait for the narrator to indulge his penchant for diachrony, Chichikov idly takes off a scarf; straightaway that scarf's potential origins are explored in detail (6:9). As if motivated by a profound concern for *causality*, Gogol is not content to record the color of a building, or even to expound infinitely on what that color is "like," but is compelled to explain *why* it is how it is: The roof of the district courthouse, for example, is "all wooden, and would even be painted red, if the office clerks hadn't added onions to the oil prepared for that purpose and eaten it, since, as it happened, it was Lent, and so the roof remained unpainted" (2:244). And like the famous story of how Odysseus got his scar and hence his heroic name, told in leisurely detail while the nurse stands holding up his leg,[8] Gogol rehearses at length the dubious derivation of Akakii Akakievich's given name while we wait to hear what was happening in a certain department (3:141–43). Gogol's diachronic urge is as Homeric as his similes.

Indeed, insofar as these expansive strategies tell stories about each descriptive detail, Gogol's discourse is, in a sense, more plotted than his stories.[9] The village dandy who flirts with the aid of a balalaika gets his girl (people fall in love and all that) long before Chichikov is even brought to articulate *his* desires. And, in a kind of infinite regress, when we do return to the actual story, the hero of *Dead Souls* is busy reenacting Gogol's diachronic expansion, fabricating "a whole life story" for each of the dead souls he acquires, not only distended and absolutely imaginary, but historically "complete" (6:136). Like his own creator, Chichikov is evidently unable to *name* without deriving in full. Iu. Ivask's astute suggestion that, should *Dead Souls* ever be filmed, these scenes of Chichikov collecting souls be depicted as Gogol himself sitting at a desk, writing on and on, testifies to his suspicion that the story tells the tale of its own verbal composition.[10]

Moreover, that this urge to expand backwards makes getting on with it nearly impossible is apparent in the story-level correlatives, the many places where the story is *about* what the discourse does. The interminable legal petitions of the "Two Ivans," for example, derive their extendedness from the same inclination on the part of the "scribblers" to account diachronically for the state of the dispute between the eponymous heroes, to rehearse in full these heroes' genealogies and the property deeds that chronicle what was inherited from whom, from whom before that, and before that still. These same hair-raising documents render closure of the case of the two Ivans impossible (2:248–50, 253–54). The events cannot go forward toward an ending because the diachronic urge keeps taking them backward to ever-receding beginnings.

Susanne Fusso, on the other hand, sees in diachrony a promise of sense available to the careful and committed reader. The tangled mess of Pliushkin's overgrown garden, for instance, is, when dissected meticulously, a "complex record of diachronic change ... that demands a complementary act of imagination on the part of the viewer or reader."[11] The extensive backtracking indulged in by the narrators (and the characters who reproduce their strategies) instructs us to disentangle what seems incomprehensible by reading back. Fusso's work on Gogol, which discerns meaning in what seems a mess, order in what more resembles chaos, and closure in the apparent open-endedness, shows us both what an ingenious reader can do and the strength of the desire to do it.[12] Everything can be explained, its sense derived, through an imaginary act of historiography.

Mann even sees the final "secret" of *Dead Souls* not in the mechanism of the scam, but in Chichikov's personal history, the biographical sources of his character and actions. In fact, Mann pinpoints having or not having a history and biography as the fundamental dividing line between characters, most of whom, he notes, have no past at all. The diachronic quality of the portrayal of Pliushkin and Chichikov thus distinguishes them, making them more important and more "alive" than the other characters.[13] But when inanimate objects have a history every bit as detailed, can we really reliably use the thickness of their portrayal as an index of either their vitality or their import? In other words, are these expeditions in reverse really any more sensible or sense-making than the "genetic" explanations given by the police sergeant for his myopia—"My mother-in-law, that is my wife's mother, can't see anything either" (3:66)?

Documentation. In addition to this earnest commitment to history and causality, there emerges a concern for verifiability that is more patently ridiculous. Rudyi Pan'ko, for instance, invites confirmation of his stories by giving detailed directions to his own residence or to the homes of the secondary narrators. In "Two Ivans," the circumstances of a specific incident are identified by invoking "common knowledge": Ivan Ivanovich's violated property line runs to "the very place where peasant women wash their pots" (2:250). The inimitable Pan'ko stores his manuscripts in a little table—"I think you know it well; it stands in the corner as you come in the door" (1:283).

But the silly characters only reproduce the author's own ostentatious gestures of rooting the fictional world in the extra-textual one. In the scholarly apparatus Pan'ko appends to each preface—an extensive listing of Dikan'ka idioms (over 70 in one list, nearly 60 in the other [1:107–9, 197–99])—"just in case" (heaven forbid!) anything should be "not fully comprehensible to everyone" (1:107), we recognize Gogol's own patented brand of "information." The vocabulary lists are excessive (Pan'ko has supplied, by his own reckoning, "almost all" of the words he could think of) and largely superfluous. And like so much Gogolian documentation, the glossaries are more stultifying than enlightening, a parody of sense-making with their "strict alphabetical order" rather than a real source of coherence.

In their extra-textual status and documentary pretensions, the vocabulary lists are a lot like the footnotes Gogol deems are "necessary" to append (and especially strange when we consider that the main text is composed of matters "superfluous to describe"). The exclusion of these particular bits of "information" from the body of the text together with their insistent inclusion, indeed showcasing, in the margins highlights again that, in the absence of any authentic principle of selection, the deployment of information is not informative. Whether these illuminating commentaries are attributed to the author (such as the solitary note in "Two Ivans" that explains, completely extraneously, that a gander is the male of the goose species [2:236]) or to his fictional compiler (such as Pan'ko's swollen marginalia at the beginning of "Christmas Eve" that purports to establish the etymology—yet another sort of genealogical account—of the verb *koliadovat'*, but the upshot of which is "I don't know, I give up" [1:201]), the footnotes are one more proof that more is not more, that addenda need not add anything.

All this substantiation obviously does little to make the accounts more viable. Instead, it mainly discredits the assumption that information is purposeful, unless its purpose is to get in the way.

Specificity. This exaggerated sense of "responsibility" in informing reaches new heights in the reverence for specificity. Evidently we must be told not only that a report was dispatched on the case of the two Ivans, but additionally that it was designated report no. 389 (2:255). With equal precision, the narrator notifies us that there were exactly eight buttons on the police chief's coat (with, naturally, the usual historical account of where and when the ninth had been torn off and what measures had been taken to recover it—supplying the most extravagant specification about what is not even there [2:256]).

If the hyperbole of this solemn commitment to specificity renders it suspect, Gogol further undercuts the seriousness of his own specifications by linking them with generalizations of the most outlandish sort. It might be overly exact, for example, to specify in a survey of a man's possessions that in his study there was a book open to page fourteen; Gogol ridicules the very specificity he has been so scrupulous in maintaining by telling us that in Manilov's study there was *always* some book open to page fourteen (6:25). The highly specified account of the inn at the beginning of *Dead Souls*, which goes on for several pages, providing excruciating detail about the patrons (and their provenance and their garments and their provenance) and the paintings (and their provenance) and the particular habits of the surly waiter, and so on, punctuates its own specifications with the periodic refrain that this is "the same as everywhere" (6:9). The narrator compiles a similarly detailed inventory of items found in another specific roadside establishment (including gilt china eggs suspended from light blue and red ribbons, a cat who had recently had kittens, a mirror that reflected four eyes instead of two and some kind of flat cake instead of a face, and dried herbs that made one sneeze), only to conclude that these idiosyncratic contents are always to be found in wooden inns (6:62).

Aside from indulging his own propensity for running on, in these absurd claims of universality about features so specific that they drastically limit the field of reference rather than constituting a useful generalization, Gogol seems to be parodying the idea of the "type," that great goal of realist prose, the sense that the typical could be discovered through astute observation of the particular.[14] It is a power of observation that, in any case, abruptly fails him, as this extreme specificity is juxtaposed right away with the chronic vagueness of *kakoi-to* (some kind of). After pages and pages of nearly as many specific details as Pliushkin has things, for instance, we are "informed" that Pliushkin's daughter eloped with someone "from God knows what cavalry regiment, and married him somewhere in a hurry, in some village church" (6:118). We are buffeted back and forth between having to process too much information to having to be content with none at all.

Walter Benjamin bans *Erklärung* and *Nachprüfbarkeit* from true storytelling, both explanation and documentation belonging more properly to the sphere of information.[15] By adopting those very categories, but filling them overfull of information so irrelevant and so frivolous that they amount to no information at all, Gogol simultaneously violates and upholds Benjamin's injunction. Like his use of footnotes to inform and document, Gogol's rhetoric of exactness is calculated less to clarify than to obscure—not unlike Ivan Ivanovich's *à propos des bottes* disquisitions on quail hunting, intended to distract his interlocutors from uncomfortable subjects (2:261). And while Gogol's play with specificity is undeniably comic, whether it continues (in its determined excess) to be any more amusing than Ivan Ivanovich's annoying diversionary tactic is debatable. Again, the "character traits" appear to be principally Gogol's own discursive proclivities with a name and patronymic (and a genealogy) attached.

Enumeration. One of Gogol's most effective mechanisms of accumulation is enumeration. I have mentioned the inventory of Pliushkin's things, the list of art supplies in Pirogov's room, the voluminous catalogue of items for sale at this or that fair, and the lists, pure and simple, of vocabulary words. The complete enumeration of Akakii Akakievich's effects at the time of his death, "namely a bundle of goose quills, a quire of white government paper, three pairs of socks, two or three buttons that had been torn off his trousers, and the 'dressing gown' already known to the reader" (3:168), is just one more of many examples that I, too, in imitation of my subject matter, could enumerate endlessly.

The most notorious Gogolian catalogue of all is probably the page-long listing of carriages, guests, apparel, and topics of conversation at the police captain's party in Mirgorod ("Two Ivans"). "Allow me to enumerate all who were there," continues the narrator, following an already very lengthy summary of vehicular varieties: "Taras Tarasovich, Evpl Akinfovich, Evtikhii Evtikhievich, Ivan Ivanovich—not *the* Ivan Ivanovich, but the other one—Savva Gavrilovich, our Ivan Ivanovich, Elevferii Elevferievich, Makar Nazar'evich, Foma Grigor'evich... I can't go on! I don't have the strength! My hand is getting tired from writing!" (2:264).

The names, as might be expected, are utterly unfamiliar (with the exception of *the* Ivan Ivanovich) and remain so (with the exception of the other Ivan Ivanovich). As sense-making information this is useless, except insofar as it reveals a certain tendency on the part of Mirgorod fathers to name their sons after themselves. It is more as nonsense syllables, as pure sound and rhythm, that it affects the reader (whether pleasantly or annoyingly). Like Gogol's mocking letter to Balabina about third and fourth spokes, this zealous cataloguing lays bare the very aspiration of exhaustiveness in presentation, as does the narrator's feigned exhaustion. And despite his protestations about his tired hand and his inability to go on, go on he does, and with a (terrible) vengeance:

And how many ladies were there! Dark and fair, tall and short, fat, like Ivan Nikiforovich, and so thin that it seemed as if each one could be hidden in the scabbard of the police captain's sword. How many bonnets! How many dresses! Red, yellow, coffee-colored, green, blue, new, turned, retailored, scarves, ribbons, reticules! Farewell, my poor eyes! You will be of no more use after that spectacle [and so on]. (2:264–65)

Even the great nineteenth-century realist novels "are not catalogues of clothes or inventories of things; no matter how extravagant the author's mimetic ambition, mimesis is always selective."[16] And yet Gogol goes to great lengths to create the impression of a speaker/observer who is unable to choose, who is incompetent to select for relevance, and who knows no moderation.

Doubling. But Gogolian discourse is swollen not only by the compulsive naming of many things. Words are multiplied as effectively by naming the same thing many times over. Nabokov is only one of many critics to point to the redundancy of expressions like "Russian muzhiks."[17] Maguire comments as well on the convulsive naming and renaming of Chichikov's revered vehicle[18]—and whether this gives the carriage greater materiality (as Maguire claims) or simply foregrounds the linguistic transaction of calling it something, the pleonastic urge inevitably delays the carriage's arrival.

As is so often the case in *Dead Souls*, Chichikov is made to reenact Gogol's discursive maneuvers. When asked to identify himself, for instance, Chichikov records his own names and titles in as many variations as possible. Gogol, not to be outdone, multiplies his own report, telling us not only that Chichikov wrote his rank, his first name and patronymic, and his surname on a piece of paper, but then specifying those three forms of identification—Collegiate Councillor Pavel Ivanovich Chichikov—landowner, adding for good measure "on private business." By naming and renaming himself, Chichikov produces (and Gogol reproduces) a calling card so exhaustive that the hero has time to go sightseeing while the waiter makes his way through the numerous morphemes (6:10–11).

The tongue-tied Akakii Akakievich, too, emerges from and reenacts the author's syntactic tic of repetition. As a copy clerk, Akakii repeats text verbatim,[19] as a son he repeats his father's name, and as a character, he inspires discursive echoing, not only in his reiterative name, but in the descriptive formulas about him (*neskol'ko riabovat, neskol'ko ryzhevat* [3:141]).[20]

Given Gogol's model of text production by verbal overdetermination, it is not surprising that the paradigmatic locus of his Dikan'ka cycle should be the "enchanted place" where each word uttered is multiplied at least two or three times (1:314).[21] Neither can we blame old granddad for wanting to abscond from that infernal echo posthaste.

Illogic: Too Random

Gogolian discourse is indiscretionary not only in its tendency to expand indefinitely in any connection. It also exhibits a remarkable capacity to elaborate at length with no connection whatsoever. Admittedly, the incoherence of "Diary of a Madman" seems to be motivated by the psychosis of the diarist, just as the "exceedingly uneven style" of the interpolated letters can be accounted for by the canine correspondents (3:203). But is this superimposed "coherence" really so different from the madman's own explication of peculiar events in terms of the national traditions of Spain? Like Rudyi Pan'ko, the madman is more an artifact of Gogolian discourse than a source of it, an inscription of Gogolian illogic rather than the reason for it.

For that matter, Gogol's "cogent" characters have little more claim on intelligibility than do his delusional clerks. The blacksmith of "Christmas Eve," who "knew how to speak like a literate man," blathers in disconnected phrases (1:234). Old granddad of "The Lost Letter," who "could talk a blue streak," produces such fine locutionary specimens as "Well, your honors, be so kind, in order to, as if so, roughly speaking, of the..." (1:187). Not incidentally, this paragon of eloquence is showcased as the master *storyteller*, the textual incarnation of narrative performance; like the characters who say too much, those who make no sense evince more than their own lack of verbal finesse. Akakii Akakievich's "incoherent medley of nonsense" (3:168)—his tendency to string together random particles and prepositions—most closely approximates his *creator's* lexical repertoire ("kak-to, kakoi-to, dazhe, neskol'ko, neskol'ko dazhe, kak-to dazhe, kazhetsia, vprochem") that effectively obscure all matters at hand;[22] Akakii's inarticulate stammering provides a portrait of this larger discursive problem.

Crazed as the mad diarist is, his wistful longing for punctuation, for periods and commas to carve out some sense in the morass of words (3:195, 202), begins to seem like an eminently comprehensible obsession, given the muddle we face. It is as if "some demon had broken the whole world into millions of little pieces and scrambled all these pieces together without sense or meaning" (3:24); Gogol's notorious phrase from "Nevskii Prospekt" describes his own text as closely as the "world" he purports to represent. Like the flagrant expansiveness, the formal problems of Gogol's skewed logic—the lack of connectivity, relevance, and control—are inscribed in the stories as matters of content. And if exhaustive enumeration is tedious, Gogol's absolutely random compilation is confounding.

Lack of Connectivity

The story matter, in imitation of the discourse, is itself syntactically disjointed. Characters take their leave as they sit down for a long visit. Card players throw out jacks when queens are required. Interlocutors demand " 'In what year?' or 'Which regiment?' without noticing that this had nothing to do with the topic of discussion" or abruptly stick decanter stoppers into pies as some kind of inexplicable rejoinder. Officers habitually query "What?" regardless of whether they really need clarification ("The Carriage," 3:185, 188–89). Hurdy-gurdies strike up one tune, but confusedly conclude with quite another (*Dead Souls*, 6:75). Ivan Ivanovich would routinely feed his mare, his turkeys, his pigs, and then, as if it followed, read a book without a title (2:239). Shpon'ka's marvelous auntie, the shrewd manager of her estate, concludes her catalogue of undergarments with an exclamation about a turnip (1:287).

The material exchanges are as indiscriminate as the verbal ones, without regard to logic or purpose. Just as he produces discourse without particular incentive, lying *bez vsiakoi nuzhdy* (6:71), Nozdrev buys up "great quantities of whatever he happens to see—horse collars, incense, calico, candles, kerchiefs for the nurse, a stallion, raisins, a silver washbasin, holland linen, wheat flour, tobacco, pistols, herring, paintings, a grindstone, pots, boots, china—until he runs out of money" (6:72). Like the incredible saga of proprietorship attributed to Anton Prokof'evich Golpopuz, who sold his house to buy three bay horses and a light carriage, which he sold, in turn, in order to acquire a fiddle and a serf girl, which he soon converted, according to some inexorable logic, into a leather tobacco pouch set with gold (2:266), exchange proceeds according to a "logic" as mysterious as the one governing the accumulation of content in the text. Gogol tenders his textual material in precisely this haphazard form, lining up knives and nurses, trousers and guns, in sequences without sense. As a storyteller, he reproduces the procedure he initiated as a historian, recording details fanatically and indiscriminately, taking thousands of pages of notes consisting entirely of isolated facts, with no attempt to posit logical connections. Bocharov claims that things enter the Gogolian text on the principle of contiguity,[23] but I think often they are contiguous on the page only.

Lack of Relevance

More troubling perhaps than the lack of relation these diffuse textual elements bear to one another is the lack of connection these elements exhibit to the *what*, the story, the matter at hand—their *relevance*, as defined by Tomashevskii, Prince, and Chatman. Despite the elaborate apologies for the attention to the "secondary characters" who have "little to do with the main story" (6:19) or the feigned relief that certain "other gentlemen" can be passed over in silence since, happily, "nothing needs to be said about them" ("The Carriage," 3:180), little of the textual matter "needs to be said," and most of it has less than "little to do with the main story." From the random but at least brief descriptions, apropos of nothing, of two-pronged forks, knife handles, and saltcellars that don't stand up (6:62), to the markedly irrelevant story of Kifa Mokievich and Mokii Kiforich who so unaccountably "peep out at the end of our *poema*," ostensibly to "testify" to something or another—but to what?—(6:243–45), most of the material has about as much relevance to the "what" as the tale of the double amputee Captain Kopeikin bears to the "who" of a man with all four limbs intact (6:199–205). Universal paraphrases aside, it is difficult to imagine any of this figuring in any retelling of the story of Chichikov, even in Barbara Herrnstein Smith's wildest "versions." Gogol encapsulates the pragmatic pitfalls of such non-related text in the image of Nozdrev's Turkish dagger: its "Turkishness" is completely undone by the inapposite inscription, "Made by Savelii Sibiriakov," engraved on the handle "by mistake" (6:75). (Nozdrev, no doubt, purchased the weapon just as unthinkingly.)

Lack of Control

Nozdrev, who obviously violates all of Grice's maxims of quality and quantity and embodies indiscriminateness of all kinds, further reenacts the text's discursive bad faith with his "complete inability to control his tongue." Like the narrator, he is unable to decline the myriad "details that assert themselves of their own accord," that represent no story and have "not only no semblance of truth, but no semblance of anything at all." Not that the Gogolian text *lies* so shamelessly. But like Nozdrev's 240 leeches, 200 of which just slither out by themselves (6:209), the text reflects a flagrant lack of control, which Gogol then addresses through Nozdrev and associates as the stuff of the story.

Lack of verbal control is embodied in the surprise of Chub, who opens his mouth to ask the mayor how he got into a sack, but instead hears himself saying "Do you rub your boots with lard or tar?" ("Christmas Eve," 1:231). It reasserts itself in the perplexity of Ivan Ivanovich, who is desperately trying to think of a way to acquire his neighbor's gun, but asks himself instead, with no less urgency, "But why is it made of iron?" (2:230).[24] As Gogol's madman says, try as you might to write "Spain," it'll always come out "China" (3:212).

Generative Models: The Story of the Discourse

Whether "Spain" or "China," the madman never truly makes it to the destination he imagined, any more than he obtains the object of his desire (the proverbial boss's daughter). Like so much Gogolian "content," this deflection of the madman's hopes and expectations reproduces the predicament of Gogol's readers, who are prevented (by the morass of material and the devices I have described) from getting either "what" or "where" they want. The excess not only complicates their access to the "story," the point behind all the elaboration, but also severely impedes their forward motion through the text. These excesses I have enumerated—from the digressive sort that strike out in a completely different direction, to the conglomerative ones that halt motion altogether by piling up insistently on one spot, to the illogical operations that trace only a discontinuous route—all prevent the reader from moving "from beginning to end in a significant way." The similes embody the problem of meandering and indirection most vividly. But the hyperbolic specificity, too, impedes motion by creating a kind of textual Zeno's paradox, perpetually splitting the distance by perpetually splitting hairs; and the convulsive backtracking of the diachrony throws forward progress relentlessly in reverse. Like the emphatic narrator of "The Nose," who concludes his story with an estimation of its value ("In the first place, it is decidedly of no use to our country; in the second place... but in the second place, too, it is of no use" [3:75]), Gogol declines to advance from the first place to the second place, from point A to point B. The trip itself, like the tale, is of "no use," neither purposeful nor directed.

Peter Brooks's book on plot is predicated on the assumption that "most viable works of literature tell us something about how they are to be read."[25] Gogol's works, we begin to understand, tell us something about how they are *difficult* to read. Beyond making movement through the text cumbersome, the discursive practices and problems are embedded as the very "content"—not only in the lightly self-referential ploys, such as the verbosity of Nozdrev and company, but most consistently in the generative models embraced throughout.

I refer here not to the obvious structural devices, such as the preface to *Arabesques* in which Gogol invokes the fiction of his unsystematic and uncritical compilation of all kinds of rubbish; or the Dikan'ka frame and its battle of competing narrators that serves less to differentiate the stories than (in the tradition of the *Decameron* and *1001 Nights*) to attribute them to someone. In this retroactively supplied "telling bee," in which the prospective narrators are gathered at the home of Rudyi Pan'ko and "simply chatter" (1:104), Gogol has been asked by his editor to do what readers regularly attempt to do for themselves: to motivate the overload.

I have in mind, rather, the discursive strategies that inhabit the content itself, that serve both to generate discourse and to comment on that overproduction, that describe both their own procedures and their problems as the very matter at hand, and that enable us to discuss the production and consumption of Gogol's texts in Gogol's own terms.

Each of the four generative models I will discuss is, in one way or another, a mark of desire—from the devil, the traditional agent of desire and instigator of urges, to food, the object of appetite, to hoarding, the overindulgence of covetous desire, to the image of non-arrival, the path of desire blocked.

Arrival: "You Can't Get There from Here"

As we have seen, the trajectory of Gogolian narrative digresses, jumps, or stands resolutely still: the path of desire is fraught with detours, potholes, and roadblocks. Even when figured as a pleasure trip, Chudakov's speeding rocket ship describes a troubling route into infinite space with no destination, no prospect of coming to rest, and no hope of getting to the point. Gogol himself names the problem: "Doezzhai-ne-doedesh'" ("Drive-and-drive-but-you'll-never-arrive," the nickname of one of Pliushkin's deceased serfs [6:125]). Not incidentally, *Doezzhai-ne-doedesh'* recalls Ivan Ivanovich's worst nightmare, *da ne doskazhesh'*, never getting to the end of the story (2:227). Gogol inscribes this narrative non-arrival in his beloved image of the road.

Narrative desire, I have said, is goal oriented: it strives to progress along a coherent path. But in Gogol, "the roadway everywhere [is] in bad shape" (*Dead Souls*, 6:11), and the problems of "getting there" are legion. In the "enchanted place" (where words multiply uncontrollably), travelers walk on and on, only to have their destination recede ever farther into the distance (1:312–13). In Gogol's works (where those same ever-multiplying words just sort of get in the way), readers often experience a similar futility. Provincial Russia's bad roads thus figure prominently in Gogol's poetics; the impassability they represent reflects graphically the reader's troubled trajectory on the narrative pathway, where the tenor of a simile is a point of departure from which there seems to be no point of arrival.

Non-arrival is almost paradigmatic in Gogol's oeuvre. As character after character discovers, "You can't get there from here." Granddad in "The Lost Letter" finds himself, after all his travels, back at the very beginning and can only start out yet again (1:190). The sorcerer of "A Terrible Vengeance" rides and rides but never arrives in Kanev; instead he finds himself in Shumsk. So he turns back to Kiev, but arrives at another town instead, even farther removed from his goal (1:277). For the entire length of "A May Night," the drunken Kalenik tries in vain to find his way home and eventually ends the story still staggering around looking for his own hut (1:180). This wandering of Kalenik is the explicit contentual analogue of the narrator's digressions: "While Kalenik is making his way to where he's going, we will without a doubt have time to say something about [the mayor]" (1:160); "But we've told you almost all that's necessary about the mayor and the drunken Kalenik still hasn't even gotten halfway there"(1:161). In "Christmas Eve," Chub and friend lose the very road in a snowstorm (1:213); Akakii Akakievich walks away from instead of toward his destination (3:152); and the Person of Consequence, who imagined he was going to his lady friend's to satisfy his desires, never gets there either (3:173). Only Gogol's madman "reaches" Spain in a mere half hour (3:211).

Much has been made of the ubiquitous road and the views it affords, less of its characteristic failure to lead anywhere.[26] In distinguishing between *doroga* and *put'*, between a spatial figure and the hero's actual movement through that space, between all potential roads and the path toward a specific goal, Lotman begins to address a certain disjunction between traveling and arriving.[27] In reading Gogol, we do indeed alternate between the thrill of the *doroga*, the "open road" (6:221–22), with its limitless possibilities, and a certain uneasiness about what this means for our own actual itinerary. But if Fanger emphasizes the goal orientation of Lotman's *put'*, its affinity with the dictates of *polza* and *tolk* (profit and sense),[28] I would argue that the outings we encounter inscribe instead the *failure* to arrive, frustration at the detour, and the collapse of the sense and purposefulness of the textual passages (passages in both senses).

Dead Souls opens with the conviction that while Chichikov's wheel might make it to Moscow, it would never get to Kazan' (6:7). More persistently obstructive to Chichikov's purposeful passage toward his destination, toward profit and sense (for him and us), however, are the machinations of his helmsman. Typical Russian driver that he is, Selifan always speeds along with his eyes closed; and though he inevitably gets *somewhere* in the end, it is rarely where Chichikov wished to go. When Selifan keeps driving, he is usually lost; when he stops, it is because he has collided with a fence and can go no farther (6:43). And when he misses his road, he simply gallops energetically off to the next one, "thinking very little about where the road he had taken would lead" (6:42). Perhaps the association of Chichikov and the amputee Captain Kopeikin is not so farfetched after all: the former is at the mercy of his creative driver, the latter subject to those English artificial legs that carry a person so far off that he is never to be heard from again (6:205).

Despite the apologetic protestations of the narrator to the contrary, Selifan is no secondary character. As he misses turns and gets hopelessly entangled en route (6:60, 90), he enacts and engenders the meanderings of the discourse.[29] By engineering its detours, Selifan traces a path that derails narrative desire and leaves us as far afield as Chichikov. So while Pletnev complains in his review of the novel that Petrushka and Selifan have no connection with *delo* (the matter at hand),[30] and while the narrator avers that he owes the story to Chichikov (6:240), I estimate that we owe at least as much of it to Selifan. And Selifan is text-producing not only insofar as he increases the extent of Chichikov's travels. His peregrinations on the road have a verbal analogue in the song he improvises as he drives along—something long and drawn out that seems to go on forever. "Everything got thrown in . . . without the slightest discrimination, just whatever happened to land on his tongue" (6:42). In every sense, Selifan runs on and on until he runs *off* the road.

Selifan is not dissimilar to the police captain of Mirgorod, whose trick leg diverts him only slightly more concretely than does his penchant for digression (2:256, 272). And while that officer's slowness to arrive drives Ivan Ivanovich mad with impatience, the latter himself regularly takes circuitous routes to the adjacent yard (2:230–31) (thereby revealing a greater tolerance for producing digression than for consuming it), and eventually he and Ivan Nikiforovich are shown to make only false starts.

Gogol militates against goal-oriented reading by problematizing arrival. It is difficult to move from beginning to end in a significant way if we are perpetually getting stuck, like Ivan Nikiforovich, in the doorway of the Mirgorod courthouse (2:251) or driven off the track as surely as if Selifan were at the helm. As we reproduce the transit history of Chichikov's vehicle (either speeding off the devil knows where or becoming hopelessly stalled and entangled), we begin to understand Akakii Akakievich's confusion about whether he is lost in the middle of a line or in the middle of a street (3:145).

All of these images of what Clarence Brown (taking a cue from Wallace Stevens) has dubbed "the not quite realized transit of Gogol" inscribe our own sense of impeded progress.[31] This "master kinetic pattern" informs all movement—physical, syntactical, and structural—in the text.[32] I would submit that it describes the pragmatic dimension equally well as we find ourselves driven by desire, but driven around by Selifan. As readers, we can only exclaim with the narrator of *Dead Souls*: "What hopelessly twisted, godforsaken, narrow, impassable roads that lead astray! . . . Where is the way out, where is the road?" (6:210–11).

Thus, when the narrator of the "Two Ivans" makes his final appearance (and final statement) by "passing through" and departing with haste, since a case with no verdict, a story with no end in sight (*da ne doskazhesh'*), is *skuchno* (boring) (2:276), we can understand the impulse. The narrator of *Dead Souls* plays on the reader's *need* to arrive at something comprehensible when he promises early on: "But the reader will learn all about this gradually and in good time, if only he has the patience to read the whole work at hand, which is very long and will expand more broadly to still greater enormity as it nears its end, which crowns the matter" (6:19). But this promised "crowning end" is the greatest joyride of them all, the speeding troika which, like Chudakov's rocket, is hurtling only God knows where. *Dead Souls* Part I ends on a great *kuda?* (whither?). The Gogolian text suppresses arrival, "coming" to rest. Admittedly Part II was to have consummated the affair. But Gogol doesn't get there.

This is not to disparage the adequacy of Gogol's endings—in fact, Fusso makes a good case for the willed closure (she calls it "promissory closure") of even such avowedly open-ended texts as *Dead Souls*.[33] It is not the endinglessness of Gogol's texts that is so troubling, but the apparent endlessness of the middle, the interminable elaboration and the resulting anxiety that, like the bewitched dancers who can never advance beyond the middle of the dance (1:311), like *Doezzhai-ne-doedesh'* (and thanks to *ne-doskazhesh'*), you might never get there. And even though arrival signifies the death of narration, if Freud is right, then beyond the pleasure principle lies the death instinct; we do have a drive toward quiescence, toward an inorganic state of rest.[34] Often, confronting Gogol's compendia of catalogues or explosions of dependent clauses, one despairs of even coming to the end of the sentence.

I might note that even Gogol becomes impatient when reading others whose routes are circuitous. He seemed to associate reading Jean Paul, for instance, whose novels exhibit many of the same discursive excesses as his own prose, with feeling unwell.[35] It is interesting that Jean Paul's "joyride" seems to produce motion sickness in Gogol when he is in the passenger seat; I regard this as partial validation of my own exasperation at being similarly propelled around by Gogol. As we have seen in the example of Ivan Ivanovich, whose own capacity for *à propos des bottes* non sequitur is great (2:261), but who cannot tolerate any such straying by others, it is much more fun to give than to receive.[36]

"The Devil Only Knows What to Make of It"

If losing the way is both a problem and a producer of more text, representing both the path of frustrated desire and the vehicle of digression, then the devil, whose specialty it is to lead astray, is the perfect agent of discursive desire. But in Gogol he is an agent provocateur, one who inflames desire only to sabotage its satisfaction.

In the Dikan'ka stories, where devilry dominates the village imagination, the devil serves nicely as the purveyor of distended discourse, the source of more and more words (particularly in the bedeviled place where all words are echoed). As a complicator of lives, too, the devil easily produces complication of plot and hence generates more story. More germane to Gogol, the most random behavior can be explained by a satanic urge ("some devil . . . made him open the door" [1:142]), thus occasioning material the relevance of which is not otherwise apparent (and each such reported action in turn brings in its wake myriad descriptive details and exclamations). Most significantly, perhaps, possession by the devil aptly motivates uncontrollable telling on the part of the textual raconteurs, like the Dnepr Cossack in "The Lost Letter" who told such stories that "there must have been a demon in him" (1:183). Foma Grigor'evich's enchanted grandfather, the paradigmatic storyteller in the Dikan'ka stories, is also a master at "treating the devil to nicknames," multiplying the names of the multiplier of words himself (1:185). Narrative activity thus becomes as frenetic as old granddad's uncontrollable dancing.[37]

Clearly the devil is more than just a frequent visitor to the town: he is a full-blown discursive strategy. The countless expressions and turns of phrase generated from the ever-productive Russian word *chert* come to life: as people "speak of the devil," these rhetorical flourishes acquire story-level existence. The characters and narrators have "a devil of a time," they "scare the devil out of themselves," "the devil made them do it," and most saliently for the often incomprehensible Gogolian oeuvre, "the devil only knows what to make of it" (1:153)—as if the availability of the expressions generates the very action (just as it is from expressions using the word "nose" that much of the action of "The Nose" proceeds). This is not a straightforward matter of story generating discourse; the discursive strategy itself creates the story: "It is the devil and not man who weaves the web of gossip," wrote Gogol. Once a word (especially *chert*) is dropped, "the word goes out for a walk . . . and little by little a tale weaves itself."[38]

But does the discourse serve the devil, or is it the other way around? Gogol's discourse, it seems, is by far the more demonic force. The devil, ironically, is just the word made flesh, the principle of proliferation clothed in a red jacket. So when Rancour-Laferriere points out that in "The Fair at Sorochintsy" the main romantic story line is interrupted by storytelling about the devil, and Driessen claims that the love story is actually a lot less central than the story of the devil's red jacket—that the very subject of the tale is a demonic principle—I suspect it is less the devil himself than the proliferation he both causes and stands for that makes him "the main figure in all of Gogol's work."[39] In casting such figures of proliferation as actual characters in the story, Gogol inscribes his own discursive strategies as content. This devil, it seems, is more metacritical than metaphysical.[40]

In Gogol's world the devil does represent a genuine threat, a real and present danger. Satan is obviously more than a whimsical figure of speech; he is a perilous force striving to turn humankind away from its true goal. But in suggesting that the disorder of Gogol's later prose is a discursive remnant of the earlier demons who "scrambled everything up," Mann recognizes an important link between the demonic and the chaotic.[41] As a usurper of power and self-control, the devil character gives us a story about loss of discursive self-possession.

The Gogolian text inscribes in this way not only its production but also some of the problems of its reception: the demonic red jacket of "The Fair at Sorochintsy," which turns up indiscriminately and disruptively (disconcerting characters and readers alike), is constantly being chopped to pieces and scattered about (because, like manuscripts, it does not burn and seems otherwise impossible to dispose of, and because, whatever Gogol may have done with Part II of *Dead Souls*, he did not burn the Dikan'ka cycle, and we are stuck with it[42]). The devil is pictured walking about despondently, picking up pieces, searching for a way to put them all together. Readers find themselves in much the same predicament, left to collect the fragments of folktales, plays, proverbs, curses, and other random verbal elements scattered throughout *Evenings* in an attempt to reconstruct an integrated whole from the chaos and profusion.

The rampant devilry, then, is both source and object of the rampant storytelling and all the complaints it inspires. And though Rudyi Pan'ko has mercifully omitted some stories, "so as not to be feared like the devil" (1:106), his powers of proliferation are every bit as fearsome; indeed, he admits, "so much printed paper has piled up already that it's hard to think of what to wrap in it" (1:103).

"Food in a Bowl" and Much, Much More

What is most persistently "wrapped" in all this paper is *food*, both in the Dikan'ka prefaces themselves and in the stories they introduce. It is Mrs. Pan'ko's batch of incomparable dinner rolls that averts an open expression of hostility between the two narrators in the first preface (1:106). It is none other than Pan'ko's renowned conversation about apple pickling that finally precipitates the huffy departure of the offended urban narrator in the second preface (1:196). In "Shpon'ka," especially, we are presented with a regular transcript of discussions of turkey parts and who should take which ones (1:299), frequent rhapsodic interludes on the varieties and virtues of melons (1:299), and crucial documents that culminate in ecstatic ejaculations about the measurements of a turnip (1:287). Conversation consists of the sonorous sucking on lamb bones (1:300), and fast friendships are forged over matters of cucumbers (1:298). "Revealing secrets" refers to the sharing of recipes for apple cheese and methods for drying pears (1:301). Even the latest development in the conspiratorial schemes for acquiring a neighbor's estate is "not the point now." What is the point? "Well, was the dinner good?" Naturally, details of the excellent repast ensue (1:302).

Gogol's fixation on the culinary is readily apparent throughout his works, and numerous critics have commented on the symbolic value of the abundant food.[43] Much less has been said, however, about its discursive function. Like the devil and the confused coachmen, food is used both to expand the prose and to convert that formidable expansiveness into the very substance of the story.

For food is not only the source of sustenance for the characters; it is enlisted to increase the bounty of the discourse. The turkey parts are not nourishment but rather information to be reflected on aloud from all possible angles (1:299); those who "take great pleasure in conversation about anything that can possibly be talked about" are actually quite silent on subjects other than pear kvass, melons, geese, cucumbers, and potatoes (1:301). And the greatest advantage of granddad's marvelous melon patch is neither the delicious fruit it produces, nor the substantial profit it turns, but rather the distended discourse it generates: it incites passing travelers to spin extravagant yarns—stories that are "like dumplings to a hungry man" ("The Enchanted Place," 1:310).

Indeed, in Dikan'ka, food is not only the subject of all conversations; it is the very substance of the communicative act. Before the relationship of Shpon'ka and his aunt ever assumed epistolary form, it existed in the dried pears and "the most delicious homemade cakes" that she used to bring him in his childhood (and later sent him during his years at school), and which are his only knowledge and memory of the kindly relative (1:287). She, in turn, imagines her absent grandnephew as a little boy asking for pie and "communes" with him by absentmindedly holding out tasty morsels to the thin air before her (1:303). I note in this gratuitous offer of food a certain parallel to the Gogolian gesture of perpetual provisioning and recognize in the incompleteness of the transaction the strong suggestion that such persistent feeding is a difficult offering to accept.

Beyond the caloric preoccupations of the food-crazed characters, the hyperbolic attention to food infests the descriptive language of the text itself. Vests are inevitably the color of wine dregs (1:170), cloaks are not merely green, but specifically the hue of pea soup

(1:105) or cold mashed potatoes (1:104–5), and the epithets attached to the fabrics are as extravagant as the repasts Gogol loves to describe. While it is hardly uncommon to characterize color in terms of fruit flavors (lemon yellow, cherry red), even in the highly refined designations of today's fashion industry the effectiveness of the categories rests on their sensual immediacy. Gogol's lavish appropriation of culinary by-products rather clutters the tableau.[44]

But if Gogol's comestibles are not in adherence to any code of fashion, what they do have in common with today's arena of conspicuous consumption is their recourse to the appetite to awaken desire. Like the upscale catalogues that boast "eggplant" trousers and "licorice" handbags, Gogol embraces food as advertising copy. In concluding his preface praising the marvelous stories and storytellers of Dikan'ka, Pan'ko puts in a good word about the treats in store for the reader who agrees to come to that hothouse of narrative:

> When you come to visit, we will serve you melons such as you have probably never eaten in your life; and, I swear, you will find no better honey on any farm. . . . And what pies my old woman will feed you! What pies, if only you knew: sugar, perfect sugar! And the butter simply melts in your mouth when you start to eat them. When you come right down to it, what masters these women are! Have you, gentlemen, ever had pear kvass flavored with sloes, or vodka with raisins and plums? Or have you ever tried rice soup with milk? Goodness gracious, what treats there are in the world! Once you start to eat, it is ecstasy, total and complete. What indescribable sweetness! Last year... But I'm getting carried away!.. Just come, come as soon as you can, and we will feed you so well that you will want to tell everyone you meet. (1:107)

On the one hand, Pan'ko admits to having gone a bit overboard (*razboltalsia*) in his lengthy tribute to the culinary arts. On the other hand, he introduces it by exclaiming: "But there, I almost forgot the most important thing" (1:106). In foregrounding the confusion between the essential and the tangential in a text in which digression is the dominant, Pan'ko's foreword does engage several questions that are not inconsequential.

First, it seems to reflect on its very function as preface. It confronts the need to tantalize the reader, to stimulate the appetite for the main course, and to propel the reader in. It is unclear, however, whether this extended and cloying promise of sweetness facilitates that propulsion any more than Rudyi Pan'ko's silly directions to his hut.

Second, this menu-as-preface gives an accurate foretaste of the stories to come from Pan'ko's larder: they are as laden with food as Pan'ko predicts, thus admitting no complaints about Pan'ko's truth in advertising. But is all we ingest really as absolutely delicious as the beekeeper personally guarantees?

Most of all, the passage demonstrates once again the unrivaled power of the palate to produce more and more words (in spite of the alleged "indescribability" of the sweetness)—not only in view of Pan'ko's tendency to "blab out of control" on the subject, but also insofar as the reader/consumer, too, will be inspired to *talk* about this food to "anyone and everyone" (*rasskazyvat' i vstrechnomu i poprechnomu*).

If *Evenings on a Farm Near Dikan'ka* opens with the promise of a feast, it closes with an awareness of how difficult the produce of a bedeviled soil may be to digest: in the enchanted place, where words sprout as uncontrollably as seeds, "it is impossible to figure out what comes up: not a watermelon, not a pumpkin, not a cucumber—the devil only knows what to make of it!" (1:316). The final sentence of the cycle brings together two prime multipliers of words (food and the devil) in an almost wistful retrospective admission that the rambling discourse is impossible to make sense of (*razobrat' nel'zia*)—as has certainly been the impression of many readers.

But the early Dikan'ka stories are only the first course. The repast continues in the Mirgorod cycle ("Stories Serving as a Continuation of *Evenings on a Farm Near Dikan'ka*," as the subtitle proclaims).[45] "Old-World Landowners" in particular is one continuous menu. It features Pul'kheriia Ivanovna, who, in perfect imitation of the Gogolian narrator, is unable to disregard anything that crosses her path (2:17) and "always liked to prepare a store for the future above and beyond what she figured to be necessary for use" (2:19). This excess is embodied in the exhaustive inventory that faithfully reproduces the bounty of her storeroom—from the innumerable sorts of preserves and delicacies she stockpiles in her larder, to the multiple types of vodka that render a man "utterly unable to control his tongue" (2:19). The very syntax of the prose imitates an annotated catalogue. Rudyi Pan'ko's vocabulary lists have become grocery lists, and the lists are interminable.

Like the dishes of Nozdrev's cook, who pitches everything at hand into his soup (while the narrator follows suit in his prose) (6:75);[46] like Rudyi Pan'ko's continuous invitation to a continuous feast in the preface to his Dikan'ka tales; like the repasts throughout Gogol's prose that prompt the narrator to "expatiate on them" ad nauseam (despite his avowed preference for "eating them" [2:271]); like the "vast scale" of the preparations for the banquet in "The Carriage," and the correspondingly vast scale of the reportage they prompt (3:179–80), food in Gogol's texts seems to have a remarkable tendency to stimulate the tongue well beyond its usual transaction with the tastebuds.

184   *Gogol: Content and Its Discontents*

Food and appetite *produce* text—and not only insofar as the young Shpon'ka must prop up a book to conceal his classroom snacking (1:285). When Akakii Akakievich's stomach begins to growl, he reaches for his ink and starts copying (3:145). The legal scribbler of "Two Ivans" fuels his own production of pages and pages of convulsive legalese by consuming nine pies in rapid succession (2:261). "Dishes become words," says Louis Marin: food is the quintessential sign.[47]

The reception of all this discourse is logically cast as consumption—stories are actually baked into pies, after all (1:283), and are "like dumplings to a hungry man" (1:310). But the dilemma of the Gogolian reader/eater is most vividly depicted in the plight of Afanasii Ivanovich, devoted husband of Pul'kheriia Ivanovna, cast (like the reader) in the role of both indefatigable listener (2:15, 16, 24, 35) and indefatigable consumer of biscuits with lard, poppy seed pies, pickled mushrooms, vodka, dried fish, porridge, butter, mushroom sauce, watermelon, pears, dumplings (naturally), berries, and a great many other things—all before (and inevitably delaying) the main agenda: dinner (2:21–23). This gluttony is reflected in the glut of details in the prose,[48] and when Afanasii Ivanovich develops a stomachache in the wake of his tremendous intake, we can relate to his distress. "Gogol's literary viands," confirms Ivask, "are fatty, calorie-laden, like dishes prepared by Pul'kheriia Ivanovna."[49] Predictably, the cure for Afanasii's bellyache is to eat some more (2:23), and the reader is served up ever more as well. We wind up with acute indigestion like the banquet-goers in "The Carriage," with a fervent need to unbutton our waistcoats (which, however, discretion and training forbid [3:181]—reading Gogol, after all, is "fun"). We are overcome, like the obese Cossack Patsiuk (who has sold his soul to the devil for food): as dumplings and turnovers fly interminably into his mouth (after dipping themselves into sour cream), he becomes so engorged that he cannot even budge. Vakula, too, who stands immobilized with his mouth open to swallow words as if they were dumplings, is as miserable as can be ("Christmas Eve," 1:224). Gogol himself, who suffered from digestive-tract problems and stomach ailments, used food as a form of self-punishment,[50] and his own terms of overconsumption suggest some of the problems of narrative overindulgence; as any psychologist will confirm, eating disorders have little to do with pleasure.

Thus, like devilry, cookery operates not only as a generative strategy, a ploy for swelling the dimensions of the discourse (as well as the characters); transactions of feeding and eating become a metaphor for both the production and the consumption of text. And in the reverse transubstantiation of the word into pies that deletes the ending of "Shpon'ka," not even "the best pies in the world" (1:283) can satisfy the hunger for what readers want most: access to the beginning, middle, and end of plot. Despite the abundance of pies, readers, like the author himself, hunger for story—*um i zheludok moi oba golodaiut*.[51]

In "A Few Words About Pushkin," where he makes the association of reading and eating explicit, Gogol himself seems to shun gluttony and concur that excess detracts from pleasure. To appreciate Pushkin's delicacy, he writes, the reader must be a "sybarite," a voluptuary of subtle flavors and dainty morsels who has renounced the larger, heavier portions of coarse fare (8:54). In this determined use of the lexicon of gastronomy to discuss reading taste, Mann recognizes Gogol's polemic with the Romantic sensibility that would divorce the aesthetic from the physical appetites.[52]

On the one hand, Gogol upholds the urgency of appetite—including appetite for *text*, figuring his readers' impatience for the next installment of *Dead Souls* as a hungry company waiting interminably for a delayed meal.[53] On the other hand, he evinces a keen awareness of the discomfort of ongoing textual *obzhorstvo i vypivka* (gluttony and drinking bouts).[54] He condemns canine correspondence, which is fixated on food, as patent "nonsense" ("as if there were nothing better to write about!" [3:202]); but are Gogol's own "doggie letters" any more worth reading than Roz Chast's kitty diary?

Gogol's intemperance leaves us wanting what we really need and staggering from the overdose of what we don't. We want more "what" for all the "how," more story for our discourse, more "nutritional value" for the servings we are constrained to swallow in bulk. The abundance of the Gogolian text is less satiating than cloying, less idyllic than horrific—indeed interminable gnawing is a "terrible vengeance," part of Gogol's vision of hell (1:282). Thus, as Gogol's "recipes" obligingly produce both plenty of food and plenty of words, we are presented with a crisis of meaning, significance, and thwarted desire, all in terms of digestive distress.

Ronald LeBlanc posits a Gogolian distinction between "tasting" (*goûter*) and "eating" (*manger*), between Manilov (the "gourmet"), who orders every dish on the menu to taste a little bit of each, and Sobakevich (the "gourmand"), who wolfs down entire portions and demands seconds without extra charge (6:63).[55] While LeBlanc cites the opposition to distinguish between feasting characters rather than reading strategies, the contrast between savoring and gobbling is suggestive at both levels. But if in Barthes's version of the opposition "gobbling" is aggressive, directed reading for the plot (as opposed to a langorous savoring of the discourse), the kind of gobbling that results from Gogolian force-feeding gets you anywhere but where you want to go. Nor is the alternative—the "dainty appetite" Gogol valorizes in the sophisticated reader of Pushkin—a live option given the cascades of produce one must ingest in the Gogolian oeuvre.

Gogol's raw material is like dough, claims Bely, and every conceivable detail is baked into the finished pie.[56] What kind of sybarite must one be to digest this doughy mess?[57] Gogol's own narrator envies the healthy appetites that can withstand limitless portions (*Dead Souls*, 6:61). But it is, in the end, only a *sow* who can gobble up everything in her path (rubbish, chicken, rinds, and so on [6:48]). Must the reader consent to eat like a pig to take in the "all sorts of rubbish" that flies by (6:21)? Sobakevich, the gobbler, insists on being served a *whole* pig, a *whole* lamb, a *whole* goose (6:99); but how are we to devour *vsiu Rus'* (the whole of Russia)? Even Rudyi Pan'ko, who while presenting his book to the reader admits in the same breath that some foods are hard to chew (1:195), acknowledges that a serving of Gogol is anything but *Reader's Digest*.

Thus, Gogolian gluttony operates (like circuitous travel and infernal temptation) both to produce unsightly discursive flab and to inscribe its own discursive procedures and problems. Ivan Ivanovich's famous melon-seed collection is not only one of many examples of the fanatical alimentary retentiveness that provides edibles for an overzealous narrator to enumerate, but also an instance that enacts its own modus operandi. Ivan Ivanovich wraps each seed in paper: recording in detail the historical coordinates of each respective melon (date of consumption, personnel present), he explicitly generates text from food, and not the most interesting text at that (2:224). When we are afforded a view within the story of Gogol's own discursive strategy, it looks fairly pathological.

Hoarding

Collectors

But obsessive hoarding, as I have noted repeatedly, is a pervasive pathology. The miserly Pliushkin is only the most completely controlled by his compulsion to collect. The retentive Ivan Ivanovich, too, is always alert to the possibility of acquiring another thing, and Pul'kheriia Ivanovna, the genius of eating disorders, keeps whatever she can find, putting away infinitely "more than is needed." Her compulsive foraging and feeding betrays an economy of hoarding and splurging not unlike the author's own collection and deployment of collectors and their respective hoards to provision his verbal prodigality. In his inscription of hoarding, the obsessive accretion of many things to motivate the naming of many things, Gogol invents Pliushkin many times over.

Chichikov may be taken aback when he encounters this arch–pack rat, but, really, his own impulses are not so very different. Quite aside from his fervent campaign to stockpile dead souls, Chichikov compulsively stuffs anything and everything he picks up into his famous box, from which nothing is ever discarded (6:161). Even as a boy, Chichikov accumulated kopecks graspingly, sewing them for safekeeping into little bags (6:226).

In this behavior he is not alone. Akakii Akakievich, too, maintains a little cache of coppers in a locked box (3:154). And the thrifty Korobochka (who in a lengthy passage of characteristically Gogolian overspecification, is nevertheless identified as one of many) does in fact represent a Gogolian commonplace: the hoarder. She is "one of those little old ladies,"

> those small land-owning ladies who are always crying about bad harvests and losses and hold their heads somewhat to one side, while at the same time accumulating, bit by bit, nice little hoards of cash, in colorful cloth bags scattered among different drawers of various bureaus. One little bag will be for silver rubles alone; another will hold the little half-ruble coins, and a third the quarter-rubles, although at first glance it will look like there's nothing in the bureau besides underwear and nightshirts, and spools of thread, and a lady's old coat with the seams ripped open, earmarked for eventual transformation into a dress, if the old one should somehow get a hole burned in it during the baking of holiday cakes and fritters with various fillings or just completely wear out on its own. But that dress will never get burned and it will never wear out on its own; thrifty is this little old lady, and the coat is fated to lie for a long, long time in its ripped-up state, and to pass by last will and testament to the niece of a second cousin, together with all kinds of other rubbish. (6:45)

As the run-on quality of the passage makes clear, this hoard is "earmarked for transformation" not into the dress Korobochka had in mind, but into *text*, and I am not persuaded that this legacy of "all kinds of other rubbish" is any more readable than the painstaking record of Ivan Ivanovich's melon-seed compulsion. The reader's impatience at having to hear about the internal arrangement of Chichikov's little box applies just as forcefully to Korobochka's drawers, Ivan Ivanovich's cupboards, and Pul'kheriia Ivanovna's pantry.

And yet cases, trunks, and cupboards are systematically emptied to produce narrative content. Thankfully, as long as they remain locked we are spared the inventory. Hence the importance of Gapka, the keeper of Ivan Ivanovich's storerooms and cellars, who secures them with locks and keys, and Ivan Ivanovich's own insistence on keeping the keys to the biggest trunk himself (2:224). And hence Agafiia Fedoseevna's first act—the appropriation of keys—upon her arrival at Ivan Nikiforovich's (2:240). Pul'kheriia Ivanovna's housekeeping, we are told, consists of continuously locking and unlocking her ample storage room (2:19), just as Shpon'ka amuses himself by repeatedly unpacking and repacking his trunk of underwear. Although *he* is never bored by this compulsive reviewing of contents (a behavior that is closely associated with his compulsive rereading of his catalogue of fortunes), we might well be. When Gogol claims to have unpacked all the trash in his desk to produce *Arabesques* (8:748), we cringe at the prospect.

Verbal Collections

The association of hoarding with verbal prodigality implied by the editorial retentiveness of *Arabesques* emerges as a proposition of the Gogolian *story*, nowhere more clearly than in the character of Akakii Akakievich. Not only does Akakii Akakievich fanatically hoard two-kopeck pieces and even collect garbage, due to his "special talent for passing under windows at the very moment when various rubbish was being thrown out of them" (3:145); what accrues in the greatest quantity on and around the figure of this copy clerk is *words*. Professionally, he reproduces them day in and day out (much like Ippolit Ippolitych and his beloved maps). And in his capacity as Gogolian character, Akakii provides a pretext for the production of more words and clauses than any reasonable sentence can accommodate (most notably in the page-long extravaganza beginning, "Even at those hours" [3:146]). In this seemingly infinite deferral of the main clause, Gogol's own procedure parallels his hero's fundamentally agoraphobic impulse to fill up empty pages with words.

"The Overcoat" seems to be largely about this discursive habit. Akakii Akakievich is a collector and proliferator of letters (both kinds). Shapely consonants are his principal love object, and the letters he copies at work inspire such admiration that he makes more and more copies for himself. Luxuriating in letters is (to apply a distinction Gogol himself makes about desire and reading) not a product of "duty," but a "genuine compulsion."[58]

Most of the "collector's items" the energetic Chichikov deposits in his trusty box are verbal as well—from fliers to anonymous letters, lists of serfs, and titles of "ownership." For that matter, even the procurement of dead souls is enacted as a scene of pure writing, the most gratifying acquisitions consisting of the unwieldy names that sprawl all over the page (6:136), or Manilov's contribution, noteworthy for its stunning calligraphy (6:140).

This story-level attention to handwriting and the proliferative powers of script is the textual counterpart of Gogol's own production methods. As if not content with the verbal explosion within each text, Gogol insisted on copying and recopying each story eight times or more in his own hand.[59] This copying—by Akakii Akakievich, Manilov, and company, as well as by Gogol himself—is only the most flagrant way of generating words not from the things they name, but just from other words. Gogol's dogged enumeration of things notwithstanding, the real prize seems to be their verbal designations.

His notebooks bear this out. Whereas Chekhov's notebooks were full of situations for potential stories, Tolstoy's with events from his own life, and Dostoevsky's with psychological observations and other notes for his novels, Gogol's notebooks were filled primarily with lists of words.[60] The raw materials he assembled were not events and existents to animate, but rather what Chudakov calls their "verbal envelopes."[61] His geography sketches, too, compile names of vegetation encountered along the road, with each plant named doubly—first in Russian, then in Latin. An undisguised list of words, Gogol's account of a journey "from Petersburg to Moscow" is a subversion of syntax only (9:309–414). His "Materials for a Dictionary of the Russian Language" (9:443–85) is only the most avowedly verbal collection.

Statistical studies of Gogol's prose have confirmed what readers feel: an unbridled overgrowth of words. Iu. S. Sorokin documents Gogol's exuberant use of regionally specific vocabulary with the certainty that this reflects not ethnographic integrity but artistic imperatives.[62] Gogol is hard to read not just because he uses odd words, but because he musters so many of them. He indulges his propensity for pleonasm by stockpiling synonyms, especially (appropriately enough) for verbal misbehavior: *briaknut'*, *pronesti*, *zagorodit' okolesinu*, *khvatit'*, and so forth.[63] The fanatical hoarding that animates Gogol's characters and provisions his prose produces a similarly verbal cache; Gogol's stories of hoarding are inexorably the story of his own agglomerative discourse.

Words and Things:
The Problem of Immateriality

To get to the point: are there many things in Gogol or just many words? In the exercise of Gogol's adamic penchant for bestowing names, collecting them, and reproducing them, what becomes of the things they refer to? Do we really sense their "solidity" and "presence," as Maguire claims? Are Gogol's words content-bearing, or are they "empty envelopes"? For Lacan, who contends that "to enter language is to be severed from . . . the real," this sense of lack and emptiness is simply the linguistic condition.[64] But Gogol's proclivity for "designation that designates nothing" (*nichego ne opredeliaiushchee opredelenie*)[65] creates a singular vacuum. Mann, like Belinsky before him, celebrates the *soderzhatel'nost'* of Gogol's prose—its richness in content—despite the "limitedness of the material."[66] I would suggest, rather, that the material is limitless, but its very materiality is in question. How contentful, how *material* is it really? How do the things behind Gogol's words fare? Do we get what we want in these envelopes?

Things (Matter: Does It Matter?)

Gogol's "thing world" hardly seems impoverished. After all, we hear unremittingly about "all kinds of rubbish," some of which is introduced long before its human counterparts,[67] and much of which exhibits unusual animation and mobility. The nose with a mind (and face, and uniform, and itinerary) of its own is perhaps the most enterprising "thing" in Gogol's repertoire, but it is not unique. On Nevskii Prospekt, too, bodily parts parade about quite disconnected. Dem'ian Dem'ianovich, the Mirgorod judge, is vexed by a perverse "autonomy on the part of his nose" (2:253), and the chief of police must devote considerable energy to counteracting the efforts of his defiant left foot. In Dikan'ka, things are avowedly demonic (bowing goblets, dancing tubs of dough, and the like). In certain venues, things threaten in their sheer profusion to encroach and smother the "living" occupants. Mirgorod is so overfull of disorderly things, says Lotman, that it has ceased to be a "space," degenerating instead into pure chaos. And in *Taras Bul'ba*, things are the enemy itself.[68]

At the very least, Gogol's things are the enemy of *sense*. The Pliushkin mansion illustrates vividly the difficulty of sense-making in the face of such profusion. It is as difficult to discern whether Pliushkin is a man or a woman as it is to make out what comprises his jumbled heaps (6:114–15). One could ask of the Pliushkin residence and most other Gogolian settings the same question that opens chapter 2 of "The Fair at Sorochintsy"—"What isn't there at the fair?" (1:115)—and the answer would be the same. What fails to materialize is significance and sense. Although Swift maintained that the "infinity of matter" in modern literature derives from the fact that we now know so much,[69] the infinite profusion in Gogol's work seems to prevent us from knowing anything at all—about the matter at hand, anyway.

Many of Gogol's things do make sense in terms of the matter at hand and thus have actual story-level existence: even the consumption of eggs in Pliushkin's household has at least some connection, however tenuous, to the *fabula*. But what of the many things that have no relation at all—spatial, temporal, or logical—to the story? These do not increase the dimensions of the *fabulnyi* sphere (as in classic, realist novels); they take up space in the discourse only. The interest of these second-tier "things" for the reader, Chudakov claims, lies not in tying them in with the story, which in any case is discontinuous and difficult, but in reveling in their unmitigated "inclusion." The greatest possible pleasure is derived from contemplating "the greatest possible quantity of things . . . illuminated by the brilliance radiating from a great mind."[70]

I have already expressed skepticism about the thrill of such unrestrained "all-inclusiveness" (*vseokhvatnost'*). But I question further the very substantiality of what Chudakov calls the "thing world": are the many things named by Gogol's texts really so "illuminated" (brilliantly or otherwise)? Are they really so present, so solid as to reflect these genial rays?

"Words, Words, Words"

Surely the abundance here is less material than verbal—not only because any text is composed of words or because a fictional world is one that by definition has no actual existence, and not even because all that signifiers can really invoke are conceptual signifieds rather than material referents, but because Gogol is so infatuated with signs that have no referents even to bracket—discourse with no story behind it and no existents or events to warrant it.[71]

Chichikov's coveted dead souls, the object of the most avid collecting, stand out as the most graphic example of "expression without corresponding content."[72] Dead and gone, they exist as name only: "Nothing is left of them but sound alone, not even perceptible to the senses" (6:102). "Such names," Akakii Akakievich's mother had originally objected to the innumerable names proposed for her son, "but there are no such people!" (3:452).[73] Indeed, even Rudyi Pan'ko recognizes that nicknames endure *veki vekov* (for all time), much longer than the bodies they ostensibly designate (1:104). And yet these dead "Probkas" and "Mikheevs" generate massive amounts of text—both in the lists they form and in the "torrents of speech" they inspire, "such an abundant flood of speech which seemed to have no end"—even though they do not exist ("you can't prop up a fence with them") [6:102–3]).

Equally insubstantial is the "land" (not to mention the river and the pond) in the Kherson province, the nonexistent destination of the nonexistent serfs described and debated at length in *Dead Souls*. Since the "peasants" Chichikov intends to settle there are only empty signifiers, the townsfolk's skepticism about Chichikov's ability to control his "turbulent rabble" articulates the broader question about Gogol's ability to control his discourse (6:147–48, 154–55). Like the officers in "The Carriage," whose war stories feature intricate detail about battles that had never been fought, and who, having finished playing cards, continue the game verbally for quite a while because the discourse of whist fills their heads longer than the cards fill their hands (3:185), Gogol seems to generate compulsively more and more words for which there are no things at all.

Pan'ko's vocabulary lists, in fact, only make explicit the nature of Gogolian discourse in general. As glosses on a text, they are signifiers that refer explicitly to words only, rather than to things. Like Akakii Akakievich's verbatim copying, like the production of text from extended wordplay,[74] the glossaries only repeat *verbal* material. The referential line is broken. Moreover, many of these so-called "vocabulary words" lack even *verbal* referents—they do not appear in the text of the stories at all. While masquerading as a source of coherence, Rudyi Pan'ko's famous vocabulary lists are as little help to the readers of the Dikan'ka stories as the abridged dream interpreter at the end of the fortune-telling book is to Shpon'ka in unraveling his incoherent dream (1:308). Like the name "Bashmachkin," which one feels should be a meaningful sign but is not, Gogol's catalogues of words testify rather to the general "destruction of connections between expression and significance."[75]

Entitlement, too, ostensibly a source of information about the textual material under its instructive aegis, is wielded by Gogol as another excuse for the most lavish "expression without corresponding content." The full title of the universally abbreviated "Two Ivans," "The Story About How Ivan Ivanovich Quarreled with Ivan Nikiforovich," does at least get around to announcing its topic—albeit in a dependent clause and after it finishes specifying the obvious (that it is a story and that the story is about something). The individual chapter titles (such as "Chapter 2, From Which One May Learn What Ivan Ivanovich Desired, the Subject of the Conversation That Transpired Between Ivan Ivanovich and Ivan Nikiforovich, and How It Ended" [2:228]) do an even more energetic imitation of eighteenth-century conventions of diction and entitlement to motivate their prolixity while nevertheless limiting their informational content. And "Chapter 6, From Which the Reader May Easily Learn All That Is Contained in It" (2:261) continues the format while containing no sense-making information at all. It is pure form, medium without message. No wonder Ivan Ivanovich favors books without titles (2:239). Titles, like the best names of dead serfs, are as insubstantial as they are extensive.

To inflate the already lopsided word-to-thing ratio, the "non-correspondence between word and thing,"[76] Gogol adds to the empty names and nouns his vast vocabulary of particles with no counterreality at all. His words do not depict a world—even a fictional one—any more than Gogol's "painter" can represent the odors and sounds of nocturnal Mirgorod.[77] Perhaps it is in this sense that Gogol could claim so forcefully that *Dead Souls* is *not* a portrait of Russia.[78]

No matter how many complaints are registered by Gogol's narrators about their tired eyes (worn out from "observing" all that is reported so scrupulously), it is difficult to speak of the superabundance of Gogol's prose as the product of perception, even from the strangest point of view. And yet visual metaphors abound in the critical attempts to account for his jumbled heaps. McLean postulates that from Gogol's vantage point in Rome, Russia was too distant for proper perspective, and "confronted only with a jumble of detail, he could get no vision of the whole." His long-range telescope distorts and magnifies things out of proportion.[79] Gary Cox, similarly, speaks of "atomic perception" which results in a "fragmented jumble of disconnected objects."[80] Proffer notes Gogol's tendency to "focus in" on peripheral detail.[81] Bely, too, concludes that Gogol has abnormal vision—his eyes are always either open "too wide" or squinted down to admit only the most minute detail.[82] And Maguire devotes a good third of his book on Gogol to the author's idiosyncratic praxis of seeing.[83] But is what Gogol writes really what he *sees*?

Although Gogol's peculiar deployment of detail may be related to the realists' and naturalists' fetishization of the eye as an organ of observation[84] (his eyes, like his writing hand, are exhausted by the spectacle), it is even more intimately connected with what can only be called a fetishization of the word. And this discursive fetish, as usual, acquires contentual status in Gogol's stories.

Verbal fetishism is, in fact, the only "story" of how Ivan Ivanovich quarreled with his neighbor. The insult he sustains is indeed arbitrary, but more saliently it is pure signifier,[85] an expression with no real corresponding content, an empty word that obscures everything else for the characters. It is a word alone—*gusak* (gander)—that causes such offense ("If Ivan Nikiforovich had not uttered that word, they would have quarreled and parted, as usual, as friends" [2:237]); it is that word alone that foils their reconciliation years later ("The word had been uttered. Everything went straight to hell" [2:273]). For a brief moment, an excellent bowl of borscht erases the fateful word from the mind of Ivan Ivanovich (who, we are told from the start, is extraordinarily sensitive to language [2:227]), but even food as a fetish cannot outweigh the power of the word (2:240).

Gogol's story is about Gogol's discourse insofar as it is about verbal fixation, which, like compulsive hoarding, looks perfectly ridiculous when put forth as a proposition. The verbal gander, in Ivan Nikiforovich's locution, is felt to be as cutting as a razor (2:226) and more injurious than the gun that precipitates the angry exchange. The lone signifier then gathers force in the "gospels" according to Ivan Ivanovich and Ivan Nikiforovich, respectively, where the word is made petition and thus commands the attention of the town administrators—at least until the silly documents are purloined by Ivan Ivanovich's sow (who thus becomes, like the sow in *Dead Souls*, a figurative reader, gobbling up everything in her path). Ivan Ivanovich's particular word-ingesting sow is referred to repeatedly as "the devil knows what." Appropriately, this demonic figure of speech, too, acquires an ascendancy of its own and inspires a fitting response to the thievery: the good functionaries hurl ink pots after her, in keeping with Luther's treatment of devilish intruders. Finally, in the hands of the professional and prolific legal scribbler, the original word is multiplied to so many pages of so much absurd jargon that it makes "any reader cough and sneeze" (2:261). Ivan Ivanovich reaffirms his attachment to text when he declines to explain the problem briefly, insisting instead on having the written complaint declaimed in full (2:248). And the ultimate proof of the complainant's gentle birth, indeed existence, is that his birth is recorded; the problem with ganderhood, we are led to believe, is that a gander cannot be inscribed in the register (2:249).

Not unlike the two Ivans, who quarrel over a verbal fowl, Chichikov and associates nearly come to blows over an act of naming even emptier than the epithet *gusak* that so offends Ivan Ivanovich. When a fellow official flings four of the emptiest words in the language at Chichikov—*Da, vot, mol, chto* (So that's what, then [6:237])—their lucrative partnership comes to an abrupt end. Even the text admits they quarreled over "nothing" (6:236). In Dikan'ka, too, as spooked as the townsfolk are of the devil, the nature of danger and salvation alike appears to be verbal.[86] And in *Dead Souls*, as we know, the power of the "aptly uttered Russian word" is portrayed as immense (6:109); the word "millionaire"—"not the millionaire himself, but precisely the word alone"—is "guilty of everything" (6:159).

Gogol's reverence for the word is well documented. "One must treat the word with the greatest respect," he writes in his essay "On the Nature of the Word" ("O tom, chto takoe slovo," 1844). "It is God's highest gift to mankind" (8:231). Gogol concurs with Pushkin that a poet's words *are* a poet's deeds. Each and every syllable must, accordingly, be considered with care (8:229). Gogol, we ought to presume then, marshals his verbal forces advisedly.

But his leadership is weak. Evidently even Gogol sensed his own lack of control, and when he talked about words "going out for walks" and spinning stories on their own, he was describing not their wonderful vitality, but rather their terrible waywardness. Moreover, he had a keen sense of the emptiness of his words, the pathetic inadequacy of human language, at least in his hands, to affirm anything real and true. It is for this reason, Maguire claims, that Gogol lapsed into silences of despair.[87]

Mute scenes notwithstanding, however, Gogol's lapses are anything but wordless. Perhaps he resorted to quantity to make up for the quality he feared was lacking. Indications are that Gogol, despairing of the content-bearing capacity of his words, turned to their orthographic and phonetic properties. Sound—assonance, alliteration, rhythm—is a formidable generator of Gogolian text, as many have noted.[88] Descriptions of landscapes are evocative not because of their visual probity, but because of the musicality of the prose.[89] This "lushness and sensuousness of the instrumentation," says Proffer, makes Gogol's prose more like poetry.[90]

But if Gogol's prose is like poetry, it is less because it sounds so musical than because it privileges word over thing. The poetic word, as Jakobson contended, is perceived as a *word* rather than as a vehicle for the object it names;[91] the "verbal envelope" is paramount. In prose, on the other hand, the word, having indicated its object, tends to recede into the shade.[92] The mention of a sail, for instance, gives rise in our minds to Lermontov's poetic line, whereas the mention of a staircase elicits Dostoevsky's image, not his exact words, which we do not recall.[93] But in Gogol's prose, the object is not available to the imagination. No one, as is often remarked, can picture the nose.

Chichikov is apparently equally difficult to visualize, even for those who have met him; his materiality is hardly increased by the fact that his acquaintances can remember him as easily without limbs as with them. As for the many, many names with no objects at all, the verbal envelope is all we get, and it is empty. The effect of Gogol's interminable inventories, comments Ivask, is "lyrical" (*liricheskoe*) rather than "proprietary" (*khoziaiskoe*)[94]—the writer is acquiring words, not the things they stand for.

So Gogol makes poetry not, as Belinsky claimed, out of the prosaic material of *life*,[95] and not even, as Proffer would have it, out of the play of sonorous phonemes, but insofar as in poetry, as Kermode's Lucinda gripes, the words just keep getting in the way. (Lucinda, we recall, finds this makes poetry unreadable.)

Gogol's deployment of so many "empty envelopes" is, in effect, confirmed by Rudyi Pan'ko's anxiety about the volume of discourse produced by his storytellers (so many printed pages that it's hard to find enough things to wrap in them [1:103]). The abundant packaging without contents figures vividly the ontological problem raised by Gogol's discourse: the dubious materiality of his existents, the precarious *soderzhatel'nost* of all this *soderzhanie*.[96] Although we keep hoping that where there is storytelling there must be story (like the exegetically inclined townsfolk in *Dead Souls* who accept that Chichikov is an abductor of young girls because "the story was spread about, so there must be some reason for it" [6:190]), we are bound to be disappointed, for Gogol's discourse not only comes first—like unsubstantiated rumor, it comes all by itself.[97] Gogol's overloaded prose presents not an "indescribable plenitude," but an "emptiness and hollowness," a realm of "Nonbeing," where the "materiality of the signifier" is the only material at all.[98] When Nozdrev "lies" in this way, producing discourse with nothing behind it, at least the townsfolk have the good taste to walk away (6:209).

Consider, for example, the great swindle that opens "Two Ivans":

> What a marvelous coat Ivan Ivanovich has! Extraordinary! And what astrakhan! Damn, what astrakhan! Frosted blue-gray! I'll bet anything that nobody else has one like it! For God's sake, just look at it, especially when he steps over to talk to somebody, look from the side: how utterly delicious! There are no words to describe it: Velvet! Silver! Fire! Lord God! St. Nikolai the Wonder-Worker, Divine Saint! Why don't I have a coat like that! He had it made even before Agafiia Fedoseevna went to Kiev. You know Agafiia Fedoseevna? The one who bit off the assessor's ear? (2:223)

As I noted at the outset, the story has nothing to do with coats. This garment works to obstruct narrative progress, to block our access to any "real" events and existents. The narrator's disingenuous disclaimer that he can find no words to describe the thing is ludicrous amidst the torrent of epithets he produces. And when the narrator modulates his unrestrained enthusiasm to "inform" us that Ivan Ivanovich acquired his remarkable garment "even before Agafiia Fedoseevna went to Kiev," we remain perplexed, since this is only the first paragraph of the story, and we still haven't the slightest idea who Agafiia Fedoseevna is (nor, at this rate, will we ever get to chapter 3, where we will find out), let alone when her journey took place. The narrator's helpful prompt, "You know Agafiia Fedoseevna? The one who bit off the assessor's ear?" is not information but a travesty of informative content.

The passage, then, is devoid of relevance and of sense-making information; more pointedly, though, it is even empty of coats. This *bekesha*, wondrous to behold (and we are exhorted repeatedly to observe, see, look, indeed gawk at it) has as little *substance* as the name Agafiia Fedoseevna, the same's trip to Kiev, or her unrestrained behavior with the tax assessor, and no more *presence* than the elusive overcoat of Akakii Akakievich's dreams. What it does (like the fabulous *shinel'* Akakii Akakievich orders from his tailor) is to awaken manifold desires for the coat—both the narrator's hankering for a similar garment ("Why don't I have a coat like that!") and our own hunger for answers ("So what's the story with the coat?"). But if Gogol's characters long for what they cannot see (their own nose), touch (dead souls), get (the dream coat, the dream girl, the perfect carriage), Gogol's readers desire—just as futilely—the solidity and presence adduced by Maguire, the "indispensable thing" coveted by Ivan Ivanovich (2:234), the ability to wrest from the verbal clutter something substantial, to see boy-get-girl (people kind of fall in love and all that) without the words kind of getting in the way. We want access: not only to get some*where* in our reading, but also to get some*thing*. The hoax of *this* plenitude is that, like the elaborately calligraphed list of dead souls, it is profoundly empty.

Threadbare Material: "The Overcoat"

And yet paraphrasable stories are told, after all. Boy meets girl and overcomes some obstacles to win her.[99] An impoverished worker seeks, gets, and loses a body covering. A rank-conscious officer loses, seeks, and gets a body part. A scheming entrepreneur seeks and gets bodiless souls. Even allowing that these are particularly reductive renderings, formulating "acceptable summaries" of Gogol's stories is problematic.[100] In the Dikan'ka cycle in particular, it is often difficult to remember what each individual tale is "about." Naturally, the only truly "acceptable summary" of any work of literature, as Tolstoy quipped about his *Anna Karenina*, is a word-for-word repetition of the whole text.[101] But Gogol's content-less discourse makes any paraphrase more than usually inadequate. The elaborate discourse not only presents a formidable obstacle to "getting on with the story";[102] much of it bears no palpable story material at all. "The Overcoat" exemplifies the problem of reading Gogol for the plot; effusive and overwhelming in the ways we have come to expect from Gogol, it both presents a problem and represents it as a matter of content. The story of "The Overcoat," along with anything else it pretends to encompass, is the problem of its own discourse.

Gogol's best-known story exhibits all the familiar characteristics— the extraneous detail, the hyperbolic specificity, the accretion and enumeration of things and attributes, the reduplicative language, the fulsome digression, the convulsive syntax, the devil as a figure of speech, and the fetishization of objects—though here the edible has been supplanted by a certain object of apparel. But the reader is teased into regarding all this verbal profusion as potentially content-bearing by the introduction of themes of genuine significance—poverty, bureaucracy, the inequity of rank, "man's" proverbial inhumanity to man, and so on.

The reader is truly invited to bewail the lamentable fate of the meek, impoverished copy clerk who, when his ancient threadbare overcoat can no longer even hold a patch, must somehow purchase a new one. After months of deprivation, shivering every evening in his room in the dark (so as to economize on candles) in his dressing gown (to keep his underwear from wearing out) and eating next to nothing, Akakii amasses the needed sum and the long-needed coat is purchased. It is invested with almost matrimonial significance by the proud Akakii Akakievich. On its first day out, however, poor Akakii is robbed of his beloved "mate." His plaintive appeals to the Person of Consequence for help in apprehending the thief and restoring the coat to its proper owner are cruelly rebuffed, and the devastated clerk returns home almost unconscious, falls into a feverish state, and soon gives up the ghost (much as Chekhov's clerk Cherviakov would succumb some forty years later).

There is clearly much more at stake here than in the tale of the two Ivans, each more ridiculous than the other, whose gander is a canard, and generations of critics (beginning with Belinsky) hastened to hail the sad story line of "The Overcoat"—and especially its digression on brotherly love—as Gogol's great humanitarian statement.

But the homily on Christian charity is as vacant as the two Ivans' verbal gander. Critics have demonstrated amply that the great "humanitarian" digression is just as much an artifact of verbal proliferation as the more frivolous asides, both in the way it is generated and in its stylistic mannerisms.[103] Eikhenbaum and Chizhevsky both read the humanitarian passage as pure device,[104] an "excuse" for more discourse, much as the new overcoat is an "excuse" for a party (3:157). Akakii Akakievich himself is not only too pathetic to take at face value[105]—he too functions, both characterologically and textually, principally as a word magnet.

In fact it could be argued that Akakii Akakievich is really little more than a verbal artifact. His very name, in spite of all the narrator's pious protestations about saints' names and inescapable derivations, has obviously been selected for its sound (and its unavoidable association with *kaka*). Moreover, Akakii Akakievich's whole life consists of words: to be sure, "besides his copying, it seemed, nothing else existed for him" (3:145). For that matter, after his untimely demise, once his copying function is taken over by someone else, it is as if he had never existed (3:169); indeed, he dies when the wind blows a quinsy into his throat and he can no longer pronounce his nonsense syllables (3:167). His greatest pleasure (since, as we know from the page-long sentence that ends in this fact, he pursues no other entertainment) comes in the form of nicely shaped letters, and the conflation of life and letters has gone so far that Akakii Akakievich is often startled to find himself "not in the middle of a line, but rather in the middle of the street" (3:145). His weak constitution is expressed in terms of his pathetic inarticulateness, and he is finally felled by the Person of Consequence's stern words (3:167). Even his death throes are linguistic (3:168). In short, Akakii Akakievich expires as he lived, in a kind of verbal hyperactivity that overtakes the plot and makes us relieved rather than saddened when the downtrodden man dies and the verbiage finally ceases.

As readers, we want there to be something behind all these words— a man behind the name, a story behind the discourse—thus the temptation to embrace the thematic "content." But our own quest for significance—for something substantial and important—is closely reenacted in Akakii Akakievich's ill-fated quest for a coat. In his seeking and losing the "thread," the meaning and the reason to go on, we recognize our own vain pursuit of sense, significance, and substance. Like the reader, Akakii Akakievich longs for good material (*inventio*) that is well crafted (*dispositio, elocutio*). But as the dismantling of Akakii Akakievich reveals, there is nothing solid to hold onto.

Can Akakii Akakievich be conflated with a desirous reader, Akakii Akakievich, whose life is replete with text, whose endless supply of rhetoric leaves him utterly sated, with no lack (*napisavshis' v-slast'* [3:147])? Indeed, the whole "point" of the page-long sentence on pleasure seeking is to exempt Akakii from the universal desires that surround him (3:146). And yet want he does; he lacks a coat and craves something *material*, something thick and substantial—a real thing in a world of overindulgent verbality. Akakii Akakievich desires like a wife "the overcoat, thickly padded and stoutly lined" (3:154), the one thing that is *prochnyi* (solid, sound, durable)—the one thing that is not language. The story of Akakii Akakievich is about the discursive problem of being awash in ever-proliferating text and desperately desiring something solid behind it.

All of Gogol's prose is diffuse. But "The Overcoat" in particular articulates (if it can be said to articulate anything definite at all) a programmatic intention not to accede to the reader's desire for substance—not to inform. The refusal in the first of many diversionary paragraphs to name the "department" directly (*luchshe ne nazyvat'* [3:141]), while masquerading as an act of discretion (not saying too much) results instead in both an inflationary digression that says much too much about something of no relevance, and the obfuscating gesture of the "certain department," which says nothing at all. The hero is at least named (at excruciating length), but "Akakii Akakievich" is but the echo of a sound, and his surname "Bashmachkin" refers to no shoe (*bashmak*) at all (3:142). The reader confronts a barrage of verbal envelopes that, like Akakii's convulsive prepositions, adverbs, and particles, "have absolutely no meaning whatsoever" (3:149).

If the exposition declines to expose because the prose is not information-bearing, the excursus on entertainment is not entertaining. This ever-expanding sentence on *razvlechenie* problematizes the entire project of "diversion" by discussing the need for escape from the "scraping of pens" with its own extravagant production of text, *bol'she dazhe chem nuzhno* (even more than is required), an infinite scraping of pens that oppresses us at least as much as it exhausts the weary office clerks. As the passage rambles on about its own formal eccentricities—the problem of having nothing worth telling and so simply repeating and proliferating text (the ostensible content is anecdote-telling off-duty clerks)—the interminable diversion is not particularly diverting. We move through all this because we would like at some point to get to the point (Akakii Akakievich's diligence)—but his diligence, too, just involves more unremitting production of text (3:146). Outside of the proliferation of words, nothing exists (3:145), not for Akakii, and not for us. This is one copy room that is *never* out of order.

In craving one *thing* in all this language, Akakii Akakievich longs for a connection with world rather than text; he seeks the one thing he might name directly, rather than just copying other words. Although he copies with zeal, even with love (3:144), he contemplates his future coat with burning *passion* (3:155). And although writing can stem a minor growl from an empty belly (3:145), only the coat ends Akakii Akakievich's prolonged fasting (3:154). As bounteous as it is, language can only mark his desire, not satisfy it. Like the kopecks he hoards to exchange for the coat, words are only *shinel'nyi kapital* ("coatly capital" [3:153]), the mediator between desire and its object, the currency one surrenders in favor of the real thing.

Aptly, Akakii Akakievich names his precious object only when he does not have it—before he takes possession of it and after it is lost. He pronounces his desire in the first scream of his life—"A hundred and fifty rubles for an overcoat!" (3:151)—outraged, as we ourselves come to be, about the unfair exchange (so much verbal "currency" for so little "thing"). After he loses the coat, he affirms sadly, "there once was an overcoat, a brand-new one" (3:166), adding more aggressively, as a corpse, "I need your *shinel'*" (3:172). His only articulation of it while the new coat is within his grasp is when, in his confusion, he disavows it, averring that it is only his old one (3:157).[106] His colleagues at work learn of the new coat's existence "by mysterious means" (3:157)—Akakii had not uttered a word. After months of debating the thing with his tailor, as soon as it is delivered, Akakii Akakievich "wanted no discussion with Petrovich" and just pays him off (3:156–57), exhausting his "capital" altogether. The brief interval of having the coat releases Akakii Akakievich from the realm of language, the prison house of empty syllables, and his empty stomach. During the one day he possesses the coat, Akakii does not talk about it, does not copy text at night, and eats with relish (*posibaritstvoval* [3:158]) what he had formerly consumed without tasting (3:144). No wonder Petrovich tests his reinforced stitches with his teeth.

This coat is emphatically solid—double stitched, multi-layered, and, in sharp contrast to the permanently dismembered cloak in Korobochka's drawer and the devil's resolutely fragmented jacket in Dikan'ka, this masterpiece of tailoring is guaranteed not to fall apart. In its unassailable integrity, Akakii Akakievich's "indispensable thing" shares the steely solidity of Ivan Nikiforovich's much-coveted gun and the fleshy firmness of Major Kovalev's fervently sought nose. In its urgency, Akakii Akakievich's desire for a real coat easily matches the pitch of the devil's frenzied attempt to reassemble his own scattered garment. And in his search for something essential, something to give his life content, Akakii Akakievich's hopeful enterprise parallels our own hunt for a story of substance and significance, something to make our own efforts worthwhile.

As Fanger has commented, there is a way in which "The Overcoat" is about "significance and nonsignificance as such."[107] It features a hyperbolically insignificant clerk, who is accorded less attention than a fly; it problematizes the relative significance of human beings when assigned according to rank; it generates text and entire characters out of puns on the word "significance" (*znachenie*); and it juxtaposes "the smallest with the largest," both in terms of people and their differing perceptions of such things as overcoats.[108] Even the investigating magistrate, the textual "reader," ignores the "main thing" and focuses on the "irrelevant" (3:163). But significance is not just shown to be relative or subjective. Like the overcoat itself, "The Overcoat" makes palpable the extent to which significance is *indispensable*; we all seek to dismiss the immaterial and grasp the significant thing.

While the coat and the story of the coat seem at first blush to offer Akakii Akakievich and us, respectively, the significant content we need, the "significant other" Akakii posits in his dream coat, the mate for life he imagines, is in reality the most fleeting of one-night stands. As a "spouse," as an enduring source of meaning, the overcoat is no more reliable than the devil's roving jacket. The coat is but a guest (*gost' v vide shineli* [3:169]), and we are left, like the needy Akakii, without coats, but with lots of disordered discourse (*besporiadochnye slova* [3:168]) about them. Discursively speaking, *insignificance* prevails.[109]

The center does not hold; the coat seems slated for removal. Even during its brief visit, this coat is most frequently shown to be taken off—first at work, then at home, at the party, at the request of the mustachioed thieves, and subsequently, from the shoulders of numerous Petersburgians, including the Person of Consequence himself. We witness no symmetrical amount of donning. Coat removal, we recall, figures prominently in Zoshchenko's plots, but the problem is much graver in Gogol. Here it signals the very disappearance of the *material*. The *soderzhanie* (content) cited by Belinsky is as threadbare as the material of the old *kapot*, too thin to hold a patch and permanently resistant to all attempts to stitch it together.

Ultimately our plight is as dire as poor Akakii's. Like him, we are deluged with discourse, one step removed from the things we crave and sorely needing something thick, real, and substantial to make the details worth telling and the hardships we endure worth enduring. Like Akakii Akakievich, we get a glimpse of the material coat ("The Overcoat," as I have said, is the most contentful of the lot), but the "real" events and "real" existents are ghosts and guests, like Akakii and his disappearing outerwear, and our patience wears as thin as the material that remains. Like the pitiable clerk, we are naked to the elements (public enemy number one in Petersburg [3:147]), buffeted about by the interminable blasts of air (whether hot air or cold), for the coat and all its material pleasures are finally absent. The nature of Akakii Akakievich's poverty is that he must do without *things*, as figured by his coatlessness. As the New York City coat murders attest, this particular form of neediness is grimly real. The stakes for the coatless reader are less dramatic, to be sure, but we, too, are keenly conscious of our need and our discomfort when the material we cling to turns out, like the emperor's new clothes, to be nothing but words.

Lost Letters ("Propavshaia gramota")

The story of "The Overcoat" is about its own discourse because it depicts a vain quest for substance in a world of proliferating text. And in losing the thread, Akakii Akakievich loses both his object and his way. Trapped in the Byzantine chain of indirect approach devised by the Person of Consequence "to increase his significance" (3:164) in a text that meanders and digresses to the peril of *its* significance, Akakii Akakievich gets lost on his way home, loses himself in his writing, loses the narrator, who capitulates finally on his protagonist's destination (3:158), and, stumbling across empty squares with his eyes closed, loses his life as he loses his coat. The reader's discontent with Gogolian content involves a similarly simultaneous loss of substance and direction, a sense that you can get neither what you need nor where you want to go.

In his "incorrigible indirection" and his poverty of possession, Akakii Akakievich embodies virtually every aspect of the discursive act.[110] He is like the text, both in his wandering and in his essentially verbal constitution. He is like the reader in his insistent need for something besides words. And he is a lot like the author in his copying, his indefatigable reproduction of words with no things attached. He resembles Gogol, too, in his proliferation of words with no direction. Taking letters home at night, Akakii Akakievich obsessively makes more and more copies for himself, impressed by the addressees, but never in contact with them (3:145–46). He perpetually copies (*perepisyvaet*), but never corresponds (*perepisyvaetsia*), producing if not actually purloined letters, then unquestionably hoarded ones, a purely verbal stash with not only the referential line broken (since Akakii Akakievich writes these letters by the verbatim reproduction of other words, with no connection to the matter at hand), but with the "conative function" disrupted as well.[111] Akakii Akakievich's collection of letters, cut off from the things that inspired them, from the addresser who composed them, and the addressee for whom they were intended, are empty and disconnected language that (like Akakii himself) bears no thing and never arrives. Like his American counterpart Bartleby the scrivener, Akakii Akakievich's vocation is in the dead-letter office.[112]

While it is the nature of the postal service to lose messages occasionally—as Derrida tells us, "une lettre n'arrive *pas toujours* à destination"[113]—the Gogolian letter is a routinely lost, *propavshaia gramota*. Like the various forms of conveyance and the characters they transport, messages do not arrive either. Gogol's postage is insufficient, perhaps because he does not weigh his words.

Akakii Akakievich's solipsistic scribbling only piles up in his room, and when he screams his voice does not carry across the square (3:161), just as Gogol writes and writes until he loses his voice and plummets into muteness. The message is lost, fallen away, and the *propavshaia gramota* is inscribed again and again as an element of story. In the tale whose title emphasizes this chronic problem, the devil absconds with the letter in question (1:185). Old granddad, who became a letter (*gramota*) carrier purely because he was literate (*gramotnyi*), performs the job inexpertly (1:182). As a result of a long and meandering story, he forgets about his message-bearing function altogether (1:183). The postmaster of *Dead Souls*, zealous civil servant that he is, delivers primarily "sacksful" of empty phrases that rival Akakii Akakievich's ("My dear sir, such a something or other, you know, you understand, you can imagine, in reference to, so to speak, after a fashion," pronounces the postmaster to no one in particular [6:157]). Unlike the Derridean "purveyor of truth," Gogolian letter carriers (thanks to the letter writers) are purveyors of junk mail and delayers of anything important, for the Gogolian letter is doubly problematic: Gogol's verbal envelopes are not only empty, they are unintelligibly addressed. They arrive without contents or they just don't come.

The corruption of the mails—figured in the "famous letters of introduction" (bribes); in the objects hoarded rather than sent on as required so as to avoid "unnecessary correspondence" (6:236); in the fact that Chichikov takes the address of petitioners, but never sends the goods (6:231)—is finally much more pernicious than the innocuous early closing time imagined by the other officials ("Your business is postal, receiving and dispatching mails! For you corruption is closing up shop a half hour early!" [6:197]). Tampering with the mail represents a fundamental disruption of the contact between the addresser and the addressee; the breach of the "postal" contract signals the dissolution of the possibility of meaningful exchange between writer and reader. The violability of the mails reflects not the sort of cynicism about public works that leads Zoshchenko to institute "norms" for how many letters may be lost, but rather a deep skepticism about language itself that in the case of Gogol would appear to be well founded.

The *vacancy* and the *vagrancy* of the Gogolian signifier doubly impede the reader's access and doubly frustrate desire, whatever we choose to call its object—pleasure or profit, story or substance, some*thing* or some*where*. The lasting hope that all this discourse will convey some content and that we will *get* it is faithlessly blighted; the "promissory note" that implies that we will be rewarded for our efforts, that relief is on the way, is as good as mail fraud.[114] Rather than initiating exchange, the Gogolian letter is a one-sided affair, serving only the self-indulgent text generator (Gogol and his copycat Akakii) whose writings are undeliverable.[115]

It has been noted that Gogol tended to write his critical prose in epistolary form.[116] I might note as well that he wrote his literary prose in the form of the numerous dead letters inscribed therein. "Diary of a Madman," too, in which "a letter is nonsense" (3:211) and yet many are written, and where correspondence is undelivered and targeted for theft (3:195, 200–1), is itself written in the form of nonsensical raving that goes nowhere. A diary, after all, is a kind of one-sided correspondence. Even the ostensible passages from "correspondence with friends" (8:213–418) are as one-sided, as monologic as they come.

This is not fun. Gogol himself complained vehemently that one-sidedness (*odnostoronnost'*) is unfair,[117] but when it comes to his prose, the pleasure is all his. Readers are hoping for something "worth it," but given the errant "itinerary" of the Gogolian signifier and its dubious content-bearing capacity, the author's protestations that "the check is in the mail" are difficult to credit.[118]

Material Needs

By the admission of even his greatest enthusiasts, Gogol's prose is marked by excess. It is expansively digressive and infinitely elaborative. It accumulates instead of progressing, dwelling on the superfluous and specifying the irrelevant. It exhibits a pleonastic tendency to name and rename things many times over; an exuberant attachment to metaphoricity that discharges extended similes like a multistage rocket;

a tendency to follow the play of sounds wherever they may lead; a passion for gratuitous documentation, calculated to obscure rather than to clarify; a flagrant lack of connectivity and control; and excursuses on every imaginable subject that usually leave their own subject far behind. In short (as Gogol would say), it collects and deploys words with unrestrained prodigality. Dante, interestingly, condemns those who hoard and dispense too freely to perpetually wheeling back and forth—in the best Gogolian tradition, Dantean dead souls are doomed never to arrive either (*Inferno* 7); the Italian, at least, has the good sense to regard this as a torment rather than as "fun."

For the "hypertrophy of information" that Burke calls a "disease" is more than that.[119] It is a hoax. The plenitude here is entirely discursive.[120] The texts are not full of "information," not full of things, not full of *soderzhanie* (content). The discursive abuse results in the disappearance precisely of the material, that which is as indispensable as Akakii Akakievich's much-needed coat, that which gives meaning to life and text—that which, in Gogol, we must do without. The stuffed, overfull quality of Gogol's prose is *zaderzhatel'nyi*, not *soderzhatel'nyi* (obstructive rather than contentful): what keeps readers from progressing also keeps them from embracing anything along the way.

This includes food. The innumerable comestibles I have enumerated nearly as exhaustively as Gogol does are as unattainable as winter coats, the plates as empty as the envelopes, the dishes as verbal as the ones on those extensive Soviet menus that long fronted for chronically ill-supplied kitchens. A horrifying exchange early in the "Two Ivans" (shortly after the lengthy passage about the chimerical coat) illustrates the problem while conveniently perpetuating it. Ivan Ivanovich confronts (as a matter of habit) the neediest of the beggars at the church door. She is starving and extends her hand in supplication. Ivan Ivanovich (who is an excellent man) speaks to her at length about the food and drink she wants and needs, but in the end, gives her neither food nor money, neither pleasure nor profit, nor the least bit of satisfaction. He whets her already healthy appetite, but serves her only names of food, a diet of words that would sustain not even the abstemious Akakii Akakievich.[121]

It is a cruel joke, but like the tragedy of the impoverished clerk who will die without his winter coat, the baiting of the hungry suppliant is just an extreme version of the contemptuous disregard for human needs. While readers' lives do not hang in the balance, they nonetheless hunger, like the beggar at the church door, for what they need most from text—sustenance for their attention—and are as cavalierly rebuffed, offered only empty words.

Barthes contends that a writer, "by citing, naming, noticing food (by treating it as notable), imposes on the reader the final state of matter, what cannot be transcended, withdrawn."[122] But the experience of reading Gogol would suggest otherwise. Gogol's storehouses and banquets do not give us "matter"; instead they keep us from anything that might really matter. Nor does Gogol's food satisfy. As old granddad—the paradigmatic storyteller and letter-loser—discovers, feasts are inferno-like affairs: no matter how impressive the spread, he can never really sink his teeth into a single forkful. Try as he might, he cannot bring his fork to his own mouth, and each tantalizing morsel disappears down some devil's gullet instead ("The Lost Letter," 1:188). Like granddad, like the beggar, we may be fed up, but we are never fed (nor, like Akakii Akakievich, clothed). Our "material" needs are not met.

To make matters worse, we are perpetually reminded that we have such desires, for Gogol takes the pursuit of appetites as his very subject, presenting us with a full complement of devilish tempters, travelers straining toward their goals, consumers straining toward promised delicacies, and greedy hoarders whose urge to collect exceeds all bounds. I have sought to satisfy my own hunger for substance and purposefulness—for story—in this discursive overload by reading these inscriptions of desires and endeavors as portraits of the problem. In seeing the machinations of the devil, the alimentary pathology, the scourge of non-arrival, and the compulsive hoarding as models of the production and consumption of problematic text, I find not exactly clarity, but at least a record of obfuscations. In the spirit of neither Maguire's first camp (seeking significance in every detail) nor his second (abdicating the search), I have elaborated a reading strategy that constructs a certain coherence from the text's documentation of its own incoherence. The relevance of much of Gogol's gab, in other words, is not in its connection to the "story" ostensibly being told, but in its reflection of the discursive dilemmas themselves. When Pul'kheriia Ivanovna conducts an inventory of her storeroom, it is above all a record of the text's compulsions. It is not, as Setchkarev claims, that the senselessness of the prose portrays the senselessness of the world,[123] but rather that the "world" Gogol concocts approximates his jumbled heaps of prose. What is "signified" is the Gogolian signifier itself.

The problem with Gogol's excessive discourse—the lack of discernible significance in so much of it—is encapsulated in Akakii Akakievich's desperate search for a real material coat, for something of substance and significance in a world of infinitely proliferating empty and disconnected syllables. The envelopes that are not only empty, but, like *Doezzhai-ne-doedesh'* and friends, never even arrive at their destinations, leave readers—textual and extra-textual—empty-handed twice over as they wait for their payoff. Instead of meaningful (pleasureable, profitable) exchange, there is one-sided swindle. And as in Chichikov's scam to mortgage dead souls, the mortgage (literally "dead pledge") is based on absent collateral; we "lend" our attention for nothing.

If reading for the plot—to get somewhere and to get something—is compelling but fruitless in the face of Gogol, it is not because, as is sometimes said, Gogol's prose is "plotless," but because the story line is inaccessible. My alternative has been to read the distended discourse itself as plotted, as the object of its own representation—to see the story of the discourse as the "real" story. If this makes all of Gogol's stories the same story, then this helps to explain why I have dealt with them less work by work than figure by discursive figure.[124]

The objection may follow that Gogol was writing about the world, not about text and reading, that especially as he grew more didactic, more convinced of his own sense of mission, he intended to communicate some kind of truth, not engage in self-referential play. But the latter does not rule out the former. In any case, language has a way of following its own plans, authorial intentions notwithstanding, as Gogol, more than anyone else, should have known (given his proclamations about the motor capacity of the word). In addition, I stress again that this is a *reading* strategy, not an account of the composition of Gogol's work. My own intentions have not been to identify Gogol's, but simply to find a way of tolerating the textual morass, to develop my own method of producing "information from noise."[125] Like Price's greedy readers who convert all content to form, I have converted (just as greedily) formal properties to content, considering the way the texts put forth as propositions the problems of their own significance. In my own writing here my use of the terms of Gogol's text to describe that text, even my tendency to make my rhetorical flourishes my substance, are in keeping with Gogol's story about discourse and discourse about itself.

Why do we need such stratagems? Because as Gogol himself concludes, strictly speaking, *razobrat' nel'zia* (it is impossible to make any sense of it all) (1:316). And yet we yearn precisely to *razobrat'* (get it) and *dobrat'sia* (get there). We want the pleasure and profit the text taunts us with but keeps beyond our reach. If a book is indeed a *Gallehault*, a go-between that stimulates desire for "delight," as the story of Paolo and Francesca in the Dantean subtext suggests, then the Gogolian text must be viewed as a *Gallehault* that serves the interest of one party only, the autoerotic text-generator who writes and writes but never delivers. As a conduit to the pleasures of textual sense, Gogolian prose is as unreliable a source of transport as the various modes of conveyance are of transportation to an end. By arousing desire it refuses to satisfy, it risks being put aside for delights that *are* accessible. It risks an end to reading that precedes the end of text. It might very well share the fate of that famous book in Canto V, when Dante's lovers opt instead for a real consummation of their desires: that day, says Francesca, with a most un-Gogolian reticence, "that day we read no more" (5:138).

CONCLUSION

Too Little and Too Much— Story and Discourse and the Pragmatics of Insignificance

"Once upon a time, they lived happily ever after."

© 1991 Tom Cheney
originally in The New Yorker
Magazine, Inc.
All Rights Reserved.

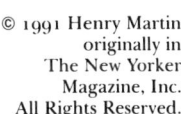

© 1991 Henry Martin
originally in
The New Yorker
Magazine, Inc.
All Rights Reserved.

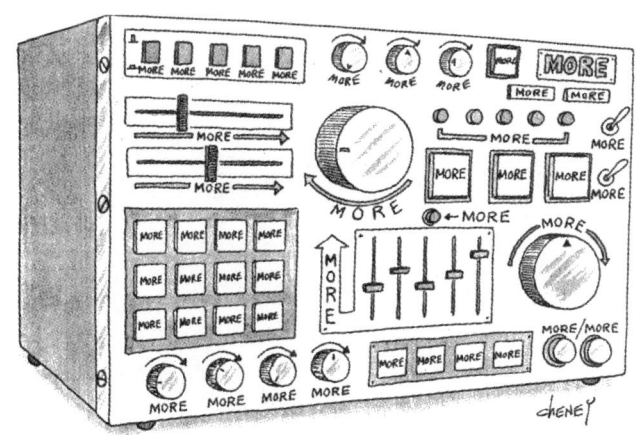

Why might we care to "read no more" of Gogol's infinite discursive embroidery, but eagerly embrace the story-level "pinpricks" of Chekhov and Zoshchenko? Why should the "insignificant"—the violation of our sense of "what's worth telling"—be less tolerable at the level of the discourse than at the level of the story?

Perhaps, in matters of text, excess is harder to take than insufficiency. Since discursive "insignificance" becomes palpable only when there is too much of it, the exasperation it occasions is protracted, and the only hope of relief is to stop reading. Telling "too much" is thus a positive affront. "Insignificant" story, conversely, tends to present its minor affair in miniature form. If in providing "too little" it produces a reading experience not wholly satisfactory, then at least the investment has been minimal, the discontent proportionately slight, and the end imminent.

But as plausible as this explanation may be, it disguises the real problem and even reverses the truth. Unfulfilled longings are at least as troubling as needs overindulged. In fact, discourse-level insignificance frustrates us precisely because in giving too much that is irrelevant and unnecessary, it gives *too little* of what a reader really needs (the chance to get somewhere and to get something). More, as I have noted, is not necessarily more. Because it impedes access to what counts most, excess creates the greatest shortage of all. "Insignificant" story, on the other hand, while appearing to offer too little, actually gives very much indeed.

At the level of story—in the classic cases of Chekhov and Zoshchenko, at any rate—the violation of minimum standards of tellability is only an apparent one. The "insignificant" story emerges as enormously significant. In Chekhov's prose, observed Bely, "small things are no longer small. . . . In its trivialities something grandiose is revealed."[1] The very fact of making a sneeze the event of a story renders it structurally pivotal, indeed, indispensable. And Zoshchenko's little coats and feet acquire the iconic significance of, well, the icon and the axe (less inspirational than the Billington dyad, perhaps, but no less consequential). Thus, readers do get plenty of the text-internal significance they desire. Insignificant story *would* be untellable if nothing happened ("Georgia O'Keeffe's ever-so-reliable poppies are still on display"), or if only the same old thing happened ("the Xerox machine has broken down again"), or if whatever happened had no appreciable effect on the status quo (whether Nikitin has married Masha or the Bolsheviks have seized power). Such occurrences are not noteworthy, not noticed, and, thus, not told. But the events of Chekhov's and Zoshchenko's miniatures reveal their own importance precisely by precipitating change and disrupting norms, by turning out either to bear unforeseen consequences or, surprisingly, to lack the gravity they ordinarily assume. The reader is treated to a revelation or a reversal. The matter is thus eminently tellable—unusual or contrary to expectations—and in the imaginative involvement it inspires, it not only invites an evaluation of the state of affairs presented, but also demands a reevaluation of the reader's (or regime's) operative categories for assessing significance. It is in this discomfiture that Lotman locates the defeated reader's "joy."

Discourse-level insignificance, by contrast, is simply defeating, without the mitigating delight. Rampant detail that bears little relevance to the matter at hand and no special semiotic burden of its own functions rather to eclipse the tellable, to get in the way as the reader tries to grasp the significance of the material and progress through the text "in a significant way."[2] In exceptional cases, trivial details do "turn out" to be laden with unexpected significance—such as the hyperbolic specificity deployed in the service of irony, or the disposition of clues and red herrings in a mystery narrative; such "loaded" details do prove to contribute to the pleasures of sense-making. But the trivia of Gogol's jumbled heap does not effect this kind of transformation from superfluous to signifying, does not reveal itself as significant, and hence does not satisfy our "passion for meaning." The narrative transaction is in this case a one-sided affair: discursive insignificance leaves us scurrying to erect for ourselves the structures of signification we crave. To satisfy our desires we must, like the readers in Dante's fifth canto, take matters into our own hands.

The sense readers seek (and, if necessary, will provide) in a narrative text relies most heavily on the logic and the content—the "somewhere" and the "something"—of its *story* line. I have gone so far in my reading of Gogol as to imagine a story about the discourse precisely because story is so essential. Too much discourse keeps us wanting because it both impedes story progress and buries story substance—the immaterial flourishes at the expense of the material. The solidity and presence Maguire touts in Gogol's prose are thus more properly attributable to Chekhov's and Zoshchenko's little stories, which fill the void between "once upon a time" and "happily ever after" (however compactly) with perceptible events and existents. Gogol's texts are rather "full" of *elocutio*, empty words that can only *zaderzhat'* (detain) when we long for the text to *soderzhat'* (contain).

The violation at the level of the discourse, then, ultimately does more damage to *story* than the "insignificant" story does. Chekhov may manipulate the magnitude of his events, and Zoshchenko may foreground the diminutive proportions of his existents, but Gogol's discursive deluge problematizes access to both of these indispensable components of story. Ironically, although Chekhov was often accused of *bessoderzhatel'nost'* (contentlessness), both Chekhov and Zoshchenko go on to make extraordinarily contentful stories out of Gogol's threadbare "Overcoat." Coming "out from under Gogol's 'Overcoat,' " Zoshchenko's "coat capers" expose the bodies that Gogol's distended discourse had obscured. And Chekhov's Cherviakov (who dies, incidentally, still wearing his new coat) succumbs to an actual *event*, whereas his predecessor, Akakii Akakievich, had died of exposure to sheer discourse. Maybe "Doonesbury"'s Ayatollah is right to make turgid prose punishable by death, for in its extreme form, it causes the death of story.

Thus I do not think, simply because the logic of story and discourse is threatened in narratives such as Gogol's, that the distinction should be abandoned in talking about them. On the contrary, it makes what is difficult about Gogol more palpable and helps to distinguish his use of the "insignificant" from that of Chekhov and Zoshchenko. Story must emerge as significant on its own terms to be worth our while; discourse feels purposeful in relation to its story. Admittedly, storytelling is not the *only* object of discursive treatment, whether measured or immoderate, and even an extravagantly detailed discourse can be deployed, as I have said, to a number of ends: to indicate ironic distance, to generate suspense, to discredit an undiscerning narrator, to endow a network of symbolic references or intertextual allusions, to suggest scrupulous verisimilitude, even to interpolate historical portraiture or social critique. But the material of the discourse must finally be proportional to the story-stuff in order not to bury it altogether.

Disproportionality is admittedly a basic component of humor. This helps to account for why many of Zoshchenko's stories and some of Chekhov's are so funny. The outrageous disproportionality of discourse to story, of container to contents, undoubtedly contributes as well to the reading of Gogol as comical. This potential for humor also explains why the *New Yorker* cartoons seem to fit here. But as even Chekhov's more somber moments testify (not to mention Varlam Shalamov's miniature horror stories from the gulag or the garish headlines from the *New York Post*), disproportionality need not be funny, and frankly, with Gogol I don't think it is.[3]

It is in this light that we must understand the impatience and irritation provoked by contentless gab. When we get too little story for our discourse (too little "what" for our "how," too little purpose for our pains), the transaction ceases to feel "worth it." Talk may be cheap, but the time it occupies and the energy it demands from the receiver are not. When we must expend too much effort for too little return, when we cannot get what we need and where we want to go, like Zoshchenko's mobile *publika* we are apt to go away instead.

But while Gogol gushes on, apparently heedless of this eventuality, Chekhov and Zoshchenko evince at every level of composition an acute awareness of the exigencies of tellability. By focusing on the dimensions and, hence, the newsworthiness of their events and existents, the latter authors pose and answer repeatedly the question of what is significant enough to merit telling. This concern also receives direct thematic treatment in the numerous characters who fail to be accordingly circumspect in their verbal contributions—Chekhov's Pecheneg, whose unending torrent is truly a torment; his Chebutykin of *Three Sisters*, whose main activity is reading aloud indiscriminately irrelevant bits of "information" from the newspaper, and the content of whose life is as unswervingly empty as the content of his "news";[4] or the infamous Ippolit Ippolitych, who, as the prototype for Chekhov's later "man in a case," embodies not only tedium in his unremarkable remarks, but lifelessness itself. Finally, Chekhov and Zoshchenko inscribe indefatigably the arbiters of significance—the listeners, the readers, the public—who make it abundantly clear that what's worth telling is in the eyes (and feet) of the receiver. "Make a long story short and leave," reads a sign posted by one of Zoshchenko's workers. Another recommends a stiff fine for each word spoken in excess. And if by chance the verbal performance is not deemed worthwhile, you can always "spit on it" (*A nam naplevat'*).[5] Spitting and sneezing are the trivial indiscretions that get Chekhov's poor clerk into such hot water, but they are shown to be very much the prerogative of the reader.

This appeal to the reader's final authority probably has a better chance of eliciting the desired approbation than the disregard exhibited by Gogol's narrators, who are oblivious to the receiver and indulgent only of themselves. But beyond acknowledging the critical role of the reader, the question of tellability raised insistently by Chekhov's and Zoshchenko's "trivial" stories addresses the largest issue of all; the question of "news value" is an inquiry into value in general. Significance, after all, is not inherent but attributed. It entails assumptions that may be ideological and gendered and motivated by any number of social, economic, political, historical, religious, ethnic, and aesthetic conditions and expectations. By laying bare our conditioned sense of consequence and its underlying values, story-level insignificance functions as a critique of what is commonly told—that is, what is noticed, deemed significant, valued—both in public and in private.

It also reveals indisputably the lunacy of legislating tellability, of regulating not only what is permissible, but also what is "interesting" enough to recount. By applying the rigorous standards of narrative eventfulness as the index of important change, "insignificant" story exposes the exclusionary limits—both implicit and imposed—that would eliminate small-scale phenomena from view and from text. Chekhov's and Zoshchenko's pinpricks and stubbed toes reveal both the problems and the conditions (or contrivances) that conceal them. Story-level insignificance thus makes conspicuous otherwise imperceptible norms of existence and norms of selection as to what is told. Its stories are about choosing well. Discourse-level insignificance, by contrast, is about not choosing at all.

Some texts that challenge the assumptions and values by which we assign significance delight their readers; others disappoint them. We have seen the lengths to which interpreters of Gogol's verbal clutter are prepared to go to ensure that it is the former rather than the latter. In the foregoing chapters on Chekhov, Zoshchenko, and Gogol, I have considered some of the operations readers perform on texts to make the material purposeful and the experience worthwhile. I have also performed a few such operations of my own.

But what makes this exercise itself worth telling? For it remains to acknowledge the obvious resonance of the question of "what's worth telling" for literary criticism as well. Must literary-critical accounts be *assertible*, in the sense of providing new information and answering outstanding questions? Or is it sufficient that they, like narratives, be *tellable*, displaying a problematic state of affairs in a form imaginative enough to engage the reader's contemplation, evaluation, and response? It is with the latter goal that I have undertaken this study, the object of which is less to "inform" than to invite the "imaginative and affective involvement" associated with tellable tales.[6] If this book is worth reading—if my personal confrontation with the pragmatic force of insignificance can be contemplated with pleasure and profit—then it is because it has succeeded in wielding its own material to a significant purpose: to tell a good story.

Reference Matter

Notes

Introduction

1. See Pratt's illuminating discussion in *Toward a Speech Act Theory*, pp. 101–6.
2. H. P. Grice, "Conversational Maxims," cited in Pratt, *Toward a Speech Act Theory*, p. 130. Omitted at the ellipses are remarks Pratt makes about Grice.
3. Pratt, *Toward a Speech Act Theory*, p. 131.
4. Ibid., pp. 134–35.
5. In his study of oral storytelling, Labov found that most narrators have a double agenda: they wish not only to recount a series of events, but also to convince their listeners that the story is "worth it." They work constantly to ward off the rejoinder "so what?" (p. 366).
6. Pratt, *Toward a Speech Act Theory*, p. 136.
7. Ibid., p. 148. Agnes Heller even goes so far as to propose repetition as a kind of index of a story's significance. We tend to tell important stories of our own many times over. This drive to frequent repetition, she suggests, "indicates that a story is *important* to us. It distinguishes the important from the less important and the unimportant" (Heller, p. 53). But although we really do retell our most beloved stories, we ordinarily do so to different audiences. *Telling* again is not the same as *hearing* again. While children enjoy the verbatim repetition of their favorite tales, conservatively spurning all variations, adult consumers of literary narrative seem typically to confront their texts with less demand for ritual reenactment and more interest in novelty. Still, Pratt is undoubtedly correct that obsolescence is not built into the "tellable" in quite the same way it is by definition in the "assertible."
8. The tradition is a long one: it goes back to Aristotle, who claimed that tragedy deals with actions that are "serious, complete, and of a certain magnitude" (*Poetics* 6, p. 51). Horace preached "decorum" and an organic unity that excludes all actions or details not strictly relevant (*Art of Poetry*, lines 1–48, pp. 9–11 [verse], pp. 43–45 [prose]). These imperatives were only strengthened in subsequent centuries by the Renaissance and neo-classical critics, who upheld the mandates of the classical theoreticians. The "unerhörte Begebenheit," literally, an "unheard-of occurrence," is Goethe's formulation of the essential feature of the novella (*Gespräche mit Eckermann*, Jan. 29, 1827, 1:228).

9. In formulating the earlier and analogous distinction between *fabula* (the basic story-stuff) and *siuzhet* (its artistic embodiment), Boris Tomashevskii, too, speaks of the *fabula* in terms of a whole vocabulary of "invention" (*izobresti*), "intention" (*zadumana*), and "composition" (*sochinit'*) (*Teoriia literatury*, p. 136, and *Kratkii kurs*, pp. 87–88).

10. The question of tellability at the level of *discourse* will be addressed separately below.

11. Lotman, *Struktura*, pp. 278, 286. Lotman uses the terms "with *siuzhet*" and "without *siuzhet*" to distinguish between eventful and non-eventful texts, respectively. I avoid this terminology here, however, because of the misleading implication that eventfulness is a function of the discourse (by analogy of story/discourse with *fabula*/*siuzhet*). The event discussed by Lotman is constituted at the level of the story. (Tomashevskii, in making approximately the same distinction between eventful and eventless texts, refers to texts "with *fabula*" and "without *fabula*" [*Teoriia literatury*, p. 134].) Lotman's example of a text "without *siuzhet*" is the telephone directory. Eventless, it simply transcribes the prevailing order. The entries in the "Diary of a Cat" register in a similar, if less obviously classificatory way, a static, uneventful, "normal" order of things in which every day might as well be "today." Note, too, that being *siuzhet*-less (eventless) does not mean being without discursive strategies (e.g., the telephone book's alphabetical order, omission of apartment numbers, use of abbreviations).

12. Morson, *Hidden in Plain View*, pp. 221, 126, 123, 130, 145, 147.

13. Ibid., p. 3. Tomashevskii, too, stresses that "the laws of plot construction have nothing to do with verisimilitude" (*Teoriia literatury*, p. 147).

14. Morson, *Hidden in Plain View*, p. 33.

15. For a more explicit treatment of the ethical implications of prosaics, see Morson and Emerson's *Mikhail Bakhtin: Creation of a Prosaics*.

16. Morson, *Hidden in Plain View*, p. 122.

17. I use "pragmatics" in Charles Morris's sense of the term. He identifies three dimensions involved in every semiotic process: the *syntactic* dimension (the way in which the signs within a given system relate to each other), the *semantic* dimension (the relations of signs to their referents), and the *pragmatic* dimension (the relations of signs to their interpreters—"and the study of this dimension will be named *pragmatics*") (pp. 6–7).

18. Warning, "Staged Discourse," pp. 53–54.

19. Lotman, *Struktura*, p. 348.

20. Size has always conveyed iconographic significance in visual representation. Likhachev documents in particular the correlation between relative size and relative importance in medieval Russian painting (p. 354).

21. The term "pinpricks," by now axiomatic in Chekhov criticism, originated with Mirsky (p. 377).

22. Warning, "Staged Discourse," p. 51.

23. Letter to A. N. Pleshcheev, Apr. 9, 1889 (Chekhov, *Polnoe sobranie sochinenii i pisem, Pis'ma*, 3:186).

24. Fish, "Normal Circumstances, Literal Language, Direct Speech Acts,

the Ordinary, the Everyday, the Obvious, What Goes without Saying, and Other Special Cases," p. 627.

25. See Chatman's *Story and Discourse*, p. 28. Most theorists agree that the deployment of detail is a function of the discourse. Many, in fact, are unwilling to attribute *any* story-level existence to non-essential detail. Umberto Eco, for instance, admits only "structurally necessary properties" to the world of the story. "Accidental properties" do not belong to the basic story-stuff "and are taken into account only by discursive structures" (p. 239). Roland Barthes, in his work on narrative structure, shares this view that those details not logically entailed by the sequence of events or not essential for our understanding of characters and atmosphere are "pure data," and as such have no real *signifié* at the level of story: they are the property of the discourse ("Introduction," pp. 10–11). Tomashevskii, too, assigns to the *fabula* only "bound motifs"—those that are compositionally necessary, impossible to omit without altering the logic and coherence of the narrative; the *siuzhet*, on the other hand, is often dominated by "free motifs"—details elaborated without logical necessity, for "artistic" purposes (*Teoriia literatury*, pp. 137–38). All these views regard the selection and arrangement of detail, whether essential or ancillary, as the function of the discourse.

26. The most frequently cited of such details involves a portion of ham and peas carried by a waiter in "Muzhiki" ("Peasants"). Since these items have no particular relevance to the story, they have drawn ample critical attention given the consistent sparseness of Chekhov's prose.

27. Shukin, p. 44. See also Chekhov's letter to A. S. Lazarev (Gruzinskii), Nov. 1, 1889 (*Pis'ma*, 3:273).

28. According to Tomashevskii, literary tradition is the chief regulator of elaborative detail, each school exhibiting its own repertoire and characteristic level of tolerance of "free motifs" (*Teoriia literatury*, p. 138).

29. Barthes, "L'Effet du réel," p. 89.

30. Barthes refers to Flaubert's "Un Coeur Simple." Obviously not all objects catalogued lack informational or symbolic content. Some, like the piano in the same descriptive passage, connote something else (bourgeois taste in living rooms, for instance). The barometer is emblematic for Barthes of all those objects reported that do not carry a heavy semiotic load according to our coded knowledge of the world and its literature.

31. Hamon, "Un discours constraint," p. 423.

32. Barthes, "Introduction," p. 7. Lotman makes essentially the same point in *Struktura*, p. 99.

33. See Crosman's "Do Readers Make Meaning?"

34. Forster, p. 17.

35. The logical anteriority of story to discourse, though fundamental to Chatman's understanding of the terms, has been strongly challenged by Barbara Herrnstein Smith and has since become a matter of heated debate. See their exchange, Smith, "Narrative Versions," and Chatman, "Reply." See also the discussion of story and discourse in Chapter 4.

Chapter 1

1. Chekhov, "Uchitel' slovesnosti," ("The Teacher of Literature"), *Polnoe sobranie sochinenii i pisem, Sochineniia*, 8:318, 319, 328. All subsequent references to this edition will be to the *Sochineniia*, unless otherwise specified, and will be noted parenthetically in the text wherever convenient. All translations are mine unless otherwise indicated.

2. Fish, "Normal Circumstances," p. 627. This principle provided the "Saturday Night Live" news team with much comic mileage from its ongoing reports that General Franco is "still dead." It also accounts for the humor in the *Tulsa World* news story and the cartoon reprinted from the *New Yorker*.

3. Letter to A. S. Suvorin, May 30, 1888 (Chekhov, *Pis'ma*, 2:280).

4. Such diverse critics as Mikhailovskii, Skabichevskii, and Govorukha-Otrok [Iu. Nikolaev, pseud.] found themselves in accord in their early exhortations to Chekhov to abandon the *melochi* and to work on something significant. The quoted passage is from Govorukha-Otrok, who repeated this criticism throughout Chekhov's career ("Ocherki sovremennoi belletristiki," cited in A. P. Chudakov, *Poetika Chekhova*, p. 159); see also Varshavskaia, p. 21.

5. [Anon.], Review of *Pestrye rasskazy, Nabliudatel'*, no. 12 (1886), cited in Chekhov, 2:476; and Skabichevskii [unsigned], Review of *Pestrye rasskazy*, p. 125.

6. Lipovskii, p. 23.

7. Mikhailovskii, "Ob otsakh i detiakh," p. 598.

8. Disterlo, "O bezvlastii molodykh pisatelei," col. 33.

9. *Bessoderzhatel'nost'* is Medvedskii's ongoing complaint (e.g., "Literaturnye zametki," p. 3). *Bezydeinost'* resounds in Medvedskii, "Zhertva bezvremen'ia," pp. 234–35, and Skabichevskii, *Istoriia noveishei russkoi literatury*, pp. 414–15, and many others; see also Aleksandrov, pp. 17–19.

10. For a more detailed comparison of the two writers' treatment of *melochi zhizni*, see Okhotina; and Kataev, *Literaturnye sviazi*, pp. 44–51.

11. Pertsov, pp. 43–44.

12. I. I. Ivanov, p. 103; Mikhailovskii, "Sluchainye zametki," p. 3.

13. Medvedskii, Review, p. 193.

14. Chudakov contends that the dominant principle of selection in Chekhov's artistic system is randomness—Chekhov, he claims, depicts the incidental as well as the essential, giving equal weight to the "significant" and the "insignificant," thus creating the illusion of non-selectivity (*Poetika Chekhova*, esp. chap. 4, pp. 138–87, also throughout chaps. 5 and 6).

15. Zel'manov [M. Iuzhnyi], cited in Chekhov, 8:423. *Otsutstvie idei* is another variation on the complaint of *bezydeinost'* voiced recurrently in the contemporary criticism of Chekhov's prose.

16. This is not to exaggerate the iconoclastic force of Chekhov's innovations. To be sure, the short story had held its own in the Russian tradition throughout the period of sovereignty of the realist novel. Writers such as Garshin had experimented with similar forms of understatement; others, like Uspenskii, influenced by the genre of the sketch (*ocherk*), had produced stories similarly

lacking in traditional plot structure and characterized by relative laconism. What distinguishes Chekhov's oeuvre is its provocational foregrounding of and structural reliance on apparent trivia.

17. J. Brooks, pp. 101–2.

18. Letter to Suvorin, May 30, 1888 (Chekhov, *Pis'ma*, 2:280); to Suvorin, Oct. 27, 1888 (*Pis'ma*, 3:46); to Suvorin, Apr. 1, 1890 (*Pis'ma*, 4:54).

19. See, for example, Aleksandrov, pp. 17–19; and Varshavskaia, pp. 40–41.

20. See Aleksandrov, p. 25; and Varshavskaia, pp. 54, 73.

21. Protopopov, pp. 112–13.

22. Vvedenskii, cited in A. P. Chudakov, *Poetika Chekhova*, pp. 175–76.

23. Disterlo, "Kriticheskie zametki," col. 1478.

24. Letter to N. A. Leikin, Jan. 12, 1883 (Chekhov, *Pis'ma*, 1:48). Chekhov's complaints about brevity are, however, less evident than his praise of its virtues. He triumphantly proclaimed a single-handed "revolt against prolixity": "Brevity is the sister of talent," he wrote. His advice to his brother Aleksandr—"Shorten it, man, shorten it!"—was an admonition to all writers. Thus his pride that "I have the ability to speak briefly on long subjects." Letter to Leikin, Jan. 12, 1883 (*Pis'ma*, 1:48); to Al. P. Chekhov, Apr. 11, 1889 (*Pis'ma*, 3:188); to Al. P. Chekhov, Apr. 30, 1893 (*Pis'ma*, 5:206). Chekhov's comment recalls Thoreau's remark: "Not that the story need be long, but it will take a long while to make it short." Letter to Harrison G. O. Blake, Nov. 16, 1857 (p. 498).

25. Skabichevskii describes Chekhov's stories as *gazetnaia boltevnia*—"minor feuilletons" for "trivial amusement" (Review of *Pestrye rasskazy*, pp. 123–24).

26. Mikhailovskii, Review of *V sumerkakh*, pp. 83–85.

27. Merezhkovksii, *Chekhov i Gor'kii*, p. 16.

28. The Pushkin prize "for the best literary work distinguished by high artistic value" was awarded by the Division of Russian Language and Letters of the Academy of Sciences for Chekhov's collection *V sumerkakh* (*In the Twilight*).

29. Some of Chekhov's work appeared in *Russkaia mysl'* and *Severnyi vestnik*.

30. Skabichevskii, "Tekushchaia literatura," cited in Chekhov, 10:375.

31. I refer to the writer in *Chaika* (*The Seagull*, 1896), who records practically everything he encounters in a little notebook in order to turn it into a story later (13:28–32).

32. Letter to F. D. Batiushkov, Dec. 15, 1897 (Chekhov, *Pis'ma*, 7:123).

33. I refer to Lotman's notion of reading as a confrontation between the perceiver's expectations and the author's model (*Struktura*, p. 348). See my Introduction.

34. The characterization of the novel is Watt's (p. 32). Teffi, whose own preferred genre was the short story, draws the contrast: in the novel, an author must "shoe, clothe, feed, water, transport to the dacha in the summer, and give [characters] the opportunity to manifest all their innate qualities." In short fiction, by refreshing contrast, "every word is weighed, every motion. What remains is only the most indispensable" (cited in Haber, p. 163).

35. Arsen'ev, "Belletristy poslednego vremeni," p. 771.
36. Pratt, "Short Story," p. 182.
37. See, for example, Pratt, "Short Story"; Eikhenbaum, "O. Genri"; Goethe, *Gespräche mit Eckermann*, Jan. 29, 1827; Sir Hugh Walpole, cited in Bates, p. 16; Jaffe and Scott, eds.; Doderer; Marler; Perrine, p. 43.
38. Govorukha-Otrok, "Literaturnye zametki," p. 3.
39. Shestov, p. 12.
40. Chekhov no doubt has in mind Dostoevsky's particularly generous use of "suddenly" (*vdrug*). See the discussions of Dostoevsky's fondness for the term by Bitsilli in "K voprosu o vnutrennei forme," pp. 9–10; and Slonimskii, "'Vdrug' u Dostoevskogo."
41. The axes correspond to the basic linguistic operations of selection and combination. In any speech act, each word is *selected* from among all possible elements in the appropriate semantic and grammatical paradigm. The chosen words are then *combined* to form a complete utterance. The axis of selection represents relations of equivalence, while the axis of combination operates on the principle of contiguity (Jakobson, "Closing Statement," p. 358).
42. Letter to Chekhov from A. V. Petrov, Jan. 4, 1882, cited in Chekhov, 2:510.
43. In "Shinel'" ("The Overcoat"), the Person of Consequence takes special pleasure in terrorizing inconsequential clerks.
44. In the *Hundred Chapters* of Pseudo-Gennadius, the favorite religious compendium in Russia since the eleventh century, mankind is reminded that although "'a worm is very humble and base, and you are very glorious and proud,'... the worm's distance from man symbolizes man's abysmal distance from God." Translated into the sphere of social interaction, "'meekness means not to annoy anyone either in words or deeds or commands, but to please every man by one's behavior.'" Servility to God and to one's betters is required (Fedotov, p. 210).
45. Barthes refers to the social showcasing ("'paraître' culturel") that characterizes the theater, in contradistinction to the dark anonymity (the "condensation humaine") of the movie house ("En sortant du cinéma," p. 105).
46. Fedotov, pp. 182–83. See also Elias, "Über das Schneuzen."
47. This usage occurs in *Ivanov*, for example: (*Lebedev*): *A ty, Nikolasha, nachikhai na vse da poezzhai k nam* (12:51).
48. Letter to Chekhov, Jan. 5, 1900 (Gor'kii, *Sobranie sochinenii*, 28:113).
49. Zoshchenko, "O komicheskom," p. 152.
50. Karlinsky, Introduction, p. 1.
51. Shklovskii, "A. P. Chekhov," p. 333.
52. Pospelov, p. 320.
53. "I know what you call psychology," exclaims Nikitin in Chekhov's "Teacher of Literature" during a heated discussion of literary psychology. "You think someone has to be sawing off my finger with a dull saw while I scream at the top of my lungs—that's what you mean by psychology" (8:315).
54. See Tolstoi, 19:349.
55. "Ne-vyrazim" means "non-expressible."

56. Al'bov, p. 105.

57. See, for example, Kacherets, p. 43.

58. Tolstoy, by contrast, in keeping with his "prosaic" mistrust of anything perceptible and attention-getting (none of which can be genuinely important), is suspicious of conscious change. Although he allows for tiny alterations in consciousness, in general, living right can only be an *unconscious* matter, and those who possess truth are unaware of their knowledge. See Morson, *Hidden in Plain View*, pp. 227, 268.

59. Mirsky, p. 378. Thomas Winner also refers to "the tension between the expected and the actual resolution which creates the aesthetic effect" (p. 5). Bitsilli suggests that this "discrepancy between expectation and realization," while certainly characteristic of Chekhov, is more broadly typical of comic works in general (*Chekhov's Art*, pp. 107–8). Poggioli argues that this "storytelling in a double key," this "changing what at first looks like an unpromising seed into a bitter, and yet ripe, fruit," is precisely what differentiates Chekhov's prose from more conventional comedy, tragicomedy, and farce—and separates his mature work from his early vaudevilles (p. 110). Kataev contends rather that the shift from *kazalos'* (it seemed) to *okazalos'* (it turned out), one of the most enduring features of Chekhov's prose, *links* his early works and his later ones. For Kataev, the *kazalos'/okazalos'* pattern is an expression of Chekhov's ongoing epistemological concerns (*Proza Chekhova*, pp. 21–30).

60. I. V. Ivanov [I. Dzhonson, pseud.], p. 244.

61. See, for example, Olesha's "Liompa" (1927) and Pasternak's "Detstvo Liuvers" ("Zhenia Liuvers's Childhood," 1918).

62. Winner has termed this characteristic Chekhovian structural feature a "zero ending" (p. 5).

63. Lotman, "Theater and Theatricality," p. 160. Such patterning and perception of life "through the filters of poetic texts" is reflected in particular in the Decembrist ideal of everyday behavior. This code, which acquired normative status among the gentry, dictated that *every* act be significant, memorable, historical—worthy, in other words, of being "inscribed" in a "poetic" text. The "prosaic" was disregarded as incommensurate, and "just as in literature," only "significant" and "daring" action was worthy of mention. The ideological assumptions here, not only about standards of behavior, but about the standards for literary content, are powerful. See Lotman's essay "The Decembrist in Everyday Life," pp. 114–19.

64. Chekhov originally called this story "Zhiteiskaia meloch'" ("A Trifle from Everyday Life"), a title he had already used in his 1886 story (discussed above) to introduce his consideration of eventfulness from disparate perspectives.

65. Readers may recognize this portrait of a corrupt and sordid hospital whose physician-in-charge is only too aware of its appalling inadequacies as a prototype for the abominations of "Palata No. 6" ("Ward Six," 1892). In the later story, the doctor is not merely *unsuccessful* at effecting change; he has taken philosophical refuge behind the stoicism of Marcus Aurelius, the passivity of Tolstoy's non-resistance to evil, and the thousand-year perspective of Schopenhauer to glorify his inactivity. Suffering, he reasons, is unavoidable

and probably necessary; constructive engagement is thus misguided. All this makes the ineffectual attempt—which is at least an attempt—of the doctor in "An Unpleasant Incident" a relative victory.

66. There may be, however, an undercurrent of attraction to Lida, whom Monsieur N. repeatedly describes as "beautiful" and who arouses impassioned responses from him in the form of irritation and heated argument. Indeed, he turns his gaze to Zhenia when he feels that Lida does not like *him*. He embraces the non-threatening passivity of the younger sister when the *activity* of Lida is beyond him.

67. Sementkovskii, col. 387. Ironically, Chekhov's ineffectual weaklings are not infrequently more humane and appealing than his socially committed activists—even those with the most laudable goals—who tend to be overbearing and tyrannical.

68. Lotman, *Struktura*, p. 283.

69. "The fact of perpetual alternation of binary situational units keeps [Olen'ka's] life condition in a constant balance," notes Pomorska (p. 462).

70. See, for example "Baby" ("Peasant Women," 1891), in which the enterprising Diudia, who maintains a lucrative trade in a wide range of commodities and services, exacts a story each night from his transient boarders, almost as part of his calculation of the payment for their lodging (in keeping with the folk motif of nocturnal storytelling in exchange for a place to spend the night). Similarly, in the frame narrative that links "Chelovek v futliare" ("The Man in a Case"), "Kryzhovnik" ("Gooseberries"), and "O liubvi" ("About Love") (1898) nights are eagerly whiled away with edifying tales. Even the weary Alekhin refrains from turning in for fear that someone will recount something interesting in his absence. Good stories—by implication these three pieces of Chekhov's, which are told in these sessions—are more worthwhile than sleep.

71. Labov, p. 366.

72. Booth, pp. 64, 196–200.

73. Varshavskaia, p. 8; Arsen'ev, "Modnaia forma belletristiki"; J. Brooks, p. 98; Erenburg, p. 89. *Forma vremeni* is Belinsky's notion of the "dominant genre" of a given epoch, a genre conditioned and shaped by the *dukha vremeni*, the spirit and exigencies of its era ("O russkoi povesti," pp. 259–72). Varshavskaia, whose agenda is to establish that the emergence of small genres with small concerns was no accident at this juncture, suggests that shorter works are indigenous to such transitional periods. When the old doctrines are stale and the new ideologies are not quite ripe, claims Varshavskaia, it is difficult to make major, all-encompassing, coherent statements—so writers deal in details and traffic in the more concrete and mobile smaller genres (p. 74). Other Soviet criticism has cited Chekhov's era as a period of "small deeds" that made more modest works of literature inevitable, in contrast to the monumental and revolutionary achievements of the Soviet period, where such little pieces are inadmissible (A. Leites, in "Razgovor o novelle," p. 211).

74. Pomorska, p. 459.

75. Durkin, p. 129.

76. A. P. Chudakov, *Poetika Chekhova*, pp. 213–17.
77. Ibid., p. 188.
78. Pomorska, p. 462.
79. Billington, p. 446.

Chapter 2

1. One of the more dramatic examples of punitive sanctions is the multimillion-dollar bounty offered by fundamentalist Iran for the assassination of "blasphemous" author Salman Rushdie (*Satanic Verses*) (spoofed in the cartoon to Chapter 4, p. 125). The Russian/Soviet authorities have dispatched innumerable writers of their own, usually with less fanfare, but with greater efficacy.

2. Admittedly, this criterion could be formulated in "too-x" terms as well—something below this threshold is "too boring," "too trivial," or, as my own analogy would have it, "too slight." But the spirit of the objection nevertheless invokes deficiency rather than excess, reflecting a kind of minimum standard of stimulation distinct from and complementary to the one that calibrates the maximum allowable irritation.

3. This became even more true in 1932 with the establishment of socialist realism "by administrative fiat" as the sole accepted mode of writing. Socialist realism prescribed a basic master plot that all novels were to recapitulate. Inventiveness was neither valued nor permitted. The object was to repeat the established litany of the socialist realist paradigm (Clark, pp. 27–45).

The novelty of this approach is remarked on as well by Nabokov, who emphasizes that "before the Soviet rule there did exist restrictions, but no orders were given to artists." However, he explains, writers in the nineteenth century had another force to contend with, quite independent of the czar's censors: the radical thinkers, the civic, utilitarian critics who, while dedicated to freeing Russia, constrained her literature with demands of their own. These enemies of dictatorship exercised their own dominion in the world of letters, requiring of literature that it be "politically correct"—socially relevant and practically engaged in the ideological battle—admirable goals, perhaps, but ones that had little to do with artistic value. In this sense, the Soviet prescription for "desirable" forms and content does have a precedent in nineteenth-century literary history, but the earlier practice was both less specific and less invested with institutional authority (*Lectures*, pp. 3–5).

4. Zhurbina, p. 20; and Maguire, *Red Virgin Soil*, p. 72.
5. Maguire, *Red Virgin Soil*, pp. 270–93.
6. A. Leites, in "Razgovor o novelle," p. 211.
7. L'vov-Rogachevskii, p. xxvi. See also Semanova.
8. See Voronskii's important article, "Na perevale," p. 322. Voronskii was not the only critic to issue a call for literature to be equal in magnitude to its great epoch, but as editor of the new thick journal, *Red Virgin Soil* (*Krasnaia nov'*), he was among the most influential.
9. The Futurists of *Lef* and the Octobrists of *Na postu* alone among the Marxists disagreed with this determination. They felt the novel, as a leftover

bourgeois artifact, was not appropriate for their all-new society. See, for example, Lelevich, p. 55.

10. Maguire, "Literary Conflicts," p. 108.

11. Voronskii, "Na perevale," p. 318.

12. Voronskii essentially voiced the appeal in "Na perevale" without actually coining the phrase, but Aleksandr Fadeev, one of the principal figures of RAPP (Russian Association of Proletarian Writers) actually made the search for a new Tolstoy an explicit part of that powerful organization's literary platform. The suggestion, though it reflected policy, was not unanimously accepted. See, for instance, Tretiakov, "Novyi Lev Tolstoi."

13. See Morson, *Hidden in Plain View*, especially the introduction and chap. 2, "Formal Peculiarities of *War and Peace*."

14. Zhits, p. 268.

15. Also inherent in the notion of "large scale" was the expectation, always an important aspect of the Russian literary tradition, that the work be of social import. The aestheticism of the Symbolists and the individualism of the Serapion Brothers were viewed as too self-focused, and consequently, too narrow.

16. Pereverzev takes this tack throughout his "Na frontakh tekushchei belletristiki."

17. Initially in the Soviet period, the function of censorship was exercised by the State Publishing House, but with the resurgence of private publishing during the period of the New Economic Policy (NEP), a new agency, Glavlit, was formed to coordinate the effort. During the greater part of the 1920s, interference from Glavlit was relatively slight, reserved principally for direct and flagrant opposition rather than for the subtleties of ideological purity. By the end of the decade, though, Glavlit became more intimately associated with the Ministry of Internal Affairs and operated much as a branch of the internal security police (Thomson, pp. 86–87).

18. For a thorough treatment of these and other literary groups actively vying for influence in this period, see E. J. Brown; Ermolaev; Maguire, *Red Virgin Soil* and "Literary Conflicts."

19. The Resolution "On Party Policy in the Field of Imaginative Literature," issued by the Central Committee of the Communist Party in 1925, officially extended the period of free competition in literature by declaring that the working class was not yet prepared to shoulder the whole burden of imaginative literature. But the assumption that literature ultimately belongs to the working class and must embody its ideology was not disputed. Even while it generously granted other forms of literature the right to exist, the Resolution of 1925 still upheld the "moral supremacy" of proletarian, "desirable" literature. See Ermolaev, pp. 45–54; Voron, p. 11; Thomson, pp. 90–91.

20. "Fellow Travelers" (*poputchiki*) were individual writers who "accepted the Revolution, each one in his own way," but for whom "the Communist ideal is foreign" (Trotsky, p. 57).

21. Shklovskii, "O Zoshchenke," p. 16.

22. See Maguire, "Literary Conflicts," pp. 108–9, and *Red Virgin Soil*, p. 67.

23. Maguire, *Red Virgin Soil*, pp. 4–5, 21–22.
24. For this reason I have chosen to focus primarily on Zoshchenko's oeuvre of the 1920s. The works of the 1930s and 1940s raise important questions of their own, but these necessitate a more extensive consideration of the dynamics of exclusion and inclusion under Stalinist censorship than the scope of the present inquiry permits.
25. Voronskii, "Na perevale," p. 315.
26. Ibid., p. 312.
27. Voronskii, Review of Zoshchenko and Slonimskii, p. 344.
28. Vsevolod Ivanov, *Vstrechi s Maksim Gor'kim*, cited in Voron, p. 39.
29. Seifullina, p. 53.
30. Voron, pp. 38–39.
31. Lezhnev, "Literaturnye zametki," p. 133.
32. Zoshchenko, "O sebe, o kritikakh," pp. 8–9.
33. Tsentral'nyi gosudarstvennyi arkhiv literatury i iskusstva (TsGALI), f. 601, op. 2, ed. khr. 3; and Zoshchenko, "O sebe, o kritikakh," p. 9. A more literal translation of *sobach'ia erunda* might be "dog drivel."
34. TsGALI, f. 601, op. 2, ed. khr. 1, l. 9.
35. Zoshchenko, "O sovremennom iumore," cited in Zoshchenko, "O komicheskom," p. 150. The first piece was drafted originally in the early 1920s for *Na perelome 1910–1920*; the second was written in 1944 but remained unpublished until this 1967 printing.
36. Zoshchenko, "O sebe, o kritikakh," p. 11.
37. Zoshchenko, "Ot avtora," *O chem pel solovei: Sentimental'nye povesti*, pp. 5–6. Also in *Sobranie sochinenii* Priboi (1929–31), 4:3 (hereafter "Priboi"). The text of this preface, in somewhat bowdlerized form, appears in the recent collected works, *Sobranie sochinenii v trekh tomakh* (1986), 2:6–7. This later edition is the most comprehensive to date, and will be used here for convenience as the basic text; subsequent references will be noted parenthetically in the text. Unless otherwise specified, all stories mentioned in my discussion can be found in this 1986 edition. Where the 1986 version differs from the text as it originally appeared, however, I will cite earlier sources instead. For this purpose, because first editions are largely unavailable, I have consulted 1920s reprintings that reproduce or closely approximate the text of the originals. Where these are missing, I rely on the early six-volume collection (Priboi) of Zoshchenko's stories of the 1920s. Since my concern is the production and reception of Zoshchenko's stories in their original 1920s context, I will consider these versions the fundamental ones, even though Zoshchenko himself often altered his own stories in subsequent editions. Substantial changes were made in particular in the stories that Zoshchenko collected and recast for his *Golubaia kniga* (*Light-Blue Book*) in 1935, reflecting the exigencies of a very different publishing climate. (For a complete transcript of the additional deletions and insertions made by the censor of *Golubaia kniga*, as well as a preliminary attempt to account for them, see "Tsenzorskaia pravka 'Goluboi knigi.'") The 1986 edition gives original publication dates for the *Golubaia kniga* stories, but prints them all in their significantly altered 1935 form.

To complicate matters further, publication data on Zoshchenko's stories is not entirely reliable—apparently Zoshchenko did not consistently clip his pieces from newspapers or keep track of dates and places of publication. This makes for some inaccuracy as to the original dates of publication, especially because many stories were released multiple times within several years in pamphlets and collections. Some stories Zoshchenko himself republished in several editions, each time citing a different date of origin (see notes to the 1986 edition, 1:536). Given these difficulties, I have relied on the dating as given in the 1986 apparatus, but without absolute confidence. Similarly hazy is the division of Zoshchenko's pieces into "stories" and "feuilletons"—each collection seems to partition the continuum differently. Thus I have not taken the distinction too much to heart. Since there are no canonical versions, no academy edition of Zoshchenko's works, and certainly no complete collection, decisions as to which versions to consider must be, and have been, made according to the goals of the particular inquiry. All translations are my own unless otherwise indicated.

38. Zoshchenko, letter to M. Gorky, cited in Murphy, p. 50.

39. Lidiia Khariton, letter to L. Lunts, Sept. 27, 1923, cited in Chudakova, p. 62.

40. Vishnev, p. 55.

41. Ibid., p. 56.

42. Murphy, p. 49.

43. Gul'binskii [I. V. Vladislavlev, pseud.], pp. 25, 116. Starkov cites even higher figures, suggesting that the 1926–27 editions totaled 950,000 (p. 5).

44. Chukovskii, p. 33.

45. The original "Galosh" appears in Zoshchenko, *Nad kem smeetes'?!*, pp. 52–54, and *Tsarskie sapogi*, pp. 131–33, among other 1920s collections, and Priboi, 2:134–37. The 1986 edition uses the altered *Golubaia kniga* version. For "The Merry-Go-Round," see *Uvazhaemye grazhdane*, p. 206, and Priboi, 1:30. The story appears in the 1986 edition in very different form as part of the *Golubaia kniga* under the title "Skol'ko cheloveku nuzhno" ("How Much Does a Person Need").

46. The terminology is Seymour Chatman's. With this pair of terms he identifies the components of a narrative's *story*: what happens ("events"), and who and what are involved ("existents"). "Existents" thus include not only characters, but also salient "things," as well as elements of setting. See *Story and Discourse*, where the chapter divisions reflect this distinction.

47. It was often claimed that Zoshchenko's stories were chaotic and unstructured, like those of so many of his contemporaries. See Murphy's discussion, p. 117; also Voronskii, "Na perevale," p. 315; and Loks, p. 84.

48. Chudakova, pp. 53–54, 140.

49. Kreps, pp. 5–6.

50. Dostoevskii, *Brat'ia Karamazovy*, *Polnoe sobranie sochinenii*, 14:216.

51. This is not to imply that Saltykov-Shchedrin was a complacent subscriber to that calendar or telephone book, but only that his own attack on the *melochi zhizni* differed in strategy from that of Zoshchenko.

52. E. J. Brown, p. 187.

53. This story also appeared several times—in Zoshchenko, *Blednolitsye brat'ia* and *Skupoi rytsar'*—under what seems to have become Zoshchenko's favorite title, "The Trifles of Life" ("Melochi zhizni"), though whether he is still quoting Saltykov-Shchedrin here or just repeating himself is hard to say.

54. I refer to the text as it appears in Zoshchenko, *Nad kem smeetes'?!*, pp. 66–69, as well as numerous other 1920s collections, and Priboi, 2:150–54. The 1986 edition uses an altered version.

55. Chudakova, p. 40.

56. Patients in waiting rooms, too, abscond regularly with coats, sometimes cloth ones, sometimes fur models, but always somebody else's. See "Avantiurnyi rasskaz" ("An Adventure Story," 1925) in *Nad kem smeetes'?!*, pp. 109–10.

57. Cf. Chekhov's ambitious *perevernut' zhizn'* (turn one's life around), diminished here to *peremenit' odezhdu* (change one's clothes [3:257]). See Chapter 1.

58. In Zoshchenko, *Uvazhaemye grazhdane*, pp. 201–2. Reproduced also in Priboi, 1:25. This story does not appear in the three-volume 1986 edition.

59. Cf. the hero of Zoshchenko's later "Sixth Tale of Belkin" ("Shestaia povest' I. P. Belkina," 1937), who accidentally acquires a medal and only later sets out to earn it (with a bullet hole in his coat and permanently disfigured hands). In this homage to Pushkin, Zoshchenko generates "adventure" by reversing the logic and the actions of his own coat and foot victims and offenders.

60. Shcheglov, "Entsiklopediia nekul'turnosti," p. 59.

61. Zholkovskii, p. 108.

62. Ibid. Zholkovskii also cites a passage by Shcheglov, nearly as entertaining as the Zoshchenko vignettes themselves, that catalogues the typical misadventures of Zoshchenko's hero in the theater: besides checking his coat, he spends his time checking out either the plumbing or the financial subtleties of the snack bar, or he cannot (or will not) pay for the ticket in the first place, or he mends his clothes during the performance rather than watching the action on stage, and so on (p. 107).

63. Lotman, "Theater and Theatricality," p. 150.

64. Lotman, "Poetics of Everyday Behavior," p. 241.

65. The other passengers complain that there are no "programs" or announcements to identify the cast (1:401).

66. In Zoshchenko, *Uvazhaemye grazhdane*, pp. 152–54. Also in Priboi, 2:44–46. Not included in the 1986 edition.

67. Uspenskij, pp. 272–73.

68. See Barthes, *Fashion System*.

69. See Gogol', "Nos," *Polnoe sobranie sochinenii*, 3:54–57.

70. Omitted from the 1986 edition. Reprinted in Zoshchenko, *Nad kem smeetes'?!*, pp. 11–13. Also in Priboi, 3:6–8.

71. Dostoevskii, *Zapiski iz mertvogo doma*, *Polnoe sobranie sochinenii*, 4:96–99.

72. Lotman and Uspenskij, pp. 8–9.

73. See Tolstoi, *Voina i mir*, *Polnoe sobranie sochinenii*, 11:123–24. Tolstoy's play (*Zhivoi trup*, 34:5–99) has entirely different concerns.

74. In this penetrating essay, Reyfman documents a whole archaeology of stylizations of Zoshchenko's models. He not only imitates Pushkin, but he realizes Leont'ev's ideas of rewriting *Tolstoy* in Pushkinian style; he also plays on Tolstoy's use of Pushkin; and, for good measure, he imitates his own earlier imitation of Pushkin in the Sinebriukhov stories.

75. Ibid., p. 408.

76. They are also functionally illiterate: (*Pol'ta, govoriat, symaite* [The charms of culture, 1:358]).

77. Zholkovskii sees in this damaged sock a parodic reference to Tolstoy's torn ball glove from *Detstvo* (*Childhood*), and hence another of Zoshchenko's caricatured "realizations" of Tolstoy's ideas (p. 127).

78. Zoshchenko, *Izbrannoe v dvukh tomakh*, 1:288–72.

79. In Zoshchenko, *Dni nashei zhizni*, pp. 168–69, in a subsection entitled "Mody" ("Fashions"). Omitted from the 1986 edition.

80. Electricity is featured, for instance, in "Bednost'" ("Poverty," 1925, Priboi, 2:41–43); "Letniaia peredyshka" ("A Summer Breather," 1929); and "Malen'kaia khitrost'" ("A Clever Little Trick," 1930, *Rasskazy*, pp. 188–89).

81. The Russian term refers both specifically to the foot and, more generally, to the entire limb.

82. Paperno points to the tendency to interpolate "boots and old galoshes" into meditations on the nature of rationality as typical of Chernyshevsky's project (p. 45), and D. Barton Johnson cites Bunin's "galoshes manifesto" (and Valentin Kataev's application of it) as an aspect of twentieth-century realism that inspires even such modernists as Sasha Sokolov (pp. 175–79).

83. As a result, the galosh enjoyed a certain currency in belles lettres. Bulgakov, in particular, portrays the Revolution and historical progress in terms of the presence and absence of galoshes—never before 1917 did a single pair of rubbers disappear, his narrator avers; by November of that year they were all gone. See *Sobach'e serdtse* (*Heart of a Dog*), throughout, but especially p. 52. Bulgakov also manipulates his characters' boots and shoes as signs of their respective ideological stances.

84. Personal communication with Chudakova.

85. Bulgakov plays on this fact as well. In a communal apartment, where the private realm is publicly shared, anyone leaving shoes—and especially galoshes—at the entryway has seen them for the last time (*Sobach'e serdtse*).

86. Hubbs, pp. 85–86.

87. See, for example Dostoevsky's "poem" about the little foot and his chapter entitled "Bol'naia nozhka" ("The Injured Foot") in *Brat'ia Karamazovy*, *Polnoe sobranie sochinenii*, 15:30, 12–20.

88. See Zoshchenko, "O sebe," in *Dni nashei zhizni*, pp. 7–8, and "O sebe, ob ideologii," pp. 28–29.

89. On Tolstoy's bootmaking, see Troyat, pp. 439–40, 465.

90. Lenin, *Shag vpered, dva shaga nazad*.

91. *Idem* can mean "we are walking/moving/marching/going" or simply "let's go"; "go, go, go" is self-explanatory. In this poem Mayakovsky also characterizes "our feet" as faster, so to speak, than a speeding bullet, more powerful

than a locomotive (*Nashi nogi—poezdov molnienosnye prokhody*). The peripatetic reaffirmation of *my idem* punctuates each verse of "Levyi marsh" as well. Mayakovsky's poster verse in particular is full of these and similar images (2:23, 43–45, 83–85, 115–48).

92. The Russian verbal system distinguishes between random, indeterminate, or back and forth motion (*khodit'*), and progress in a specific direction (*idti*).

Chapter 3

1. Dostoevskii, *Zapiski iz podpol'ia*, *Polnoe sobranie sochinenii*, 5:130–32. Dostoevsky's episode on Petersburg's main street is itself a well-known parody of a similar street scene in *Chto delat'?* (*What Is to Be Done?*) where Chernyshevsky's "new man" has no difficulty making his presence palpable; he triumphantly tosses his opponent off the road. The association of Zoshchenko's numerous pedestrian encounters with the long-standing tradition of *vseobshchaia kommunikatsiia*, the *gulian'e Peterburga* (the circulation of people on Nevskii Prospekt), tacit in many stories, is made explicit in "Kitaiskaia tseremoniia" ("The Chinese Ceremony," 1924), Zoshchenko's story about the conventions of encountering and touching other strollers on that famous boulevard (shaking hands rather than rubbing noses). Many of Zoshchenko's stories in one form or another replay the Dostoevskian primal scene, though far less dramatically—see, for example, "A Trivial Incident from Private Life," in which the dilemma is that of going unnoticed when strolling down the street.

2. Although the reference is probably inadvertent, the terms of this man's resolution echo the accusation leveled at Chekhov by his critics—that he would simply "go out for a walk in life" and fail to notice whether "a man was being murdered or just champagne was being served." See Chapter 1.

3. Koffka, p. 184.

4. Chvany, p. 252.

5. Reinhart, p. 788.

6. Shcheglov, "Mir Mikhaila Zoshchenko," pp. 111, 123, 124, 132–33. In this earlier version of his "Entsiklopediia nekul'turnosti," Shcheglov discusses the function of the pervasive *nekul'turnost'*, to which he assigns the central role in Zoshchenko's fictional universe. The "Entsiklopediia nekul'turnosti" elaborates Shcheglov's systematic typology of *nekul'turnost'* further, in its diverse story- and discourse-level manifestations.

7. And how much more ludicrous the stringent demands on costume appear in light of this.

8. Not included in the 1986 edition. It appeared in many of Zoshchenko's collections in the 1920s, including *Nervnye liudi*, pp. 64–66; and *Veselye rasskazy*, pp. 30–33. Also in Priboi, 2:164–66.

9. Zoshchenko, "The Wedding," in *Nad kem smeetes'?!*, p. 69; Priboi, 2:154. The 1935 text reproduced in the 1986 edition eliminates this portion of the ending.

10. Shklovskii, "O Zoshchenke," p. 22; Starkov, p. 33.

11. The Soviet cult of the hero, while fostered as emblematic of the new,

heroic era, actually has a distinguished history in Russian letters. See Mathewson's book, *The Positive Hero in Russian Literature*, for both his delineation of the specifically Soviet outlines of the type, as well as his detailed discussion of its roots in nineteenth-century literary criticism.

12. "I'm not in the habit of" (*ia ne privyk*) even becomes an automatic (comic) defense against all accusations: I'm not in the habit of stealing watches ("Chasy" ["The Watch"], 1926, 1:332); I'm not in the habit of putting a mop in my tea ("Stakan" ["The Glass"], 1925, 1:306).

13. The statement echoes Dostoevsky's "definition" of man as a "creature that can get used to anything"—including prison (*Zapiski iz mertvogo doma, Polnoe sobranie sochinenii*, 4:10, 56). Raskol'nikov as well concludes with disgust that "man gets used to everything, the scoundrel"—including the prostitution of a beloved daughter (*Prestuplenie i nakazanie*, 6:25). Zoshchenko's implicit comparison of everyday Soviet life to incarceration and prostitution is anything but flattering.

14. In Zoshchenko, *Nad kem smeetes'?!*, pp. 49–51, and Priboi, 2:131–33.

15. Zoshchenko, "O sebe, o kritikakh," p. 11.

16. See Chekhov's "Skripka Rotshil'da" (8:297–305).

17. He has no story, just his catarrh. Again, chronic incommodity is the opposite of story—it is the norm and precludes telling. Cf. the hero of "Wisdom," whose reclusiveness has two possible but antithetical explanations: chronic catarrh or a good story. Similarly, illness is norm rather than news in "Bol'nye" ("Sick people," 1928), which presents the small talk of hypochondriacs as idle banter consisting of "How's your illness?" "Oh, it's fine, thanks" (1:416–17). *Good* health, by contrast, would be not only tellable, but assertible.

18. In Zoshchenko, *Uvazhaemye grazhdane*, pp. 149–51, *Sobachii niukh*, pp. 16–18, and numerous other collections, as well as Priboi, 2:41–43. Also published as "Elektrifikatsiia" ("Electrification"). The story does appear in the 1986 edition as part of the *Golubaia kniga* under the title "Poslednii rasskaz" ("The Final Story"), but with its tenor completely reversed. In this 1935 reworking, the electrification of the apartment changes everyone's life for the better, and thus is heralded as a "great event," the dawning of a new day, as worthy of inscription in gold ink, and so on (3:438–40).

19. I cite the original version in Zoshchenko, *O chem pel solovei*, pp. 69–70; also in Priboi, 4:140–41.

20. For the original text see Zoshchenko, *O chem pel solovei*, p. 141, or Priboi, 4:67. The later manifestation is in the 1986 edition, 2:49.

21. Morson, *Hidden in Plain View*, p. 126. Blanchot, on the other hand, would agree that the "everyday" is by definition "unperceived," but, unlike Tolstoy, rules that it "belongs to insignificance." As for making this aspect of existence "interesting" (the achievement Morson claims for Tolstoy), Blanchot expresses some skepticism: the "everyday become manifest" amounts to "boredom"—"as a consequence of having lost its essential—constitutive—trait of being *unperceived*" (pp. 14, 17).

22. Tolstoi, "Dlia chego liudi odurmanivaiutsia" ("Why Do People Stupify

Themselves?"), *Polnoe sobranie sochinenii*, 27:280. Morson cites this passage in *Hidden in Plain View*, p. 220.

23. *Skaz* is the Russian term for a written narrative that imitates an *oral* tale by foregrounding a narrator who is clearly not identical with the implied author, and whose language, values, and social background are conspicuously non-standard. This marked discourse makes the narration itself an object of curiosity and forces an evaluation of the stance of the teller as well as of the events under consideration. "Broken intonation" is Bocharov's characterization of Zoshchenko's narrative voice (" 'Veshchestvo sushchestvovaniia,' " p. 342).

24. See Bakhtin's *Problemy poetiki Dostoevskogo* and "Slovo v romane" for a discussion of such stylization and other forms of "double-voicing" and their destabilizing effect on authoritative discourse.

25. Zoshchenko, "Kak ia rabotaiu," p. 110.

26. Zoshchenko, "O komicheskom," p. 152.

27. Cf. Chudakova's and Kreps's insistence that plot in Zoshchenko is unimportant, and only language counts.

28. In Zoshchenko, *Uvazhaemye grazhdane*, pp. 234–36, and Priboi, 3:128–30. Not included in the 1986 edition.

29. Cf. the edict of Doonesbury's Ayatollah, reproduced on the opening page of Chapter 4.

30. In Zoshchenko's *Uvazhaemye grazhdane*, p. 203, and Priboi, 1:27. The 1986 collection omits this story.

31. See Zoshchenko's forward to *Pis'ma k pisateliu* (*Letters to the Writer*, 1929), in which he claims that although he did not author the volume, he had the most difficult task—to select the interesting material from the vast stock of boring discourse (p. 8).

32. McLean calls Zoshchenko's disquisitions on these subjects digressive and irrrelevant (Introduction to Zoshchenko, p. xxi). But, as one such "digression" makes clear, they contain the most essential components of Zoshchenko's *plots*. We are told, for example, that in the sixteenth century duels were not an event; they were the order of the day. They proceeded from simply *going out for a walk* (more of Zoshchenko's pedestrian duels, we note). They occasioned no wailing and no gnashing of teeth; on the contrary—they were not noticed. Such, the narrator suggests, is the nature of the human animal. Whatever kind of life is in progress, people will accustom themselves brilliantly—and whoever cannot must "go to the side and not get underfoot" (*otkhodiat v storonu i ne putaiutsia pod nogami*) (2:180–81). In other commentaries feet are the measure of historical progress, coats function as violation, and clothes establish identity. In Zoshchenko's work, none of this is trivial or marginal.

33. Chudakova, p. 193.

34. See, among many other stories, "Something Special" (1:405), "Home Remedy" ("Domashnee sredstvo," 1929, 1:515), "Guests" (1:363), "A Summer Breather" (1:430), "Cockroaches" (1:473), "A Trivial Incident" (1:370), "Lemonade" (1:362), "It's Bearable" (1:518), "A Trick of Nature" (1:508), "The

Merry-Go-Round" (Priboi, 1:30), "Not Funny" ("Ne zabavno," 1928, 1:513), "Thank You" ("Spasibo," in *Dni nashei zhizni*, p. 83). The oddity of presenting material as a matter "of course" rather than as news is most apparent in "Metaphysics" ("Metafizika," 1922), which introduces alternate paragraphs with *udivitel'no* (surprisingly) and *konechno* (naturally, of course), respectively (1:113).

35. "Fog" is actually about literacy and legibility rather than literary discernment, but the point is made nevertheless.

36. Shcheglov draws the comparison with a Greek chorus in "Mir Mikhaila Zoshchenko," p. 128, and "Entsiklopediia nekul'turnosti," p. 62.

37. These public rulings are too numerous to record with any thoroughness here, but such instances of audience participation can be found in "Administrative Ecstasy," "The Actor," "The Lady Aristocrat," "The Bottle," "The Watch," "The Downfall of a Man," "NEP Grimace," "The Merry-Go-Round," "A Trivial Incident," "Casting Bait," "Who Needs Relatives?" "An Unpleasant Story" ("Nepriatnaia istoriia," 1927, in Zoshchenko, *Semeinyi kuporos*, pp. 23–27), "The Charms of Culture," "An Occurrence" ("Proisshestvie," 1929), "Work Clothes," "The Power of Talent," "The Lilacs Are Blooming," "An Incident in the Provinces," "Dog Scent," "A Terrible Night," "Theater Life," "Theater for Oneself," "Street Incident." In all of these works the public "of course" has its say on the question of what is noticeable, eventful, and important and most often votes with its feet—by stopping or walking on.

38. See Sarnov.

39. Barmin, p. 40.

40. Chekhov's "Lady with the Little Dog" contains a famous watermelon-eating scene in which Gurov, the hero, pays no attention to the tears of his paramour, concentrating instead on his piece of fruit.

41. Zoshchenko, "Americans," in *Uvazhaemye grazhdane*, p. 235, and Priboi, 3:129.

42. In Zoshchenko, *Uvazhaemye grazhdane*, pp. 59–62. The 1986 edition reprints the *Golubaia kniga* version under the title "Rasskaz o pis'me i o negramotnoi zhenshchine" ("The Story About the Letter and the Illiterate Woman") and with significant embellishments.

43. Ol'shevets, p. 3; and Vishnev, p. 57.

44. Gorky, letters to Zoshchenko, Sept. 16, 1930; Oct. 3, 1930; Mar. 25, 1936 (*Gor'kii i sovetskie pisateli*, pp. 159, 163, 167–68).

45. Maguire discusses in detail the debate about generality and particularity—especially as it concerned literary *characters*—in "Literary Conflicts."

46. The first comment is from Loks, p. 84, the second from Voronskii, "Na perevale," p. 320. Neither critic cites Zoshchenko specifically here, but both would include him as one of the Fellow Travelers whose work was under discussion.

47. Zoshchenko, "'Meloch',' kotoraia mnogo znachit," p. 17. Each detail deployed, says Zoshchenko, must be *nuzhna* (essential).

48. Chudakova, p. 7.

49. Maguire, *Red Virgin Soil*, p. 99.

50. Morson, *Hidden in Plain View*, pp. 145–48.
51. Voronskii, "Na perevale," p. 316.
52. Vishnev, p. 56; and Voronskii, "Literaturnye otkliki," p. 321. The suitability of *byt* for literary subject matter is the object of a continuing debate. See, for instance, the series of articles entitled "Proza byta i bytie prozy" that appeared weekly in *Literaturnaia gazeta* from Aug. 13 to Oct. 29, 1980.
53. Stewart, p. 111.
54. Arvatov, p. 66.
55. Clark, pp. 37–40. The essay by Bakhtin she refers to is "Epos i roman."
56. Ibid., pp. 3–16.
57. See, for example, "O sebe, ob ideologii":

> Nowadays a writer's supposed to have an exact ideology. . . .
> Will someone please tell me how I can possibly have an "exact ideology" if not a single party appeals to me?
> From the point of view of the Party types, I'm unprincipled. So be it. I'll tell you myself. I'm no Communist, no S-R, no monarchist, I'm just Russian. And moreover, I'm politically dissolute. . . .
> I don't hate anyone. That's my exact ideology. (p. 28)

His stories, too, poke fun at the demand that every work of literature be an ideological lesson. See, for example, the "exposé" of petit bourgeois tendencies in "A Hidden Treasure" ("Klad," 1929, in Zoshchenko's *Dni nashei zhizni*, pp. 52–54).

58. Vishnev, p. 57.
59. Chumandrin, "Chei pisatel'—Mikhail Zoshchenko." Although Zoshchenko was consistently reproached for his subject matter throughout the 1920s, his critics became particularly strident about his motives toward the end of the decade. By 1929, when any nonconformity was suspect, Zoshchenko's irreverence was countered even more vociferously.

Chumandrin's question, "Chei pisatel'?" (Whose writer?), was later adopted by the emigré community as a kind of mark of honor. Just after the writer's death in 1958, a small commemorative volume echoing this title but very much in homage to Zoshchenko appeared in Munich: Sven, *Chei drug i chei vrag Mikhail Zoshchenko?* (Whose friend and whose enemy is Mikhail Zoshchenko?).

60. "Respected citizens" (*Uvazhaemye grazhdane*) refers to the title of Zoshchenko's popular 1928 collection, which itself plays on the polite formula for addressing an audience. "Lit-entsiklopediia v sharzhakh."
61. *Pervyi Vsesoiuznyi s''ezd sovetskikh pisatelei*, p. 221.
62. This view of Zoshchenko has found permanent expression in some of the more recent editions of his works. The 1927 preface to *Sentimental'nye povesti*, for instance (where he acknowledges his focus on "small" themes and "insignificant" individuals), is reproduced in later editions with the epithet "philistine" (*obyvatel'*) inserted every time Zoshchenko refers to his themes and heroes. See, for example, Zoshchenko, *Izbrannoe v dvukh tomakh*, 1:371–72. The 1986 edition follows this practice (2:6–7). "Philistine" does not appear in the 1927 publication (pp. 5–6), nor in the text of the 1930 Priboi version

(4:34). The extended commentary on how, mercifully, the philistine element is now dying out is also a later addition.

63. See the treatment of satire in *Literaturnaia gazeta*: Lezhnev, "Na puti k vozrozhdeniiu satiry"; Blium, "Vozroditsia li satira?"; Iakubovskii, "O satire nashikh dnei"; [unsigned], "O putiakh sovetskoi satiry"; Rogi, "Puti sovetskoi satiry."

64. Voronskii, Review of Zoshchenko and Slonimskii, p. 344.

65. This was all true for the duration of the 1920s, in any case. Later, Zoshchenko did participate in centrally organized literary endeavors to glorify very large projects (such as the White Sea Canal). Opinions differ as to the meaning of Zoshchenko's "capitulation." McLean regards it as strategic, a means to keep the critics at bay in the repressive 1930s (Introduction to Zoshchenko, p. xvi). Nadezhda Mandel'shtam, on the other hand, firmly believes that Zoshchenko had accepted the Soviet arrangement and had become nicely indoctrinated by that time (p. 403). Whichever view is closer to the truth, Zoshchenko's paeans to the glories of Communism and his children's stories about Lenin did not keep him from devoting himself to his autobiographical and extremely self-focused *Before Sunrise*, which was anything but the model Soviet novel.

66. Voronskii, "Na perevale," p. 322.

67. Morson, *Hidden in Plain View*, pp. 42–46.

68. See in particular Stifter's preface to *Bunte Steine*, in *"Bergkristall" und andere Erzählungen*, pp. 9–16. Interestingly, the synecdochic relationship of small to large, of part to whole, posited so reverently by Stifter, resurfaces in the New Historicist move to "reveal through the analysis of tiny particulars the behavioral codes, logics, and motive forms controlling a whole society" (Veeser, p. xi). New Historicism, however, lacks both Stifter's reverence and his inspiring faith in the tender goodness of the social whole.

69. See Berman, chap. 5. Berman claims that Stifter talks about order so much precisely because it is so tenuous.

70. Loks in particular warned of the danger of seizing upon individual details and "blowing them up way out of proportion" (p. 85).

71. Clark, p. 16.

72. Maguire, *Red Virgin Soil*, p. ix.

73. Jameson, p. 20.

Chapter 4

1. Gogol', "Povest' o tom, kak possorilsia Ivan Ivanovich s Ivanom Nikiforovichem" (1835), fourth story in the *Mirgorod* cycle, hereafter referred to more simply as "Two Ivans" (2:223). All further references to Gogol's works will be included parenthetically in the text wherever convenient. Unless otherwise indicated, the translations are my own.

2. Admittedly, "Shinel'" ("The Overcoat," 1842), perhaps Gogol's most famous story and the subtext for Zoshchenko's many coat capers, does have a coat at its thematic center. As I will argue in my later discussion of "The

Overcoat," though, the materiality (and immateriality) of both coats and content is precisely at issue.

3. This scene takes place at the inn, at night, while Chichikov is in fact asleep, but the narrator, like the tireless shoe fanatic, is not inclined to rest. Henry Fielding in particular had utilized the device of the inn as a kind of interlude between chapters to disrupt the linear progression and temporality and to expand on a "Wordsworthian 'spot of time' " (Black, pp. 71–72). Gogol uses the nocturnal interlude, I would suggest, to expand not time, but text.

4. Consider, for example, the parodic etymology of Akakii Akakievich Bashmachkin's surname, a source of sense that makes none: "It is clear from the name itself that it must have originally derived from the word *bashmak* [shoe], but when, during what period, and how exactly it came from 'shoe' is completely unknown. His father, his grandfather, and even his brother-in-law, and absolutely all the Bashmachkins wore boots, simply resoling them about three times a year" (3:142).

5. William Todd astutely identifies the lieutenant's self-absorbed heel inspection in *Dead Souls* as distinctly autoerotic activity, a characterization I would (and will) extend to the self-indulgences of the *narrator* (*Fiction and Society*, p. 257).

6. Thus the relevance of Garry Trudeau's "Doonesbury" suggestion that the Ayatollah might dispatch an assassin in response to a writer's *stylistic* excesses. Censorship has traditionally concerned itself with a work's substance, the *what* rather than the *how*. Gogol's violation of decorum here is discursive rather than contentual.

7. Belinskii, "O russkoi povesti," pp. 288–91.

8. Gogol', "Neskol'ko slov o Pushkine" ("A Few Words About Pushkin," 1832), 8:54.

9. Mann, *V poiskakh zhivoi dushi*, p. 169.

10. See, for example, the reviews of *Dead Souls* by Masal'skii, pp. 7, 10, 19–26; and Polevoi, pp. 36–41. Although Gogol's stylistic idiosyncrasies did not really become the main issue until the publication of *Dead Souls*, the earlier Dikan'ka and Mirgorod stories and other works had already prompted similar observations from Polevoi and his contemporaries (see Polevoi's review of *Vechera na khutore bliz Dikan'ki* vol. 1, pp. 94–95). Some critics objected less to the profusion than to the gratuitous "dirtiness" of the details (Iurkevich [P. M-skii], p. 30; and Grech, pp. 34–35); others more graciously forgave the accumulation of unnecessary detail as a manifestation of Gogol's "lavish Russian generosity," a laudable propensity to give and give beyond what is called for (Shevyrev, p. 214).

11. The "naturalism" argument was advanced by Belinsky in "O russkoi povesti," pp. 267, 271, 292–95, and "Otvet 'Moskvitianinu,' " pp. 242–55; and by Pletnev in his review of "Rim," p. 42. Both critics applauded the verisimilitude and perfect representation of life enabled by the inordinate amount of detail.

Gogol himself makes the now famous boast of all-inclusiveness, first in his letter to A. S. Pushkin, Oct. 7, 1835 (10:375), and again, later, to V. A.

Zhukovskii, Nov. 12, 1836 (11:74). Mann makes much of Gogol's intention to grasp the "entirety" (*tseloe*) (*V poiskakh zhivoi dushi*, p. 8), and A. P. Chudakov locates the "intrigue" of Gogol's text in its ingenious *vseokhvatnost'* (all-encompassing grasp) and the "absolute vision" it provides ("Veshch' v mire Gogolia," pp. 278–79). Proffer, in turn, treats the distended similes as precisely a means to achieving this ambitious project of all-inclusiveness, motivating the accretion by giving it a point of departure (p. 81).

Slonimskii devotes an entire monograph to explicating Gogol's use of detail as a technique of the *comic* (*Tekhnika komicheskogo*), while Mann treats the profusion as evidence of an attenuated fantastic in the world of *byt*. Mann implies that the radical unmotivatedness of so much of the material, the alogism, and the arbitrary outbursts of characters and narrators alike are vestiges of the more explicit strangeness of Gogol's early works; that the lack of discursive control mirrors the loss of control at the hands of supernatural powers, the more corporeal demons who "scramble everything up." This attachment to "fantasy," moreover, is not whimsical, but rather "true to life," embodying what Gogol called the "hubbub, hurlyburly, and incoherence" of the real world. Mann, in effect, sees the unruly detail as at once profoundly fantastic and mimetic (*Poetika Gogolia*, pp. 9, 79, 81, 106, 110–26, 282–83, 308).

The "symbolism" argument is Bely's (see, for example, *Masterstvo Gogolia*, pp. 43–45), "plenitude" is Aksakov's, and vices are Merezhkovskii's ("Gogol'," p. 166). Merezhkovskii sees Gogol's technique of overspecification as a feat of fine moral differentiation. Ermilov cites social commentary (pp. 186, 212, 213), and carnivalization is Bakhtin's explanation ("Rable i Gogol' "). Vinogradov points to linguistic development in the 1830s and 1840s and locates Gogol's abuses of verbal decorum in terms of the intermingling of levels of diction (pp. 286–88).

For an excellent survey of the history of Gogol's reception, see Maguire's introduction to his *Gogol from the Twentieth Century*, pp. 3–54. For the reactions of Gogol's contemporaries, see Debreczeny. For the actual texts of some of the more salient early reviews of Gogol's work, see the anthology edited by Zelinskii, *Russkaia kriticheskaia literatura o proizvedeniiakh N. V. Gogolia*, esp. vols. 1 (*1829–1842*) and 2 (*1842–1855*).

12. Personal communication.

13. A major exception to this has been the Soviet literary establishment, for whom social relevance (and, hence, realism) was the primary source of literary value. Soviet critics traditionally projected a Gogolian oeuvre that exposes the injustices of serfdom, bureaucracy, poverty (along with other associated evils of the czarist regime), and the stultifying *poshlost'* of contemporary life, through a realistic portrayal of these social problems. Today, however, in some of the most imaginative criticism on Gogol, Russian scholars are presenting his work as anything but straightforward realism; most Western critics as well have dismissed the portrait of Gogol as a realist or naturalist writer. Still, it was in these terms that his contemporaries first discussed (and praised) his work. See Maguire, Introduction to *Gogol from the Twentieth Century*, pp. 6, 16–17.

14. Maguire, "Reading *Dead Souls*," pp. 21, 23. The gun-shaped pin from Tula makes its inexplicable appearance on the first page of *Dead Souls*.

15. See Kermode, "Secrets and Narrative Sequence," pp. 91–97.

16. See Proffer, pp. 83–86; Woodward; and Rancour-Laferriere, *Out from Under Gogol's "Overcoat."*

17. I. D. Ermakov had, in fact, commented that the proliferation of apparently "irrelevant" detail in Gogol's works provides exactly the same kind of material for interpretation as an analysand's "random" chatter gives the psychoanalyst, namely the key to underlying meaning. Every word of Gogol's, he claimed, is a sign, an indicator of profound significance (pp. 11–12).

18. Foucault, pp. 139–40.

19. Setchkarev, *Gogol*, p. 11. Expressions of this kind abound throughout Setchkarev's book. Acknowledging, for instance, that Gogol introduces characters and even entire episodes that have no connection to anything else, Setchkarev nevertheless lauds the "unity" of the work in question: "Gogol tells the story in such detail, that one involuntarily assumes something and is captivated by it" (p. 109). Even when we are led so far afield by the digressions that we forget the plot, Setchkarev contends, the details provide all the unity we could desire (p. 185).

20. Schor, *Reading in Detail*, p. 7.

21. "Semiotic totalitarianism" is Morson's phrase and refers to the tendency to assign meaning to everything, to see every detail as the sign of an underlying order or system. I make reference not only to Morson's *Hidden in Plain View* (which addresses the issue of reading for significance in *War and Peace*), but also to his "Prosaics and *Anna Karenina*," in which he expresses a general suspicion of any perceptual stance that fails to admit the random or accidental.

22. This tendency traces its most illustrious roots to Eikhenbaum's view of Gogol's plots as an excuse for the deployment of verbal device ("Kak sdelana 'Shinel'" Gogolia").

23. Fanger, *Creation of Nikolai Gogol*, p. 235.

24. Erlich, p. 221.

25. Bocharov, "O stile Gogolia," p. 441. Bocharov's formulation comes from Iurii Lotman's characterization of Gogolian space that, in the Petersburg stories, has only "bureaucratic" and no "topographical" reality, reflecting empty administrative categories rather than concrete, physical reality. It is Lotman who cites in this connection Tvardovskii's couplet "Oboznacheno v meniu,/A v nature netu" (Listed on the menu/But nonexistent in reality) (Lotman, "Problema khudozhestvennogo prostranstva," p. 39).

26. A. P. Chudakov, "Veshch' v mire Gogolia," pp. 271–73.

27. Ibid., pp. 273–76. Masal'skii, too, spent many pages of his original review of *Dead Souls* reproducing and ridiculing this simile and others like it (see esp. p. 26).

28. Potebnia, p. 294.

29. Belyi, *Masterstvo Gogolia*, p. 277.

30. A. P. Chudakov, "Veshch' v mire Gogolia," p. 277.

31. Fanger, *Creation of Nikolai Gogol*, p. 261.

32. Mirsky, p. 157.
33. See Senkovskii, p. 29.
34. Zhukhovskii, diary entry of Jan. 6, 1839, cited by Mann, *V poiskakh zhivoi dushi*, p. 42. Zhukovskii's reference to pain is no doubt an expression of his anguish and compassion at the recognition of some of the more lamentable aspects of Russian life, but I find it captures something of the reading process as well, more effectively than the rhetoric of "unadulterated" fun or unremitting hilarity.
35. I. Mandel'shtam, pp. 75–76.
36. Proffer, p. 78; Belyi, *Masterstvo Gogolia*, p. 70.
37. Fish outlines his theory of "interpretive communities" in "Introduction," p. 14. I owe this comparison to Duffield White's considered response to my argument.
38. Mann, *Poetika Gogolia*, p. 401. Mann's agenda is clearly to rid the world of the very idea of a "flawed" Gogol.
39. The term is Freud's and refers to the retrospective conferral of meaning.
40. This image of the fence with a miscellany of objects displayed on it reappears in "Koliaska" ("The Carriage," 1836), 3:178.
41. P. Brooks, pp. 4–5.
42. Bernheimer, p. 55.
43. Barthes, *Pleasure of the Text*, p. 13. In reviewing the Mirgorod stories, one of Gogol's contemporaries as well identifies two kinds of readers: those who read for the plot, and those who are able to revel in the writing and the style itself. Ladies, who belong to the first group, will not enjoy Gogol. *Educated* readers, however, will. A.v.m.l., cited in Debreczeny, p. 9.
44. Letter to S. T. Aksakov, Aug. 18, 1842 (12:91).
45. Mann characterizes this relationship to artifacts of culture as "mechanized" rather than pleasure-seeking (*Poetika Gogolia*, p. 144).
46. Robert Belknap proposes that this boy represents one manifestation of the narrator-perceiver of the whole interaction of the two Ivans. In Belknap's view, the story is in fact very well-ordered indeed, reflecting a linear progression of narrators who mature from boy to young man to older sojourner. Absence of plot thus does not preclude a strong organizing structure: we watch the narrator growing old before our very eyes. Belknap's reading may be idiosyncratic, but like all ingenious readings of Gogol, it testifies eloquently to the readerly urge to link the disparate in a sensible way.
47. Barthes, *S/Z*, pp. 75–76; P. Brooks, p. 104. Brooks allows that all texts, like all trips, must "take time," and that a premature climax is hardly the most gratifying. But that reading is governed by an urgency to move forward toward that outcome is basic to his understanding of the process (pp. 101–4). For placing such great emphasis on endings, for locating textual pleasure in the satisfaction of the reader's desire for "consummation" after interest is "aroused," Brooks has been ably taken to task by feminist critics who find his assumptions about pleasure profoundly male. See, for example, Winnett.
48. Forster, pp. 17–18.

49. P. Brooks, p. 37.
50. Barthes, "Introduction," p. 27.
51. Morson, *Boundaries of Genre*, p. 42. This is from Morson's pre-prosaics work.
52. "Uchebnaia kniga slovesnosti dlia russkogo iunoshestva" ("Textbook on Literature for Russian Youth," 1844–45?), 8:470. The complaint about Dostoevsky's verbosity comes from Gogol's letter to A. M. V'el'gorskaia, May 14, 1846 (13:65–66). Interestingly, in this same letter, while he castigates the young Dostoevsky for his lack of "conciseness," Gogol urges his correspondent to omit nothing at all in her own accounts: "Don't leave anything out from now on! Talk about everything, even things about which there's almost nothing to say, and describe to me every trifle [*pustotu*] that surrounds you: I need everything."
53. "Avtorskaia ispoved'" ("An Author's Confession," 1847), 8:453.
54. His letters to his mother are full of predictions and fervent hopes for a work of great magnitude. *Dead Souls*, in particular, was part of a mission to produce something of genuine significance that would demonstrate his importance as a writer (letter to Zhukovskii, June 26, 1842 [12:70]).
55. *Kakaia raznoobraznaia kucha! Vsia Rus' iavitsia v nem!* Letter to Zhukovskii, Nov. 12, 1836 (11:74).
56. Letter to M. P. Pogodin that accompanied the manuscript, Jan. 22, 1835 (10:348).
57. We know, in fact, that Gogol's collection was composed a lot less haphazardly than he liked to pretend. Susanne Fusso argues persuasively for its order and coherence ("Landscape of *Arabesques*").
58. In the essay on Pushkin, Gogol evinces a particular awareness of the dangers of alienating one's audience (8:52–55), anticipating in this disdain for the "crowd" his famous diatribe in chap. 7 of *Dead Souls*.
59. Mirsky, p. 123.
60. Leont'ev, pp. 17, 21, 23, 29, 30, 81–83, 89–98, 112, 133. Tolstoy himself favored Pushkin's spare, succinct style and strove to attain the standard of clarity established by the earlier writer.
61. Zoshchenko, "Shestaia povest' I. P. Belkina," p. 25.
62. Rozanov, *Legenda o Velikom Inkvizitore*, pp. 15–23.
63. Gor'kii, *Literaturno-kriticheskie stat'i*, p. 583.
64. Proffer, p. 19.
65. Digression—*parekbasis* (to step to the side)—which denotes moral transgression, came to refer initially in literary theory to a stylistic fault or excess. Subsequently the notion of *digressio* was absorbed into classical rhetoric as a structurally conventional part of an oration. Cicero includes digression as one of five basic components of a speech (*De Inventione*), and Quintilian follows suit (Black, pp. 12–13). Black himself treats digression as a way of achieving a balance between a text's organizing and disorganizing tendencies (pp. 49, 270).
66. Swift, in his "Digression in Praise of Digression," points to his era's emphasis on knowledge and its proliferation rather than on novel and well-

constructed stories (*Tale of a Tub*, pp. 60–64). The "effect of the real" is Barthes's phrase ("L'Effet du réel," p. 89).

67. Carnochan, p. 56.

68. Chatman, *Story and Discourse*, p. 144.

69. On the role of digression in the seventeenth and eighteenth centuries, see Black, p. 30. Gogol's infamous digression on "a certain department" delays the opening of "The Overcoat" (3:141).

70. Letter to M. P. Balabina, Oct. 12, 1836 (11:67–71). The "nothing worth telling" index reappears in other letters as a justification for a lapse in the correspondence. See, for instance, Gogol's letter to Zhukovskii of Nov. 12, 1836, in which he excuses in this way his irregularity in writing letters, just before going on to proclaim, with considerable enthusiasm, that *all* of Russia, without particular discrimination, will appear in his forthcoming novel, whether it is "worth telling" or not (11:73–74).

71. Shepard, pp. 113, 120, 123, 127, 141.

72. Food is indeed the bearer of social, psychological, and cultural information, and the generous detail Gogol provides is not "empty" in this sense. Still, as I will suggest in Chapter 5, the function of Gogol's ample menus, like the ones Bocharov cites, is less referential than self-referential.

73. Iurkevich [P. M-skii], p. 30.

74. Khrapchenko, pp. 131, 133.

75. Todd, *Fiction and Society*, p. 188. Todd's observation is not intended to enlist Gogol as a realist, however.

76. Maguire, Introduction to *Gogol from the Twentieth Century*, p. 16. Fanger suggests that this was due in large part to the particular imaginative exigencies of critics like Belinsky, for whom social vision was paramount and who tended to read their own concerns into Gogol's works ("Gogol and His Reader," pp. 70, 75).

77. "O Sovremennike" ("On *The Contemporary*," 1846), 8:425.

78. I borrow here Maguire's paraphrase of Horace's *dulce et utile* ("Reading *Dead Souls*," p. 23).

79. *Vechera na khutore bliz Dikan'ki* (1831 and 1832) consists of eight relatively unconnected stories in two volumes. Volume 1 contains a preface, "Sorochinskaia iarmarka" ("The Fair at Sorochintsy"), "Vecher nakanune Ivana Kupala" ("Saint John's Eve"), "Maiskaia noch', ili utoplenitsa" ("A May Night, or the Drowned Maiden"), and "Propavshaia gramota" ("The Lost Letter"). Volume 2, which also begins with a preface, consists of "Noch' pered Rozhdestvom" ("Christmas Eve"), "Strashnaia mest'" ("A Terrible Vengeance"), "Ivan Fedorovich Shpon'ka i ego tetushka" ("Ivan Fedorovich Shpon'ka and His Auntie"), and "Zakoldovannoe mesto" ("The Enchanted Place"). This particular passage is from the second preface (1:196).

80. Kulish, 1:90–91.

81. The suggestion that characters most often provide the eyes and occasion for textual observations is Hamon's. Hamon is dealing primarily with Zola, however, who scrupulously provides the proper lighting and ample windows

through which each "viewing" occurs and by means of which virtually every description becomes a motivated one ("Qu'est-ce qu'une description?").

82. Bernheimer, p. 54.
83. Mukařovský, pp. 194, 181, 197–99, 203.
84. Polevoi, Review of *Vechera na khutore bliz Dikan'ki* vol. 2, p. 263.
85. Although it is customary to note the development and maturation of Gogol's art from the earlier stories to the later ones, I would emphasize the striking continuity in Gogol's inclination to "grasp and encompass much." (The more palpable evolution is in reader response from consternation to delight as the audience became more accustomed to the verbal avalanche.)
86. Bakhtin, *Problemy poetiki Dostoevskogo*, esp. pp. 179–224.
87. Bakhtin, "Rable i Gogol'," pp. 485, 492.
88. P. Brooks, pp. 48, 53, 58, 61.
89. Lacan actually says it a good deal less succinctly. This is Elizabeth Wright's restatement of Lacan's argument in his "Seminar on 'The Purloined Letter'" (Wright, p. 160).
90. P. Brooks, pp. 89, xiii, 37, 48, 52.
91. Smith, *On the Margins of Discourse*, p. 117.
92. Letter to Pushkin, Oct. 7, 1835 (10:375).
93. Morson, *Boundaries of Genre*, p. 42.
94. Kermode, *Genesis of Secrecy*, pp. 53, 56–57, 9.
95. Price, "Fictional Contract," pp. 155, 174.
96. Burke, p. 157.
97. The cycle, which begins with an expression of love (*liubliu*), fades by the end into eternal boredom (*skuchno*) (McLean, "Nikolai Gogol's Retreat from Love," pp. 242–43).
98. Burke, p. 183.
99. *Boswell's Life of Johnson*, 2:175. Morson refers to the same passage in connection with Tolstoy's extravagant amassing of "irrelevant" material in *War and Peace* (*Hidden in Plain View*, p. 49).
100. P. Brooks, p. 21.
101. Common sense tells us as much; but the Formalists found this an important enough point to make an explicit issue of it. See Tomashevskii, *Teoriia literatury*, pp. 132–33.
102. P. Brooks, p. 93.
103. Paulson, p. 145.
104. Todd describes with great subtlety Gogol's manipulation of the forms of "polite talk" that the "polite society" of his time had elevated to a veritable art form. See *Fiction and Society*, esp. the introduction, chap. 1, and chap. 5 ("*Dead Souls*: 'Charmed by a Phrase'").
105. Letter to Balabina, Feb. 17, 1842 (12:37).
106. Karlinsky, *Sexual Labyrinth*, pp. 232–33, 270; and Chizhevsky, [Tschiževskij], "Skovoroda–Gogol." Chizhevsky finds this attitude especially evident in *Dead Souls* Part I, and identifies its possible source in Horace, Skovoroda, and Pushkin.

107. The amazing simile runs: "The sunbeams, catching here a blue or a green sleeve, there a red cuff or a piece of gold brocade, or playing on the tip of the sword, turned it into something unusual, like the puppet show put on in villages by wandering vagrants, especially when a densely packed crowd gazes at King Herod in his golden crown or at Anton leading the goat; backstage the fiddle squeals; a gypsy claps his hands on his lips as on a drum, as the sun goes down and the fresh coolness of the southern night imperceptibly presses itself more insistently against the fresh shoulders and bosoms of the stout village women" (2:229).

108. See Chapter 5 for a discussion of the narrative implications of this perpetual feeding.

109. See the endless sentence (2:20–21) to the effect that however much was stolen, pilfered, nibbled, etc., there was such abundance that none of this determined misappropriation made even the slightest dent.

110. I borrow the Schillerian terminology from Mann, *Poetika Gogolia*, p. 160.

111. Chizhevsky, "About Gogol's 'Overcoat,'" p. 301.

112. Smith, *On the Margins of Discourse*, pp. 117–18.

113. Personal communication.

114. Barthes, *Pleasure of the Text*, p. 11.

115. This reflects, admittedly, my own attempt to make some of this textual "information" useful.

116. Maguire, "Reading *Dead Souls*," pp. 16, 19.

117. Perhaps this marked and characteristic lack of comprehension is what leads Bocharov to comment that there is no real dialogue in Gogol ("O stile Gogolia," p. 431).

118. Mirsky, p. 155. Mirsky has in mind, as did Gogol, actual readings, oral performances of the texts.

119. Smith, *On the Margins of Discourse*, p. 108.

120. Ibid., pp. 196–97; and Smith, "Narrative Versions," p. 230.

121. Smith, *On the Margins of Discourse*, p. 108.

122. Smith's vivid example contrasts a television news broadcast, in which listeners are best served by conciseness, with storytelling while killing time on a commuter train, a context in which the more drawn out the tale, the better ("Narrative Versions," p. 230).

123. P. Brooks, p. 43.

124. Price, "Irrelevant Detail," pp. 69, 77.

125. Aristotle, *Poetics* 24, p. 64.

126. Warning, "Ironiesignale," p. 419.

127. Culler, *Structuralist Poetics*, p. 148.

128. Tomashevskii, *Kratkii kurs*, p. 85.

129. Kintsch and van Dijk, p. 365.

130. This particular version of this classic blurb comes from Dan Aykroyd's endorsement of the book by Judith Jacklin Belushi, *Samurai Widow* (*New York Times Book Review*, June 10, 1990, p. 31).

131. See, for example, Sade, pp. 194, 196, 197, 210, 219, 226, 239, 241,

254, 309, 570, 578, 673. In fact what is surprising about this horrifying work is how explicitly it is *about* storytelling.

132. Literature, says Paulson, *is* the noise of culture. In its noise is its potential to create something new (pp. ix, 145). In essential agreement, Barthes comments that narrative communication is precisely not "idyllic," i.e., sheltered from any noise (*S/Z*, p. 131). "Necessary surplus" is what "allows for the conservation of information that 'noises' may suppress" (Suleiman, pp. 120, 122). The "disease" diagnosis is Burke's (pp. 182–83).

133. O'Faolain, pp. 66–67. In Chekhov's stories, O'Faolain claimed, "everything is to the point." Gogol's, on the other hand, are not "skillfully written," and we do not go back to them for their "technique"—"any modern editor would have asked him to compress" (p. 493).

134. Morson, *Boundaries of Genre*, p. 42. He goes on to acknowledge that not all details are of *equal* relevance, and that part of the reading process consists of ranking them in terms of their relative centrality.

135. Chatman, *Story and Discourse*, pp. 21–22.

136. Tomashevskii, *Teoriia literatury*, pp. 144–45.

137. Ibid., pp. 137–39.

138. Prince, pp. 68–69. Smith, however, takes strong issue with the notion that such a universal paraphrase exists, emphasizing that we select "important" motifs according to our particular needs. See her "Narrative Versions." See also my discussion in the next section of the present chapter.

139. Culler, *On Deconstruction*, p. 215.

140. Chatman, *Story and Discourse*, p. 20. Here Chatman follows Tomashevskii, who claimed that "one and the same *fabula* admits many different ways of telling it" (*Kratkii kurs*, p. 87).

141. Smith, "Narrative Versions," p. 217.

142. Ibid., pp. 221–22, 228.

143. Culler, *Pursuit of Signs*, pp. 186, 171–72, 215.

144. The gravity/levity opposition is Black's.

145. George Khairallah, "Our Latest Master Of The Arts," in *Academe* (Beirut, 1979), p. 49; cited by Kermode, "Secrets and Narrative Sequence," p. 79; reprinted here by permission of the author.

146. Barthes emphasizes the impulse to posit something "behind" the words and the ineluctable urge to get to it (*S/Z*, p. 122).

Chapter 5

1. Schaarschmidt, p. 172.

2. As J. Hillis Miller puts it more fully, there is "no intrinsic limit to a given subject. To represent it completely would be to retrace an infinite web of relevant relations extending to the horizon and beyond, in every direction. . . . It would appear, however, that this problem could be solved by the arbitrary drawing of a boundary line establishing an edge beyond which the writer will not allow himself to go. The fundamental act of form-giving is the establishment of a periphery" (p. 108).

3. Chizhevsky, "About Gogol's 'Overcoat,'" p. 300.

4. See esp. Proffer, Setchkarev (*Gogol*), and A. P. Chudakov ("Veshch' v mire Gogolia").

5. Tomashevskii identifies this penchant for preterition as a legacy of Pushkin's "Grobovshchik" ("The Undertaker"), or more directly as a reaction to the same 1830s tradition Pushkin himself was responding to (*Teoriia literatury*, p. 138).

6. Chatman, *Story and Discourse*, p. 223.

7. Maguire, "Gogol and the Legacy of Pseudo-Dionysius," p. 51.

8. *Odyssey*, 19:392–468. See Auerbach's discussion, "Odysseus' Scar," in *Mimesis*, pp. 3–23.

9. K. P. Stepanova, too, notes that Gogol's very description becomes *siuzheten* (plotted) (p. 44).

10. Ivask, p. 174.

11. Fusso, "The Landscape of *Arabesques*," pp. 123–24.

12. See also Fusso's "*Mertvye Dushi*," and her book, *Designing Dead Souls: An Anatomy of Disorder in Gogol*, the very title of which testifies vividly to its own impulses to discern order or create it.

13. Mann, *Poetika Gogolia*, pp. 309–12, 331.

14. For a discussion of the "type" and its importance in realist aesthetics, see Wellek, pp. 242–47, 253. In Russia, Belinsky especially developed the notion of the "typical" as a delicate (if shifting) balance between the particularity of a representation and the universality of its significance. See Terras, *Belinskij*, pp. 147–48.

15. Benjamin, p. 39.

16. Schor, *Zola's Crowds*, p. 57.

17. Nabokov, *Nikolai Gogol*, p. 76. Actually much earlier was Vengerov, 2:139; also, Belyi, *Masterstvo Gogolia*, p. 82. "Russian muzhiks" is redundant because "muzhiks" alone refers to Russian peasants. The specification is also unnecessary, since it is unlikely that peasants of Irish or Italian extraction would be lolling about the Russian countryside.

18. Maguire, "Reading *Dead Souls*," p. 21.

19. Indeed, the one time Akakii Akakievich is asked to change the language of a document slightly, he is so stricken with anxiety that he begs to return to straight copying (3:144–45).

20. Bernheimer cites this particularly rhythmic example, which translates loosely as "somewhat on the pock-marked side, somewhat on the red-haired side" (p. 56).

21. John Kopper discusses the role of multiplication and reduplication in the Dikan'ka tales as a point of relation between noumenal and phenomenal worlds (pp. 47–49).

22. Belyi, *Masterstvo Gogolia*, p. 245. Rozanov claims, on the contrary, that Gogol could not have done without a single one of them (*Sredi khudozhnikov*, p. 281).

23. Bocharov, "O stile Gogolia," p. 443.

24. V. F. Odoevskii notes this particular instance of discursive perversity (p. 39).

25. P. Brooks, p. xii.

26. Fanger in particular discusses the importance of the *view* from the road (*Creation of Nikolai Gogol*, p. 169). I note also that the beneficiary of these views is invariably *proezzhii* or *prokhozhii* (3:177–78)—always walking by, passing through, "driving around" (6:19) rather than getting there. "The Carriage" even introduces a vehicle that is itself perpetually "lost"—as each officer loses it in cards to the next, it simply makes the rounds of the regiment without conveying anyone anywhere (3:178).

27. Lotman, "Problema khudozhestvennogo prostranstva," p. 47.

28. Fanger, "Chichikov's Journey."

29. Bely, too, noted that the development of the action owes much to these *bokovye khody*, these side trips that lead "away" from the desired destination (*Masterstvo Gogolia*, p. 95). Mann, in keeping with his own purpose of showing the novel to be animated by *opposing* structural principles, cautions against reading the trajectory as wholly disruptive, as *all* digression and diversion from itinerary. The itinerary itself *must* be sensible if the departure from it is to be palpable (*Poetika Gogolia*, p. 306). Mann also attributes the loss of control embodied in the *dorozhnaia putanitsa i nerazberikha* (muddle and confusion on the road) to the devolved fantastic he finds determining in Gogol's later work. The fact that "you can't get there from here" is an attenuated form of being waylaid by supernatural powers (p. 113).

30. Pletnev, "Chichikov ili Mertvye dushi Gogolia," p. 24.

31. Judith Deutsch reads these instances of impeded motion rather as windows of opportunity, moments "to pause on the threshold and glimpse the world beyond." She sees stopping as liberating, not frustrating (p. 14).

32. C. Brown, p. 41.

33. See her "*Mertvye Dushi*." Nevertheless, there *is* a certain emptiness to the way the stories conclude: arrival, as the narrator tells us in *Dead Souls*, is "always a letdown" (6:241). Gogol's conclusions range from mute scenes ("The Fair at Sorochintsy"), to endings torn off and baked into pies ("Shpon'ka"), to drunken, confused wanderers who *still* cannot find their way ("A May Night"), to landing back where you started, accompanied by uncontrolled dancing that simply cannot be stopped ("The Lost Letter"), to driving around in search of new things ("Old-World Landowners"), to the boredom of irresolvability ("Two Ivans"), to the capitulating *razobrat' nel'zia* of incomprehensibility ("The Enchanted Place," 1:316), to Chichikov's notorious flying troika—"Where are you flying to, answer! She gives no answer" (6:247).

34. P. Brooks, pp. 51–52.

35. Letter to Balabina, Feb. 17, 1842 (12:37). After complaining at length about his own illness and commiserating with her about hers, he wishes her improved health, hoping to find her soon "reading not Jean Paul Richter, but Shakespeare and Pushkin," both of whom can be read "in a healthy state." Jean Paul (Johann Paul Friedrich Richter [1763–1825]), the early theoretician of German Romantic aesthetics, was also the author of paradigmatically "excessive" novels. What remains unclear is the extent to which Gogol was personally familiar with Jean Paul's novels. G. I. Chudakov does not include

Jean Paul in the list of foreign authors known to have been read by Gogol (in translation or in the original). Eight works of Jean Paul did, however, appear in translation in the 1820s and 1830s in journals Gogol read regularly (G. I. Chudakov, pp. 125–30, 23).

36. In his own exhortation to writers to cultivate a *mnogoznachitel'noe kratkoslovie* (significant laconism), in fact, Gogol decries the overspecification "without which a German won't take a step or set out on the road," urging prospective deployers of words instead (in terms that at once confirm the association of reading, writing, and traveling and disregard his own call for *kratkoslovie*) to "gallop forth at an even and measured pace, not speeding up or slowing down, fleetingly, like a good coachman, who overexcites neither his horses nor himself and who flies forward not in a base trot, nor at full speed, nor at a breakneck pace, but rather in the kind of flight that gladdens the heart, just as he began the trip, and arrives at the station without foundering his steeds or overtaxing himself. Otherwise," concludes Gogol, "we do not enjoy the trip" (*Inoi ezdy my ne liubim*) ("Textbook on Literature for Russian Youth," 8:469–70).

37. Gary Cox sees the grandfather's bewitched dancing as an analogue to his storytelling; they are parallel expressions of his "inability to control his art" ("Geographical, Sociological, and Sexual Tensions," p. 229).

38. Letter to A. O. Smirnova, Dec. 6, 1849 (14:154).

39. Rancour-Laferriere, "All the World's a *Vertep*," p. 362; Driessen, pp. 65–66. The final phrase is from Setchkarev, "From the Golden to the Silver Age," p. 144.

40. Terras sees in Gogol's devil the "manifestation of the metaphysics of Nonbeing" ("Nabokov and Gogol," p. 195); other well-known treatments of Gogol's penchant for demonic figures tend likewise to emphasize the supernatural, metaphysical, or evil powers of the creatures rather than their discursive properties. See: Mann, *Poetika Gogolia*, pp. 23–28; Holquist; Merezhkovskii, *Gogol' i chert*; Emerson-Topornin; Gippius, especially the chapter on "Demonologiia i fars," pp. 25–39; and Stender-Peterson.

41. Mann, *Poetika Gogolia*, pp. 81, 106, 110–26.

42. Geir Kjetsaa has argued that the "legend" of the burning of Part II of *Dead Souls* by the author is precisely that.

43. LeBlanc in particular establishes a whole set of social, economic, political, and psychological oppositions invoked by the various types of fare ("Dinner With Chichikov") as well as the broader symbolic relevance of "appetite" ("Satisfying Khlestakov's Appetite"). Alexander Obolensky sees in the many meals a device to differentiate the characters by what and how they eat, and Lynn Visson explicates these gastronomic differences specifically in terms of the Slavophile-Westernizer debate. Mann contends that, far from being "meaningless" or bothersome or excessive, Gogol's culinary transactions mean far *more* than the obvious, carrying a kind of Kermodian secret; that feeding and eating, ironically, refer to deep, genuine spirituality, feeling and goodness (*Poetika Gogolia*, p. 162). McLean, conversely, reads the hyperbolic attention to food as an index of trivialization ("Gogol and the Whirling

Telescope," p. 96). McLean also discerns in the persistent eating an expression of regression to the oral stage of libidinal development ("Nikolai Gogol's Retreat from Love," p. 237). Kolb-Seletski, similarly, sees in food the object of sublimated sexual desire. Garrard suggests that food stands for the vulgar, fleshy aspects of life that forestall spiritual progress, the counterforce to the speeding troika that carries "man" forward (p. 855). But, as we have seen, forward motion in Gogol is never unimpeded.

44. Interestingly, a cartoonist in a recent *New Yorker* makes fun of the arcane lexicon of color in today's mail-order catalogues by creating an ad for lavish articles of attire available in the shades "Knell," "Rib-Eye," and "Taras Bulba" (Danny Shanahan, "Enigmas: Fall/Winter Catalogue" [Dec. 31, 1990], p. 30). Shanahan may just have hit upon a random odd name, but it is appropriate that Gogol should occur to the artist reaching for a descriptive term that gets in the way rather than making vivid.

45. *Mirgorod*, which appeared in 1835, consists of four works of differing lengths: vol. 1, "Old-World Landowners" and *Taras Bul'ba*; and vol. 2, "Vii" and "Two Ivans."

46. This practice unwittingly confirms Swift's observation that digression is like "ragout" (*Tale of a Tub*, p. 60).

47. Marin, *Food for Thought*, pp. 125, xv, 4–5. Marin adduces the Eucharist as the most powerful illustration of food's capacity to stand for, indeed to become, something else: "What is edible is always to a certain extent a little bit of all three of the following: a desirable erotic body awaiting consummation, an economically appropriated possession, and a linguistic sign exchanged within a system of communication" (pp. 124–25). I am not sure that this is "always" the case, or even self-evidently so; in fact, it would seem that the confusion of these things is part of what makes Gogol's prose both unusual and untenable.

48. See Karlinsky's aptly entitled "Portrait of Gogol as a Word Glutton."
49. Ivask, p. 178.
50. Driessen, p. 50.
51. "My mind and belly are both starving," comments Gogol in his letter to Pushkin about "hungering" for a plot. Oct. 7, 1835 (10:375).
52. Mann, *Poetika Gogolia*, p. 170.
53. See Gogol's letter to S. T. Aksakov (Mar. 6, 1847) in which he develops an extended parable about the cooks who take forever to produce a meal (to the ravenous impatience of the consumers) as a metaphor for his own long, drawn-out "preparation" of *Dead Souls* Part III (and the corresponding intensity of his readers' impatience for the sequel) (13:241–42).
54. Belyi, *Masterstvo Gogolia*, p. 168.
55. LeBlanc, "Dinner With Chichikov," p. 73. See also his "Satisfying Khlestakov's Appetite," p. 486. LeBlanc credits Ronald Tobin for the *manger/goûter* opposition ("Les mets et les mots," p. 135).
56. Belyi, *Masterstvo Gogolia*, p. 79.
57. A mass that expands like rising dough, Gogol's prose recalls the folkloric "devil in a doughpan," a figure of uncontrolled reduplication and ever-

increasing bulk. See "Potan'ka" ("The Devil in a Doughpan"), in Afanas'ev, pp. 74–75.

58. Letter to Balabina, Feb. 17, 1842 (12:37).
59. Berg, p. 125.
60. Fanger, *Creation of Nikolai Gogol*, p. 20. See Gogol's "Zapisnye knizhki," esp. 1842–44 (9:539–57).
61. A. P. Chudakov, "Veshch' v mire Gogolia," p. 259.
62. Sorokin, pp. 19–20. A. P. Chudakov, too, recognizes the ethnographic pose and echoes Sorokin in calling it a matter of stylistic play rather than scientific rigor ("Veshch' v mire Gogolia," pp. 266–67).
63. Sorokin, pp. 12, 21. I. Mandel'shtam, too, remarks on Gogol's deliberate use of new words each time he designates the same things (pp. 73–74).
64. Lacan speaks of the constant slippage of meaning. For a particularly lucid treatment of Lacanian theory, see Eagleton, pp. 163–74. The text I have cited is on p. 168. For Lacan's own discussion of "full" and "empty" speech, see sec. 1 of "The function and field of speech and language in psychoanalysis" (1953), pp. 40–56. For his treatment of the "rupture" between the signifier and the signified (as opposed to the unity posited by Saussure) and the resulting slippage of meaning, see "The agency of the letter in the unconscious or reason since Freud" (1957), pp. 149–59. On the incapacity of language to signify an object, which object is then always missing and thus always the object of desire, see "The subversion of the subject and the dialectic of desire in the Freudian unconscious" (1960), pp. 298–324. All of the above essays are in Lacan's *Ecrits*.
65. Vengerov, 2:139. Bely, too, speaks of "something said" in which nothing is said (*Masterstvo Gogolia*, p. 82).
66. Mann, *V poiskakh zhivoi dushi*, p. 169. Belinsky applauds Gogol's *soderzhanie* in his review of Aksakov, pp. 257–59.
67. Ivan Ivanovich, we are told in the opening of "Two Ivans," has a marvelous coat—but who is Ivan Ivanovich?
68. Lotman, "Problema khudozhestvennogo prostranstva," p. 32.
69. Swift, pp. 61–62.
70. A. P. Chudakov, "Veshch' v mire Gogolia," pp. 271–74, 278.
71. "Unfortunately," laments Prosper Mérimée, "Monsieur Gogol gets so caught up in his orchestration of minute details that he neglects to attach them to any coherent action" (p. 4).
72. I refer to Bocharov's description of the Gogolian signifier ("O stile Gogolia," p. 441). See the discussion in Chapter 4.
73. This exchange, as Bocharov points out, appears in the manuscript of "The Overcoat," but not in the published text ("O stile Gogolia," p. 409).
74. See, for example, the extensive punning on the word *znachitel'nyi* (significant) that arises from the designation "Person of Consequence" (*znachitel'noe litso* [3:164]).
75. Bocharov, "O stile Gogolia," p. 442.
76. Novikov, p. 53.
77. See, for example, 2:242, where Gogol's narrator rhapsodizes about how

vividly he would paint what amounts to sound, scent, movement, dreams, and black on black, none of which can be expressed in that medium.

78. Letter to N. M. Iazykov, Jan. 8, 1846 (13:30).
79. McLean, "Gogol and the Whirling Telescope," pp. 87, 97.
80. Cox, "Writer as a Stand-up Comic," p. 53.
81. Proffer, p. 40.
82. Belyi, *Masterstvo Gogolia*, p. 151.
83. See Maguire's forthcoming book, *Placing, Seeing, Speaking: A Study of Nikolai Gogol*.
84. Schor, *Zola's Crowds*, p. 57.
85. See Fanger, *Creation of Nikolai Gogol*, p. 103.
86. See "The Fair at Sorochintsy" (1:116): The fair youth reassures the skittish maiden, who fears his words come from the "Evil One," that he will *say* nothing to harm her. When she comes to share his ardor, the two of them are finally left alone to negotiate their perfect union solely because her obtrusive father suddenly hears the word "wheat," and "that magic word" spirits him away from the lovers.
87. Maguire, "Gogol and the Legacy of Pseudo-Dionysius," pp. 52–53.
88. See, for example, Bely on sound and rhythm in Gogol's prose (*Masterstvo Gogolia*, pp. 71–76, 218–27). Setchkarev, by the same token, claims that the paintings on Sobakevich's walls are hanging there purely because of the sound of the names of the warriors they depict: Mavrokordato, Kolokotroni, Miauli, Kanari, Bobelina (*Gogol*, p. 198). Gogol, who was a great performer himself and reveled in the art of reading aloud, was profoundly attentive to the tonal qualities of his words, and "sometimes he would apparently put in some sonorous word solely for the harmonious effect" (D. A. Obolenskii, p. 944).
89. Driessen, p. 68.
90. Proffer, p. 20.
91. Jakobson, "What Is Poetry?" p. 750.
92. A. P. Chudakov, "Veshch' v mire Gogolia," p. 259.
93. A. P. Chudakov, "Predmetnyi mir literatury," pp. 289–90.
94. Ivask, p. 174.
95. Belinskii, "O russkoi povesti," pp. 289–92.
96. That is, the "contentfulness" of all this "content." Todd, too, concludes that "all this extravagantly detailed materiality" lacks the "ontological status" granted by the realists to their details of setting. But in understanding Gogol's many "things" as a facet of the characterization of their owners, Todd's "psychologization of the material world" nevertheless posits a materiality that is simply the product rather than the determinant of personality (*Fiction and Society*, pp. 188–89).
97. "Rumor," Warren Johnson has remarked, "fills up the void between the sign and the signified" (p. 93). More precisely, perhaps, rumor—lone discourse—occupies the void of the *absent* signified. Rumor is the only meaning that inhabits the dead souls, just as "rumors" and "complaints" are the only substance of Akakii Akakievich's ghost (3:169–70).
98. The contrast between plenitude and emptiness is Terras's ("Nabokov

and Gogol," p. 195). The "materiality of the signifier" is Lacan's expression from his "Seminar" (p. 194).

99. This describes, albeit formulaically, the basic armature of "The Fair at Sorochintsy," "A May Night," and "Christmas Eve."

100. The notion of the "acceptable summary" is from Prince, p. 69.

101. Tolstoy, letter to N. N. Strakhov, Apr. 23 and 26, 1876 (42:268).

102. This difficulty in moving forward through the Gogolian text, the fact that "you can't get there from here," may contribute to what critics describe as the "static quality" of his stories. See Driessen, who compares in this regard Gogol's "Two Ivans" with Narezhnyi's parallel, yet infinitely more dynamic "Dva Ivana ili strast' k tiazhbam" ("Two Ivans, or a Passion for Litigation") (p. 179).

103. O'Toole points to the combinations of vagueness and specificity, the elevated declamatory style, and the hyperbole: "All the digressions in the story, whether 'lyrical,' 'linguistic,' 'sociological' or 'philosophical,' contribute to the story's rich verbal texture and to the flirtatious relationship between the author/narrator and his readers; none can claim any priority as thematic" (pp. 23–24).

104. Eikhenbaum, "How Gogol's 'Overcoat' is Made," p. 282; Chizhevsky, "About Gogol's 'Overcoat,'" p. 296.

105. Bryusov discusses the hyperbolic nature of Gogol's portraiture that precludes our taking Akakii with a straight face (p. 106).

106. The act of naming the new overcoat is foregrounded by the rechristening of the old one by Akakii Akakievich's coworkers, who substitute the inglorious *kapot* (dressing gown) for the more noble *shinel'* (3:147). Appropriately, this threadbare material, not much of a "thing" at all, is marked by a proliferation of names, more text for less textile; the more words, the more recessive the things.

107. Fanger, "Gogol and His Reader," p. 87.

108. Bocharov, "Petersburg Tales," p. 164; and Chizhevsky, "About Gogol's 'Overcoat,'" p. 310. Chizhevsky points to the discrepancy between Akakii Akakievich's perspective ("great," "enormous," "significant") and the reader's perceptions that the same things are "tiny," "insignificant," "little."

109. Zholkovskii comments that the insignificance seems to triumph *stylistically* (p. 128).

110. "Incorrigible indirection" is Derrida's characterization of the itinerary of the purloined letter in Poe's story of that title ("Purveyor of Truth," p. 204).

111. Jakobson's "conative function" refers to the relation of the "message" to the *addressee* ("Closing Statement," p. 355).

112. See Melville, p. 45.

113. A letter, says Derrida, can always *not* arrive ("Purveyor of Truth," p. 187). This is Derrida's rewriting of the conclusion of Lacan's "Seminar"—"a letter always arrives at its destination" (p. 53).

114. Fusso speaks of "promissory closure" as Gogol's way of escaping the reader's desire for a final word (*"Mertvye Dushi,"* pp. 32, 35).

115. Even the textual correspondence that does go both ways is a travesty

of any real exchange. See, for example, the utterly non-responsive letters between Shpon'ka and his auntie that "answer" questions never posed (1:287–88).

116. Todd, "Gogol's Epistolary Writing," p. 51.

117. "O teatre, ob odnostoronnem vzgliade na teatre i voobshche ob odnostoronnosti" ("On the Theater, on One-Sided Views of the Theater, and on One-Sidedness in General," 1845), one of Gogol's own one-sided "letters" (8:267, 277).

118. The "itinerary of a signifier" is Lacan's expression ("Seminar," p. 29).

119. Burke, p. 183.

120. Plenitude, as understood by Lacan, is that elusive state of primordial fullness where no gap has yet opened up between the signified and the signifier.

121. The dialogue in full is as follows:

> "Greetings, you poor woman!" he usually said, seeking out the most crippled beggar woman in a tattered dress made of stitched together patches. "Where do you come from, you poor thing?"
>
> "I've come from the village, kind sir; I haven't had a thing to drink or eat for three days; my own children kicked me out."
>
> "Poor wretch! Why did you come here?"
>
> "To beg for alms, kind sir, in case anyone might give me something at least for bread."
>
> "Hm! So would you like some bread?" Ivan Ivanovich would usually ask.
>
> "Of course I would. I am as hungry as a dog."
>
> "Hm!" Ivan Ivanovich usually replied, "so maybe you would like some meat too?"
>
> "Yes, anything your worship may give will satisfy me."
>
> "Hm! Would meat be better than bread?"
>
> "It is not for a hungry beggar to be choosy. Anything that you graciously give will be good." With this the old woman would usually hold out her hand.
>
> "Well, be off then, and God be with you," Ivan Ivanovich would say. "What are you standing here for? I am not beating you, am I?" And having conducted such inquiries with a second and a third, finally he returns home or drops in for a glass of vodka with his neighbor, Ivan Nikiforovich, or the judge, or the police captain. (2:225)

122. Barthes, *Pleasure of the Text*, p. 45.

123. Setchkarev, *Gogol*, p. 204. Analogously, Chizhevsky claims that the exuberance of the discourse is designed to imitate the characters ("About Gogol's 'Overcoat,'" p. 300). I think rather that the discourse itself produces scenes and characters like this. Discursive requirements produce Pliushkin.

124. This procedure may well be the only way to approach anything like "acceptable summaries" of the Gogolian tale.

125. Paulson, p. 113.

Conclusion

1. Belyi, *Arabeski*, p. 403.
2. P. Brooks, p. 89.
3. See Shalamov's *Kolymskie rasskazy* (Kolyma tales).
4. See Chekhov's *Tri sestry* (13:122, 147, 148).
5. See Zoshchenko's "Americans" (Priboi, 3:128–30).
6. Pratt, *Toward a Speech Act Theory*, p. 136.

Works Cited

Afanas'ev, A. N., ed. *Narodnye russkie legendy*. London: n.p., 1859.
Aksakov, K. S. "Neskol'ko slov o poeme Gogolia: 'Pokhozhdeniia Chichikova ili Mertvye dushi.'" Moscow, June 16, 1842. Reprinted in K. S. Aksakov and I. S. Aksakov, *Literaturnaia kritika*. Moscow: Sovremennik, 1981, pp. 141–50.
Al'bov, V. "Dva momenta v razvitii tvorchestva A. P. Chekhova: Kriticheskii ocherk." *Mir Bozhii*, no. 1 (1903): 84–115.
Aleksandrov, B. I. *A. P. Chekhov: Seminarii*. Moscow: Prosveshchenie, 1964.
Aristotle. *Poetics*. Trans. S. H. Butcher. In Hazard Adams, ed., *Critical Theory Since Plato*. New York: Harcourt Brace Jovanovich, 1971, pp. 48–66.
Arsen'ev, K. K. "Belletristy poslednego vremeni." *Vestnik Evropy*, no. 12 (1887): 766–84.
———. "Modnaia forma belletristiki." *Vestnik Evropy*, no. 4 (Apr. 1889): 679–94.
Arvatov, B. "Iazyk poeticheskii i iazyk prakticheskii (K metodologii iskusstvoznaniia)." *Pechat' i Revoliutsiia*, no. 7 (Dec. 1923): 58–67.
Auerbach, Erich. *Mimesis: The Representation of Reality in Western Literature*. Trans. Willard R. Trask. Princeton, N.J.: Princeton University Press, 1974.
A.v.m.l. "Moi kommerazhi o sochinenii Gogolia *Mirgorod*." *Literaturnye pribavleniia k Russkomu invalidu*, no. 33 (1835). Cited in Paul Debreczeny, *Nikolay Gogol and His Contemporary Critics*. Transactions of the American Philosophical Society (n.s.), vol. 5, part 3. Philadelphia: American Philosophical Society, 1966.
Bakhtin, M. M. "Epos i roman (o metodologii issledovaniia romana)." In *Voprosy literatury i estetiki: Issledovaniia raznykh let*. Moscow: Khudozhestvennaia literatura, 1975, pp. 447–83.
———. *Problemy poetiki Dostoevskogo*. Moscow: Khudozhestvennaia literatura, 1972.
———. "Rable i Gogol' (Iskusstvo slova i narodnaia smekhovaia kul'tura)." In *Voprosy literatury i estetiki*, pp. 484–95.
———. "Slovo v romane." In *Voprosy literatury i estetiki*, pp. 72–233.
Barmin, A. G. "Puti Zoshchenki." In *Mikhail Zoshchenko: Stat'i i materialy*. Leningrad: Academia, 1928, pp. 27–50.
Barthes, Roland. "L'Effet du réel." *Communications* 11 (1968): 85–90.
———. "En sortant du cinéma." *Communications* 23 (1975): 104–7.

---. *The Fashion System*. Trans. Matthew Ward and Richard Howard. New York: Hill and Wang, 1983.
---. "Introduction à l'analyse structurale des récits." *Communications* 8 (1966): 1–27.
---. *The Pleasure of the Text*. Trans. Richard Miller. New York: Hill and Wang, 1975.
---. *S/Z*. Trans. Richard Miller. New York: Hill and Wang, 1975.
Bates, H. E. *The Modern Short Story: A Critical Survey*. Boston: The Writer, 1941.
Belinskii, V. G. "O russkoi povesti i povestiakh g. Gogolia ('Arabeski' i 'Mirgorod')." In *Polnoe sobranie sochinenii*. 13 vols. Moscow: Izdatel'stvo Akademii nauk, 1953–59, 1:259–307.
---. "Otvet 'Moskvitianinu.'" In *Polnoe sobranie sochinenii*, 10:221–69.
---. Review of K. S. Aksakov, "Neskol'ko slov o poeme Gogolia: 'Pokhozhdeniia Chichikova ili Mertvye dushi.'" In *Polnoe sobranie sochinenii*, 6:253–60.
Belknap, Robert. "Narrative Time in the Nineteenth Century." Paper presented at the AATSEEL Annual Meeting, New York, Dec. 1986.
Belyi, Andrei. *Arabeski: Kniga statei*. Moscow: Musaget, 1911.
---. *Masterstvo Gogolia: Issledovanie*. Moscow-Leningrad: Gosudarstvennoe izdatel'stvo khudozhestvennoi literatury, 1934. Reprint. Ann Arbor, Mich.: Ardis, 1982.
Benjamin, Walter. "Der Erzähler." In *Über Literatur*. Frankfurt: Suhrkamp, 1975, pp. 33–61.
Berg, N. V. "Vospominaniia o N. V. Gogole." *Russkaia starina*, no. 5 (1872): 118–28.
Berman, Russell A. *The Rise of the Modern German Novel: Crisis and Charisma*. Cambridge, Mass.: Harvard University Press, 1986.
Bernheimer, Charles C. "Cloaking the Self: The Literary Space of Gogol''s 'Overcoat.'" *PMLA* 90 (1975): 53–61.
Billington, James H. *The Icon and the Axe: An Interpretive History of Russian Culture*. New York: Alfred A. Knopf, 1968.
Bitsilli, P. M. *Chekhov's Art: A Stylistic Analysis*. Trans. Toby W. Clyman and Edwina Jannie Cruise. Ann Arbor, Mich.: Ardis, 1983.
---. "K voprosu o vnutrennei forme romana Dostoevskogo." In Donald Fanger, ed., *O Dostoevskom: Stat'i*. Brown University Slavic Reprint 4. Providence, R.I.: Brown University Press, 1966, pp. 1–71.
---. "Zoshchenko i Gogol'." *Chisla*, no. 6 (1932): 211–15.
Black, Joel. "The Second Fall: The Laws of Digression and Gravitation in Romantic Narrative and Their Impact on Contemporary Encyclopaedic Literature." Ph.D. diss., Stanford University, 1978.
Blanchot, Maurice. "Everyday Speech." Trans. Susan Hanson. *Yale French Studies: Everyday Life* 73 (1987): 12–20.
Blium, B. "Vozroditsia li satira?" *Literaturnaia gazeta*, May 27, 1929, p. 2.
Bocharov, S. G. "O stile Gogolia." In Ia. E. El'sberg, et al., eds., *Teoriia literaturnykh stilei: Tipologiia stilevogo razvitiia novogo vremeni (klassicheskii stil':*

sootnoshenie garmonii i disgarmonii v stile). Moscow: Nauka, 1976, pp. 409–45.
———. "Petersburg Tales." *Soviet Literature* (Issue devoted to Gogol), no. 4 (1984): 155–64.
———. "'Veshchestvo sushchestvovaniia': Vyrazhenie v proze." In N. K. Gei, et al., eds., *Problemy khudozhestvennoi formy sotsialisticheskogo realizma*. 2 vols. Vol. 2: *Vnutrenniaia logika literaturnogo proizvedeniia i khudozhestvennaia forma*. Moscow: Nauka, 1971, pp. 310–50.
Booth, Wayne C. *The Rhetoric of Fiction*. Chicago: University of Chicago Press, 1961.
Boswell's Life of Johnson. Ed. George Birkbeck Hill. Rev. and enl. ed., L. F. Powell. 6 vols. Oxford: Clarendon Press, 1934.
Brooks, Jeffrey. "Readers and Reading at the End of the Tsarist Era." In William Mills Todd III, ed., *Literature and Society in Imperial Russia, 1800–1914*. Stanford, Calif.: Stanford University Press, 1978, pp. 97–150.
Brooks, Peter. *Reading for the Plot: Design and Intention in Narrative*. New York: Vintage, 1984.
Brown, Clarence. "The Not Quite Realized Transit of Gogol'." In Joachim T. Baer and Norman W. Ingham, eds., *Mnemozina: Studia Literaria Russica in Honorem Vsevolod Setchkarev*. Munich: Fink, 1974, pp. 41–45.
Brown, Edward J. *Russian Literature Since the Revolution*. Rev. and enl. ed. Cambridge, Mass.: Harvard University Press, 1982.
Bryusov, Valerii. "Burnt to Ashes." In Robert A. Maguire, trans. and ed., *Gogol from the Twentieth Century: Eleven Essays*. Princeton, N.J.: Princeton University Press, 1974, pp. 105–31.
Bulgakov, M. A. *Sobach'e serdtse*. Paris: YMCA, 1969.
Burke, Kenneth. *Counterstatement*. New York: Harcourt, Brace, 1931.
Carnochan, W. B. *Confinement and Flight: An Essay on English Literature of the Eighteenth Century*. Berkeley: University of California Press, 1979.
Chatman, Seymour. "Reply to Barbara Herrnstein Smith." In W. J. T. Mitchell, ed., *On Narrative*. Chicago: University of Chicago Press, 1981, pp. 258–65.
———. *Story and Discourse: Narrative Structure in Fiction and Film*. Ithaca, N.Y.: Cornell University Press, 1978.
Chekhov, A. P. *Polnoe sobranie sochinenii i pisem*. 30 vols. Moscow: Nauka, 1974–83.
Chizhevsky, Dmitry. "About Gogol's 'Overcoat.'" In Robert A. Maguire, trans. and ed., *Gogol from the Twentieth Century: Eleven Essays*. Princeton, N.J.: Princeton University Press, 1974, pp. 295–322.
——— [Tschižewskij, D.]. "Skovoroda–Gogol': Y. G. Shevelov zum 60. Geburtstag." *Die Welt der Slaven* 13 (1968): 317–26.
Chudakov, A. P. *Poetika Chekhova*. Moscow: Nauka, 1971.
———. "Predmetnyi mir literatury (k problemam kategorii istoricheskoi poetiki)." In M. B. Khrapchenko, et al., eds., *Istoricheskaia poetika: Itogi i perspektivy izucheniia*. Moscow: Nauka, 1986, pp. 251–91.
———. "Veshch' v mire Gogolia." In V. V. Kozhinov, et al., eds., *Gogol': Istoriia*

i sovremennost' (k 175–letiiu so dnia rozhdeniia). Moscow: Sovetskaia Rossiia, 1985, pp. 259–80.

Chudakov, G. I. *Otnoshenie tvorchestva Gogolia k zapadno-evropeiskim literaturam*. Kiev: Univ. St. Vladimira, 1908.

Chudakova, M. O. *Poetika Mikhaila Zoshchenko*. Moscow: Nauka, 1979.

Chukovskii, Kornei. "Iz vospominanii." In A. Smolian and N. Iurgeneva, eds., *Mikhail Zoshchenko: V vospominaniiakh sovremennikov*. Moscow: Sovetskii pisatel', 1981, pp. 13–66.

Chumandrin, M. "Chei pisatel'—Mikhail Zoshchenko." *Zvezda*, no. 3 (1930): 106–19.

Chvany, Catherine V. "Backgrounded Perfectives and Plot Line Imperfectives: Toward a Theory of Grounding." In Michael S. Flier and Alan Timberlake, eds., *The Scope of Slavic Aspect*. UCLA Slavic Studies, vol. 12. Columbus, Ohio: Slavica Publishers, 1986, pp. 247–73.

Clark, Katerina. *The Soviet Novel: History as Ritual*. Chicago: University of Chicago Press, 1981.

Clyman, Toby W. "The Hidden Demons in Gogol''s *Overcoat*." *Russian Literature* 7 (1979): 601–10.

Cox, Gary. "Geographic, Sociological, and Sexual Tensions in Gogol's Dikan'ka Stories." *Slavic and East European Journal* 24 (Fall 1980): 219–32.

———. "The Writer as a Stand-up Comic: A Note on Gogol and Dickens." *Ulbandus Review* 2 (Fall 1979): 45–61.

Crosman, Robert. "Do Readers Make Meaning?" In Susan R. Suleiman and Inge Crosman, eds., *The Reader in the Text: Essays on Audience and Interpretation*. Princeton, N.J.: Princeton University Press, 1980, pp. 149–64.

Culler, Jonathan. *On Deconstruction: Theory and Criticism after Structuralism*. Ithaca, N.Y.: Cornell University Press, 1982.

———. *The Pursuit of Signs: Semiotics, Literature, Deconstruction*. Ithaca, N.Y.: Cornell University Press, 1981.

———. *Structuralist Poetics: Structuralism, Linguistics, and the Study of Literature*. Ithaca, N.Y.: Cornell University Press, 1975.

Dante Alighieri. *The Divine Comedy: Inferno*. Trans. Allen Mandelbaum. New York: Bantam, 1980.

Debreczeny, Paul. *Nikolay Gogol and His Contemporary Critics*. Transactions of the American Philosophical Society (n.s.), vol. 5, part 3. Philadelphia: American Philosophical Society, 1966.

Derrida, Jacques. "Le Facteur de la vérité." In *La Carte postale: de Socrate à Freud et au delà*. Paris: Flammarion, 1980, pp. 439–524. Translated and abridged as "The Purveyor of Truth." Trans. Alan Bass. In John P. Muller and William J. Richardson, eds., *The Purloined Poe: Lacan, Derrida, and Psychoanalytic Reading*. Baltimore, Md.: Johns Hopkins University Press, 1988, pp. 173–212.

Deutsch, Judith. "Perspective from the Threshold: The Troika of *Dead Souls*." *Ulbandus Review* 5 (Fall 1987): 3–17.

Disterlo, R. A. [R. D.]. "Kriticheskie zametki." *Nedelia*, no. 46 (1889). Cited in A. P. Chudakov, *Poetika Chekhova*. Moscow: Nauka, 1971, p. 175.

———. "O bezvlastii molodykh pisatelei (Novogodnie razmyshleniia)." *Nedelia*, no. 1 (1888). Cited in Chudakov, *Poetika Chekhova*, p. 178.
Doderer, Klaus. *Die Kurzgeschichte in Deutschland: Ihre Form und ihre Entwicklung.* Wiesbaden, 1953. Reprint. Darmstadt: Wissenschaftliche Buchgesellschaft, 1969.
Dostoevskii, F. M. *Polnoe sobranie sochinenii v tridtsati tomakh.* Leningrad: Nauka, 1972–90.
Driessen, F. C. *Gogol as a Short-Story Writer: A Study of His Technique of Composition.* Trans. Ian F. Finlay. The Hague: Mouton, 1965.
Durkin, Andrew R. "Chekhov's Narrative Technique." In Toby W. Clyman, ed., *A Chekhov Companion.* Westport, Conn.: Greenwood, 1985, pp. 123–32.
Eagleton, Terry. *Literary Theory: An Introduction.* Minneapolis: University of Minnesota Press, 1983.
Eco, Umberto. *The Role of the Reader: Explorations in the Semiotics of Texts.* Bloomington: Indiana University Press, 1979.
Eikhenbaum, B. M. "Kak sdelana 'Shinel'' Gogolia." *Skvoz' literaturu: sbornik statei.* Leningrad, 1924. Reprint. The Hague: Mouton, 1962. Translated as "How Gogol's 'Overcoat' is Made." In Robert A. Maguire, trans. and ed., *Gogol from the Twentieth Century: Eleven Essays.* Princeton, N.J.: Princeton University Press, 1974, pp. 269–91.
———. "O. Genri i teoriia novelly." In *Literatura.* Leningrad: Priboi, 1927, pp. 166–209.
Elias, Norbert. "Über das Schneuzen." In *Über den Prozess der Zivilisation: Soziogenetische und psychogenetische Untersuchungen.* 2 vols. Munich: Francke, 1969, 1:194–207.
Emerson-Topornin, Alexis E. "Šinel'—The Devil's Ovals—Motif of the Doubles." *Forum at Iowa on Russian Literature* 1 (Fall 1976): 34–56.
Erenburg, I. *Perechityvaia Chekhova.* Moscow: Khudozhestvennaia literatura, 1960.
Erlich, Victor. *Gogol.* New Haven, Conn.: Yale University Press, 1969.
Ermakov, I. D. *Ocherki po analizu tvorchestva N. V. Gogolia: Organichnost' proizvedenii Gogolia.* Moscow: Gosudarstvennoe izdatel'stvo, 1923.
Ermilov, V. V. *N. V. Gogol'.* 2d ed., rev. and enl. Moscow: Sovetskii pisatel', 1953.
Ermolaev, Herman. *Soviet Literary Theories 1927–1934: The Genesis of Socialist Realism.* University of California Publications in Modern Philology, vol. 69. Berkeley: University of California Press, 1963.
Fanger, Donald. "Chichikov's Journey, Gogol's Road, Russia's Progress." Paper presented at The Metaphor of the Journey—The Myth and Meaning of Russian Space: A Symposium, New Haven, Conn., Oct. 20, 1988.
———. *The Creation of Nikolai Gogol.* Cambridge, Mass.: Belknap, 1979.
———. "Gogol and His Reader." In William Mills Todd III, ed., *Literature and Society in Imperial Russia, 1800–1914.* Stanford, Calif.: Stanford University Press, 1978, pp. 61–95.

Fedotov, George P. *The Russian Religious Mind.* 2 vols. Vol. 1: *Kievan Christianity—The 10th to the 13th Centuries.* Belmont, Mass.: Nordland, 1975.

Fish, Stanley E. "Introduction, or How I Stopped Worrying and Learned to Love Interpretation." In *Is There a Text in This Class?* Cambridge, Mass.: Harvard University Press, 1980, pp. 1–17.

———. "Normal Circumstances, Literal Language, Direct Speech Acts, the Ordinary, the Everyday, the Obvious, What Goes without Saying, and Other Special Cases." *Critical Inquiry* 4 (Summer 1978): 625–44.

Forster, E. M. *Aspects of the Novel and Related Writings.* London: Edward Arnold, 1927.

Foucault, Michel. *Discipline and Punish: The Birth of the Prison.* Trans. Alan Sheridan. New York: Vintage, 1977.

Fusso, Susanne. *Designing Dead Souls: An Anatomy of Disorder in Gogol.* Stanford, Calif.: Stanford University Press, 1993.

———. "The Landscape of *Arabesques.*" In Susanne Fusso and Priscilla Meyer, eds., *Essays on Gogol: Logos and the Russian Word.* Evanston, Ill.: Northwestern University Press, 1992, pp. 112–25.

———. "*Mertvye Dushi*: Fragment, Parable, Promise." *Slavic Review* 49 (Spring 1990): 32–47.

Garrard, John G. "Some Thoughts on Gogol's 'Kolyaska.'" *PMLA* 90 (Oct. 1975): 848–60.

Gippius, Vasilii. *Gogol'.* Leningrad: Mysl', 1924. Reprint. Providence, R.I.: Brown University Press, 1966.

Goethe, Johann Wolfgang von. *Gespräche mit Eckermann.* In Johann Peter Eckermann, *Gespräche mit Goethe in den letzten Jahren seines Lebens.* Ed. Gustav Moldenhauer. 2 vols. Leipzig: Philipp Reclam, n.d.

Gogol', N. V. *Polnoe sobranie sochinenii.* 14 vols. Moscow: Izdatel'stvo Akademii nauk SSSR, 1937–52.

Gor'kii i sovetskie pisateli. Literaturnoe nasledstvo, vol. 70. Eds. I. I. Anisimov, et al. Moscow: Akademiia nauk SSSR, 1963.

Gor'kii, M. *Literaturno-kriticheskie stat'i.* Moscow: Gosizdat, 1937.

———. *Sobranie sochinenii.* 30 vols. Moscow: Khudozhestvennaia literatura, 1949–56.

Govorukha-Otrok, Iu. N. [Iu. Nikolaev, pseud.]. "Literaturnye zametki: Nigilizm." *Moskovskie vedomosti*, no. 83 (Mar. 25, 1893): 3–4.

———. "Ocherki sovremennoi belletristiki." *Moskovskie vedomosti*, no. 345 (Dec. 14, 1889). Cited in Chudakov, *Poetika Chekhova*, p. 159.

Grech, G. Review of *Mertvye dushi. Severnaia pchela*, no. 137 (1842). In V. Zelinskii, ed., *Russkaia kriticheskaia literatura o proizvedeniiakh N. V. Gogolia: Khronologicheskii sbornik kritiko-bibliograficheskikh statei.* Vol. 2: *1842–1855.* Moscow: Tipografiia A. G. Kol'chugina, 1893, pp. 33–40.

Gul'binskii, I. V. [I. V. Vladislavlev, pseud.]. *Literatura velikogo desiatiletiia, 1917–1927.* 4 vols. Vol. 1: *Khudozhestvennaia literatura.* Moscow-Leningrad: Gosudarstvennoe izdatel'stvo, 1928.

Haber, Edythe C. "Teffi as Miniaturist: An Examination of 'Ke Fer?' and 'Slepaja.'" In Joachim T. Baer and Norman W. Ingham, eds., *Mnemozina:*

Studia Literaria Russica in Honorem Vsevolod Setchkarev. Munich: Fink, 1974, pp. 163–70.
Hamon, Philippe. "Qu'est-ce qu'une description?" *Poétique* 12 (1972): 465–85.
———. "Un discours constraint." *Poétique* 16 (1973): 411–45.
Heller, Agnes. *A Theory of History*. Boston: Routledge, 1982.
Holquist, James M. "The Devil in Mufti: The *Märchenwelt* in Gogol's Short Stories." *PMLA* 82 (1967): 352–62.
Homer. *The Odyssey*. Trans. Richmond Lattimore. New York: Harper & Row, 1965.
Horace. *The Art of Poetry*. Trans. Burton Raffel (verse) and David Armstrong (prose). Albany: State University of New York Press, 1974.
Hubbs, Joanna. *Mother Russia: The Feminine Myth in Russian Culture*. Bloomington: Indiana University Press, 1988.
Iakubovskii, G. "O satire nashikh dnei." *Literaturnaia gazeta*, July 8, 1929, p. 3.
Iurkevich, P. D. [P. M-skii]. Review of *Mirgorod*. *Severnaia pchela*, no. 115 (1835). In V. Zelinskii, ed., *Russkaia kriticheskaia literatura o proizvedeniiakh N. V. Gogolia: Khronologicheskii sbornik kritiko-bibliograficheskikh statei*. Vol. 1: *1829–1842*. Moscow: Tipografiia A. Gatskuka, 1889, pp. 30–32.
Ivanov, I. I. "Zametki chitatelia: Sovremennyi geroi." *Artist*, no. 1 (1894): 97–110.
Ivanov, I. V. [I. V. Dzhonson, pseud.]. "Chekhov i ego rasskaz 'Nevesta.'" *Pravda: Ezhemesiachnyi zhurnal iskusstva, literatury i obshchestvennoi zhizni*, no. 5 (1904): 232–44.
Ivask, Iu. "O Gogole: Vykhod iz odinochestva." *Mosty* 12 (1966): 171–80.
Jaffe, Adrian H. and Virgil Scott, eds. *Studies in the Short Story*. New York: Sloane, 1949.
Jakobson, Roman. "Closing Statement: Linguistics and Poetics." In Thomas A. Sebeok, ed., *Style in Language*. Cambridge: The Technology Press of Massachusetts Institute of Technology, and New York: John Wiley, 1960, pp. 350–77.
———. "What Is Poetry?" Trans. M. Heim. In Stephen Rudy, ed., *Roman Jakobson: Selected Writings*. 8 vols. The Hague: Mouton, 1962–88, 3:740–50.
Jameson, Frederic. *The Political Unconscious: Narrative as a Socially Symbolic Act*. Ithaca, N.Y.: Cornell University Press, 1981.
Johnson, D. Barton. "The Galoshes Manifesto: A Motif in the Novels of Sasha Sokolov." *Oxford Slavonic Papers*, n.s., 22 (1989): 155–79.
Johnson, Warren. "Spontaneous Generation: The Rumor in Gogol'." *Russian Language Journal* 37 (Winter-Spring 1983): 87–95.
Kacherets, G. *Chekhov: Opyt*. Moscow, 1902.
Karlinsky, Simon. Introduction to *Anton Chekhov's Life and Thought: Selected Letters and Commentary*. Ed. Simon Karlinsky, trans. Michael Henry Heim. Berkeley: University of California Press, 1973, pp. 1–32.
———. "Portrait of Gogol as a Word Glutton, with Rabelais, Sterne, and Gertude Stein as Background Figures." *California Slavic Studies* 5 (1970): 169–86.

———. *The Sexual Labyrinth of Nikolai Gogol.* Cambridge, Mass.: Harvard University Press, 1976.
Kataev, V. B. *Literaturnye sviazi Chekhova.* Moscow: Izdatel'stvo Moskovskogo universiteta, 1989.
———. *Proza Chekhova: Problemy interpretatsii.* Moscow: Izdatel'stvo Moskovskogo universiteta, 1979.
Kermode, Frank. *The Genesis of Secrecy: On the Interpretation of Narrative.* Cambridge, Mass.: Harvard University Press, 1979.
———. "Secrets and Narrative Sequence." In W. J. T. Mitchell, ed., *On Narrative.* Chicago: University of Chicago Press, 1981, pp. 79–97.
Khrapchenko, Mikhail. "The Great Realist." *Soviet Literature* (Issue devoted to Gogol), no. 4 (1984): 129–37.
Kintsch, Walter and Teun A. van Dijk. "Toward a Model of Text Comprehension and Production." *Psychological Review* 85 (Sept. 5, 1978): 363–94.
Kjetsaa, Geir. "Soviet Contemporary Views of Gogol." Paper presented at the IV World Congress of Slavic and East European Studies, Harrogate, Eng., July 22, 1990.
Koffka, K. *Principles of Gestalt Psychology.* New York: Harcourt, Brace, 1935.
Kolb-Seletski, Natalia. "Gastronomy, Gogol, and His Fiction." *Slavic Review* 29 (1970): 35–57.
Kopper, John. "The 'Thing-in-Itself' in Gogol's Aesthetics: A Reading of the Dikan'ka Stories." In Susanne Fusso and Priscilla Meyer, eds., *Essays on Gogol: Logos and the Russian Word.* Evanston, Ill.: Northwestern University Press, 1992, pp. 40–62.
Kreps, M. *Tekhnika komicheskogo u Zoshchenko.* Benson, Vt.: Chalidze, 1986.
Kulish, P. A. *Zapiski o zhizni Nikolaia Vasil'evicha Gogolia.* 2 vols. St. Petersburg: V tipografii Aleksandra Iakobsona, and v tipografii Iliusa Shtaufa, 1856.
Labov, William. *Language in the Inner City.* Philadelphia: University of Pennsylvania Press, 1972.
Lacan, Jacques. *Ecrits: A Selection.* Trans. Alan Sheridan. New York: W. W. Norton, 1977.
———. "Seminar on 'The Purloined Letter.'" Trans. Jeffrey Mehlman. In John P. Muller and William J. Richardson, eds., *The Purloined Poe: Lacan, Derrida, and Psychoanalytic Reading.* Baltimore, Md.: Johns Hopkins University Press, 1988, pp. 28–54.
LeBlanc, Ronald D. "Dinner With Chichikov: The Fictional Meal as Narrative Device in Gogol's *Dead Souls.*" *Modern Language Studies* 18 (1988): 68–80.
———. "Satisfying Khlestakov's Appetite: The Semiotics of Eating in *The Inspector General.*" *Slavic Review* 47 (Fall 1988): 483–98.
Lelevich, G. "Otkazyvaemsia li my ot nasledstva?" *Na postu,* nos. 2–3 (1925): 43–59.
Lenin, V. I. *Shag vpered, dva shaga nazad (krizis v nashei partii).* In *Polnoe sobranie sochinenii.* 55 vols. Moscow: Izdatel'stvo politicheskoi literatury, 1967, 8:185–414.
Leont'ev, K. *Analiz, stil' i veianie: O romanakh gr. L. N. Tolstogo.* In *Sobranie*

sochinenii K. Leont'eva. Moscow: Izdanie V. M. Sablina, 1912, vol. 3. Reprint. Providence, R.I.: Brown University Press, 1965.
Lezhnev, A. "Literaturnye zametki." *Pechat' i Revoliutsiia,* no. 7 (Oct.–Nov. 1925): 133–38.
―――. "Na puti k vozrozhdeniiu satiry." *Literaturnaia gazeta,* Apr. 22, 1929, p. 2.
Likhachev, D. S. *Poetika drevnerusskoi literatury.* Leningrad: Nauka, 1967.
Lipovskii, A. "Predstaviteli sovremennoi russkoi povesti i otsenka ikh literaturnoi kritikoi." *Literaturnyi vestnik,* no. 5 (1901): 19–26.
"Lit-entsikopediia v sharzhakh." *Literaturnaia gazeta,* July 15, 1929, p. 3.
Loks, K. "Sovremennaia proza." *Pechat' i Revoliutsiia,* no. 5 (Aug.–Sept. 1923): 82–86.
Lotman, Ju. M. "The Decembrist in Everyday Life: Everyday Behavior as a Historical-Psychological Category." Trans. C. R. Pike. In Ju. M. Lotman and B. A. Uspenskij, *The Semiotics of Russian Culture.* Ed. A. Shukman. Michigan Slavic Contributions, no. 11. Ann Arbor, 1984, pp. 71–123.
―――. "The Poetics of Everyday Behavior in Russian Eighteenth-Century Culture." Trans. N. F. C. Owen. In *Semiotics of Russian Culture,* pp. 231–56.
―――. "Problema khudozhestvennogo prostranstva v proze Gogolia." *Uchenye zapiski Tartuskogo gosudartvennogo universiteta,* no. 209 (1968): 5–50.
―――. *Struktura khudozhestvennogo teksta.* Providence, R.I.: Brown University Press, 1971.
―――. "The Theater and Theatricality as Components of Early Nineteenth-Century Culture." Trans. G. S. Smith. In *Semiotics of Russian Culture,* pp. 141–64.
Lotman, Ju. M., and B. A. Uspenskij. "The Role of Dual Models in the Dynamics of Russian Culture (Up to the End of the Eighteenth Century)." Trans. N. F. C. Owen. In *Semiotics of Russian Culture,* pp. 3–35.
L'vov-Rogachevskii, V. L. Introduction to A. P. Chekhov, *Izbrannye proizvedeniia.* Moscow: Gosudarstvennoe izdatel'stvo, 1928, pp. iii–xxvi.
McLean, Hugh. "Gogol and the Whirling Telescope." In Lyman H. Legters, ed., *Russia: Essays in History and Literature.* Leiden, Netherlands: E. J. Brill, 1972, pp. 79–99.
―――. Introduction to Mikhail Zoshchenko, *Nervous People and Other Satires.* Trans. Maria Gordon and Hugh McLean. Bloomington: Indiana University Press, 1963, pp. vii–xxvii.
―――. "Nikolai Gogol's Retreat from Love: Toward an Interpretation of *Mirgorod.*" In *American Contributions to the Fourth International Congress of Slavicists.* The Hague: Mouton, 1958, pp. 225–44.
Maguire, Robert A. "Gogol and the Legacy of Pseudo-Dionysius." In Robert L. Belknap, ed., *Russianness: Studies on a Nation's Identity* (In Honor of Rufus Mathewson, 1918–1978). Ann Arbor, Mich.: Ardis, 1990, pp. 44–55.
―――, ed. and trans. *Gogol from the Twentieth Century: Eleven Essays.* Princeton, N.J.: Princeton University Press, 1974.
―――. "Literary Conflicts in the 1920s." *Survey* 18 (Winter 1972): 98–127.

———. *Placing, Seeing, Speaking: A Study of Nikolai Gogol*. Stanford, Calif.: Stanford University Press, forthcoming.

———. "Reading *Dead Souls.*" *Teaching Language Through Literature* 26 (Apr. 1987): 10–23.

———. *Red Virgin Soil: Soviet Literature in the 1920's*. Princeton, N.J.: Princeton University Press, 1968.

Maiakovskii, Vladimir. *Polnoe sobranie sochinenii v trinadtsati tomakh*. Moscow: Gosudarstvennoe izdatel'stvo khudozhestvennoi literatury, 1956.

Mandel'shtam, I. *O Kharaktere gogolevskogo stilia: Glava iz istorii russkogo literaturnogo iazyka*. Helsingfors: Novaia Tipografiia Guvudstadsbladet, 1902.

Mandel'shtam, Nadezhda. *Vtoraia kniga*. Paris: YMCA, n.d.

Mann, Iu. *Poetika Gogolia*. 2d ed. Moscow: Khudozhestvennaia literatura, 1988.

———. *V poiskakh zhivoi dushi: "Mertvye dushi": Pisatel'-kritika-chitatel'*. Moscow: Kniga, 1984.

Marin, Louis. *Food for Thought*. Trans. Mette Hjort. Baltimore, Md.: Johns Hopkins University Press, 1989.

Marler, Robert. " 'Bartelby, the Scrivener' and the American Short Story." *Genre* 6 (Dec. 1973): 428–47.

Masal'skii, K. P. Review of *Mertvye dushi*. *Syn otechestva*, no. 6 (1842): 1–30.

Mathewson, Rufus W., Jr. *The Positive Hero in Russian Literature*. 2d ed. Stanford, Calif.: Stanford University Press, 1975.

Medvedskii, K. P. "Literaturnye zametki: Nechto o g. Chekhove i 'futliarakh.'" *Moskovskie vedomosti*, no. 215 (Aug. 7, 1898): 3.

———. Review. *Nabliudatel'*, no. 9 (1892). Cited in A. P. Chekhov, *Polnoe sobranie sochinenii i pisem*. 30 vols. Moscow: Nauka, 1974–83, *Sochineniia*, 8:423.

———. "Zhertva bezvremen'ia (Povesti i rasskazy Antona Chekhova)." *Russkii vestnik*, no. 7 (July 1896): 231–45.

Melville, Herman. "Bartleby the Scrivener." In Harrison Hayford, Hershel Parker, and G. Thomas Tanselle, eds., *The Writings of Herman Melville*. 15 vols. The Northwestern-Newberry ed. Evanston, Ill.: Northwestern University Press, 1968–89, 9:13–45.

Merezhkovskii, D. S. *Chekhov i Gor'kii*. N.p.: Izdanie M. V. Pirozhkova, 1906.

———. *Gogol' i chert: Issledovanie*. Moscow: Skorpion, 1906. Reprinted in *Polnoe sobranie sochinenii*. 24 vols. St. Petersburg-Moscow: Izdanie T-va M. O. Vol'f, 1911–14, 10:163–209. Translated as "Gogol and the Devil." In Robert A. Maguire, trans. and ed., *Gogol from the Twentieth Century: Eleven Essays*. Princeton, N.J.: Princeton University Press, 1974, pp. 57–102.

———. "Gogol': Tvorchestvo, zhizn' i religiia." In *Polnoe sobranie sochinenii*, 10:163–286.

Mérimée, P. "Nicholas Gogol." In *Oeuvres complètes*. 12 vols. Paris: Librairie Ancienne Honoré Champion, 1927–33, 11:1–50.

Mikhailovskii, N. K. "Ob otsakh i detiakh i o g. Chekhove." In *Literaturno-kriticheskie stat'i*. Moscow: Gosudarstvennoe izdatel'stvo khudozhestvennoi literatury, 1957, pp. 594–607. [Orig. pub. as "Pis'ma o raznykh raznostiakh." *Russkie vedomosti*, no. 104 (Apr. 18, 1890): 2–3.]

———. Review of *V sumerkakh: Ocherki i rasskazy*. *Severnyi vestnik*, no. 9 (1887): 81–85.

———. "Sluchainye zametki: 'Palata No. 6.'" *Russkie vedomosti*, no. 335 (Dec. 4, 1892): 2–3.

Miller, J. Hillis. "The Figure in the Carpet." *Poetics Today* 1 (Spring 1980): 107–18.

Mirsky, D. S. *A History of Russian Literature from Its Beginnings to 1900*. Ed. Francis J. Whitfield. New York: Vintage, 1958.

Morris, Charles. *Foundations of the Theory of Signs*. Chicago: University of Chicago Press, 1938.

Morson, Gary Saul. *The Boundaries of Genre: Dostoevsky's "Diary of a Writer" and the Traditions of Literary Utopia*. Austin: University of Texas Press, 1981.

———. *Hidden in Plain View: Narrative and Creative Potentials in 'War and Peace.'* Stanford, Calif.: Stanford University Press, 1987.

———. "Prosaics and *Anna Karenina*." *Tolstoy Studies Journal* 1 (1988): 1–12.

Morson, Gary Saul, and Caryl Emerson. *Mikhail Bakhtin: Creation of a Prosaics*. Stanford, Calif: Stanford University Press, 1990.

Mukařovský, Jan. "Detail as the Basic Semantic Unit in Folk Art." In John Burbank and Peter Steiner, trans. and eds., *The Word and Verbal Art: Selected Essays by Jan Mukařovský*. New Haven, Conn.: Yale University Press, 1977, pp. 180–204.

Murphy, A. B. *Mikhail Zoshchenko: A Literary Profile*. Oxford: Willem A. Meeuws, 1981.

Nabokov, Vladimir. *Lectures on Russian Literature*. Ed. Fredson Bowers. New York: Harcourt Brace Jovanovich, 1981.

———. *Nikolai Gogol*. Norfolk, Conn.: New Directions, 1944.

Novikov, A. A. "Khudozhestvennoe slovo Gogolia (Stilisticheskii analiz 'Povesti o tom, kak possorilsia Ivan Ivanovich s Ivanom Nikiforovichem')." *Russkii iazyk v shkole*, no. 1 (Jan.-Feb. 1984): 48–55.

Obolenskii, D. A. "O pervom izdanii posmertnykh sochinenii Gogolia." *Russkaia starina*, no. 8 (Dec. 1873): 940–53.

Obolensky, Alexander P. *Food-Notes on Gogol*. Winnipeg, Man.: Trident, 1972.

Odoevskii, V. F. "Dve zametki o Gogole." In *O literature*. Moscow: Sovremennik, 1982, pp. 39–40.

O'Faolain, Sean, ed. *Short Stories: A Study in Pleasure*. Boston: Little, Brown, 1961.

Okhotina, G. A. "Saltykov-Shchedrin i Chekhov (problema 'melochei zhizni')." *Russkaia literatura*, no. 2 (1979): 117–27.

Olesha, Iurii. "Liompa." In *Izbrannoe*. Moscow: Khudozhestvennaia literatura, 1974, pp. 191–94.

Ol'shevets, M. "Obyvatel'skii nabat (O 'Sentimental'nykh povestiakh')." *Izvestiia*, Aug. 14, 1927, p. 3.

"O putiakh sovetskoi satiry." *Literaturnaia gazeta*, July 15, 1929, p. 1.

O'Toole, L. Michael. *Structure, Style and Interpretation in the Russian Short Story*. New Haven, Conn.: Yale University Press, 1982.

Paperno, Irina. *Chernyshevsky and the Age of Realism: A Study in the Semiotics of Behavior.* Stanford, Calif.: Stanford University Press, 1988.
Pasternak, Boris. "Detstvo Liuvers." In *Sobranie sochinenii v piati tomakh.* Moscow: Khudozhestvennaia literatura, 1989– , 4:35–86.
Paulson, William R. *The Noise of Culture: Literary Texts in a World of Information.* Ithaca, N.Y.: Cornell University Press, 1988.
Pereverzev, V. F. "Na frontakh tekushchei belletristiki." *Pechat' i Revoliutsiia,* no. 4 (June-July 1923): 127–33.
Perrine, Laurence. *Literature: Structure, Sound, and Sense.* 3d ed. New York: Harcourt Brace Jovanovich, 1978.
Pertsov, P. "Iz''iany tvorchestva (Povesti i rasskazy A. Chekhova)." *Russkoe bogatstvo,* no. 1 (1893): 39–71.
Pervyi Vsesoiuznyi s''ezd sovetskikh pisatelei. Stenograficheskii otchet. Moscow: Khudozhestvennaia literatura, 1934.
Pletnev, P. A. "Chichikov ili Mertvye dushi Gogolia." *Sovremennik,* no. 27 (1842): 19–61.
———. Review of "Rim." *Sovremennik,* no. 26 (1842): 41–44.
Poggioli, Renato. *The Phoenix and the Spider: A Book of Essays about Some Russian Writers and Their View of the Self.* Cambridge, Mass.: Harvard University Press, 1957.
Polevoi, N. A. Review of *Mertvye dushi. Russkii vestnik,* nos. 5–6 (1842): 33–57.
———. Review of *Vechera na khutore bliz Dikan'ki* vol. 1. *Moskovskii telegraf,* no. 17 (Sept. 1831): 91–95.
———. Review of *Vechera na khutore bliz Dikan'ki* vol. 2. *Moskovskii telegraf,* no. 6 (1832): 262–67.
Pomorska, Krystyna. "On the Structure of Modern Prose: Čexov and Solženicyn." *PTL: A Journal for Descriptive Poetics and Theory of Literature* 1 (1976): 459–65.
Pospelov, G. N. *Problemy literaturnogo stilia.* Moscow: Izdatel'stvo Moskovskogo universiteta, 1970.
Potebnia, A. A. *Iz zapisok po teorii slovesnosti.* Khar'kov: M. Zil'berberg, 1905. Reprint. The Hague: Mouton, 1970.
Pratt, Mary Louise. "The Short Story: The Long and the Short of It." *Poetics* 10 (1981): 175–94.
———. *Toward a Speech Act Theory of Literary Discourse.* Bloomington: Indiana University Press, 1977.
Price, Martin. "The Fictional Contract." In Frank Brady, John Palmer, and Martin Price, eds., *Literary Theory and Structure* (Essays in Honor of William K. Wimsatt). New Haven, Conn.: Yale University Press, 1973, pp. 151–78.
———. "The Irrelevant Detail and the Emergence of Form." In J. Hillis Miller, ed., *Aspects of Narrative: Selected Papers from the English Institute.* New York: Columbia University Press, 1971, pp. 69–91.
Prince, Gerald. *Narratology: The Form and Functioning of Narrative.* New York: Mouton, 1982.
Proffer, Carl R. *The Simile and Gogol's 'Dead Souls.'* The Hague: Mouton, 1967.

Protopopov, M. A. "Zhertva bezvremen'ia: Povesti g. Antona Chekhova." *Russkaia mysl'*, no. 6 (1892): 95–122.
"Proza byta i bytie prozy." *Literaturnaia gazeta* (Aug. 13–Oct. 29, 1980, weekly).
Rancour-Laferriere, Daniel. "All the World's a *Vertep*: The Personification/Depersonification Complex in Gogol's *Soročinskaja jarmarka*." *Harvard Ukrainian Studies* 6 (Sept. 1982): 339–71.
———. *Out from Under Gogol's "Overcoat."* Ann Arbor, Mich.: Ardis, 1982.
"Razgovor o novelle (Obrabotannaia stenogramma soveshchaniia, organizovannogo redaktsiei zhurnala 'ZNAMIA' 28 noiabria 1934g)." *Znamia*, no. 1 (Jan. 1935): 197–215.
Reinhart, Tanya. "Principles of Gestalt Perception in the Temporal Organization of Narrative Texts." *Linguistics* 22 (1984): 779–809.
Reyfman, Irina. "Shestaia povest' Belkina: Mikhail Zoshchenko v roli Proteia." In Boris Gasparov, Robert P. Hughes, and Irina Paperno, eds., *Cultural Mythologies of Russian Modernism: From the Golden Age to the Silver Age*. California Slavic Studies 15. Berkeley: University of California Press, 1992, pp. 393–414.
Rogi, M. "Puti sovetskoi satiry." *Literaturnaia gazeta*, July 22, 1929, p. 3.
Rozanov, V. V. *Legenda o Velikom Inkvizitore F. M. Dostoevskogo. Dve stat'i o Gogole*. St. Petersburg: Izdatel'stvo M. V. Pirozhkova, 1906. Reprint. Slavische Propyläen, vol. 67. Munich: Wilhelm Fink, 1970.
———. *Sredi khudozhnikov*. St. Petersburg: Tipografiia T-va A. S. Suvorina "Novoe vremia," 1914.
Sade, Marquis de. *The 120 Days of Sodom*. In *The 120 Days of Sodom and Other Writings*. Trans. Austryn Wainhouse and Richard Seaver. New York: Grove, 1966, pp. 183–674.
Saltykov-Shchedrin, M. E. *Melochi zhizni*. In *Sobranie sochinenii*. 20 vols. Moscow: Khudozhestvennaia literatura, 1965–77, vol. 16, bk. 2.
Sarnov, Benedikt. "Russkaia proza iz zapasnikov: XX vek." *Ogonek*, no. 11 (Mar. 1989): 18.
Schaarschmidt, Gunter. "Text Theory and Stylistic Filters." In J. Douglas Clayton and Gunter Schaarschmidt, eds., *Poetica Slavica* (Studies in Honor of Zbigniew Folejewski). Ottawa: University of Ottawa Press, 1981, pp. 163–73.
Schor, Naomi. *Reading in Detail: Aesthetics and the Feminine*. New York: Methuen, 1987.
———. *Zola's Crowds*. Baltimore, Md.: Johns Hopkins University Press, 1978.
Seifullina, L. N. "Chetyre glavy." In *Sobranie sochinenii*. 4 vols. Moscow: Khudozhestvennaia literatura, 1968–69, 1:53–98.
Semanova, M. *Chekhov i sovetskaia literatura*. Moscow-Leningrad: Sovetskii pisatel', 1966.
Sementkovskii, R. I. "Chto novogo v literature?" *Ezhemesiachnye literaturnye prilozhenia k zhurnalu "Niva,"* no. 6 (1896), cols. 379–400.
Senkovskii, O. I. "Pokhozhdeniia Chichikova ili Mertvye dushi." *Biblioteka dlia chteniia*, no. 53 (1842): 24–54.
Setchkarev, Vsevolod. "From the Golden to the Silver Age (1820–1917)." In

Robert Auty and Dimitri Obolensky, eds., *An Introduction to Russian Language and Literature*. Cambridge, Eng.: Cambridge University Press, 1977, pp. 133–84.

———. *Gogol: His Life and Works.* Trans. Robert Kramer. New York: New York University Press, 1965.

Shalamov, Varlam. *Kolymskie rasskazy.* London: Overseas Publications Interchange, 1978.

Shcheglov, Iu. K. "Entsiklopediia nekul'turnosti (Zoshchenko: rasskazy 1920-kh godov i 'Golubaia kniga')." In A. K. Zholkovskii and Iu. K. Shcheglov, eds., *Mir avtora i struktura teksta: Stat'i o russkoi literature.* Tenafly, N.J.: Hermitage, 1986, pp. 53–84.

———. "Mir Mikhaila Zoshchenko." *Wiener Slawistischer Almanach* 7 (1981): 109–54.

Shepard, Elizabeth C. "The Society Tale and the Innovative Argument in Russian Prose Fiction of the 1830s." *Russian Literature* 10 (Aug. 15, 1981): 111–61.

Shestov, Leon. "Anton Tchekhov (Creation from the Void)." In *Anton Tchekhov and Other Essays.* Trans. S. Koteliansky and J. M. Murry. London: Maunsel, 1916, pp. 3–60.

Shevyrev, S. P. Review of *Mertvye dushi. Moskvitianin*, no. 7 (1842): 207–28.

Shklovskii, Viktor. "A. P. Chekhov." In *Povesti o proze: Razmyshleniia, razbory.* 2 vols. Moscow: Khudozhestvennaia literatura, 1966, 2:333–35.

———. "O Zoshchenke i bol'shoi literature." In *Mikhail Zoshchenko: Stat'i i materialy.* Leningrad: Academia, 1928, pp. 13–25.

Shukin, S. "Iz vospominanii ob A. P. Chekhove." *Russkaia mysl'*, no. 10 (1911): 37–61.

Skabichevskii, A. M. *Istoriia noveishei russkoi literatury (1848–1890).* St. Petersburg: Tipografiia gazety "Novosti," 1891.

——— [unsigned]. Review of *Pestrye rasskazy. Severnyi vestnik*, no. 6 (1886): 123–26.

———. "Tekushchaia literatura: Novye rasskazy Antona Chekhova: 'Chelovek v futliare,' 'Kryzhovnik,' 'O liubvi.'" *Syn otechestva*, no. 238 (Sept. 4, 1898). Cited in A. P. Chekhov, *Polnoe sobranie sochinenii i pisem.* 30 vols., Sochineniia, 10:375.

Slonimskii, A. *Tekhnika komicheskogo u Gogolia.* Petrograd: Academia, 1923. Reprint. Providence, R.I.: Brown University Press, 1963.

———. "'Vdrug' u Dostoevskogo." *Kniga i Revoliutsiia*, no. 8 (1922): 9–16.

Smith, Barbara Herrnstein. "Narrative Versions, Narrative Theories." In W. J. T. Mitchell, ed., *On Narrative.* Chicago: University of Chicago Press, 1981, pp. 209–32.

———. *On the Margins of Discourse: The Relation of Literature to Language.* Chicago: University of Chicago Press, 1978.

Sorokin, Iu. S. "Slovarnyi sostav 'Mertvykh dush' Gogolia." In M. P. Alekseev, et al., eds., *Gogol': Stat'i i materialy.* Leningrad: Izdatel'stvo Leningradskogo universiteta, 1954, pp. 11–38.

Starkov, A. *Iumor Zoshchenko.* Moscow: Khudozhestvennaia literatura, 1974.

Stender-Peterson, Ad. "Der Ursprung des Gogolschen Teufels." *Göteborgs Högskolas Årsskrift (Minneskrift)* 26 (1920): 72–87.
Stepanova, K. P. "Funktsii opisanii v siuzhete povesti N. V. Gogolia 'Sorochinskaia iarmarka.' " In I. A. Dubashinskii, et al., eds., *Voprosy siuzhetoslozheniia: Sbornik statei*. Riga, Latvia: Zvaignze, 1978.
Stewart, Susan. *On Longing: Narratives of the Miniature, the Gigantic, the Souvenir, the Collection*. Baltimore, Md.: Johns Hopkins University Press, 1984.
Stifter, Adalbert. *"Bergkristall" und andere Erzählungen*. Frankfurt am Main: Insel, 1980.
Suleiman, Susan Rubin. "Redundancy and the 'Readable' Text." *Poetics Today* 1 (1980): 119–42.
Sven, Viktor. *Chei drug i chei vrag Mikhail Zoshchenko?* Munich: Izdanie tsentral'nogo ob''edineniia politicheskikh emigrantov iz SSSR, 1958.
Swift, Jonathan. *Tale of a Tub: Written for the Improvement of Mankind*. New York: Columbia University Press, 1930.
Terras, Victor. *Belinskij and Russian Literary Criticism: The Heritage of Organic Aesthetics*. Madison: University of Wisconsin Press, 1973.
———. "Nabokov and Gogol: The Metaphysics of Nonbeing." In J. Douglas Clayton and Gunter Schaarschmidt, eds., *Poetica Slavica* (Studies in Honor of Zbigniew Folejewksi). Ottawa: University of Ottawa Press, 1981, pp. 191–96.
Thomson, Boris. *The Premature Revolution: Russian Literature and Society 1917–1946*. London: Weidenfeld and Nicolson, 1972.
Thoreau, Henry David. *The Correspondence of Henry David Thoreau*. Eds. Walter Harding and Carl Bode. New York: New York University Press, 1958. Reprint. Westport, Conn.: Greenwood, 1974.
Tobin, Ronald. "Les mets et les mots: gastronomie et sémiotique dans *L'École des femmes*." *Semiotica* 51 (1984): 133–45.
Todd, William Mills, III. *Fiction and Society in the Age of Pushkin: Ideology, Institutions, and Narrative*. Cambridge, Mass.: Harvard University Press, 1986.
———. "Gogol's Epistolary Writing." *Columbia Essays in International Affairs* 5 (1969): 51–76.
Tolstoi, L. N. *Polnoe sobranie sochinenii*. Ed. V. Chertkov, et al. 90 vols. Moscow: Gosudarstvennoe izdatel'stvo khudozhestvennoi literatury, 1928–58.
Tomashevskii, Boris. *Kratkii kurs poetiki*. Moscow: Gosudarstvennoe izdatel'stvo, 1928.
———. *Teoriia literatury. Poetika*. 4th ed. Moscow: Gosudarstvennoe izdatel'stvo, 1928. Reprint. New York: Johnson Reprint Corp., 1967.
Tretiakov, S. "Novyi Lev Tolstoi." *Novyi Lef*, no. 1 (1927): 34–38.
Trotsky, Leon. *Literature and Revolution*. Trans. Rose Strunsky. New York: International Publishers, 1925.
Troyat, Henri. *Tolstoy*. Trans. Nancy Amphoux. Garden City, N.J.: Doubleday, 1967.
"Tsenzorskaia pravka 'Goluboi knigi' M. M. Zoshchenko: Publikatsiia S. Pecherskogo." *Minuvshee* 3 (1987): 355–91.

Uspenskij, B. A. "Tsar and Pretender: *Samozvančestvo* or Royal Imposture in Russia as a Cultural-Historical Phenomenon." Trans. David Budgen. In Ju. M. Lotman and B. A. Uspenskij, *The Semiotics of Russian Culture*. Ed. Ann Shukman. Michigan Slavic Contributions, no. 11. Ann Arbor, 1984, pp. 259–92.

Varshavskaia, K. O. "Malye zhanry v literature 80-90kh godov i proza A. P. Chekhova." Diss., Tomsk, 1969.

Veeser, H. Aram. Introduction to *The New Historicism*. Ed. H. Aram Veeser. New York: Routledge, 1989, pp. ix–xvi.

Vengerov, S. A. *Sobranie sochinenii*. 5 vols. St. Petersburg: Prometei, 1911–19.

Vinogradov, V. V. "Iazyk Gogolia." In V. V. Gippius, ed., *N. V. Gogol': Materialy i issledovaniia*. 2 vols. Moscow: Izdatel'stvo Akademii nauk SSSR, 1936, 2:286–376.

Vishnev, V. "Razgovor po dusham." *Na literaturnom postu*, nos. 11–12 (June 1927): 55–58.

Visson, Lynn. "Kasha vs. Cachet Blanc: The Gastronomic Dialectics of Russian Literature." In Robert L. Belknap, ed., *Russianness: Studies on a Nation's Identity* (In Honor of Rufus Mathewson, 1918–1978). Ann Arbor, Mich.: Ardis, 1990, pp. 60–73.

Voron, D. D. "Osobennosti siuzhetiki sovetskoi prozy 20-kh godov." Diss., Minsk, 1973.

Voronskii, Aleksandr. "Literaturnye otkliki: o gruppe pisatelei 'Kuznitsa'—obshchaia kharakteristika." *Krasnaia nov'*, no. 4 (June-July 1923): 309–34.

———. "Na perevale." *Krasnaia nov'*, no. 6 (Oct.-Nov. 1923): 312–22.

———. Review of Mikhail Zoshchenko, *Rasskazy Nazara Il'icha gospodina Sinebriukhova*, and Mikhail Slonimskii, *Shestoi strelkovyi*. *Krasnaia nov'*, no. 6 (Nov.-Dec. 1922): 343–45.

Vvedenskii, A. I. [Ar.]. "Zhurnal'nye otgoloski." *Russkie vedomosti*, no. 333 (Dec. 3, 1888). Cited in Chudakov, *Poetika Chekhova*, pp. 175–76.

Warning, Rainer. "Ironiesignale und ironische Solidarisierung." In Wolfgang Preisendanz and Rainer Warning, eds., *Das Komische*. Poetik und Hermeneutik, no. 7. Munich: Wilhelm Fink, 1976, pp. 416–23.

———. "Staged Discourse: Remarks on the Pragmatics of Fiction." Trans. Tom Beebe. *Dispositio* 5 (Winter-Spring 1980): 35–54.

Watt, Ian. *The Rise of the Novel: Studies in Defoe, Richardson and Fielding*. Berkeley: University of California Press, 1957.

Wellek, René. *Concepts of Criticism*. Ed. Stephen J. Nichols, Jr. New Haven, Conn.: Yale University Press, 1963.

Winner, Thomas. *Chekhov and His Prose*. San Francisco: Holt, Rinehart and Winston, 1966.

Winnett, Susan. "Coming Unstrung: Women, Men, Narrative, and Principles of Pleasure." *PMLA* (Special Topic: The Politics of Critical Language) 105 (May 1990): 508–18.

Woodward, James. *Gogol's 'Dead Souls.'* Princeton, N.J.: Princeton University Press, 1978.

Wright, Elizabeth. "Modern Psychoanalytic Criticism." In Ann Jefferson and

David Robey, eds., *Modern Literary Theory: A Comparative Introduction*. Totowa, N.J.: Barnes & Noble, 1982, pp. 145–65.
Zelinskii, V., ed. *Russkaia kriticheskaia literatura o proizvedeniiakh N. V. Gogolia: Khronologicheskii sbornik kritiko-bibliograficheskikh statei*. 3 vols. Moscow: Tipografiia A. Gatskuka, and Tipografiia A. G. Kol'chugina, 1889–96.
Zel'manov, M. G. [M. Iuzhnyi, pseud.]. "Rasskaz g. Chekhova." *Grazhdanin*, no. 89 (Apr. 12, 1893). Cited in A. P. Chekhov, *Polnoe sobranie sochinenii i pisem*. 30 vols., *Sochineniia*, 8:423.
Zhits, Fedor. Review of Viktor Shklovskii, *Teoriia prozy. Krasnaia nov'*, no. 1 (1926): 267–69.
Zholkovskii, A. K. "Lev Tolstoi i Mikhail Zoshchenko kak zerkalo i zazerkal'e russkoi revoliutsii." *Sintaksis* 7 (1986): 103–28.
Zhurbina, Evgeniia. "Mikhail Zoshchenko." In Mikhail Zoshchenko, *Sobranie sochinenii*. 6 vols. Leningrad: Priboi, 1929–31, 1:1–20.
Zoshchenko, Mikhail. *Blednolitsye brat'ia*. Moscow: Ogonek, 1927.
———. *Dni nashei zhizni*. Riga, Latvia: Gramatu drauts, 1929.
———. *Izbrannoe v dvukh tomakh*. Leningrad: Khudozhestvennaia literatura, 1978.
———. "Kak ia rabotaiu." *Literaturnaia ucheba*, no. 3 (1930): 107–13.
———. *Melochi zhizni*. Leningrad: Krasnaia gazeta, 1927.
———. "Meloch', kotoraia mnogo znachit." *Literaturnaia Rossiia*, no. 29 (June 16, 1965): 16–17.
———. *Nad kem smeetes'?!* 3d ed. Moscow-Leningrad: Zemlia i fabrika, 1928.
———. *Nervnye liudi*. Khar'kov: Proletarii, 1927.
———. *Nervous People and Other Satires*. Trans. Maria Gordon and Hugh McLean. Bloomington: Indiana University Press, 1963.
———. *O chem pel solovei: Sentimental'nye povesti*. Moscow-Leningrad: Gosudarstvennoe izdatel'stvo, 1927.
———. "O komicheskom v proizvedeniiakh Chekhova." *Voprosy literatury*, no. 2 (1967): 150–55.
———. "O sebe, ob ideologii i eshche koe o chem." *Literaturnye zapiski*, no. 3 (1922): 28–29.
———. "O sebe, o kritikakh i o svoei rabote." In *Mikhail Zoshchenko: Stat'i i materialy*. Leningrad: Academia, 1928, pp. 5–11.
———. *Pis'ma k pisateliu*. Leningrad: Izdatel'stvo pisatelei v Leningrade, 1929.
———. *Rasskazy*. Moscow: Khudozhestvennaia literatura, 1974.
———. *Semeinyi kuporos*. Berlin: Petropolis, 1929.
———. "Shestaia povest' I. P. Belkina." *Zvezda*, no. 1 (1937): 25–32.
———. *Skupoi rytsar'*. Riga, Latvia: Literatura, 1928.
———. *Sobachii niukh*. Moscow: Ogonek, 1926.
———. *Sobranie sochinenii*. 6 vols. Leningrad: Priboi, 1929–31.
———. *Sobranie sochinenii v trekh tomakh*. Leningrad: Khudozhestvennaia literatura, 1986.
———. *Tsarskie sapogi*. Riga, Latvia: Literatura, 1927.
———. *Uvazhaemye grazhdane*. 9th ed. Moscow-Leningrad: Zemlia i fabrika, 1928.
———. *Veselye rasskazy*. Paris: Imprimerie Scientifique et Commerciale, 1927.

Index

In this index "f" after a number indicates a separate reference on the next page, and "ff" indicates separate references on the next two pages. A continuous discussion over two or more pages is indicated by a span of numbers. *Passim* is used for a cluster of references in close but not consecutive sequence.

Acmeism, 58
Adaptation, 101–4. See also Norm
Aksakov, K. S., 132, 242
Alibis, 140–43
Aristotle, 153, 221
Arsen'ev, K. K., 24
Assertibility, 4–5, 19, 217, 221
Audience, see Reader
Aurelius, Marcus, 227
Authority, 111, 122–24, 137
Axes of selection and combination, 28–29, 226

Bakhtin, Mikhail, 111, 120, 142, 237, 242
Balabina, M. P., 138
Balzac, Honoré de, 138
Barmin, A. G., 115
Baroque, 136. See also Literature: in seventeenth and eighteenth centuries
Barthes, Roland, 80, 207, 226; on reality effect, 12, 223; on noise of narrative, 13, 249; on pleasure of reading, 133, 149–50; on desire for meaning, 134, 185, 249
Begemot (The Hippo), 63, 69
Belinsky, V. G., 228, 250; on Gogol's naturalism, 128, 196, 198, 241, 246; on Gogol's informativeness, 132, 190, 202, 254
Belknap, Robert, 149, 244

Bely, Andrei: on Gogol, 131f, 186, 193, 242, 251, 254f; on Chekhov, 213
Benjamin, Walter, 168
Berman, Russell, 240
Bernheimer, Charles, 132, 141, 250
Biedermeier, 123
"Big literature," see Monumentality
Bitsilli, P. M., 74, 227
Black, Joel, 245
Blanchot, Maurice, 236
Boccaccio, Giovanni: *Decameron*, 174
Bocharov, S. G., 130, 172, 237, 243–48 *passim*, 254
Body, exposure of, 76, 82, 215
Bolsheviks, see Communist Party; Soviet ideology
Booth, Wayne, 49
Boredom, 48–49, 150f, 236, 247
Boundary, 162; Lotman's model of, 7, 28; crossing of, 30, 35, 71, 84; of tellability (upper and lower), 55, 58–59, 115–22 *passim*, 162; of noticeability, 96, 98. See also Event; Noticing; Tellability; Trivia
Brevity, see Conciseness; Short forms
Brooks, Jeffrey, 21
Brooks, Peter, 133f, 144–51 *passim*, 174, 244
Brown, Clarence, 177
Brown, Edward, 69
Bryusov, Valerii, 25

Budil'nik (Alarm Clock), 22
Bulgakov, Mikhail, 234
Bunin, Ivan, 88, 234
Burke, Kenneth, 146, 206, 249
Buzoter (The Roughneck), 63
Byt, 78, 120, 239

Carnival, 129, 142–43
Catastrophe theory, 28
Censorship, 55–59 *passim*, 65, 104, 122, 229ff, 241. *See also* Communist Party; Soviet ideology
Challenge, *see* Boundary; Event; Noticing; Tellability; Trivia
Chaos, 119–20. *See also* Randomness
Character, 7, 47, 162, 199–200, 246. *See also* Narrator
Chatman, Seymour, 154, 156, 172, 223, 232, 249
Chatter, 47, 140, 153, 161, 243
Chekhov, Anton: use of trivia, 6–13 *passim*, 19f, 27–33, 213–17 *passim*; structure of events and nonevents, 8, 10, 22, 25–26, 35–36, 46, 50, 65f, 214–17 *passim*; critical reception, 9–10, 20–25 *passim*, 30–31, 37–38, 49–50, 56–57, 224–27 *passim*, 235; brevity in, 10, 12, 19, 223, 225; confrontation with reader, 14, 21, 24, 38, 41–42, 49–50, 216; emphasis on tellability, 24, 47–48, 153, 213–17 *passim*, 228; strategies of eventfulness, 26–27, 46; maximizing the minimum, 26–33; minimizing the maximum, 26, 33–38; disparate perspectives, 26–27, 38–40, 227; withholding of promised events, 26, 40–46; subversion of categories of significance, 27, 33–38, 50–51, 55, 122–23; psychology, 31, 226; opinion of social engagement, 43, 45, 228; despondency, 51; compared to Zoshchenko, 66, 69, 71, 77, 105, 109f, 112, 119; compared to Gogol, 128, 135, 151, 189, 198. *See also* Clerks; Cockroach; Frame narrative; "Little man"; Perspective; "Pinpricks"; Sneeze; Tellability; "Zero ending"

Chekhov, Anton, works of: "About Love" ("O liubvi"), 228; "Aniuta," 43; "At Home" ("Doma"), 23; "The Betrothed" ("Nevesta"), 37; "The Bishop" ("Arkhierei"), 48; "A Boring Story" ("Skuchnaia istoriia"), 47ff; "The Darling" ("Dushechka"), 47; "Death of a Clerk" ("Smert' chinovnika"), 27–31, 32, 46, 215; "The Event" ("Sobytie"), 38–39, 49; "Gooseberries" ("Kryzhovnik"), 48, 228; "Grisha," 40; "Gusev," 47; "The House with the Mansard" ("Dom s mezoninom"), 43–45, 228; "In Exile" ("V ssylke"), 43; "In the Cart" ("Na podvode"), 33; "The Kiss" ("Potselui"), 46, 48; "The Lady with the Little Dog" ("Dama s sobachkoi"), 36–37, 77, 238; "The Man in a Case" ("Chelovek v futliare"), 49, 228; "Misery" ("Toska"), 49; "Misfortune" ("Neschast'e"), 43; *Multicolored Stories (Pestrye rasskazy)*, 22; "The Murder" ("Ubiistvo"), 47; "The Nightmare" ("Koshmar"), 36, 42, 46; "Peasants" ("Muzhiki"), 223; "Peasant Women" ("Baby"), 228; "The Pecheneg," 47, 49, 149, 216; "The Requiem" ("Panikhida"), 48; "Rothschild's Fiddle," 105; "Sancta Simplicitas" ("Sviataia prostota"), 48, 69; *The Seagull (Chaika)*, 225; "Sleepy" ("Spat' khochetsia"), 47, 49; "Small-Fry" ("Meliuzga"), 31–32; "The Student," 33, 48; "The Teacher of Literature" ("Uchitel' slovesnosti"), 19, 34–35, 226; *Three Sisters (Tri sestry)*, 216; "Transgression" ("Bezzakonie"), 45–46; "A Trifle from Everyday Life" ("Zhiteiskaia meloch' "), 40; "An Unpleasant Incident" ("Nepriatnost' "), 42–43, 227–28; "Ward Six" ("Palata No. 6"), 43, 227; "The Wife" ("Supruga"), 41
Chernyshevsky, Nikolai, 88, 234f
Child, perspective of, 27, 38–40, 221. *See also* Perspective

Chizhevsky, Dmitry, 147, 149, 162, 199, 247, 256f
Chudakov, A. P., 20, 50, 130f, 157, 175, 189, 191, 224, 242, 254
Chudakov, G. I., 251–52
Chudakova, M. O., 67, 74, 88, 113, 237
Chumandrin, M., 239
Chvany, Catherine, 98
Cicero, 245
Classicism, 221
Clerks, insignificant, 31, 198, 203. *See also* "Little man"
Cloakroom attendants, 70–71, 78, 81–82, 84. *See also* Clothing; Coats
Clothing: as plot, 72–73, 75; as identity, 74, 80–81, 237; conventions of, 78ff, 84; semiotics of, 80; index of exclusion, 81, 84
Coats—in Zoshchenko: symbol of interdictions, 70–71, 81–84; tellability of, 71–79, 84–87 *passim*, 100, 202, 215, 233, 237; eventfulness of, 72–84 *passim*
—in Gogol: as verbal obstacle, 127, 196–97, 240–41; as significant object, 199–200, 201ff, 207, 215
Cockroach, significance of, 31–32, 86, 90, 102, 112, 114
Collecting, as discursive strategy, 143, 186–89. *See also* Gogol, Nikolai; Hoarding
Communal apartments, 104–9 *passim*, 116, 234
Communist Party, 76, 109, 117–18; literary policy of, 58f, 67f, 123, 230. *See also* Revolution of October 1917; Soviet ideology
Conative function, 204, 256
Conciseness, 112–13, 119–20, 135f, 139, 225, 252. *See also* Verbosity
Control, lack of, *see* Gogol, Nikolai: wordiness, distended discourse, narrators; Verbosity
Costumes, 79–82, 84. *See also* Clothing; Coats
Cox, Gary, 193, 252
Crosman, Robert, 13
Culler, Jonathan, 155, 156–57

Dante Alighieri, 82, 206, 208–9
Death, 82–83
Decembrists, 227
Deconstructive criticism, 123–24
Defamiliarization, 78, 110
Defoe, Daniel, 137, 139
Derrida, Jacques, 204, 256
Description, 12, 162–64. *See also* Trivia
Desire, 75, 87, 147–48, 178–85 *passim*, 207, 253; and narrative, 15, 134, 144–57 *passim*, 174–78 *passim*, 197, 205, 209. *See also* Narrative; Pleasure, of reading; Reader; Reading
Details, insignificant, *see* Trivia
Detective fiction, 153
Deutsch, Judith, 251
Devil, as discursive strategy, 178–80, 252
Diachrony, 164–66
"Diary of a Cat," 1, 3, 25, 69, 185, 222
Digressions, 144, 147, 153, 182, 245, 253; in Gogol, 13, 127–33 *passim*, 137–41 *passim*, 148, 198, 205, 256; in Zoshchenko, 113, 237; in seventeenth- and eighteenth-century literature, 138, 246. *See also* Irrelevance; Superfluity; Trivia; Verbosity
Discourse, 45–46; definitions of, 6, 11, 155–57, 223, 237; as obstruction of story in Gogol, 14–15, 128–33 *passim*, 141, 155–57, 161, 165, 191–99 *passim*, 205–8, 213–17 *passim*, 250, 257; and tellability in Zoshchenko, 111–15; reader's relation to in Gogol, 143, 150–51, 155–57; generative strategies of in Gogol, 173–89; as disease, 206. *See also* Collecting; Devil; Food; Hoarding; Narrative; Rocket ship; Sleep; Story
Disproportionality, 215
Disterlo, R. A., 22
Documentation, *see* Gogol, Nikolai: rhetoric of exactness, lists
"Dog drivel," *see* Sobach'ia erunda

"Doonesbury," 125, 215, 229, 237, 241
Dostoevsky, Fyodor: and Gogol, 24, 135, 137, 153, 189, 195, 245; and Chekhov, 29, 226; and Zoshchenko, 68, 74, 82–83, 95, 122, 235f; and feet, 89, 234
Double-voicing, 237
Dress, *see* Clothing
Driessen, F. C., 179, 256
Durkin, Andrew, 50

Eagleton, Terry, 254
Eco, Umberto, 223
Eikhenbaum, Boris, 199, 243
Enumeration, 168–70. *See also* Gogol, Nokolai: lists
Epic, 67–71 *passim*, 120, 135, 137; shrunken, 68–69, 71, 87. *See also* Monumentality
Epideictic, 137–38
Erlich, Victor, 130
Ermakov, I. D., 243
Ermilov, V. V., 242
Eroticism, 74–75, 77, 85, 89, 241, 253
Event: definitions of, 6–10 *passim*, 22–26 *passim*, 154f, 222, 232; maximization of, 27–33, 65–72 *passim*, 78, 105, 110; as challenge of boundaries, 30, 32–33, 46–48, 58–59, 66f, 71, 75, 89, 95–96, 98, 114, 118–19, 214, 217; minimization of, 33–38, 105–11 *passim*, 122; audience/reader's reception of, 38–46 *passim*, 48–51, 115–18; absence of in Gogol, 128, 189, 191, 196–97. *See also* Clothing; Coats; Eventlessness; Feet; Shoes; Significance; Sneeze; Tellability; Theater; Trivia; Trivialization
Eventfulness, *see* Event; Eventlessness; Trivia
Eventlessness, 19–27, 33–38, 40–46, 50–51. *See also* Event; Significance; Trivia; Trivialization
Excess, *see* Superfluity; Trivia: superfluity of
Existents: significance of in Zoshchenko, 66, 118; Chatman's definition of, 154–55, 232; absence of in Gogol, 189, 191, 196–97
Exposure, in literature, 75–86 *passim*

Fabula, 130, 191, 222f, 249. *See also* Story
Fadeev, Aleksandr, 230
Fanger, Donald, 130f, 176, 202, 246, 251
Fashion, *see* Clothing; Coats
Feet, 71–72, 90, 119, 234–38 *passim*; eventfulness of, 68, 85–91, 95–96, 109, 128, 213; tellability of, 86ff, 101–2; political subversiveness of, 89, 108–9, 113, 118, 122, 237. *See also* Shoes
Fellow Travelers, 59, 122, 230, 238
Feminist criticism, 244
Fielding, Henry, 241
Fish, Stanley, 10, 132, 244
Flaubert, Gustave, 223
Folklore, 30, 142
Food, 141, 246, 252–53; as discursive strategy, 180–86, 206–7
Formalist criticism, 110, 247
Forster, E. M., 14, 134
Frame narrative, 105–6, 141, 228
Freud, Sigmund, 30, 178, 244, 254
Freudian criticism, 30, 130, 254
Fun, 131–32, 140–44 *passim*, 161, 205. *See also* Pleasure, of reading
Fusso, Susanne, 165, 178, 245, 250, 256
Futurism, 58, 229

Galosh, *see* Feet; Shoes
Garrard, John, 253
Garshin, Vsevolod, 224
Genre, 57. *See also* Short story
Gestalt theory, 98–99
Gladkov, Fedor, 61
Glavlit, 230. *See also* Censorship
Goethe, Johann Wolfgang von, 24, 69, 221
Gogol, Nikolai: insignificant details, 6, 14, 151, 155–57, 172–73, 202, 205; superfluous details, 12f, 128–34, 137, 143, 152–54, 161–

62, 166, 205; digressions, 13, 127–28, 131–33, 137–38, 140–43, 147f, 175, 200, 205, 246, 256; discursive strategies, 14–15, 144, 173f; critical reception, 25, 57, 128–32, 134, 139–46, 198–99, 207, 241–46 *passim*; and Zoshchenko, 72–75, 80, 83–84, 112, 122, 127–28, 149, 151; wordiness, 127, 129, 135–37, 150–51, 162; reader's experience of, 129–56 *passim*, 161f, 173–78, 187, 196–97, 203, 205–9, 213–17, 245, 247, 256; and realism, 129, 137–39, 168, 193, 198–99, 241f, 255; distended discourse, 130–31, 136, 139, 155–57, 162–64, 169–70, 213–17, 257; similes, 130–37 *passim*, 147, 163, 165, 174, 205, 242, 247–48; story about discourse, 132–34, 157, 161, 165, 171, 173–74, 179, 189, 194–99, 205–8, 214–17, 250, 255; theory of literature, 134–36, 139; attitude toward other writers, 135–40, 185–86, 245; collecting, 136, 143, 186–89, 206f; self-referential details, 139, 190–97, 246; narrators, 140f, 162, 168, 173; food, 141, 180–86, 206–7, 246, 252–53; space, 142–43, 176, 190, 243; painting, 163–64, 193, 254–55; rhetoric of exactness, 166–68, 174, 206; lists, 166–69 *passim*, 189, 192; randomness, 170–72; non-arrival of plot, 174–78, 207, 251, 256; and devil, 178–80, 207, 252; endings, 178, 251; empty signifiers, 190–97, 199–207, 214; sound of prose, 195, 255; tellability, 213–17, 246. *See also* Diachrony; Frame narrative; "Little man"; Pleonasm; Preterition; Rocket ship; Tula pin

Gogol, Nikolai, works of: *Arabesques*, 136, 174, 188; "The Carriage" ("Koliaska"), 171f, 183f, 192, 244, 251; "Christmas Eve" ("Noch' pered Rozhdestvom"), 142, 167, 171, 175, 184, 256; *Dead Souls* (*Mertvyi dushi*), 74, 83–84, 127–37 *passim*, 144–54 *passim*, 161–78 *passim*, 183–96 *passim*, 204, 245, 251; "Diary of a Madman" ("Zapiski sumasshedshego"), 147, 170, 176, 205; "The Enchanted Place" ("Zakoldovannoe mesto"), 141f, 181, 251; *Evenings on a Farm Near Dikan'ka* (*Vechera na khutore bliz Dikan'ki*), 128, 140–43, 162, 166, 170, 174, 178–86 *passim*, 190–201 *passim*; "The Fair at Sorochintsy" ("Sorochinskaia iarmarka"), 142, 162, 179–80, 191, 251, 255f; "A Few Words About Pushkin" ("Neskol'ko slov o Pushkine"), 128, 135, 185, 245; "Geographical Sketches" ("Materialy po geografii"), 189; "Ivan Fedorovich Shpon'ka and His Auntie" ("Ivan Fedorovich Shpon'ka i ego tetushka"), 141, 162, 171, 180, 185, 188, 192, 251; "The Lost Letter" ("Propavshaia gramota"), 171, 175, 179, 203–4, 207, 251; "Materials for a Dictionary of the Russian Language" ("Materialy dlia slovaria russkogo iazyka"), 189; "A May Night, or the Drowned Maiden" ("Maiskaia noch', ili utoplenitsa"), 150, 162, 175, 251, 256; "Nevskii Prospekt," 143, 168, 171, 190; "The Nose" ("Nos"), 80, 128, 147–52 *passim*, 174; "Notebooks" ("Zapisnye knizhki"), 189; "Old-World Landowners" ("Starosvetskie pomeshchiki"), 148, 183–88 *passim*, 207, 251; "On the Nature of the Word" ("O tom, chto takoe slovo"), 195; "The Overcoat" ("Shinel' "), 72–75, 132, 165–71 *passim*, 175–76, 184–91 *passim*, 197–207, 215, 226, 241, 250, 255–56; "The Portrait" ("Portret"), 128; "Saint John's Eve" ("Vecher nakanune Ivana Kupala"), 142, 152; *Selected Passages from Correspondence with Friends* (*Vybrannye mesta iz perepiski s druz'iami*), 205, 257; "The Story of How Ivan Ivanovich Quarreled

with Ivan Nikiforovich" ("Povest' o tom, kak possorilsia Ivan Ivanovich s Ivanom Nikiforovichem"), 73, 127, 146–50 *passim*, 163–72 *passim*, 177, 184–98 *passim*, 206, 250, 254, 257; *Taras Bul'ba*, 30, 190; "A Terrible Vengeance" ("Strashnaia mest' "), 175; "Textbook on Literature for Russian Youth" ("Uchebnaia kniga slovesnosti dlia russkogo iunoshestva"), 135, 252
Gorky, Maxim, 31, 61, 118f, 137
Gosizdat, 115
Govorukha-Otrok, Iu. N. (pseud. Iu. Nikolaev), 224
Grice, H. P., 3, 5, 13, 114, 173

Hamon, Philippe, 246–47
Hawthorne, Nathaniel, 25
Heller, Agnes, 221
Hierarchy, 122, 124, 142, 155f
History, 109, 114, 118–21 *passim*
Hoarding, 136f, 139, 186–89
Homer, 135, 137, 164–65
Horace, 151, 221, 247
Humor, 11, 64, 132, 153, 215
Hundred Chapters (*Stoglav*; Pseudo-Gennadius), 226

Ideology, *see* Soviet ideology
Illiteracy, 100, 107, 117–18, 234, 238
Immateriality of content, 190–97, 199–203, 205–8, 255
Imposture, 80
Information, relevance of in narrative, 3ff, 115, 144, 146, 164–70
Information theory, 145, 153–54
Insignificance, *see* Significance; Trivia
Interpretive communities, 132, 244
Ippolit Ippolitych, 19–23 *passim*, 34–38 *passim*, 43, 47, 51, 55, 63, 99, 112, 127, 188, 216
Irony, 46, 153, 214f
Irrelevance, 14, 146, 152–57, 172–73. *See also* Event; Gogol, Nikolai: superfluous details, digressions; Significance; Trivia; Tula pin

Irving, Washington, 25
Ivask, Iu., 165, 184, 196

Jakobson, Roman, 28–29, 195, 226, 256
James, Henry, 132
Jameson, Frederic, 124
Jean Paul, *see* Richter, J. P. F.
Johnson, D. Barton, 234
Johnson, Samuel, 146
Johnson, Warren, 255

Kant, Immanuel, 133
Karamzin, Nikolai, 69
Karlinsky, Simon, 31, 147
Kataev, V. B., 227
Kataev, Valentin, 234
Kermode, Frank, 145, 157, 196, 252
Khvoshchinskaia, Nadezhda, 24
Kjetsaa, Geir, 252
Kokorev, Ivan, 24
Kolb-Seletski, Natalia, 253
Kopper, John, 250
Krasnaia gazeta (*Red Newspaper*), 97
Krasnaia nov' (*Red Virgin Soil*), 229
Kreps, Mikhail, 67, 237

Labov, William, 4, 49, 65, 108, 221
Lacan, Jacques, 144, 190, 247, 254, 256f
Laclos, Pierre Ambroise François Choderlos, 69
Laconism, *see* Conciseness; Short forms
Language, emptiness of, 191–207 *passim*, 214, 254
Laughter, 31, 111
LeBlanc, Ronald, 185, 252f
Lef (Left Front of Literature), 59, 229
Length, of narrative, *see* Monumentality; Short forms
Lenin, V. I., 89, 114
Leont'ev, K., 136, 234
Lermonotov, Mikhail, 195
Lessing, Gotthold Ephraim, 34f
Letters (mail), significance of, 118, 203–5, 256–57
Likhachev, D. S., 222

Literature: social relevance of, 42, 56, 227, 230, 242; and propaganda, 58–59; as exposure, 75–76; in seventeenth and eighteenth centuries, 137f, 193, 221, 246; as noise, 249
—in nineteenth century, 24, 136ff, 169; as model for Soviet critics, 57–58, 67, 236; Zoshchenko's parodies of, 72, 83
—*See also* Communist Party; Exposure; "Little man"; Monumentality; Neoclassicism; Physiologies; Realism; Romanticism; Society tale; Soviet ideology
"Little man," in Russian literature, 24, 100–101. *See also* Literature: in nineteenth century; Realism
Local color, 142
Loks, K., 240
Lotman, Iurii: events and boundaries, 6ff, 28, 42, 59, 222; reader/author relation, 9, 214, 225; theater, 42, 78; space, 176, 190, 243; codes of behavior, 227
Luther, Martin, 194

McLean, Hugh, 146, 193, 237, 240, 252–53
Maguire, Robert, 164, 195, 238; on reader response to Gogol, 129, 134, 140, 146, 150, 207; on significance of Gogol's details, 129f, 169–70, 190, 193, 197, 214
Mail, *see* Letters
Mandel'shtam, I., 132, 254
Mandel'shtam, Nadezhda, 240
Mann, Iu., 132, 166, 180, 185, 242, 244, 251f
Marin, Louis, 184, 253
Marriage, 72, 89f, 100; as non-event, 34–35, 37, 47
Marxist criticism, *see* Communist Party; Soviet ideology
Masal'skii, K. P., 132, 243
Mathewson, Rufus, 236
Mayakovsky, Vladimir, 89–90, 234–35
Melville, Herman, 204
Merezhkovskii, D. S., 22, 242

Mérimée, Prosper, 254
Metaphors, literalization of, 90
Mikhailov, Mikhail, 24
Mikhailovskii, N. K., 20f, 224
Miller, J. Hillis, 249
Mimesis, 142, 153, 169. *See also* Realism; Trivia: as mimetic
Miniature, *see* Conciseness; Short forms; Trivia
Minimalism, *see* Conciseness; Short forms; Trivia
Mirsky, D. S., 37, 131, 136, 140, 151, 222, 248
Modernism, 58
Monumentality, as paradigm for literature, 56–58, 61, 67, 120, 122–24, 228
Morris, Charles, 222
Morson, Gary Saul, 120, 122, 134; on prosaics, 7–8, 110; on semiotic totalitarianism, 130, 243; on relevance of details, 145, 154, 236, 247, 249
Motifs, bound and free, 155, 223
Motion: in narrative, 90–91, 96; in reading, 144–45, 173–75. *See also* Gogol, Nikolai, non-arrival of plot; Road
Mukařovský, Jan, 142
Mukhomor (The Toadstool), 63
Myth, 121

Nabokov, Vladimir, 169, 229
Nachtrglichkeit, 132
Na postu (On Guard), 229
Narrative, 8, 25, 47–49, 111, 132f; and noise, 13, 154, 249; as economic transaction, 14f, 151–52, 156, 208, 214, 216, 228; and sleep, 49, 228; and desire, 134, 144–48, 208–9; as a road, 175–78, 251. *See also* Discourse; Food; Information, relevance of in narrative; Motion; Reader; Story
Narrator, 49, 111–12, 118, 140–41, 144, 162–63, 221. *See also* Skaz
Naturalism, 139, 193. *See also* Realism
Nekul'turnost', 77, 99, 101, 235

Neo-classicism, 138, 221. *See also* Literature: in seventeenth and eighteenth centuries
New Economic Policy (NEP), 70, 76, 79, 81, 116, 230
New Historicism, 240
New Soviet man, 121. *See also* Communist Party; Soviet ideology
New Yorker, 41, 63, 98, 224, 253
Nikolaev, Iu., *see* Govorukha-Otrok, Iu. N.
Nineteenth-century literature, *see* Literature: in nineteenth century
1920s, *see* Soviet Union: atmosphere in 1920s
Noise, and literature, 13, 154, 249
Norm, and tellability, 6–10; and noticeability, 98–106 *passim*. *See also* Event: as challenge of boundaries to rules of tellability; Trivia: as challenge
Noticeability: as index of tellability, 65–66, 95–96, 104–6; of trivia, 91, 98, 102, 106, 110, 121–22; of October Revolution, 106, 109, 121–22; of narrative voice, 112. *See also* Perceptibility
Noticing, poetics of, 11; as an act of challenge, 97, 102–3, 119; as event, 112, 116
Novel, 19, 57, 224f, 229–30. *See also* Literature: in nineteenth century; Monumentality; Realism
Novella, 221
Novoe vremia (*New Times*), 22

Obolensky, Alexander, 252
Ocherk (sketch), 224
Octobrists, 59, 229
Odoevskii, V. F., 250
O'Faolain, Sean, 249
O'Keeffe, Georgia, 19, 25, 213
Olesha, Iurii, 39
Opoiaz, 58
Oskolki (*Splinters*), 22
Ostranenie, see Defamiliarization
O'Toole, L. Michael, 256

Paperno, Irina, 234
Parody, 77, 111, 241

Pass, the (Pereval), 59
Pasternak, Boris, 39
Paulson, William, 146–47, 249
Pedestrians, *see* Feet; Motion
Perceptibility, 108, 110–11, 122. *See also* Noticeability
Pereverzev, V. F., 60
Perspective, 27, 38–40, 122, 221
Pertsov, P., 20f
Peter the Great, 80
Physiologies, 138. See also Literature: in nineteenth century; Realism
Pigs, in narrative, 73–74, 186, 194
"Pinpricks," 24, 26, 50, 122–23, 217, 222
Pisarev, Dmitrii, 88
Pisemskii, Aleksei, 24
Plato, 32
Pleasure, of reading, 131–34 *passim*, 140–51 *passim*, 205, 208, 244
Pleasure principle, 178
Plenitude, 196, 206, 255, 257
Pleonasm, 169–70, 189, 205, 250
Pleshcheev, Aleksei, 10, 24
Pletnev, P. A., 241
Plot, *see* Story
Poe, Edgar Allan, 25, 256
Poggioli, Renato, 227
Polevoi, N. A., 142, 241
Political ideology, *see* Soviet ideology
Pomorska, Krystyna, 50, 228
Poshlost', 35
Pospelov, G. N., 31
Potebnaia, A. A., 131
Pragmatics, 9, 66, 101, 110, 115, 173, 177, 222
Pratt, Mary, 3ff, 221
Preterition, 163, 250
Price, Martin, 145, 152, 156, 208
Prince, Gerald, 155, 172
Privacy, 115
Proffer, Carl, 129, 132, 137, 163, 193–96 *passim*, 241
Proletarian literature, 59, 60, 230
Proletkul't, 59
Propaganda, *see* Soviet ideology
Prosaics, 7, 8, 110, 222
Protopopov, M. A., 22
Puns, 87–88, 202, 254

Pushkin, Alexander, 25, 247, 250; parodied by Zoshchenko, 83–84, 88, 233f; foot fetish, 89; as paradigm of conciseness, 128, 135ff, 139, 185f, 195, 245

Quintillian, 245

Rabelais, François, 137
Rancour-Laferriere, Daniel, 130, 179
Randomness, 20–21, 170–72, 224
Rank, 27–28, 30
RAPP (Russian Association of Proletarian Writers), 230
Reader, 3, 13, 15, 40, 50–51; as arbiter of tellability, 9, 21, 49–50, 114–18, 122, 124, 216, 238; "defeated," 9, 38, 214; frustrated by author, 41–42, 129–40 *passim*, 144, 148–56 *passim*, 173–78, 187, 196–97, 202–9 *passim*, 216; boredom of, 48–49, 150f; desire for meaning and plot, 132–34, 143–57 *passim*, 161, 173–74, 185, 196–209 *passim*, 213–16, 244; desire for closure, 133–34, 145–46, 152, 177–78, 244, 256; desire for pleasure, 133–34, 140, 143–44, 149–51, 205, 208, 244; as consumer, 133, 151–52, 184, 186. *See also* Chekhov, Anton: confrontation with reader; Event; Gogol, Nikolai: reader's experience of; Story; Tellability; Trivia; Tula pin; Zoshchenko, Mikhail: relation to reader/audience
Reading: and desire, 144–51; as transaction, 151–52, 208; as consumption, 133, 151–52, 184, 186. *See also* Desire; Narrative; Reader
Realism, 19–20, 224, 234, 250; as paradigm for Soviet critics, 57, 242; use of detail in, 137–39, 169, 191, 193, 255. *See also* Gogol, Nikolai: and realism; "Little man"; Literature: in nineteenth century; Physiologies; Society tale
Reality effect, 12, 137

Reception, 9, 15, 117, 148–51. *See also* Chekhov, Anton: critical reception; Gogol, Nikiolai: critical reception; Reader; Trivia: critical response to; Zoshchenko, Mikhail: critical reception
Recusatio, 79, 99, 122
Redundancy, *see* Pleonasm
Referents, 191–92, 222
Renaissance literary theory, 221
Repetition, 41, 66, 170, 221
Revolution of October 1917: as paradigm for narrative event, 56–62 *passim*; and feet, 86, 89, 234; Zoshchenko's trivialization of, 106–11, 113, 119–22 *passim*. *See also* Soviet ideology
Reyfman, Irina, 83, 234
Richardson, Samuel, 146
Richter, Johann Paul Friedrich (Jean Paul), 178, 251–52
Road, as narrative pathway, 175–78, 251
Rocket ship, discourse as, 130–31, 157, 175
Romanticism, 24, 136, 185, 251
Rozanov, V. V., 137, 250
Rumor, 255

Sade, Marquis de, 153
Saltykov-Shchedrin, Mikhail, 20, 69, 120, 232
Satire, 121, 240
Saussure, Ferdinand de, 254
Schlegel, Friedrich, 136
Schopenhauer, Arthur, 227
Schor, Naomi, 130
Seifullina, L. N., 61
Semiotics, 80, 222f
"Semiotic totalitarianism," 130f, 243
Senkovskii, O. I., 132
Serapion Brothers, 59, 61, 230
Setchkarev, Vsevolod, 130, 207, 243, 255
Shalamov, Varlam, 215
Shcheglov, Iu. K., 77–78, 233, 235, 238
Shestov, Lev, 25–26
Shklovskii, Viktor, 31, 110

Shoes, 85, 88, 101, 127, 241; as index of eventfulness, 89, 109; political significance of, 109, 113, 234. *See also* Feet

Short forms, literary genre of, 19–25 *passim*, 56–62 *passim*, 67–68, 228

Short story, 24–25, 224f

Shrunken epic, *see* Epic

Sign, 191, 222

Significance: norms of, 3, 10, 23, 38, 84, 202, 221; hierarchy of, 8, 110, 124, 216–17; and size, 10, 222; made insignificant, 11, 33–38. *See also* Event; Irrelevance; Trivia; Trivialization

Signified and signifier, 130, 191–92, 194, 205, 207, 254ff

Similes, extended (Homeric), 130–32, 135, 137, 147, 163, 165, 174, 205, 242, 247–48

Siuzhet, 222f. *See also* Discourse

Skabichevskii, A. M., 20, 22–23, 224f

Skaz, 111–12, 237. *See also* Narrator

Sketch, *see* Ocherk

Skovoroda, Grigorii, 247

Sleep, as reader response, 49, 150, 228. *See also* Reader

Slonimskii, A., 131, 242

Smallness, *see* Conciseness; Short forms; Trivia

Smith, Barbara Herrnstein, 145, 149–52 *passim*, 156, 173, 223, 248f

Smithy, 59

Sneeze, 19; as tellable event, 7, 10, 35, 213; as transgression, 27–31 *passim*

Sobach'ia erunda ("Dog drivel"), 62, 75, 84, 102

Social Democrats, 37

Socialism, *see* Communist Party; Soviet ideology

Socialist realism, 121, 229

Society tale, 138

Sokolov, Sasha, 234

Sorokin, Iu. S., 189, 254

Soviet ideology (requirements for literature): social relevance, 21, 59, 242; monumentality, 56f, 60–61, 64, 120, 122–24, 228ff; revolutionary themes, 58, 106–9, 121; significant events, 59, 114ff; image of strides, 89–90; cult of hero, 235–36. *See also* Censorship; Communist Party; Revolution of October 1917; Socialist realism

Soviet Union: atmosphere in 1920s, 11, 56, 59f, 79, 99, 123; atmosphere in 1930s, 121

Specificity, *see* Gogol, Nikolai: rhetoric of exactness, lists

Speech act theory, 3–4, 226

Stanislavsky, Konstantin, 78

Stepanova, K. P., 250

Sterne, Laurence, 137

Stevens, Wallace, 177

Stifter, Adalbert, 123, 240

Story: definitions of, 6–14 *passim*, 155–57, 223, 232; Chekhov's construction of, 23, 29, 37, 50, 128, 213–17 *passim*; Zoshchenko's construction of, 67, 75–76, 112, 128, 213–17 *passim*, 237; as expression of discourse in Gogol, 128–34 *passim*, 146, 155–57, 161, 165, 171–79 *passim*, 188–99 *passim*, 205–8, 213–17, 250, 255; as object of reader's desire, 133, 144–46, 155–57, 161, 173, 185, 196, 205. *See also* Discourse; Fabula; Narrative; Reader

Storytelling, 8, 48, 114, 168, 221, 228

Strekoza (*Dragonfly*), 22

Superfluity, 129, 132, 137, 152–57 *passim*, 161, 205. *See also* Gogol, Nikolai: superfluous details; Trivia: superfluity of

Supernatural, 128, 139

Suvorin, A. S., 22

Sven, Viktor, 239

Swift, Jonathan, 191, 245, 253

Symbolist movement, 21, 58, 230

Synechdoche, 120

Talkativeness, 47, 112, 140–41. *See also* Chatter; Gogol, Nikolai: wordiness, narrators; Verbosity

Teffi, Nadezhda, 225
Tellability, 3–13 *passim*, 49, 77, 221; of the unlikely, 6f, 25, 37, 214, 236; and the reader, 9, 48–49, 115–18; of the trivial event, 19, 30, 32f, 65, 86–91 *passim*, 99, 101; Chekhov's challenges to the rules of, 24, 38, 47–48, 213–17; of non-events, 41–45 *passim*; Zoshchenko's challenge to the boundaries of, 55, 64, 71, 84, 113, 122–24, 213–17; politics of, 59, 107, 123–24; and noticeability, 95–96, 104–6, 110; Gogol's discursive challenge to, 128f, 154, 213–17, 246. *See also* Chekhov, Anton: emphasis on tellability; Coats; Event; Feet; Noticeability; Theater; Trivia
Terras, Victor, 252, 255–56
Theater, 80, 82, 90, 115, 226; as place of strict codes, 29–30, 76–81; as locus of tellable events, 42, 70–71, 76–82 *passim*, 87, 90, 99, 233
Thoreau, Henry David, 225
1001 Nights, 133–34, 174
Tobin, Ronald, 253
Todd, William Mills, III, 241, 246f, 255
Tolstoy, Lev, 24, 30, 32, 73, 105, 121, 136, 198, 245; use of ordinary events, 7–8, 110–11, 189, 227; as paradigm for Soviet critics ("Red Lev Tolstoy"), 57–58, 61, 78, 120, 230; and Zoshchenko, 69, 78, 83–84, 89, 110–11, 122, 234
Tomashevskii, Boris, 110, 155, 172, 222f, 249f
Topos, 66, 142–43
Transaction, narrative, 14, 151–52, 156, 208, 214, 216, 228
Trifles, *see* Trivia
Trivia: as challenge to rules of tellability and significance, 6–12, 27–33, 71, 78, 95–96, 113, 123–24, 202, 214, 216–17; discursive use of, 6–7, 13–15, 141, 223; critical response to, 9, 20–21, 57–61, 63, 119–21, 129–32; monumental significance of, 10, 25, 27–33, 66–72 *passim*, 83, 88, 108, 122–24; superfluity of, 12–13, 128–36, 140–43, 151–54, 213–16; as story-level event, 13, 23, 27, 33, 50, 76, 213–17 *passim*; comparison of, in Chekhov, Zoshchenko, and Gogol, 12, 14–15, 213–17; as politically provocative, 31, 33, 55, 65, 68–70, 110, 118–24, 217; as empowerment of reader, 48–50, 115–18, 122, 124, 216, 238; reader's desire for significance of, 129–34, 140, 145–46; as self-referential signifiers, 130f, 139, 191, 246; as mimetic, 137–39, 142, 153. *See also* Clothing; Coats; Cockroach; Event; Feet; Irrelevance; Noticeability; Reader; Shoes; Significance; Sneeze; Tellability; Tula pin
Trivialization, of the "officially significant," 33–38, 96, 106–11, 122–24
Tula pin, 129–30, 146, 154, 243
Turgenev, Ivan, 24
Tvardovskii, Aleksandr, 243

Ukrainian folklore, *see* Folklore
Uspenskii, Gleb, 224
Utilitarian literature, 56, 88. *See also* Soviet ideology

Varshavskaia, K. O., 228
Verbosity, 112, 127, 129, 135, 137, 139, 150–51, 193, 225. *See also* Conciseness
Vinogradov, V. V., 242
Visson, Lynn, 252
Voronskii, Aleksandr, 57, 60, 122, 229f

Warning, Rainer, 9
White, Duffield, 244
Winner, Thomas, 227
Woodward, James, 129
Wordiness, *see* Verbosity
Wordsworth, William, 24, 241
Wright, Elizabeth, 247

Zeno's paradox, 174
"Zero ending," 227
Zhits, Fedor, 58
Zholkovksii, A. K., 78, 233f, 256
Zhukovskii, Vasilii, 132, 244
Zola, Emile, 246–47
Zoshchenko, Mikhail: 231–32, 240; provocative use of trivia, 6, 13, 55, 58, 63, 68–71, 119–20, 122–24, 237f; subversion of norms of eventfulness, 8, 64–71 *passim*, 96–106 *passim*, 110–11, 122–24, 213–17; poetics of noticing, 11, 65–66, 95–98, 102–6, 110–12, 122; critique of official ideology, 11, 59, 61–62, 67–68, 90–91, 96–124 *passim*, 239; short forms, 12, 62, 67–69, 71, 87; proto-deconstruction, 14, 123–24; parodies of literary predecessors, 31, 68–74 *passim*, 78–84 *passim*, 89, 95, 105, 232ff; political context, 55–56; critical reception, 55, 63–64, 119, 121, 232, 239; conciseness, 62, 112–13, 119–20, 136; critique of Soviet society, 64–65, 69, 82, 95–104 *passim*, 236; compared to Chekhov, 66, 69, 71, 77, 105, 109f, 112, 119; relation of story to discourse, 66–67, 111–13, 237; clothing, 71–85 *passim*, 202, 213, 233, 237; theater, 76–81, 90, 115, 233; feet, 85–91, 127–28, 213, 237–38; relation to reader/audience, 114–18, 122, 124, 149, 216, 238; compared to Gogol, 127–28, 149, 151, 202, 205. *See also* Digression; Monumentality; Revolution of October 1917; Short forms; Soviet ideology
Zoshchekno, Mikhail, works of: "Absence of Malice" ("Dushevnaia prostota"), 65, 68f, 86, 95–96, 99, 102f; "The Actor" ("Akter"), 80, 238; "Administrative Ecstasy" ("Administrativnyi vostorg"), 73, 79, 99, 114, 238; "An Adventure Story" ("Avantiurnyi rasskaz"), 233; "Americans" ("Amerikantsy"), 112; "The Bathhouse" ("Bania"), 64, 81–83; *Before Sunrise* (*Pered voskhodom solntsa*), 69, 240; "The Bottle" ("Butylka"), 100, 238; "The Cap" ("Shapka"), 90, 97; "Capital Item" ("Stolichnaia stuchka"), 113; "Casting Bait" ("Na zhivtsa"), 86, 88, 238; "The Charms of Culture" ("Prelesti kul'tury"), 76f, 79, 238; "The Chinese Ceremony" ("Kitaiskaia tseremoniia") 109, 235; "Cockroaches" ("Tarakany"), 86, 112, 114, 237; "Comrade Gogol" ("Tovarishch Gogol'"), 74; "Confession" ("Ispoved'"), 75; "The Crisis" ("Krizis"), 104; "The Czar's Boots" ("Tsarskie sapogi"), 109; "The Dictaphone" ("Diktafon"), 79; "Dog Scent" ("Sobachii niukh"), 75, 100, 102, 238; "The Downfall of a Man" ("Gibel' cheloveka"), 96, 116, 238; "The Earthquake" ("Zemletriasenie"), 87, 111; "The Economy Campaign" ("Rezhim ekonomii"), 79, 107; "Electrician" ("Monter"), 78; "Electrification" ("Elektrifikatsiia"), 107, 236; "The Event" ("Sobytie"), 116; "The Fantasy Shirt" ("Rubashka-fantazi"), 103; "Fog" ("Tuman"), 114, 238; "Fortunetelling" ("Khiromantiia"), 99, 114; "The Galosh" ("Galosha"), 64, 87; "Galoshes and Ice Cream" ("Kaloshi i morozhenoe"), 87; "Green Production" ("Zelenaia produktsiia"), 104, 116; "The Glass" ("Stakan"), 117, 236; "Guests" ("Gosti"), 74, 113f, 237; "Happiness" ("Schast'e"), 104, 108; "Hard Labor" ("Katorga"), 104; "The Hero" ("Geroi"), 75; "A Hidden Treasure" ("Klad"), 239; "A Historic Tale" ("Istoricheskii rasskaz"), 113f; "Home Remedy" ("Domashnee sredstvo"), 115, 237; "Hypnosis" ("Gipnoz"), 99; "The Incident" ("Sluchai"), 79; "An Incident in the Provinces" ("Sluchai v provintsii"), 80, 102, 116, 238; "It Happens" ("Byvaet"), 100; "It's Bearable" ("Terpet'

mozhno"), 100, 237; "The Lady Aristocrat" ("Aristokratka"), 77, 80, 238; "Lemonade" ("Limonad"), 99, 237; *Letters to the Writer* (*Pis'ma k pisateliu*), 115, 237; "Liaisons dangereuses" ("Opasnye sviazi"), 69, 77; *Light-Blue Book* (*Golubaia kniga*), 71, 118, 231; "The Light Fixture" ("Kolpak"), 103; "The Lilacs Are Blooming" ("Siren' tsvetet"), 101, 113, 238; "A Little Mistake" ("Oshibochka"), 102, 107, 114; "The Living Corpse—A True Story" ("Zhivoi trup—Istinnoe proisshestvie"), 69, 83; "Love" ("Liubov'"), 73, 84, 87; "Man of Literature" ("Literator"), 89; "'Meloch', kotoraia mnogo znachit"), 119; "The Merry-Go-Round" ("Karusel'"), 65, 109, 238; "Metaphysics" ("Metafizika"), 238; *Michel Siniagin*, 69, 108, 113, 117f; "Misfortune" ("Beda"), 73; "NEP Grimace" ("Grimasa nepa"), 79, 116; "Nervous People" ("Nervnye liudi"), 65, 108f, 117; "Not Funny" ("Ne zabavno"), 238; "An Occurrence" ("Proisshestvie"), 238; "Operation" ("Operatsiia"), 79, 85–86; "O sebe," 89; "O sebe, ob ideologii i eshche koe o chem," 89, 239; "O sebe, o kritikakh i o svoei rabote," 61–62, 104; "The Patient" ("Patsientka"), 113; "Pelegeia," 117–18; "People" ("Liudi"), 107; "Philistines" ("Meshchane"), 81; "Poor Liza" ("Bednaia Liza"), 69; "Poverty" ("Bednost'"), 107, 236; "The Power of Talent," 87, 238; "The Prayer" ("Molitva"), 113; "The Quality of the Production" ("Kachestvo produktsii"), 99; *Respected Citizens* (*Uvazhaemye grazhdane*), 117, 121, 239; "A Scientific Phenomenon" ("Nauchnoe iavlenie"), 87; *Sentimental Tales* (*Sentimental'nye povesti*), 62, 231; "Sixth Tale of Belkin" ("Shestaia povest' I. P. Belkina"), 83, 136, 233; "Slippers" ("Baretki"), 87; "Small-Fry" ("Melkota"), 63, 88, 102, 114; "Something Special" ("Chto-nibud' osobennoe"), 114, 237; "Street Incident" ("Ulichnoe proisshestvie"), 96, 100, 116, 238; "Strong Medicine" ("Sil'noe sredstvo"), 77; "The Sufferings of Young Werther" ("Stradanie molodogo Vertera"), 69; "A Summer Breather" ("Letnaia peredyshka"), 109, 237; "A Swine Affair" ("Svinoe delo"), 73–74; "Swinishness" ("Svinstvo"), 73–74; *Tales of Nazar Il'ich, Mr. Sinebriukhov* (*Rasskazy Nazara Il'icha gospodina Sinebriukhova*), 60, 62; "A Terrible Night" ("Strashnaia noch'"), 90, 108, 238; "Thank You" ("Spasibo"), 238; "Theater for Oneself" ("Teatr dlia sebia"), 88, 90, 238; "Theater Life" ("Teatral'naia zhizn'"), 76, 238; "The Thief" ("Vor"), 74; "A Trick of Nature" ("Igra prirody"), 97, 114, 237; *The Trifles of Life* (*Melochi zhizni*), 63, 69, 72, 103; "A Trivial Incident" ("Melkii sluchai"), 63, 69–71, 72, 76f, 85, 101, 113, 237f; "A Trivial Incident from Private Life" ("Melkii sluchai iz lichnoi zhizni"), 74–75, 77, 87f, 235; "A Trivial Occurrence" ("Melkoe proisshestvie"), 63, 97, 116; "An Unpleasant Story" ("Nepriatnaia istoriia"), 238; "Victim of the Revolution" ("Zhertva revoliutsii"), 86; "The Watch" ("Chasy"), 236, 238; "Weak Packaging" ("Slabaia tara"), 109; "The Wedding" ("Svad'ba"), 72; "What the Nightingale Sang" ("O chem pel solovei"), 63, 113; "Who Needs Relatives?" ("Ne nado imet' rodstvennikov"), 79, 238; "Wisdom" ("Mudrost'"), 77, 106, 108, 113; "Woman's Happiness" ("Bab'e schast'e"), 116; "Work Clothes" ("Rabochii kostium"), 81, 85, 238

Zoshchenko, Vera Vladimirovna, 88

Zritel' (*Spectator*), 22

Library of Congress Cataloging-in-Publication Data

Popkin, Cathy
  The pragmatics of insignificance : Chekhov, Zoshchenko, Gogol /
Cathy Popkin.
    p.   cm.
  Includes bibliographical references and index.
  ISBN 0-8047-2209-9 (alk. paper)
  1. Russian fiction—19th century—History and criticism.
2. Russian fiction—20th century—History and criticism.
3. Discourse analysis, Narrative.   4. Chekhov, Anton Pavlovich,
1860–1904—Criticism and interpretation.   5. Zoshchenko, Mikhail,
1895–1958—Criticism and interpretation.   6. Gogol', Nikolai
Vasil'evich, 1809–1852—Criticism and interpretation.   I. Title.
PG3095.P59   1993
891.709′003—dc20   93-7021
                                                                 CIP